Conserving Bogs
The Management Handbook

UNIVERSITY OF
WOLVERHAMPTON
KNOWLEDGE · INNOVATION · ENTERPRISE

Harrison Learning Centre
City Campus
University of Wolverhampton
St. Peter's Square
Wolverhampton
WV1 1RH
Telephone: 0845 408 1631
Online Renewals: www.wlv.ac.uk/lib/myaccount

Telephone Renewals: 01902 321333 or 0845 408 1631
Online Renewals: www.wlv.ac.uk/lib/myaccount
Please return this item on or before the last date shown above.
Fines will be charged if items are returned late.

CONSERVING BOGS

THE MANAGEMENT HANDBOOK

Edited by

Rob Stoneman and Stuart Brooks

EDINBURGH: THE STATIONERY OFFICE

Editorial Steering Group: Stuart Brooks, Philip Immirzi, Lucy Parkyn, Alastair Sommerville and
Rob Stoneman

The Stationery Office Limited
South Gyle Crescent, Edinburgh EH12 9EB

First published 1997

Applications for reproduction should be made to The Stationery Office Limited

British Library Cataloguing in Publications Data

A catalogue record for this book is available from the British Library

ISBN 0 11 495836 X

CONTENTS

Part 4
Monitoring and Site Assessment

Part 5
Methods and Techniques for Management

Part 6
Practical Examples of Bog Conservation

Appendices

GENERAL ACKNOWLEDGEMENTS

This book was researched and written under the auspices of the Scottish Raised Bog Conservation Project, which was funded under the European Union *Life* regulation. Whilst the majority of the book was completed during the project, additional funding was gratefully received from Scottish Natural Heritage and the Royal Society for the Protection of Birds to aid its completion. A great many people have given advice, encouragement and above all their enthusiasm to assist the authors in the production of this book. Special thanks go to Alastair Sommerville (SWT) for his continual support, guidance and inspiration, and to Lucy Parkyn (SWT), Philip Immirzi (SNH) and Paul José (RSPB) for their substantial input during the lengthy editing process. We also thank all the bog managers and members of the 'peatland community' who have given so willingly of their time and expertise. Thanks also go to Arlene Foreman, Agnes Mitchell and Sally Clarke for typing the manuscripts, Finally, thank you to all those whom we have failed to mention here for their help in the preparation of this book.

CONTRIBUTORS

Introduction
Rob Stoneman (SWT)

Part 1 The Values and Uses Of Bogs
1.1–1.5   Rob Stoneman
1.6   Margaret Cox (Bournemouth University) and Rob Stoneman
1.7   Rob Stoneman and Pete Pollard (SWT)
1.8–1.14   Rob Stoneman

Part 2 Distribution and Ecology
2.1–2.4   Rob Stoneman
2.5   Olivia Bragg (Dundee University)
2.6   Hamish Anderson (MLURI)

Part 3 Planning Conservation Management
3.1   Rob Stoneman and Margaret Cox
3.2   Rob Stoneman
3.3   Stuart Brooks (SWT)
3.4   Rob Stoneman

Part 4 Monitoring and Site Assessment
4.1   Stuart Brooks
4.2   Peter Hulme (MLURI) and Dick Birnie (MLURI)
4.3   Russell Anderson (Forest Authority)
4.4   Hamish Anderson
4.5–4.6   Peter Hulme and Dick Birnie
4.7   Stuart Brooks and Jonathan Hughes (SWT)

Part 5 Methods and Techniques for Management
Stuart Brooks

Part 6 Practical Examples of Bog Conservation
6.1, 6.8, 6.9, 6.12, 6.14–6.16, 6.20, 6.24
             Lucy Parkyn (SWT)
6.6, 6.7, 6.19, 6.21, 6.22, 6.25–6.28
             Mandy Clothier
6.2, 6.3, 6.5, 6.10, 6.11, 6.13, 6.17, 6.22, 6.23
             Emma Wilson (SWT)
6.4   Rob Stoneman
6.29   Stuart Brooks

Appendix 3 Site Assessment of Bogs from the Damage Sustained
Rob Stoneman, Fiona Everingham, Stuart Brooks and Philip Immirzi (SNH)

Appendix 4 Health and Safety
Stuart Brooks

Appendix 6 Common Methods
A6.2   Dick Birnie and Peter Hulme
A6.3   Russell Anderson
A6.4   Peter Hulme and Dick Birnie

All illustrations by Stuart Brooks

The following people provided invaluable help and assistance in the research and production of Part 6.

Cors Beet (Staatsbosbeheer), Sally Blyth (SNH), Berndt Bölscher (Technical University of Braunschweig), Bill Burlton (FE), Alexander Buttler (University of Neuchâtel), Andrew Coupar (SNH), Joan Daniels (EN), John Davies (CCW), Catriona Douglas (OPW), Ian Douglas (Northumberland Wildlife Trust), Graeme Elliott (RSPB), Peter Foss (IPCC), Philip Grosvernier (University of Neuchâtel), Andreas Grünig and Roland Haab (Swiss Federal Institute for Forest, Snow and Landscape), Tim Jacobs (SNH), Reinhard Lohmer (BUND), Dieter Maas (Munich Technical University), Robert Masheder (Northumberland Wildlife Trust), Frank Mawby (EN), Gilles Mülhauser (EcoConseil), Richard Ninnes (SNH), Catherine O'Connell (IPCC), Andrew Panter (SNH), Robin Prowse (EN), John Rook (EN), Peter Rowarth (EN), Jim Ryan (OPW), Jos Schouwenaars (University of Groningen), Peter Singleton (EN), Chris Smith (Sinclair Horticulture), Keith Stanfield (DOE Northern Ireland), Peter Staubli, Nico Straathof (Natuurmonumenten), Jan Streefkerk (Staatsbosbeheer), Stewart Taylor (RSPB) and Melvyn Yeandle (EN).

FOREWORD

Responding to the force of gravity, the rain which falls on the surface of the Earth makes its inexorable way down to the sea. Where its progress is impeded, wetlands come into existence and peat can begin to form: marsh, callow or fen, poor fen and bog – its natural order, the natural succession. Each plant community mirrors the hydrogeology of the landscape, each community drier and more acid than the first – the once open water gradually being replaced by the wonder of our boglands. The true magic of this, the hydrosere, is that as the peat forms, it records the whole process of change in the minutest of detail – as pollen grains, spores and much more besides, neatly stacked into a living history book.

It was the conquest of the wetland forests of the Tigris and Euphrates which enabled the beginnings of irrigated agriculture and the birth of the first civilisations of the world, some 5,000 years ago. Since then, humankind has waged a continuous war of attrition against the wetlands of the world. This war has left many catchments sour and subject to erosion and catastrophic flooding. To date, these problems have been alleviated only by 'civil' engineers and the massive application of lime and fertiliser – costly, energy consuming measures, often causing more problems than they solve.

The drainage and destruction unfortunately continue apace, yet countries as diverse as Thailand, Spain, the Netherlands and the UK have truly begun to recognise the value of our wetlands as reservoirs of biodiversity, as carbon stores and as natural filters of pollution; their role in catchment control and management is being recognised by the varied opinions of environmentalists and insurers alike. What is more, words are being put into action: schemes large and small, even whole river systems, are being returned to their 'natural' order, restoring their natural wonder and their natural values.

Europe's wetland heritage is second to none; in particular Europe's boglands, from the ice-filled palsas of northern Scandinavia to the classic concentric domes forming the raised bogs skirting the Baltic. The added twist of the environmental mis-management tale is the creation of blanket bog. In the high rainfall areas of the Atlantic seaboard, our ancient ancestors stripped the forest cover from the hills and glens causing excessive soil leaching; only the bog mosses, the Sphagna, could grow, thus healing the landscape to stem the tide of erosion and attrition.

This timely book is a distillation of the best of peaty knowledge relating to the management and rehabilitation of bogs. This new volume in the peaty archive must turn the tide of destruction and ensure that the diversity of bogland is maintained and restored, allowing the sustainability of all the plants, animals and livelihoods that depend on the bogs. Not least, it should allow the continued formation of peat to maintain the living encyclopaedia – this time recording good management not mismanagement.

This book gives the recipe for 'good health' to all the peaty catchments of Europe.

Slàinte mhath to all who helped to produce it.

Dr David Bellamy
Chairman of the Royal Society for Nature
Conservation: The Wildlife Trust
Bedburn, Durham
January 1997

INTRODUCTION

INTRODUCTION

HANDBOOK FORMAT

This handbook is, above all, a practical manual: a cookbook of methods and techniques to help people effectively manage and conserve bogs. The handbook has been written with peatland conservationists in mind, although it is as useful to any land manager who has control of bogland. Above all, it is hoped that this handbook can inspire and guide people towards bog conservation.

The handbook has been laid out in six parts (*see* Figure I.1). Part 1 concerns 'The values and Uses of Bogs'. The positive values considered here include: biodiversity and landscape, a carbon store, an educational resource nature reserves, the peat archive and catchment hydrology. Alternatively, bogs are viewed as an economic resource or as wasteland to be 'improved'. Only recently has the former attitude become more prevalent; many bogs have suffered considerable damage. These uses are also outlined in Part 1. By looking at the damaging uses to which bogs have been put, a damage assessment can be made. A detailed description of various damaging activities is, therefore, included in Appendix 3. This allows a detailed site assessment to be made as a tool for management planning (*see* Part 3).

In Part 2, 'Distribution and Ecology', an introduction to bog ecosystems is given. Sections on classification, distribution, raised and blanket bog

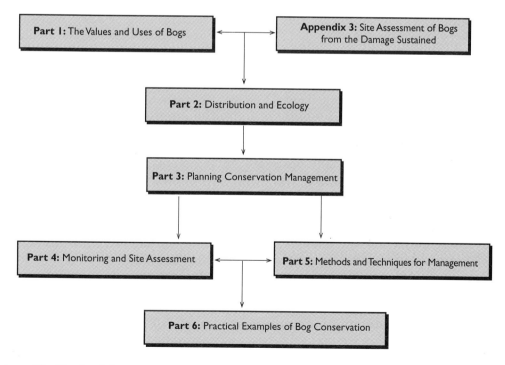

Figure I.1   The Handbook Structure.

and their formation, bog vegetation, bog hydrology and bog chemistry are laid out. These are all summaries and, if detail is required, specialist texts should be sought.

Part 3 details the ways in which management plans should be prepared for bogs. The management plan format adopted is that developed by the Nature Conservancy Council and its successor bodies, which is succinctly summarised in *Site Management Plans for Nature Conservation – A Working Guide* (NCC, 1988). The basic structure is restated before going on to show how this structure can be used for bog management.

Given that each site has its own unique set of characteristics, guiding bog managers to effective management strategies is difficult. However, the types of damage that bogs may have sustained are common across many sites and often require common solutions. Thus section 3.3 describes the varying types of damage, ecohydrological effects that ensue and how the effects of such damage can be recognised. This section – 'Action Plan (Prescriptions), Damaging Impacts and Solutions' – forms the linchpin of the handbook, as it links damage (Part 1; Appendix 3) to the actual methods and techniques which could be used for conservation management (Parts 4 and 5). Thus section 3.3 gives a variety of options available to ameliorate the effects of damaging activities.

Cross-linking of different sections in the handbook is a common feature throughout. This allows managers, who come to the subject with differing levels of experience, to navigate through the volume at different speeds according to their knowledge. A manager with many years of experience could thus skip quickly from a description of a particular type of damage straight through to necessary techniques. If one's experience is less, then it would be worth going through each section more slowly. It is important to remember that the handbook structure is defined by such cross-linking of sections (although contents and index lists are provided also).

Each technique for monitoring and management is laid out in Parts 4 and 5 respectively; they effectively form the main parts of the handbook. Techniques can be considered on their own, and

pages should be easily photocopyable to be used in the field. Again, though, the reader should be aware of extensive cross-referencing to other parts of the handbook. Management techniques may, for example, be cross-linked to a monitoring method designed to test the effectiveness of such management. Particularly useful cross-references take the reader to the final part of the handbook. Part 6 sets out a number of case-studies which illustrate the majority of the methods and techniques laid out in Parts 4 and 5. The complexity of each case-study could never be fully explored in this handbook. The approach, then, is to briefly describe the site and its management objectives and then highlight a particular method or technique which has been practised there. If there is any doubt over when, where or how a technique should be applied, a manager could always contact the personnel involved. In this way, networking of information around peatland conservationists can be further enhanced.

MANAGING BOGS

Ecologists look at bogs as one of the most limiting of ecosystems – highly acidic, nutrient-poor and, of course, waterlogged – and delight in their biodiversity and landscape. Climatologists consider the vast store of carbon that peat bogs contain and the effects that this must have on global carbon cycling. Archaeologists gain insights from the beautifully-preserved organic remains. Environmental historians extract detailed records of human culture and environmental change. For many, bogs are a source of fuel, whilst for others bogs represent a profitable industry.

Yet, all across the globe, bogs have been damaged and modified. In some countries, such as the Netherlands and Germany, bogs have been modified so greatly to leave only fragmentary remains; mere clues to the past watery richness of this once common landscape. In Britain and Ireland, the blanket bogs which envelop the north and west still remain, although they are now much modified. In the lowlands, the raised bogs have become one of Britain's rarest habitats – having been afforested, 'reclaimed' for agriculture and cutaway for gro-bags and the horticultural industry.

Only recently has society begun to recognise the true significance of Europe's peat bogs. Gradually, nature protection has checked the progressive destruction of this natural asset. For many bogs, however, legislative protection is not enough. To conserve a site, management is needed.

In Europe, conservation management of bogs was first practised in the Netherlands and Germany. In the Netherlands, initial management works concentrated on preserving two semi-intact blocks, Engbertsdijksvenen and Bargerveen, in the 1960s. In Germany, management concentrated on rehabilitating industrially worked bogs. One of the first bog management works in Britain was carried out at Danes Moss (Meade, 1992), although fen management for conservation purposes has long been practised (for example, at Wicken Fen since the 1890s). A devastating fire at Glasson Moss, a Nature Conservation Review site (Ratcliffe, 1977), spurred the Nature Conservancy Council to switch from protection to active management of the site. The success of the works at Glasson – the site now has some of the finest raised bog vegetation in Britain – demonstrates the potential of such management.

An important impetus to peatland management came as a result of *The Peatland Management Handbook* (Rowell, 1988). As published material relating to peatland management was so scarce, Rowell culled much of the information for this volume directly from people interested in, or practising, peatland conservation management. Rowell's aims were to review present knowledge, stimulate improved management, and encourage an interchange of ideas and experience between conservation managers of peatlands.

The Peatland Management Handbook proved to be extremely successful in achieving its aims and led to a flurry of bog management initiatives throughout the country. As Rowell realised, some of the techniques and methods presented were new and relatively untested. It was specifically noted that 'some sections of the Handbook will become out of date quite rapidly' (p. 2). To counteract this, the handbook was designed to be easily updated. Today though, peatland management has moved on dramatically and a new handbook is now required, especially in the light of the *Habitats Directive* and the Biodiversity Convention which commit the European governments to conserving Europe's biodiversity (see, for example, Juniper, 1994).

In this volume, the focus lies on the management of ombrotrophic (literally rain-fed) peatland systems only, in other words bogs. In addition, there is an undisguised emphasis on the conservation management of north-west European bogs, and, in particular, British bogs. This is the result of the experience of the authors and of the data available.

Before writing this handbook, a thorough review of bog management work was undertaken. Firstly, questionnaires were sent to all interested parties. Seventy-six questionnaires were returned covering 150 sites. This information was transferred on to a database to allow effective access to the dataset. The questionnaires were then followed up with site visits in the UK, Ireland, Switzerland, Germany and the Netherlands. Extra information and expertise was garnered through contracting people to write certain sections in which the editors had less expertise (see Acknowledgements and List of Contributors).

A PLEA FOR GOOD REPORTING

This handbook is part of a process towards pushing forward the effectiveness of peatland conservation management. In Britain, Rowell's extremely useful *Peatland Management Handbook* (1988) laid the framework for a more professional approach to the subject. Projects such as English Nature's Lowland Peatland Project (1992–6) and the Scottish Wildlife Trust's Raised Bog Conservation Project (1993–5) have been networking information around the bog management community via workshops, reports, site visits, newsletters and, of course, long telephone conversations. The alliance of practical experience with academic research has brought bog conservation to a threshold. We are now in a position to move from crisis management – conserving our best sites – to reversing the progressive degradation of our peatland resource.

If we are to achieve this, management will need further refinement. Many techniques are still experimental and need to be evaluated. Evaluation can only be achieved if good records are kept and management is monitored to test its effectiveness.

THE VALUES AND USES OF BOGS

Part 1 looks at the ways in which bogs are valued and used, and is split into the following sections:

THE VALUES AND USES OF BOGS

1.1 INTRODUCTION

A walk across the high ground of Britain nearly always involves a walk on water since the black 'soil' beneath, topped with a mat of cotton grasses and bog mosses, is peat. Given that wet peat is mostly water (90%), this is 'land' stretched to the edge of its definition; this is bogland. The bogs of the world span the high latitudes and parts of the tropics to cover 3% of the world's land area (Figure 1.1) – an area roughly equal to the size of India and Pakistan combined. Billions of tonnes of carbon are locked away in peatlands, and it is surmised that peatlands may be involved in triggering ice-ages (Pearce, 1994).

In some areas, peatlands dominate the landscape (Figure 1.2). In the north-west of Scotland, blanket bog (*see* 2.3) covers the land, intertwining with the country's culture and economy. The rolling moorlands, the flavour of whisky, the dyes for tartan, and peat-fuelled fires all relate to boglands (SNH, 1995). Bogs are variously viewed as a natural wonder or as an economic asset.

The ways in which bogs are viewed are changing. At one time, bogs were highly regarded

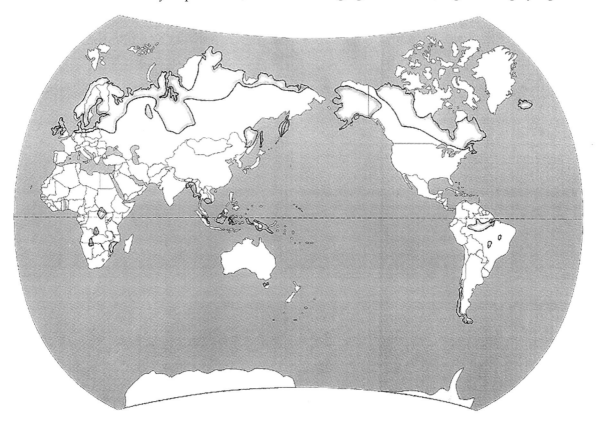

Figure 1.1 The shaded areas represent a generalised distribution of mires around the world. Data is taken from various sources.

Figure 1.2   An aerial view of the Flow Country, Scotland. (S. G. Moore and R. A. Lindsay)

as a source of fuel and early spring 'bite' for cattle and sheep. As agricultural and the Industrial Revolution changed land practices, bogs came to be viewed as wasteland (Smout, 1996). Today this view is giving way as people begin to appreciate the natural and cultural heritage of bogland.

In Part 1, the values of bogs, and the uses to which they have been put, are considered. This helps countryside managers both to assess the state of the bog in terms of the damage it has sustained and to consider what use the site should be put to. In effect, a site assessment can be undertaken to form the site description of a conservation management plan and set objectives for the site (*see* Part 3).

Conservation management of bogs most often relates to ameliorating the effects of past damage. The types of damage sustained by sites are often widespread. Therefore, by considering the ways in which a bog has been used and the damage ensuing from that use, solutions to countering the effects of damage can be formulated. The potentially damaging uses outlined below are, therefore, considered in much more detail in Appendix 3.

Part 1 is split into positive values (or functions) – biodiversity, carbon store, education, nature reserves, catchment hydrology and archive – alongside potentially damaging uses: peat extraction, agriculture, forestry, development and recreation. The effects of pollution and the cumulative effects of many small-scale damaging activities are also discussed.

1.2   BIODIVERSITY AND LANDSCAPE

All across the northern latitudes, particularly in Canada, Scandinavia and Russia, peatlands dominate the scene, from the treeless blanket bogs of Scotland to the perma-frosted bogs of the North to the great forested bogs of the Siberian Taiga. In South-East Asia, much of the remaining pristine

1.2

rainforest grows on a blanket of tropical wood peat (Figure 1.3).

Bogs throughout the world act as a significant part of global biodiversity. The remarkably specialised conditions of waterlogging, low nutrient status and high acidity combine to create a specialised flora and associated fauna. The carnivorous plants serve as an example (Figures 1.4 and 1.5). In European countries, sundews (*Drosera* spp.) and butterworts (*Pinguicula* spp.) are found mostly on mires. In North America,

Figure 1.4 The carnivorous sundew, *Drosera rotundifolia*, supplements its diet by catching insects on the sticky hairs of its leaves. (G. Cambridge)

has experienced a dramatic decline in the last fifteen years, possibly because of intensive pesticide and fertiliser use. Raised bogs, despite damage, now host significant populations. Indeed, lowland bogs can form a wildlife oasis in an increasingly sterile (for wildlife) agricultural landscape.

Figure 1.3 From an isolated granite extrusion, tropical peat swamp forest can be seen to stretch out to the horizon in every direction. However, this forest in Kalimantan, Indonesia is now threatened by huge logging and agricultural schemes. (Rob Stoneman)

bogs nurture *Sarracennia* spp. whose leaves form funnels of enzyme-rich water to trap and digest insects. Most beautiful are the pitcher plants (*Nepenthes* spp.) of South-East Asian boglands.

Alongside such specialised biodiversity, bogs are host to a large array of species which are found in other habitats. Dunlin and golden plover feeding on the mud-flats of eastern England, for example, may have spent their summer breeding on the boglands of northern Scotland or the far northern tundra. Even the damaged raised bogs of the British lowlands have a significant part to play in conserving regional biodiversity. By way of an example, a recent survey (Trubridge, 1994) of lowland raised mires in central Scotland revealed high numbers of skylark. This species

Figure 1.5 Carnivorous pitcher plants, *Nepenthes ampullaria*, digest insects that fall into the watery enzyme-rich soup that collects in the base of the pitcher. (Rob Stoneman)

1.3 A CARBON STORE

Peatlands are unbalanced ecosystems. The rate of addition of dead organic matter exceeds that lost by decay. As a consequence, layers of organic matter and water (forming peat) develop to form mires. Effectively, mires sequester carbon dioxide from the atmosphere and preserve the carbon as peat in the developing mire.

Although peatlands are highly threatened in some parts of the world (England, for example), they still cover a vast area globally (Immirzi et al., 1992).

This huge area of peatland thus represents a gigantic store of carbon which may otherwise reside in the atmosphere. Immirzi et al. (1992) estimate that peatlands hold between 330 and 530 billion tonnes of carbon ($3-3\frac{1}{2}$ times the carbon pool of tropical rainforests, and about a fifth of all soil carbon), and would have sequestered about 100 million tonnes of carbon per year. Exploitation of peatlands for agriculture and forestry and peat extraction has now turned the world's peatlands from a sink to a source of carbon. Possibly, as much as 600 million tonnes of carbon dioxide are released into the atmosphere every year due to peatland exploitation.

1.4 BOGS AS AN EDUCATIONAL RESOURCE

In an effort to inform and educate the public of the need to conserve peatlands, some conservation organisations have focused on environmental education as an integral part of their campaigns. In Britain and Ireland, Friends of the Earth, the Scottish Wildlife Trust and the Irish Peatland Conservation Council (IPCC), the Department of the Environment (Northern Ireland) and Scottish Natural Heritage have all produced peatland education packs for this purpose. These packs demonstrate that bogs are a rich educational resource ranging from botany through to archaeology to poetry and painting. Indeed, the IPCC found that the value of their pack far exceeded their expectations, proving to be useful in teaching environmental education at primary and secondary levels.

The IPCC peatland education pack (IPCC, 1992) is split into six modules spanning science, history, geography, art, craft and design, English and Gaeilge, reflecting the breadth of subjects which peatland study can offer. The content of each module is summarised below:

- Science module – focuses on the bog as a habitat for ecological studies.
- History – considers bogs as preservers of archaeology.
- Geography – focuses upon the conservation issue and wise use of peatland resources.
- Art, craft and design – explores how bogs can be used as inspiration for artistic work.
- English – a broad-based module which looks at nature conservation and the value of natural and cultural heritage by basing the module around a core text, *Rua, the Red Grouse*.
- Gaeilge – uses the bogland theme for issues in Gaeltacht areas (obviously fairly specific to Ireland).

Another example is a small-scale educational facility in Somerset. The Peat Moors Visitor Centre is a multi-faceted provision which includes aspects such as the environmental history of the Somerset Levels, its present value for nature conservation, the history of peat extraction and the archaeology of the area.

Many peat bog sites are now nature reserves which can be used for educational purposes. Some sites have been specifically developed for educational purposes, for example, Langlands Moss in Scotland and Peatlands Park (*see* 6.20). Obviously, in using peat bogs as an educational resource, care must be taken not to damage the bog significantly and to conduct safe visits. Access facilities (*see* 5.6) are clearly important in this respect.

1.5 NATURE RESERVES AND WILDERNESS AREAS

Bogs can make fascinating natural and cultural reserves. They have intriguing wildlife being home to bog specialists, a refuge for wetland species and a significant part of an area's biodiversity. Their natural interest is complemented by archaeological finds and palaeoecological research. The two interests have been successfully combined at some reserves (such as, Shapwick Heath: *see* 6.4).

This combination of factors has led to the creation of many peatland-based nature reserves. Additionally, peatlands are now so threatened that, in some countries, nature reserve designation forms the mainstay of peatland conservation programmes. In the Netherlands, for example, nearly all remnants of the once extensive Bourtangermoor are now conserved as nature reserves.

Types and uses of reserves vary considerably. Peatlands Park (*see* 6.20) attracts many thousands of visitors a year and has become Northern Ireland's second most popular tourist attraction. The emphasis at the park is on access, interpretation, education and recreation which run alongside conservation of intact bog and fen habitat. Many peat-bog nature reserves have been created as wildlife havens only. These reserves are thought to be too sensitive to disturbance to breeding birds and so on and to trampling damage to allow visitor access. Some of these problems can be alleviated by provision of well-planned access facilities (*see* 5.6).

On a wider scale, where peatland is dominant in the landscape, the nature of the environment forces low-intensity agricultural practices. 'Wilderness' areas of Britain are mountains or peatland. These large, sparsely-inhabited areas such as the Flow Country (Figure 1.2) or the peatlands of the Cairngorm Plateau have immense wildlife value. They are home to very rare breeding birds such as golden plover, red-necked phalarope, red-throated diver, black-throated diver and wood sandpiper. The vast wilderness peatland areas of Scandinavia, Siberia and Canada perform the same function. An interesting parallel to northern latitude bogs is the South-East Asian bogs, which now contain a large proportion of the world's orang-utan population. Wilderness areas are very important in terms of recreation. These areas can be sustainably exploited for tourism, providing a calming land of natural wonder when set against frantic urban lifestyles.

1.6   THE PEAT ARCHIVE

1.6.1   Introduction

The study of the peatland archive originated with discoveries in the Swiss lakes region in the 1850s, inspiring workers such as Arthur Bulleid, who sought and found a lake village site in the Somerset Levels in 1892. In recent times, the importance and enhanced value of wet sites over dry sites has been realised because of more detailed studies (such as, Godwin, 1981). As techniques develop, the archaeological value of waterlogged deposits is likely to grow, so it is imperative that these records be conserved. Once lost, this rich archaeological archive cannot be restored or rehabilitated.

The last twenty-five years have seen a considerable growth in the study of wetland archaeology. This reflects both the increasing threats to wetlands and the increasing realisation that wetlands, particularly peat bogs, with their unique qualities of preservation of organic material (including the palaeoenvironmental record), can augment and very often lead to a reinterpretation of human activity in the past, particularly in prehistory (for example, Coles and Coles, 1986). Peat substrates have a low pH and are anaerobic, prohibiting the activity of those microbes (bacterial and fungal) responsible for the decay of organic materials (these include wood, pollen, textiles and human bodies).

During the last five years, some aspects of archaeology have become less human-orientated. Today, many archaeologists consider the palaeo-environmental or palaeoecological record to be important in its own right and not merely as an add-on to site-based studies. Wetland sites are particularly important in that cultural evidence is within its contemporary environmental context. This can be either 'natural' or anthropogenic.

1.6.2   The Nature of the Resource

The archaeological record preserved in wet sites should not be understated:

- Extensive water-logged deposits can contain whole landscapes and conserve the palaeo-environmental record on a regional, as well as a local level.

- Wet sites have often engulfed and preserved pre-existing land surfaces.
- On a temporal level, dry sites can occasionally, and at best, contain deposits of a few hundred years; wet sites can contain evidence over much of the Holocene and beyond.
- Wetland sites preserve artefacts extraordinarily well, providing information about past lives in wetland areas.

The following subsections give a brief overview of various aspects of the archive.

A Sacred Place

Human activity in bogs has been varied. It has been a place to placate the deities, as attested at Flag Fen (Pryor, 1991) with offerings of high-status goods. Less palatable today is overt human sacrifice, as attested archaeologically from the Iron Age in bogs such as Lindow Moss in Cheshire (Figure 1.6) (Stead et al., 1986).

Figure 1.6   Lindow Man is a wonderfully preserved bog body. He lay undiscovered in a bog in Cheshire for 2000 years. (Copyright British Museum)

Prehistoric Exploitation of the Wetland Resource

Fens in particular, were considered to be a rich resource in the past. 'The fatness of the earth gathered together at the time of Noah's Flood' is an early seventeenth-century description of the East Anglian fens. Such areas could be rich in food-stuffs such as fish and fowl, and provide useful raw materials such as reeds and rushes. In Somerset, hunting platforms were constructed

upon the mire surface as early as the Neolithic (Coles and Coles, 1986). Such activity has continued through time, culminating in the duck-decoy pools of the post-medieval period.

Trackways, Communication and Access

Bogs and marshes can be treacherous places; consequently, people living in adjacent areas have made efforts to cross them safely since the early Neolithic period. The earliest known trackway in the UK is the Sweet Track (3807–6BC) in the Somerset Levels (Figure 6.7). To date, over 1,000 wooden trackways have been located in peat in Ireland, Britain, the Netherlands, Germany and Denmark (for example, Figure 1.7). Analysis of

Figure 1.7   Abbots Way, a wonderfully preserved wooden trackway in the Somerset Levels dating back to 2000 BC. (Margaret Cox)

wooden artefacts and structures from peat bogs has demonstrated the highly-developed skills acquired by our ancestors in terms of woodworking technology and woodland management. Both areas of expertise were advanced by the early Neolithic.

Water Transport

Archaeological evidence from peat bogs demonstrates the use of boats in and around the wetlands of the past. Several examples of log boats exist from Somerset and elsewhere in Europe and North America (Figure 1.8).

Prehistoric Settlement

There is little evidence to suggest that people lived within mires or marshes in the past. The majority

Figure 1.8   A log boat discovered at Shapwick Heath dating to 350 B.C. (Margaret Cox)

of the settlements associated with prehistoric exploitation of wetlands took place upon the adjoining dry lands. In Somerset, two exceptions to this rule are the lake village sites at Glastonbury and Meare. Both sites date from the Iron Age and offer an insight into life at that time.

A Palaeoenvironmental Resource

Examination of the peat substrate for palaeoenvironmental information includes varied analyses. The waterlogged deposits facilitate excellent preservation and a more complete palaeoenvironmental record than dry sites. The organic nature of peat facilitates radio-carbon dating which enhances the value of the deposits. Radio-carbon dates can often be supplemented and enhanced by tephra chronology and dendrochronology. Tree-ring dating can achieve an impressive degree of accuracy for some timber going back to the Neolithic. For example, it is known that the Sweet Track was constructed, through a reedmarsh, in the winter of 3807–6BC (Hillam et al., 1990).

Vegetational change can be detected at two levels. Macrobotanical remains (seeds, fruits, nuts, leaves and so on) indicate local and wider environmental conditions, whilst pollen analysis offers more general information about vegetation change and provides evidence of the environ-

mental (hydrological, climatic, anthropogenic) implications of such change. Wood deposits are extremely useful, not only as environmental indicators, but because wood lends itself to dendrochronology (tree-ring dating) which can be accurate to the year of felling. Microfauna are usually sensitive to environmental oscillations and adapt quickly; larger animals are slower to react. The study of insect remains, in particular beetles and weevils, is particularly appropriate to peat soils as their exoskeletons survive very well in the acidic anaerobic environment of waterlogged peat.

The calcium carbonate shells of land and marine molluscs can survive in some peats (pH-dependent) and reflect local conditions. Bone, however, rarely survives in acidic peats.

Other microscopic remains examined from peat samples are Foraminifera (one-celled organisms) from sediments resulting from marine transgressions and diatoms (unicellular algae whose siliceous walls survive). Both enhance our understanding of the environment and environmental change.

The types of analyses described above can be used to build up an understanding of the past environment. This can be used to demonstrate environmental change both spatially and through time, particularly when combined with radiocarbon dates.

Historic Exploitation of the Wetland Resource

In most peatland areas, the more modern peats were removed by the hand cutters (Figure 1.9) of the past for use as fuel or as deep litter (prior to the 1950s). The earliest known peat-cutting in Somerset, for example, is from Romano-British briquetage mounds, where peat was used as fuel in the salt production process (Leech et al., 1983). The medieval period saw efforts at wetland exploitation in such areas as the Somerset Levels where monastic influence irreversibly altered the landscape via drainage regimes. The post-medieval period witnessed the impact of the great Dutch drainage engineers in areas such as the English Fens (Hall and Coles, 1994). Exploitation of the resource has continued up to the present, more recently for horticultural purposes and in

Figure 1.9   Women digging peat by hand in the late nineteenth century. (Anon)

many areas very intensively. Past exploitation has largely restricted archaeological examination of peat deposits from the historic period. Nevertheless, the present landscape reflects both ancient and modern drainage systems and land tenureship.

The Industrial Heritage

Historic exploitation and management of peatlands have resulted in the present historic and industrial landscape. The growth in the study of post-medieval and industrial archaeology places an emphasis upon landscape and architectural features previously considered to be of little value (for example, Figure 1.10).

Figure 1.10   The old peat cutting factory at Fenns Moss (see 6.1) has been preserved for its industrial archaeological interest. (Margaret Cox)

1.7   CATCHMENT HYDROLOGY

The hydrology of bogs (*see* 2.5) lies within the framework of the river catchment. A peat bog's influence may be small if it composes a small part of the catchment. Often, though, bogs play an important and sometimes dominant role in catchment hydrology. The River Sebangau's catchment in Kalimantan, for example, is wholly contained within a peat bog. In Scotland, virtually all major rivers have their source in peat or peaty soils of the uplands and Highlands (Figure 1.11). Three influences between bogs and river catchments are considered here: land use, water chemistry and hydrology.

Figure 1.11   Many Scottish rivers have their origins within peatland catchments. (SNH)

Land use

Many extensive areas of upland bog support only low-intensity land use. Whilst the ecology of Scotland's upland blanket bog (*see* 2.3.2) has been altered by burning and grazing, the basic functioning and ecology of these areas remain intact. Consequently, water courses coming out of these upland areas tend to be little disturbed and fairly 'wild'-running. However, where upland bog has been heavily drained, afforested or eroded (*see* 1.14), water sources are altered and downstream effects occur. For example, heavy erosion of south Pennine (UK) blanket bog has resulted in a dramatic silting-up of reservoirs (*see* 4.5.6). Hydrological regimes of waters emana-ting from drained bogs are different from more natural watercourses.

Water Chemistry

Water draining from peat bogs tends to be cool, oligotrophic and acidic and to contain a high concentration of organic substances (*see* 2.6). This is because, for deep peats, underlying mineral deposits play no part in the chemistry of surface waters. Acidity and nutrient status are, therefore, dependent upon the peat and the wet and dry atmospheric deposition of salts. Given such a low pH, storm events and acid deposition have less effect than might be found in waters emanating from non-peat catchments.

Where acid-sensitive mineral soils abut peaty soils, the presence of high concentrations of organic substance in surface waters is important in counteracting the effects of 'acid rain', as one of the most important causes of acid-water toxicity is high concentrations of aluminium. Organic compounds form complexes with aluminium helping to ameliorate the toxic effects of acid rain.

Catchment Hydrology

Intact peat bogs have a fairly 'flashy' water discharge regime characterised by large differences between low and high flows and a rapid rise in the hydrograph following storm events. This is because most of the peat bog is saturated. Only a thin layer (the acrotelm) is available for changes in storage (*see* 2.5). However, a low baseflow is always maintained, sustained by lateral seepage from the peat body. The 'flashiness' of bog waters is often restrained because of the gently undulating topography of bog areas, in contrast to shallow mineral soils on steep slopes.

Manipulation of bog hydrology for conservation purposes may also affect areas which receive drainage, or run-off, from the bog. Landowners may be concerned about the possibility of flooding adjacent fields and about patterns of river discharge (which differ between peaty and non-peaty catchments).

1.8 PEAT EXTRACTION (*see* A3.2)

1.8.1 Introduction

Peat is light, is high in organic matter, has excellent water-retention properties and is easy to cut. Because of these properties, peat has been cut for many thousands of years. Peat has long been used as fuel. Hand-cut peat banks, a traditional feature of Scottish and Irish peatlands, are long established for fuel-cutting (Figure 1.9). These small-scale activities contrast to the highly mechanised extraction of peat for peat-fired power stations in Ireland and Finland (Figure 1.12).

Figure 1.12 Vast wet black deserts have been created where peat is commercially harvested for fuel or horticultural use. This is typified in Ireland where bogs have been stripped, drained and harvested (foreground) to fuel electricity generating power stations (background). (Stuart Brooks)

In the twentieth century, peat has also been cut commercially to provide bedding material for horses and cattle and, more recently, to provide a potting and soil substitute for professional and amateur gardening (Figure 1.13). This use has had dramatic effects on Europe's lowland peat bogs in the last thirty years.

Figure 1.13 Gro-bags containing peat for amateur gardening. (Nigel Doar)

Whatever the past or present uses of peat, a conservation manager nearly always has to contend with some form of damage from peat extraction. There are four main types of cutting techniques : domestic cutting, extrusion (sausage cutting), sod or baulk/hollow cutting and milling.

1.8.2 Domestic Cutting

This is the traditional method of cutting peat. Peat is cut out to form a bank which then proceeds forwards as peat is cut away (Figure 1.9). The upper vegetated layer is discarded and thrown behind the working face. This has the desirable effect of revegetating the bare peat left behind the face, hence maintaining bog vegetation and giving a firmer surface to work on.

The effects of domestic cutting can be significant. As peat is removed, the size and shape of the peat body changes and so the hydrological properties of the bog (*see* 2.5.3) alter. Water levels fall next to the peat-cutting area or may be altered across the whole bog. Widespread cutting results in an uneven surface characterised by drier heath vegetation and wetter boggy pools with occasional areas of fen where the peat has been almost completely cut away.

1.8.3 Sausage Cutting or Extrusion

Traditional cutting is being superseded by tractor-driven machines which cut slits beneath the surface, extracting a 'pipe' of peat and laying it on to the surface (Figure 1.14).The 'sausages' of peat are then left to dry before being cut up as burning briquettes. Bogs, cut in this way, are effectively drained by the creation of sub-surface drainage channels whilst the peat structure is disturbed as cutting continues. Sites, cut in this way on a commercial basis, are drained and the vegetation is stripped to allow easier machine access and to stop 'sausages' becoming entangled in vegetation.

1.8.4 Baulk and Hollow (Sod) Cutting

Up until recently, most commercial peat operations used a baulk and hollow pattern of cutting, initially by hand and lately by machine, to extract peat. Bogs are drained by a rectilinear sequence of drains to allow peat to be extracted from

Figure 1.14   Mechanised sausage cutting is now a common method of peat harvesting. Sites cut in this fashion are particularly difficult to manage as much of the active drainage is sub-surface. This method of cutting is beginning to replace more traditional techniques particularly in Ireland and the Scottish Highlands. (Julian Anderson)

rectangular 'fields' or hollows which are bordered by drains. The blocks of cut peat are dried on intervening baulks. Baulk and hollow cutting leaves a distinctive pattern (Figure 1.15).

Figure 1.15   The distinctive pattern left by baulk and hollow peat cutting. After abandonment, the hollows often re-colonise with vegetation characteristic of wet bog whilst drier baulks are colonised by scrub or dry heath. (Peter Rowarth)

1.8.5   Peat Milling

Most commercial extraction operations today utilise peat milling. The first phase of a milling operation is to drain the surface layers with a series of regularly-spaced deep drains. After the upper peat has dried sufficiently to allow machines to pass over, the surface vegetation is removed to create vast bare, black fields (Figure 1.16). The top layers are then rotavated (milled) to allow drying before being bulldozed into long ridges. The peat is then removed for bagging or transported directly into power stations. On cessation of extraction, the bare peat fields are inhospitable to vegetation establishment although, with careful management, wetland can be created. Without management, peat fields slowly succumb to scrub.

Figure 1.17   Many peatlands are 'improved' for grazing by implementing a regime of burning and drainage. This tends to produce a vegetation dominated by heather to the detriment of other typical bog species, notably *Sphagnum* moss. (Fiona Everingham)

Figure 1.16   Vast, black deserts are created as the bog is stripped of its vegetation and drained prior to mechanical harvesting. (Lucy Parkyn)

1.9   AGRICULTURE (see A3.3)

Much bogland has some agricultural value, principally for light grazing. In an effort to improve grazing, there has been a long tradition of burning and drainage to dry the ground and improve the vegetation (Figure 1.17).

These activities are intensified through more drainage, fertilising and seeding, gradually diminishing any peatland character. At its most extreme, peat is simply cut away to leave a thin layer which is ploughed into underlying clays to create arable land.

However, in many areas bogs are used for marginal agriculture only. This causes a change in species composition although it need not be irreversible.

1.10   FORESTRY (see A3.4)

In continental climates, hot and dry summer weather allows trees to establish on bogs to become part of the site's natural flora. In more oceanic climates, such as Britain and Ireland, trees are very rarely a natural component of bog vegetation. However, bogs have been widely afforested as technology has allowed foresters to exploit peatland areas (Figure 1.18).

Trees, often non-native species such as lodgepole pine and sitka spruce, can be established on sites through drainage and fertiliser application (Figure 1.19). As trees mature and form a closed canopy, interception of rainwater (up to 30%) acts to maintain sufficiently dry conditions for tree growth. The afforested bog is transformed from open bogland to monotonous monocultures of non-native conifers overlying a bare, shaded

Figure 1.18   Many peatlands have been afforested in the last fifty years. This is a typical example of a raised bog (Carnwable Moss) that has been truncated by a railway and afforested on one side. (S. G. Moore)

Figure 1.19   Prior to planting, extensive drainage and fertilisation is required before trees can begin to grow on deep peat. This is a view of the Flow Country in Scotland, which, in the 1980s was the centre of a debate between conservationists and foresters. (S. G. Moore)

surface covered with dead needles. On rides and unplanted blocks, some of the character of the former bog can remain, suggesting that rehabilitation is possible (*see* 5.3).

1.11   DEVELOPMENT (see A3.5)

Bogs can form a barrier to development and are, therefore, modified or cut away to allow development to take place. As with many other habitats, bogland is lost to roads, railways, housing, industry, mining and waste disposal. Open-cast mining and waste disposal have had a particularly serious impact on Britain's lowland raised bogs (Figure 1.20). In some cases, developments are localised (such as roads), but in many cases, development leads to the outright destruction of the site.

Figure 1.21   Bogs are susceptible to damage from unmanaged access. A pathway is quickly created, even through relatively robust vegetation such as this. (Stuart Brooks)

Figure 1.20   Many lowland raised bogs have been destroyed by open cast coal mining and landfill operations. (Julian Anderson)

Other forms of recreational damage include:

- Shooting – localised pollution from lead shot and clays;
- Duck decoys – where pits are dug into the bog;
- Planting of rhododendron to provide cover for pheasants;
- Trampling on footpaths; and
- Vehicle damage from off-road vehicles.

1.12   RECREATION (see A3.6)

The use of bogs for recreation and enjoyment is a significant stimulus to their conservation. Shooting on British blanket bogs is an important economic activity, whilst many upland footpaths take the walker through bog landscapes. However, unmanaged recreational pressure can have a considerable impact through trampling, pollution and land management (Figure 1.21). In Britain, grouse moor management, for shooting, involves burning and limited drainage to encourage a multi-aged patchwork of heather.

1.13   POLLUTION (see A3.7.1)

The types of uses discussed above have mostly direct and fairly obvious forms of damage associated with them. However, bogs are also damaged from other, less obvious sources. Particularly worrying is pollution. Pollutants can enter bog systems in different ways:

- Via the atmosphere; from industrial and vehicular emissions or fertiliser drift from agriculture. As bogs receive all their inputs from the atmosphere, they are extremely nutrient-deficient and hence very sensitive to atmospheric pollution. Nitrogen pollution appears to be particularly significant.

- Via drains or surface run-off where drains direct water into a site from an adjacent enriched/polluted source.
- Via direct application for agricultural improvement.
- Via faecal enrichment from bird roosts and grazing animals or enrichment from dead animals.

Some of these effects are localised, but all significantly alter vegetation composition generally from oligotrophic (nutrient-poor) to mesotrophic or eutrophic (nutrient-rich) vegetation.

1.14   CUMULATIVE IMPACTS (see A3.7.2)

The cumulative impacts of many differing small-scale damaging activities may be the most significant but least understood cause of peatland degradation (in wildlife terms). The relationships between flora, fauna, peat and hydrology are complex and inextricably interlinked (see 2.5); changes in one affect all the others. For example, peat removal from one side of a raised bog could eventually affect the vegetation on the other side of the bog. The time-scale over which these changes occur is unknown but may be very slow given the extremely slow movement of water in the lower saturated catotelm layer (see 2.5.3).

As a consequence, it is sometimes quite difficult to identify the main causes of degradation to a site. It may just be the cumulative effect of centuries of small-scale damaging activities.

Another form of possible degradation manifests itself as peat erosion – a widespread phenomenon on upland blanket peats (see 4.5.6).

It is generally considered that no single mechanism can explain the erosion of bog peat in the British Isles. Anthropogenic influences such as sheep grazing (see 1.9, A3.3.3), burning (see 1.9, A3.3.5) and atmospheric pollution (see 1.13, A3.7.1) may be causative factors, although erosion may just be a natural phenomenon due to the dynamic nature and inherent instability of peatland systems (Tallis, 1985; Stevenson et al., 1990). For example, higher stocking rates of sheep can increase erosion and prevent eroding peat from stabilising and becoming revegetated (Birnie and Hulme, 1990; Birnie, 1993).

The two main types of erosion processes are those predominated by running water (more common) and those relating to mechanical failure and mass movement of peat. Water erosion produces linear and dendritic/reticulate channel systems depending on local topography. Linear channels generally occur on the steeper slopes and only occasionally intersect one another, whereas reticulate channels form a dense network around blocks of vegetation-capped peat. Extensive areas of bare peat are generally preceded by reticulate erosion or may result from severe fires. Although mass movements of peat occur relatively in-frequently, they can have a major impact. They are characterised by slumping and/or debris flow features known as bog bursts (Werritty and Ingram, 1985). Large blocks of peat, which may be several tens of metres across, become detached at the margin of peat-covered plateaux or on steep slopes, to slide or flow down-slope. This catastrophic event is triggered by major rainstorms.

DISTRIBUTION AND ECOLOGY

Bogs are unusual habitats, and an understanding of their ecology is key to effective conservation management. Part 2 acts as an introduction to bog ecosystems, and is divided into the following sections.

2.1   **Classification**

2.2   **Distribution**

2.3   **Raised and Blanket Bogs and their Formation**

2.4   **Bog Vegetation**

2.5   **Bog Hydrology**

2.6   **Bog Chemistry**

DISTRIBUTION AND ECOLOGY

2.1 CLASSIFICATION

Peatlands include a rich diversity of habitats. The range and variability of these habitats can be confusing. It is, therefore, useful to classify sites. For mires, many different criteria for classification are used (Moore, 1984). Classification systems are looked at in detail in Heathwaite and Göttlich (1993), Moore (1984), Moore and Bellamy (1974) and Gore (1983) among others.

A good starting point is the term 'mire', which simply describes any peat-forming ecosystem. Mires are commonly then subdivided into 'fens' and 'bogs' (Tansley, 1939). Fens are mires which are influenced by groundwater (that is, they are rheotrophic), whilst bogs are fed solely by precipitation (ombrotrophic). However, in England this simple system becomes slightly confused, as some valley fens are called bogs (for example, in the New Forest). More detailed classification schemes relate to different criteria. Moore (1984) describes seven different features which are used either separately or together to classify mires. These are: floristics, vegetation physiognomy, morphology, hydrology, stratigraphy, chemistry and peat characteristics. Of these, shape (morphol-

ogy), chemistry, plants (floristics) and structure are most widely used.

Shape

An early classification scheme was developed by Osvald (1925), who distinguished continental, Baltic, Atlantic and upland raised bogs. Baltic raised bogs are considered as classic with an outer lagg zone, a distinctive sloping rand and a gently domed cupola (Figure 2.1). Continental bogs are similar but forested. In more oceanic areas, Osvald noted that the surface of the dome was much flatter, forming a plateau rather than a dome; these were distinguished as Atlantic raised bogs. Upland raised bog is now not regarded as raised because they are unconfined, that is, they have no recognisable rand. Raised bogs are usually limited in extent and have a recognisable boundary (the rand). These unconfined peatlands are termed 'blanket bog' (Gore, 1983).

Shape is also used to subdivide 'raised' bogs into concentric (broadly symmetrical) and eccentric bogs. Most raised bogs in Britain are concentric, although some eccentric bogs do exist, for example, Claish and Kentra Mosses, Argyll.

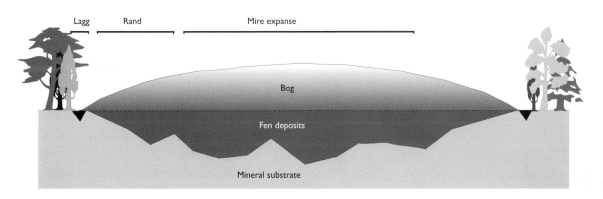

Figure 2.1   Profile of a classic 'Baltic' type raised bog.

Chemistry

The broad subdivision between bog and fen is reflected chemically, as fens are usually more eutrophic because of the nutrients within ground-water. Bogs are nutrient-poor because they are rain-fed. However, the amount of nutrients coming into a bog relates to the quantity of rainfall and distance from the sea. Sea-spray on to bog surfaces increases the nutrient status of a bog, whilst high rainfall serves to increase the total amount of nutrients falling onto a bog. These chemical variations partly account for a distinct east–west differentiation of blanket bogs in the British and Irish Isles (Ratcliffe, 1977).

Plants

A valuable approaches to mire classification is based on floral composition (Moore, 1984). Classifying mires on a botanical basis alone has been extensively used in Central Europe (for example, Rybnicek, 1984). This highly compart-mentalised approach used in Central Europe is less commonly adopted in Britain, where a continuum concept (Goodall, 1963) is more generally used. However, the recent National Vegetation Classification (Rodwell, 1991) is encouraging British ecologists to classify bogs in a more ordered way. The NVC classifies mires into thirty-eight different categories (termed noda), each of which is further subdivided. Whilst other NVC types may be found within bog habitat, the main bog vegetation communities are represented by seven NVC types:

M1   *Sphagnum auriculatum* bog pool community,
M2   *Sphagnum cuspidatum/recurvum* bog pool,
M3   *Eriophorum angustifolium* bog pool community,
M17 *Scirpus cespitosus – Eriophorum vaginatum* blanket mire,
M18 *Erica tetralix – Sphagnum papillosum* raised and blanket mire,
M19 *Calluna vulgaris – Eriophorum vaginatum* blanket mire, and
M20 *Eriophorum vaginatum* blanket and raised mire.

It should be noted that, as with any classi-fication, the NVC is an approximation and not a definitive description. It may be necessary to use different, or more focused, classification schemes.

Structure

A more abstract way of classifying bogs is to consider active structural or morphometric units. Ivanov (1981) suggests a four-stage bog classi-fication scheme: (1) mire microform such as a hummock or hollow; (2) mire microtope – a group of microforms making up a surface patterning on a bog; (3) mire mesotope – a body of peat which makes up a single hydrological unit such as a raised bog; and (4) mire macrotope which relate to situations where mesotopes have coalesced. Insight into the functioning of a bog ecosystem can sometimes be gained by considering it at these various levels.

For example, Lindsay et al. (1985) describe a series of labelled microforms (= microtopes) (Figure 2.2). These can sometimes be used to assess the hydrological condition of a bog.

For many years, the classification of bogs in Britain has been rather informal. The National Peatlands Resource Inventory (NPRI) represents a first attempt to map and classify all of Britain's peat deposits. The classification system used is deliberately simple: peatland is divided into fen, blanket bog, raised bog and intermediate bog (but *see* Wheeler and Shaw, 1995). Blanket bog in Britain is widespread, reflecting a highly oceanic climate. In the lowlands, a less oceanic climate has led to the development of raised bogs: discrete units of peat which are distinctly domed. Their shape and form, though, have often been highly modified by human activities. In some areas, where the distribution of raised and blanket bog coincide, the distinction is less easy to make. Particularly common are domed mantles of peat lying on hill tops or on ridges. Moore and Bellamy (1974) describe these bogs as ridge-raised mire, whilst Hulme (1980) terms them semi-confined mires. The NPRI simply classifies these types of bogs as intermediate bog, which can be confusing as the term 'intermediate bog' is also used to describe sites in transition from fen to bog (*see* 2.3.1).

2.2   DISTRIBUTION

2.2.1   World-wide Peatland Distribution

On a world-wide scale, mires cover an extensive area. Problems with definition and mapping make

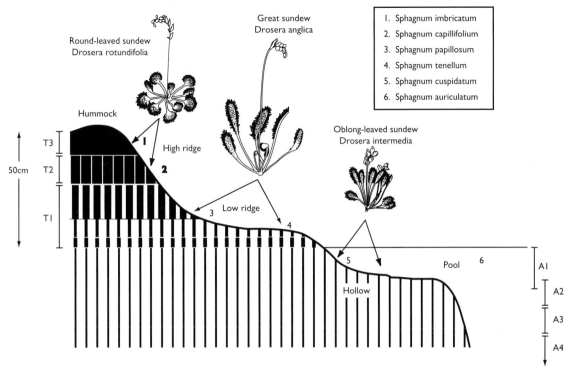

Figure 2.2 Generalised distribution of microforms and an idealised distribution of species found on northern British bogs (adapted from Lindsay et al.,1988).

it difficult to give a precise figure, although estimates suggest there are around 4 million square kilometres (for example, Immirzi et al., 1992). Figure 1.1 shows the global distribution of mire. The northern boreal countries have the highest concentrations of mire: principally Canada, the USA, Russia, Finland, China, Sweden and Norway. Huge areas of peatland are also found in the tropics, principally in Indonesia and Malaysia.

2.2.2   British Peatland Distribution

Britain's mires show considerable diversity. Taylor (1983) gives examples of valley mires, schwing-moors, raised bogs, upland blanket bog, lowland blanket bog and basin mires. A variety of factors (including high oceanicity; the existence of high-altitude peneplanation surfaces; glacial history; Holocene sea-level rise; and the impact of human culture at a time of deteriorating climates) have conspired to give rise to 8.4% of Britain's land surface being covered with mire (Taylor, 1983). The greatest areas of peat development are in the north-west, reflecting a highly oceanic climate. The relatively more continental climate of the south-east is less favourable to peat development.

In this handbook, only bogs are considered. Of the British bogs, there are clear differences between north-western or upland blanket peats and predominantly lowland raised bogs in terms of their setting, shape, flora and fauna (*see* 2.1).

Figure 2.3 shows the historical distribution of blanket, raised and intermediate bog as classified by the National Peatlands Resource Inventory. Today, many of the lowland bogs have been severely modified and are now unrecognisable as peatland ecosystems, that is, they are afforested or used as pasture or arable land.

The map shows clearly that raised bog is a restricted habitat in Britain. In sharp contrast, blanket bog is the dominant habitat in large areas of the country, especially in the uplands and the north and north-west.

Peat soils in Great Britain

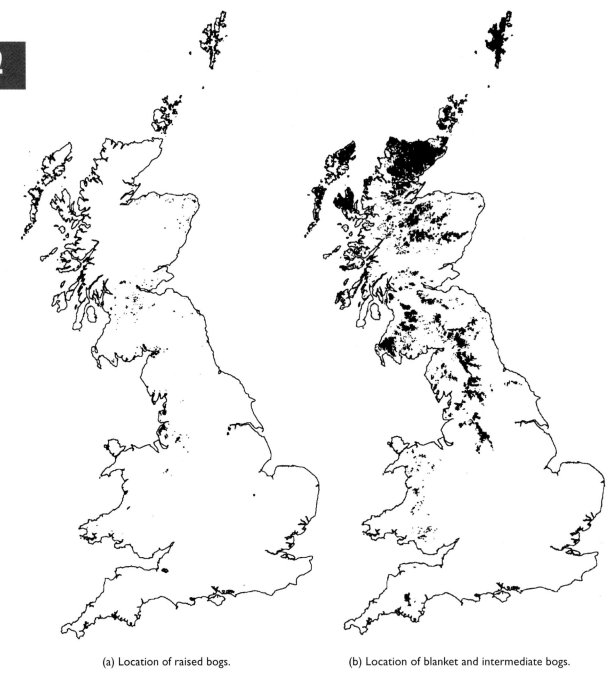

(a) Location of raised bogs.

(b) Location of blanket and intermediate bogs.

Figure 2.3   British bog distribution. From the National Peatland Resource Inventory. The boundaries derived from British Geological maps, plus additional information where necessary. Produced with permission of British Geological Survey and The controller HMSO; © Crown Copyright.

2.2.3 Blanket Bog – Global and British Distribution

The predominance of blanket bog over large areas of Britain is, globally, unique. Formation of blanket peat requires a climate which is both wet and cool. Indeed, rather exacting climatic conditions are required for blanket bog formation. Lindsay et al. (1988) point to a combination of a minimum annual rainfall of 1,000 mm, a minimum of 160 wet days and a cool climate (mean temperature below 15°C for the warmest month) for blanket peat formation. Superimposed on this climatic pattern is the role of human cultures in initiating blanket peat development (Moore, 1973). Lindsay et al. (1988) indicate parts of the globe where blanket bog has been recorded (Figure 2.4).

The diagram clearly shows that, on a global scale, blanket bog is a very limited resource.

Lindsay et al. (1988) tentatively estimate a total global resource of about 1.3 million ha, of which 13% is found in Britain. Britain and Ireland are considered as the classic region for blanket bog development.

Arguably the finest area of blanket bog in Britain occurs in Caithness and Sutherland – the great Flow Country (Figure 1.2). A combination of an extremely oceanic climate and a fairly level topography has resulted in 4,000 km² of almost continuous blanket bog. Ratcliffe and Osvald (1987) sum up its international significance:

- it is the largest and most intact known area of blanket bog in the world;
- it is a tundra-like ecosystem in a relatively southern region;
- it has developed unusually diverse systems of patterning;
- it has a unique floristic composition;
- it has a tundra-type breeding bird assemblage;

2.2

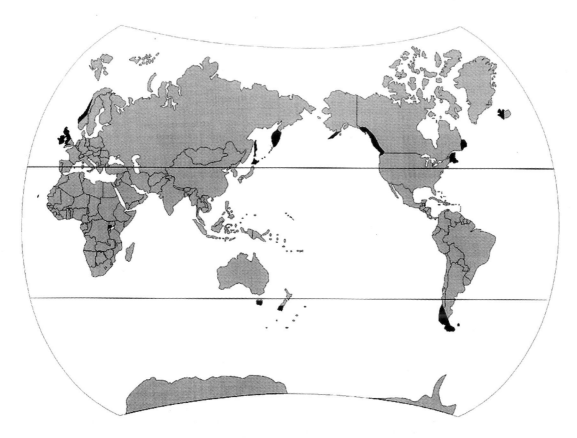

Figure 2.4 The global distribution of blanket mire. Blacked areas represent regions where blanket bog has been recorded.(adapted from Lindsay et al., 1988).

- it has significant fractions of notable bird species; and
- it has insular ecological adaptations by several bird species which may represent incipient evolutionary divergence in Britain.

2.2.4   Raised Bog – British Distribution

In contrast to blanket bog, 'classic' or 'type-site' raised bogs are the *Hochmoor* (literally translated as high moor = raised bog) of the Baltic region (*see* 2.1). In Britain, the dome of peat is less pronounced, with cupolas which are often flat. The margins of bogs are often less sloped, grading gently down to the mineral soil. In addition, lagg fen systems are rarely found, which is probably due to drainage of lagg fen systems for agriculture (*see* 1.9, A3.3).

However, raised bogs can be distinguished from blanket bog. They are generally found in the lowlands; they exist as discrete peatland units in a non-peat landscape, are raised above the general land surface and have a surface topography which is mostly independent of sub-surface topography.

Raised bogs are largely found in the north and west of England, and the lowlands of Scotland. A few raised bogs are also found in Wales, with outliers in east and south-west England. The original resource, shown in Figure 2.3, has now been severely depleted through conversion to agriculture, afforestation and more recently peat extraction for horticulture (*see* 1.8 – 1.14). Today, raised bogs, which are still dominated by 'near-natural' flora, are found mainly in central Scotland with a few other examples around the Solway Firth and in Wales.

Twenty per cent of the whole British resource of raised bog is found in the Upper Forth carselands. Here, eighteen raised bogs exist, of which six are SSSIs and one – East Flanders Moss – represents one of the largest expanses of 'intact' raised bog in Scotland.

2.3   RAISED AND BLANKET BOGS AND THEIR FORMATION

2.3.1   Raised Bogs

Raised bogs often develop over shallow basins formed during the last Ice Age. After the ice retreated from northern parts of Europe, the landscape was littered with many depressions within a mantle of often impermeable glacial debris or till. These basins formed lakes and were colonised by a fringe of fen vegetation. In-washed material formed lake sediments which, when mixed with dead and undecayed plant material, eventually led to many lakes completely infilling. Classically, it was thought that this sequence of succession gradually led to the development of forest over the former lake (for example, Tansley, 1939). Walker (1970), however, showed that this sequence of succession is rare.

Instead, as the lake basin is filled with fen peats and sediment, the plants at the centre are cut off from nutrients at the lake margins, making conditions rather nutrient-poor. *Sphagnum* bog mosses thrive in nutrient-poor and waterlogged conditions such as these, and can dominate in these situations (Figure 2.5).

Sphagnum leaves are characterised by large and empty hyaline cells sandwiching much smaller photosynthetic cells. The hyaline cells act as water-conducting systems, to allow *Sphagnum* spp. to cope with waterlogging, and create a large surface area for cation exchange (Daniels and Eddy, 1990). Cation exchange is the mechanism by which *Sphagnum* (and other plants) absorb nutrients dissolved in water. *Sphagnum*'s unusual physiognomy means that the genus has a high cation exchange ability, swapping scarce nutrients for hydrogen ions. As a result, *Sphagnum* species gradually acidify their surroundings (Clymo 1963). High acidity favours *Sphagnum* over many other species, further allowing Sphagna to dominate the infilled former lake.

Sphagna grow from the top of the plant – the apices – and die at the base. As a result, dead organic material is left in a waterlogged zone to form peat; Sphagna are efficient peat-formers. Water can move only very slowly through the peat, as it has a low hydraulic conductivity (Ingram, 1982). In effect, it is difficult for rainfall to leave the site, and waterlogged conditions are maintained.

The stage is now set for a dome of peat to form above the former lake-level and away from the influence of groundwater. *Sphagnum* growth continues in conditions of low nutrients, high

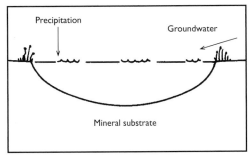

1. A hollow or depression fills with water.

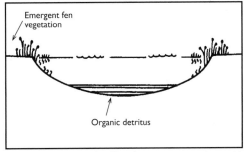

2. The open water gradually infills with organic or inorganic material.

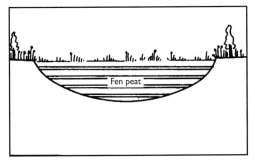

3. The depression completely infills. At this stage it is still influenced by mineral-rich groundwater.

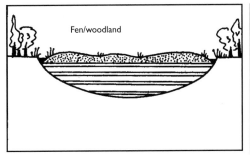

4. Inputs now become dominated by precipitation alone. Vegetation changes from minerotrophic to ombrotropic species.

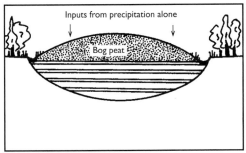

5. Bog peat is laid down by specialist plant communities. All input is now from precipitation alone as the dome extends above the surrounding land.

Figure 2.5   Hydroseral succession leading to the development of a raised bog.

acidity and waterlogging to accumulate layers of peat which rise above the landscape. Once a half-metre layer has formed above the former lake-level, the surface becomes isolated from ground-water (Granlund, 1932). The bog now becomes dependent upon rainwater alone, that is, the system becomes ombrotrophic (rain-fed). Rain-fed bogs derive all their nourishment from the atmosphere; bogs are highly nutrient-deficient systems.

2.3.2   Blanket Bog

In cool, moist and mild airstreams, ground can become so waterlogged that dead vegetation cannot decompose fully, leading to the formation of peat directly on to mineral surfaces (paludification). This process is dramatically illustrated in north-west Scotland, where peat forms directly upon large, isolated glacial erratics – bogs on rocks (Figure 2.6). Usually, however this process – paludification – proceeds upon highly podzolised glacial tills. Constant precipitation allied to low evaporation rates leads to podzol formation, eventually forming an iron-pan. Once an iron-pan forms, the soil above is prone to waterlogging to form a peaty-gleyed podzol. Decay processes are often slowed enough to form peat. After this stage,

Figure 2.6   A peat mound growing on an isolated boulder - an extreme example of blanket peat formation. (Rob Stoneman)

the peat itself holds water back because of low hydraulic conductivity, allowing layer upon layer of peat to build to a considerable thickness, eventually blanketing the landscape.

In Britain and Ireland, there is evidence to suggest that podzolisation and the eventual development of blanket peat was partly or, possibly, wholly the result of human intervention (Moore, 1973). Under the warmer and drier climatic conditions of the early Holocene (9000–6000 years BP), deciduous forest (across most of Britain) or pine forest (in northern Scotland) developed to cover most of the landscape. An exception may be the Northern Isles and parts of northern Scotland. Following deforestation by prehistoric farmers and an accompanying deterioration of climatic conditions in the mid- to late Holocene (between 5,000 and 2,000 years BP), exposed brown earth soils, which had developed under a forest canopy, became podzolised, eventually leading to peat formation. Whether climatic conditions would have led to forest decline and peat formation directly, without human intervention, is open to debate. Certainly, in the Flow Country, pine forest had developed on peat surfaces but eventually succumbed to wetter climatic conditions irrespective of human land use (Charman, 1994).

Once peat forms, the same set of processes described for raised bogs (*see* 2.3.1) operates on blanket bogs. Sphagna acidify the environment and efficiently form peat whilst peat formation

itself maintains waterlogging. The surface eventually becomes rain-fed, and takes on the bog characteristics of high-acidity, low-nutrient status and waterlogging.

Such peat formation can proceed on even quite steep slopes given appropriate climatic conditions. In the north-west Highlands, peat forms on slopes as steep as 35° (Lindsay, 1995). The distribution of blanket bog is clearly controlled by climate.

In addition to paludification, other processes of mire formation can occur in blanket bog landscapes. Terrestrialisation of open water bodies via hydroseral succession to bog – usually raised bog – leads to domed, apparently raised bog units within a blanket bog landscape. Additionally, water courses are enveloped in fen vegetation and fen peats form. Blanket bog, in fact, is rather a misnomer as the landscape is often composed of a mixture of ombrotrophic (bog) and rheotrophic (fen) units (Figure 2.7). A more accurate expression is blanket mire, as this includes all peatland elements. In this volume, the term 'blanket bog' is retained for familiarity purposes. However, it should be recognised that blanket bog is actually a highly diverse landscape.

The diversity of blanket bog landscapes is reflected by their hydrology. Lindsay et al. (1988) recognise the importance of morphology in controlling the hydrology of blanket peats by classifying mesotopes (mire units) according to their hydromorphology (*see* 2.1). Broad categories include:

• Watershed bog	Truly ombrotrophic peats developed on the tops of hills.
• Saddle bogs	These may have developed from terrestrialisation of pools within saddles. Saddle bogs are partly rheotrophic as they receive water from surrounding hillsides.
• Valleyside peats	These peats are often thin, depending upon the angle of slope. Vegetation reflects higher rates of flushing and is generally less 'ombrotrophic' with a lower cover of *Sphagnum* mosses.

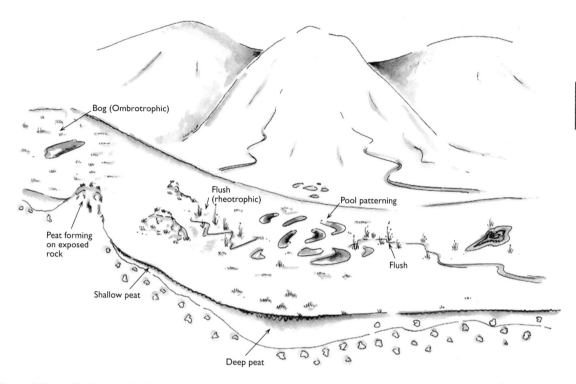

2.4

Figure 2.7   Blanket bog landscape features (adapted from Lindsay, 1995).

- Spur bogs   These combine features of saddle and valley side bogs.
- Ladder fens   A special category of mire found in the Flow Country, which has affinities to ribbed fens found in eastern Canada (Charman, 1993).
- Minerotrophic fens   These form in water collection areas.

2.4   BOG VEGETATION

2.4.1   Introduction

The conditions of high-acidity, low-nutrient status and waterlogging lead to a distinctive vegetation type. Commonly-found vegetation include *Sphagnum* bog mosses, sedges (cotton grass and deer sedge in particular) and various heathers. The nutrient-poor conditions are exemplified by sundews and butterworts which gain extra nutrients (particularly nitrogen) by catching and absorbing insects.

On a European continental scale, the range of vegetation types across bogs is, unsurprisingly, large. Eastern, continental bogs are tree-covered. In southern Germany, mountain pine (*Pinus mugo*) grows as a low-spreading prostrate shrub. In more continental climates, such as Siberia, trees dominate bogs entirely. In western Europe, a transition from the south to the north is noticeable. In Britain, vegetation variation relates mainly to east–west rainfall variation (hyper-oceanic to oceanic climates) and to altitude. Good descriptions of bog vegetation types can be found in Rodwell (1991) and McVean and Ratcliffe (1962).

Four broad categories of bog vegetation are commonly encountered in Britain: western blanket bog, eastern and high-level blanket bog, lowland bog and damaged bog.

2.4.2   Western Blanket Bog

Western blanket bog occurs in very wet (hyper-oceanic) parts of Britain (over 2,000 mm per year and over 200 wet days per year), although it is

2.4

generally found below 500 m where frost is infrequent. From a distance, deer grass and purple moor grass appear dominant. On closer inspection, the ground layer is rich in bryophytes, particularly *Sphagnum papillosum*, *S. capillifolium*,whilst hare's tail cotton grass, heathers (ling heather and cross-leaved heath especially) and, sometimes, bog myrtle are common. Wetter areas in these communities are represented by a high percentage of *Sphagnum* species, common cotton grass and bog asphodel. The wettest parts have bog pools which are colonised by white-beaked sedge and *Sphagnum auriculatum*. The driest areas may have an increased abundance of *Racomitrium lanuginosum* and *Cladonia* spp. The most western blanket bogs differ by the presence of black bog rush, common in western Ireland and on the Scottish island of Islay.

2.4.3   High-level or Eastern Blanket Bog

At higher altitudes or in eastern areas, where rainfall is between 1,200 and 2,000 mm p.a. with 160–200 wet days per year, blanket bog vegetation is characterised principally by hare's tail cotton grass and ling heather. This type of vegetation is prevalent across the Scottish Eastern Highlands and Southern Uplands and the English Pennines. Under a regime of burning and grazing with high levels of atmospheric pollution, hare's tail cotton grass becomes dominant. Indeed, in the southern Pennines, heather is lost almost completely. On high areas, mountain shrubs occur like cranberry, cowberry, northern (bog) bilberry, small crowberry, bearberry, dwarf birch and the herb, cloudberry.

2.4.4   Lowland Bog

In the less oceanic lowlands of north-western Europe, bog vegetation is characterised by a carpet of *Sphagnum* mosses, in particular, *S. magellanicum*, *S. papillosum*, *S. capillifolium*, *S. tenellum*, *S. cuspidatum* and, sometimes, *S. imbricatum*, *S. fuscum* and *S. pulchrum*. The multicoloured patterning of *Sphagnum* mosses is delightful. In the mix of mosses, vascular plants such as hare's tail cotton grass, common cotton grass, ling heather and cross-leaved heath are common with bog rosemary, bog asphodel, deer grass, cranberry and round-leaved sundew all commonly found. Wetter areas are characterised by pools of *S. cuspidatum* and *S. recurvum*.

The lowland bog vegetation type is most frequently found on raised bogs, although it can be found on intermediate bogs and where blanket bog extends over saddles and deep depressions (*see* 2.3.2).

2.4.5   Damaged Bogs

Though commonly found, this type is more rarely described. Unfortunately, land managers are probably more familiar with various types of damaged bogs than the relatively pristine communities described above. Appendix 3 describes the ecological effects of various types of damage and the types of vegetation likely to be encountered. Broadly, though, the main changes relate to changes in water level, from drainage, abstraction, peat-cutting and so on, and chemical conditions, from eutrophication, atmospheric pollution, burning, grazing and so on.

On pristine bogs, the water level is high – only centimetres below the surface. Only in very dry weather do water levels drop below 10–20 cm. On damaged bogs, water levels are often lower and vegetation communities are typified by heath and woodland. Particularly common is a decline in *Sphagnum* mosses and an increase in heathers and/or sedges. This is followed or accompanied by scrub invasion by pine or birch. Many very dried-out or cut-over bogs are now colonised by open-canopy birch or pine woodland. Another common element in today's modified bogs is rhododendron. This common exotic can establish itself on wet bogs. Rhododendron thrives on drained bogs, spreading rapidly to become a monotonous dense thicket.

The effects of eutrophication are less clear. Direct eutrophication from contaminated waters is unusual unless the bog has been cut or waters are deliberately pumped onto the surface (*see*, for example, 6.4). However, atmospheric pollution (particularly nitrogen) may be having a greater effect than perhaps realised. In Scotland, many lowland bogs are devoid of *S. magellanicum*, although *S. recurvum* is abundant. This appears to be especially so near roads, suggesting that atmospheric pollution may be an important factor. In central Europe, Twenhoven (1992) has found a similar replacement of *S. magellanicum* by *S. fallax* (= *S. recurvum*), and he also postulates atmospheric pollution as the cause (*see* A3.7.1).

2.5 BOG HYDROLOGY

2.5.1 Inputs and Outputs

Peat is mainly water occupying space between soil particles or filling pools on the surface. The bog's water-table is shaped as a dome – indeed, it is the dome of water which shapes the peat-body. Understanding how the water-table adopts a domed profile is key to the understanding of bog ecosystems.

On the dome of the bog itself, the only water which reaches the surface comes from above as rain, snow or fog entering the bog as meteoric water and leaving the bog as groundwater. Water is lost from the system via a number of routes.

As *evapotranspiration*: rainwater can be caught by vegetation and is simply evaporated straight back into the atmosphere. The rainwater which is not evaporated falls onto and infiltrates the bog surface. Again, some of this is directly evaporated back to the atmosphere. Another part of the water is taken up by plants to be returned to the atmosphere via transpiration. The total effect is termed 'evapotranspiration', a process that occurs readily on warm, sunny or windy days.

As *seepage*: the remaining water occupies pores between plant material, within *Sphagnum* hyaline cells and between soil particles. The water within the pores can move as long as it has the energy to do so, that is, has hydraulic potential. On bogs, this potential is fired by gravity; not surprisingly, water moves downhill from the centre to the edges of the peat dome. The rate at which it moves partly depends upon the ability of the water to move through the pore spaces. If the pores are small or the number of channels are few, the hydraulic conductivity is low and the water passes through slowly. The amount of water moving out of the bog is termed 'seepage', which can be vertical (out through the base) or lateral (out through the sides).

2.5.2 The Water Balance

The various inputs and outputs can be expressed by the water balance equation. Essentially, the amount of precipitation must equal the amount lost by evapotranspiration, lateral seepage and vertical seepage, balanced by any change in the total volume of water stored in the bog itself. This is more commonly written as the water balance equation:

$$P - E - U - G - \Delta W = 0$$

where P = precipitation, E = evapotranspiration, U = lateral seepage, G = vertical seepage and ΔW = the change in storage. Of these variables, vertical seepage is usually low as peat bogs often sit on impermeable bases – glacial clays or saturated sediments – whilst changes in storage are often quite small. Evapotranspiration and lateral seepage are, therefore, the most important ways in which a bog balances the precipitation coming in.

2.5.3 The Hydraulic System

Given that lateral seepage is important, consider the way in which it varies across the bog. The centre of the bog receives water from precipitation alone (Figure 2.8i). The peat around this central portion receives water from precipitation and from seepage emanating from the central area (Figure 2.8ii). Moving outwards, each successive ring, away from the centre, receives progressively more and more water. To disperse these increasing volumes of water, the slope of the water-table has to increase, that is, the water in the bog must take the form of a dome – a groundwater mound (Figure 2.8iii) or, to put it another way:

> A raised mire is sustained by… discharge, which creates a groundwater mound in the catotelm, whose hydrodynamics mould the profile of the intact peat deposit to a hemi-ellipse. (Ingram, 1992)

The groundwater mound can be modelled (Bragg and Brown, in preparation) although the equations are complex. Most important though, is that alteration of one part of the dome must affect the rest of the system. The whole peat body constitutes a single hydrological system unified by the lateral seepage of water.

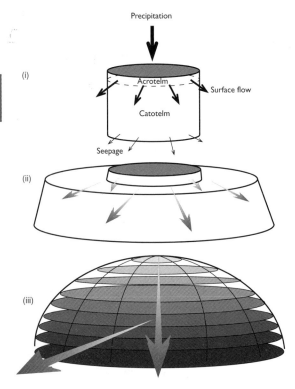

(i)

2.5

(ii)

(iii)

Figure 2.8   The variation of lateral seepage in successive rings around the central core of the bog.

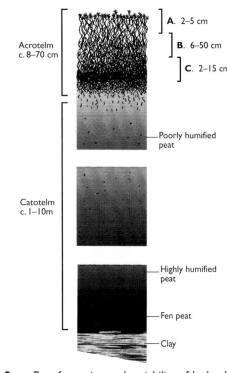

Acrotelm
c. 8–70 cm

A. 2–5 cm

B. 6–50 cm

C. 2–15 cm

Poorly humified peat

Catotelm
c. 1–10m

Highly humified peat

Fen peat

Clay

Figure 2.9   Peat formation and variability of hydraulic conductivity through the profile. **A**—Plants are alive and photosynthetic – 90% of volume is void, 10% water filled. Gas and water moves very freely through this structure. **B**—Material is gradually buried by apical growth of *Sphagnum* above – most of the plant material is dead. Water can still move freely between plants which are largely intact. **C**—Progressive decay and an increased load from above causes dead plant stems to collapse. Dry bulk density increases five fold and hydraulic conductivity is increased 625-fold. The flow of water beneath this layer is thus very slow and it remains permanently waterlogged.

2.5.4   Hydrology and Ecology

On European bogs, *Sphagnum* mosses are dominant, growing as tightly packed carpets of individual stems gently undulating across the surface as hummocks and pools. By taking a core of surface peat, the peat formation process is exposed (Figure 2.9).

On the collapse of stems, the pore-space dramatically decreases, making seepage increasingly difficult – the hydraulic conductivity declines 625-fold (Clymo, 1992). The effect is of great consequence, as water movement slows to such an extent that the peat becomes permanently waterlogged. During dry weather, when water levels drop into the zone of low hydraulic conductivity, seepage is extremely slow. Only in wet weather is rapid seepage possible through the upper, more open, layer of peat.

The two layers of the peat profile are clearly very different. The upper layer – the *acrotelm* – is partly alive, only semi-waterlogged, is where the peat forms and contains the water level. In sharp contrast, the lower layer, which forms the vast majority of the peat – the *catotelm* – is permanently waterlogged and virtually dead.

2.5.5   The Water-table

The dynamics of this system are reflected by changes in the water-table which convey changes in the total amount of storage in the system. By referring back to the water balance equation, it can be seen that a rapid decline in the water level (a reduction in water storage) can only be achieved by either high rates of evapotranspiration or, and more likely, a high rate of lateral seepage. The water level recorder at Cors Caron shows this pattern (Figure 2.10). Generally, the water-table stays at a similar level. On raining, the water level increases rapidly but then falls back fairly quickly to a constant level (about 5 cm below the surface). The pattern reflects lateral seepage draining the bog which slows when water levels fall back towards the catotelm. Only during the summer, when evapotranspiration rates are particularly high, can water levels drop further. This pattern, where the bog water-table is more or less constant throughout the year, reflects a relatively intact situation. Deviations from this pattern reflect alteration of the bog.

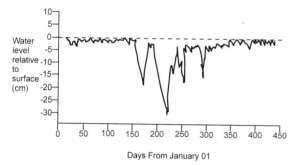

Figure 2.10 The water-level as recorded at Cors Caron SE bog in 1992.

2.6 Bog Chemistry

2.6.1 Peat Hydrochemistry

Peat chemistry is generally dictated by peatland vegetation and the influence of its microbial communities. It is also strongly influenced by human activities. Peat chemistry influences human agricultural and forestry activities and also has a bearing on water quality. This can be very important; in Scotland, for example, 95% of the country's drinking water is derived from peatland-rich catchments.

In peatlands, the process of humification produces organic acids as end-products which are key to the understanding of bog chemistry. Molecules are usually composed of two parts: a positively-charged cation which is attracted to a negatively-charged anion.

These organic acids neutralise incoming alkaline anions such as bicarbonates (the only relatively strong base found in natural surface waters) and, therefore, become the dominant anions in peat hydrochemistry alongside hydrogen and sodium cations with smaller contributions from magnesium, potassium and calcium. Sulphate usually forms the major *in*organic anion, arising from the oxidation of organic matter containing sulphur, such as, amino acids. However, since the Industrial Revolution, much sulphate has derived from human activities, for example, as acid rain from power stations.

In all cases, soluble organic matter is the dominant anion although, in oceanic bogs, sodium and chloride are evident because of marine salt inputs in rainwater. The soluble organic matter gives rise to drainage water pH values of around 4.2–4.4 in ombrotrophic peatlands (very acidic). Drainage waters from undisturbed peatlands are usually moderately coloured but rich in dissolved organic matter. Disturbance, by erosion or cultivation of the surface, for example, leads to increased suspended sediment, that is, particulate peat, and also to deeply-coloured drainage waters which can contain elevated levels of organic matter.

2.6.2 Peat Soil Chemistry

The dominant components of peat are water (mainly) and humic substances.

These humic substances are mostly mixtures of plant and microbial-derived macromolecules formed from building blocks of *poly*saccharides, lignin and *poly*peptides. Some humic substances are water-soluble. Others are insoluble poly-carboxylic acids (fulvic and humic acids) which form a variety of molecules. Some of these molecules react with calcium, thereby removing bony structures from animal remains buried in peat, and also react with substances such as skin and hair, causing a tanning process which helps to preserve these. Peat also contains waxy residues (up to 40% dry weight). The high wax content makes it difficult to rewet dried peat.

2.6

The macromolecules are prone to oxidation when exposed to air, releasing nitrogen (usually as ammonium), sulphate and carbon into drainage waters from disturbed peatlands, for example, where ditches have been dug or where the bog has been cut away. The carbon output is usually in the form of colloidal humic substances. One of the down-stream effects of such run-off is the precipitation of dark-coloured surface coatings on stream-bed sediments, especially where bog drainage mixes with calcium- and iron-rich (due to liming) run-off from improved land. This can be confused with visibly similar iron ochre deposition which may have equally severe effects on stream-bed ecology.

PLANNING CONSERVATION MANAGEMENT

The various planning stages are outlined in the following sections:

DEVISING A MANAGEMENT PLAN

Devising a Management Plan

Part 3 discusses the management planning process and how it could be applied to bogs. On intact sites, the objectives for management are simple – to maintain the natural functioning of the bog; it may be that a 'do-nothing' plan is all that is required. Almost all bogs are damaged, and conservation management is usually required. The most effective way to pursue such management is first to devise a plan (even if a do-nothing policy is the outcome). These plans are often structured into the four planning stages shown below:

1. Description	The description acts as a summary statement which outlines the important features of the site and its ecology.
2. Evaluation and Setting Objectives	The second stage is an evaluation of the site to outline clearly-identified and stated objectives for management.
3. Action Plan Prescriptions	For each objective, outline prescriptions (tasks) which would achieve that objective are identified. Each outline prescription is then converted into one, or usually more, units of work often called projects.
4. Reporting, Monitoring and Evaluation	Projects can be listed within a project register. Forward planning can be achieved by detailing annual work plans which state all projects and their associated resource implications. The progress of work can then be monitored by setting up a project recording system. This has been formalised and computerised in the Countryside Management System.

These stages are in reality a cyclical continuum allowing the plan to be reviewed annually and updated every five years to ensure that the plan remains relevant. Monitoring and survey is essential to monitor the effectiveness of the plan and management works. At best, each management project would have a monitoring project attached to it. In practice, this is often far too time-consuming. However, monitoring is required to evaluate whether original objectives of the plan are being realised.

Management plan preparation can be a lengthy and time-consuming process. To avoid getting tangled up in management planning at the expense of actual conservation management, begin with short and simple plans which can be expanded, if necessary, at a later date. For small and uncomplicated sites, plans need only be small – a couple of pages. This can then be built upon to form more detailed documents when plans are reviewed annually or overhauled.

The following sections go through the planning stages outlined above to indicate the methods and techniques which may be used to formulate an effective plan and monitor progress. The techniques are described, in more detail, in Parts 4 and 5.

PLANNING CONSERVATION MANAGEMENT

3.1 DESCRIPTION

3.1.1 Introduction

The description of the site is usually a collation process of known information on which the evaluation exercise can be based. This process allows shortfalls within the data to be identified and gaps made up through appropriate survey. However, for bogs, management can be ineffective without an adequate baseline dataset. The complexities of bog management requires various types of data. For example, a knowledge of hydrology, peat depth, underlying geology, topography, water chemistry and type of peat would all have to be gathered if the restoration of a commercial peat extraction site was considered.

Vegetation, hydrology, topography and safety/hazards information is all important for effective management planning. However, a high level of detail is not always required; plan preparation or actual management need not be held up by a complex, expensive and time-consuming data collection exercise.

It is clear that baseline data collection is often a map-based exercise. A large-scale map is extremely useful for recording any information. It is recommended that 1:10,000 maps are used, though for small sites these can be enlarged to cover most of an A3 page (it is worth noting by how much the map has been enlarged to get a correct scale). Large sites may need to be split onto several pages or represented using a smaller scale (1:25,000 for example). The value of Geographical Information Systems (GIS) for managing sites is increasingly being recognised as it allows quick and easy data manipulation. Equally importantly, maps concerning various aspects of site management can fairly easily be generated (although bear in mind the cost of a plotter).

3.1.2 Vegetation

Bog management often relates to setting up appropriate conditions to maintain or encourage various types of vegetation. A vegetation map is, therefore, central to decision-making. A practical way to describe the vegetation a site is to divide it into compartments of fairly homogenous vegetation types. Compartments can be defined by three methods:

1. On small sites, walking around the site with a map may be all that is required. On more damaged sites, man-made features such as walls, fences, tracks, drains, forest boundaries, peat-cuts and so on can be used as the boundary between compartments. If there are few features on the ground for adequate orientation, a grid system may need to be installed (*see* A6.2.2.4).

2. For larger sites, it may be impractical to walk round the whole site for mapping purposes. In these cases, aerial photographs should be purchased or borrowed. Interpretation of these images can then be used for initial mapping. Aerial photograph interpretation (API) of bogs should always be backed up with ground truthing since contrasting vegetation types may be indistinguishable on the photograph (*see* 4.6.4).

3. Very large areas of blanket bog are much more difficult to compartmentalise. One method, used by Scottish Natural Heritage to map blanket bog (although for inventory rather than management purposes), is the use of satellite imagery. Blocks of image pixels with a similar frequency (colour) are checked in the field to provide a classification system which can then be applied to the whole image (*see* 4.6.5, A6.4.5.3).

The detail to which a site may be compartmentalised depends both on the likely management of the site and available resources. Swiss managers have described sites in immense detail. API of false colour 1:10,000 or 1:5,000 aerial photographs can be used to map individual hummocks and pools, through this level of detail is rarely required. A sensible mapping policy would be to compartmentalise areas of broader vegetation communities. Note that UK National Vegetation Classification (NVC) mire communities are not necessarily the best way of compartmentalising a site for management purposes.

Once a site is compartmentalised, vegetation information can be collected from each compartment. As ever, the amount of vegetation survey is dependent upon time and expertise available. A few quadrats (*see* 4.6.3) per compartment may suffice where the vegetation is rather similar. A more accurate survey would require a greater number of quadrats.

This information can then be used to prepare a vegetation map. In Britain, NVC maps (*see* 2.1) are commonly prepared. These are not always appropriate for damaged bogs since the NVC describes 'natural' vegetation communities which may not necessarily be represented. Accordingly, it may be more useful to devise a site-specific scheme to describe the main variation within the site. An example is shown in Figure 3.1.

3.1.3   Hydrology

Bog management is nearly always tied to manipulating a site's hydrological regime. Accordingly, hydrological information is required. This has various uses:

- The existing hydrology needs to be assessed before it can be altered. An imperfect understanding of the hydrology of a site can lead to poor hydrological control and, thus, wasteful use of scarce resources.
- Before management measures are implemented, the manager ought to know the possible implications of management around the site. For example, drain-blocking may cause the majority of a site's discharge to exit via a different channel. That channel may not be able to cope with extra flow, thus flooding neighbouring land (an unpopular move!).
- Alteration of the hydrology of one part of the site may have significant effects in other parts of the site. Drain-blocking of one area to raise water levels to the surface may cause unexpected backing up and flooding. More commonly, water simply finds another exit via a different part of the site, causing the failure of a management scheme.

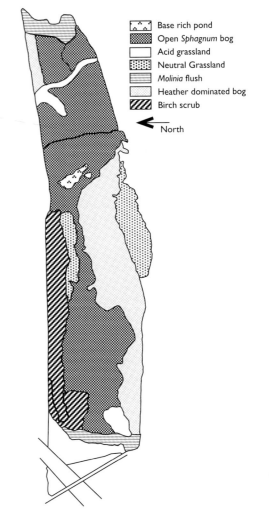

Base rich pond
Open *Sphagnum* bog
Acid grassland
Neutral Grassland
Molinia flush
Heather dominated bog
Birch scrub

North

Figure 3.1   Vegetation compartment map of Tailend Moss, Scotland.

The simplest way to assess the hydrological regime of a site is to draw up a hydrological map (Figure 3.2). This map could detail the following features:

- route and direction of flows (streams, erosion channels, flushes, seepage lines) – topographical survey may be required;
- all anthropogenic drainage features: ditches, pipes, mine-shafts, channels, cracks, tile-drains and so on;
- the main water catchments within a site;
- all inflows and outflows;
- water shedding and water collecting areas;

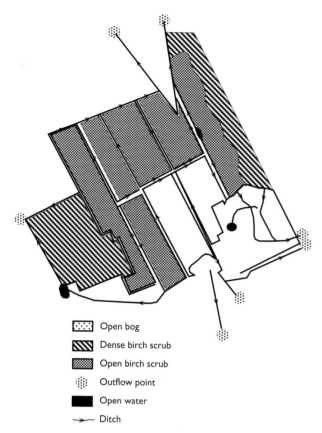

Open bog

Dense birch scrub

Open birch scrub

Outflow point

Open water

Ditch

Figure 3.2   Hydrological map of Lenzie Moss, Scotland.

- diffuse flows; and
- any areas of permanent standing water on the site.

A useful approach is to combine stereo aerial photography and ground mapping. API can be used to map all the obvious hydrological features. Ground survey is then required to assess the direction of flow. This can be ascertained by accurate levelling (*see* 4.2, A6.2) or, more simply, by going out on a rainy day and seeing which way the water flows. Once the main routes and directions of flow have been mapped, main catchments can also be mapped.

Another type of useful baseline hydrological survey has been carried out successfully on Fenns and Whixhall Mosses (*see* 6.1). There, summer and winter areas of open water were mapped.

When carrying out these types of mapping it is worth bearing in mind the following points:

- On an undamaged bog, most of the flow is through the surface semi-aerated '*acrotelm*' layer (*see* 2.5.4). Flow is diffuse and direction of flows on often fairly level surfaces are difficult to detect. Piezometer networks (*see* 4.3.4.3) may be the only way to gauge flow direction.
- On reasonably 'natural' raised bogs, flow is generally from the centre to the edge of the bog exiting into a surrounding lagg stream or fen. However, since most raised bogs are far from 'natural', flow patterns are usually highly altered. On Flanders Moss (Stirlingshire, Scotland) for example, drains, cut into the edge of the bog, act as water-collecting foci for the area immediately surrounding the drain. Increased flow in these areas seems to have caused the formation of a poorly-defined channel running back towards the centre of the Moss. Thus, the channel now has a large catchment area. These types of problems are not always obvious; ideally a detailed contour map should be drawn (*see* 4.2.9, A6.2).
- The hydrology of 'natural' blanket bog is much more complex than raised bogs. Sub-surface piping, complex pool systems, variable topography, sink holes, springs and so on all serve to create hydrological complexity. At its simplest, water travels by diffuse flow within surface layers in the direction of the slope. Many areas of blanket bog within Britain have been moor-gripped to improve grazing (*see* 1.9, A3.3.2), creating an artificial hydrological regime.
- Saturated peat is not impermeable but does exhibit a very low hydrological conductivity (*see* 2.5). Water seeps very slowly through peat barriers, and this may be an important pathway in some sites. Different types of peat have different conductivities. White or less humified upper peats (*see* 4.5.5.1) are more permeable than black, highly humified peat.
- Sub-surface piping is a common feature on blanket mire and has been found on raised bogs (such as, at Flanders Moss). If water appears to 'disappear' on a site, have a good poke around with a stick to check for the existence of these pipes.
- Water can often be found upwelling onto the mire surface (*see*, for example, 6.14). Peat bogs may even initially form as spring-fed peat mounds (for example, Red Lake Peatlands, N. America: Glaser et al., 1981). Water may also exit within the bog. On Moss Moran (Fife, Scotland), most of the water exits into old mine workings located in the centre of the bog.
- Where most of the peat has been stripped away to leave only thin layers of peat overlying mineral ground, surface water may exit the bog through the sub-surface. This only happens

3.1

where the mineral strata below the peat are permeable. On Thorne Moors (*see* 6.19), underlying sandy deposits were probably originally saturated. Land drainage and water abstraction have caused groundwater levels to drop considerably, allowing water to seep through the thin layer of peat remaining (after peat extraction) and exit into the ground aquifer. Similar problems are experienced at Engbertsdijksvenen (*see* 6.12).

3.1.4   Topography

Hydrological control also requires a knowledge of the topography of a site. At its simplest, this could just involve sketching topography onto a site map. Often, more detailed topographical survey is required. As a minimum, it is worth levelling (*see* 4.2, A6.2.2, 3.1.3) the main water routes in the site, such as, drains, erosion channels and so on. This will help in deciding where to locate dams, for example (*see* 5.1.2.1). More detailed topographical survey may also be required in areas which are likely to receive intensive management. For example, the topography of a block (sod) cut area may need surveying for effective management.

For large and complex sites, where a high level of hydrological manipulation is required, it may be worthwhile to survey the whole site to provide a baseline information set. This can be carried out in two ways. The site can be surveyed using levelling equipment (*see* 4.2, A6.2) which often requires a grid system (the greater the number of grid points, the more accurate the survey is). Alternatively, aerial photogrammetric mapping (*see* A6.2.2.1) can be used to automatically produce contour maps. Note that these are expensive (£5,000–£7,000 on a 40–100ha site) and their precision relates to the type of vegetation cover.

Detailed topographic maps can also be used to assess the groundwater mound of raised bogs (*see* 2.5.3). Careful modelling of the bog (Bragg and Brown, in preparation) can be used to solve conservation problems.

> It is important to note that surveying topography is an expensive and time-consuming. Topographic survey should only be contemplated if the results are genuinely required.

3.1.5   Special Interest – Fauna and Flora

Bogs harbour unusual vegetation given their extreme conditions of low pH, low nutrients and waterlogging (*see* 2.4). In addition, there are a number of particular species which are now rare and restricted to a few sites. For example, Rannoch Moor (Scotland) contains the only British locality for *Scheuzeria palustris* (Rannoch Rush).

It is often useful to record exactly where these species grow on a site to ensure that future management operations do not drastically affect the population.

Similarly, particularly rare fauna should also be mapped. Many bogs are important invertebrate sites (*see* 4.7.3). Sometimes, their preferred habitat has resulted from damage. Management objectives to conserve a bog and invertebrate communities can conflict. Compromises and prioritising are then necessary (*see* 3.2).

Mapping of rare species is of interest to assessing the effects of management (which may encourage an expansion of these populations) and also acts as a management constraint map. Management operations can be tailored to take cognisance of the distribution of rare species.

3.1.6   Safety and Hazards

Bogs can be dangerous places (*see* Appendix 4). Whilst the oft-quoted tales of coach and horses being subsumed into the mire may be an exaggeration, there is a record of a man on horseback found, perfectly preserved, in a bog on the Slamannan Plateau, Scotland. More recently, a small boy drowned in a bog pool in a Norwegian bog nature reserve. Most bogs, however, are far too dry nowadays to present this sort of risk, although artificial pools (such as dammed-up drains) present a safety hazard.

More commonly, on damaged bogs, the dried shrubby vegetation on dry peat presents a serious fire risk. Glasson Moss (Cumbria, England) burned for four months in the dry summer of 1976 as a fire slowly burned within the peat (Lindsay, 1977).

The forbidding and hazardous nature of bogs has been both an advantage and disadvantage for their conservation. On the one hand, this aspect has kept people off sites, so leaving some sites in a remarkable 'natural' state. However, this view of bogs has also contributed to unchecked exploitation. Clearly, to alter this view, people should be encouraged to visit bog nature reserves. Given the inherent dangers associated with bogs, a baseline hazard/safety survey is essential.

A convenient way to collate this information is onto a map (*see* 6.1). Safety/hazard information should include:

- drain network indicating particularly deep and/or hazardous drains (for example, drains which have vegetated over) and crossing points;
- deep pits or fire-pools;
- areas of unstable peat;
- areas of severe fire risk;
- hazards from derelict machinery or equipment;
- game shooting areas;
- wooded areas – danger from falling trees in high winds (trees on peat are always shallow-rooted and are susceptible to wind-throw); and
- emergency telephone locations.

In addition, consult with the local fire-brigade to produce a fire-hazard map. This would detail access routes, areas of deep water, areas of high fire-risk, firebreaks, turning points for fire appliances and adjacent fire hydrants.

3.1.7 Archaeological, Palaeoecological and Historical Interest

Part of the interest in bogs relates to the richness of the archive found within the peat. The significance of these types of remains should be considered as equal to the nature conservation significance of the site. Usually, conservation of the two areas of interest requires the same types of management (Coles, 1995). Rarely, conflicts may arise. For example, in the peat fields which enclose the remains of the Sweet Track at Shapwick Heath (*see* 6.4), the water levels were allowed to drop to allow mowing of meadows famed for their floristic and invertebrate interest. This could have damaged the trackway. In response, nature conservation management has now been altered to accommodate both interests.

Occasionally, there may be times where the two interests conflict. To identify potential conflicts and find appropriate solutions, it is important to undertake a baseline survey of existing archaeo-

logical/palaeoenvironmental/historical interest. Again, mapping of these interests is useful. Information which could be mapped includes:

- peat-cutting pattern;
- locations of archaeological finds;
- probable routes (corridors) of trackways;
- coring locations for palaeoenvironmental research (if known);
- intactness of peat column – on cut-over sites it is useful to indicate areas which have large parts of the profile remaining; and
- structures of archaeological or historical interest.

3.2

3.2 EVALUATION AND SETTING OBJECTIVES

Evaluating the features of interest of a bog and setting management objectives need not be a difficult process. The approach taken in this handbook is to evaluate the damage a bog has suffered, set objectives and define actions (prescriptions) which ameliorate the effects of the damage (*see* 3.3). This approach entails the assumption that the desired objective of bog management is to switch bogs back to as 'natural' a state as possible. For European raised bogs and much blanket mire, 'natural' systems are ombrotrophic and *Sphagnum*-dominated. Whether this type of ecosystem can be recreated from a damaged bog depends upon a number of different factors.

Starting Conditions

The degree of damage a bog has sustained affects what can be achieved. Objectives set should be realistic. For example, peat extraction may expose underlying clays. Acidic, ombrotrophic vegetation cannot recolonise these surfaces. Instead, wetland restoration may lead to the development of fen communities which in turn *may*, after hundreds or thousands of years, lead to the development of raised bog.

An assessment of the starting condition through the baseline survey (*see* 3.1) is, therefore, useful. If, after assessing damage the bog has sustained and the resultant habitat, it is realised that a 'natural' bog system cannot be recreated, rehabilitated or maintained, then more realistic objectives should be set.

Legislative Responsibilities

Various legal and land-use constraints should be checked whilst setting objectives. Of note are planning, wildlife, archaeological, hydrological and health and safety regulations. The following should be considered:

1. On (former) peat extraction sites, land may be subject to planning controls specifying working practice and after-use. Checks should be made with the relevant local authorities. Also, check for other possible constraints such as shooting rights, grazing rights, turbary rights, riparian rights, rights of way, common land and public utilities (pipelines and pylons in particular).
2. Wildlife legislation may also affect what objectives are set. In particular, due regard must be given to (in Britain) species specially protected under the Wildlife and Countryside Act and associated amendments, and (in the EU) the Habitats and Species Directive and the Birds Directive.
3. Additionally, British archaeological sites may have been designated under the Ancient Monuments and Archaeological Areas Act (1979). Similar legislation applies in other European countries.
4. The protection of archaeological and palaeo-environmental sites is, at present, rather weak (in Britain, at least). This is because legislation applies to structures rather than more abstract concepts such as peat stratigraphy or potential or even likely archaeology. Given such inadequacies, site managers should seek to fill the 'gap'. It is useful to consider the following when planning site management:

   - Undertake a baseline archaeological and palaeoenvironmental survey; this can be a field or desk-top survey.
   - Ask or fund archaeologists to undertake watching briefs if peat extraction occurs.
   - Liaise with archaeologists in the management planning process.
   - Check on the palaeoenvironmental significance of the site with experts from local universities (usually located within geography or biology departments).

4. For large-scale hydrological management, licences need to be obtained for water impoundment (greater than 25,000 m^3 in the UK), abstraction, discharging water (in some circumstances) and works affecting land drainage.
5. Health and safety regulations (for example, the UK's Health and Safety Act, 1974) and subsequent regulations also impact on setting realistic objectives.

Finance

An obvious constraint for bog conservation management is finance. However, setting desired objectives despite a lack of funding is important given that a good management plan can be used as a tool to seek funding. As a step towards achieving those ideal objectives, a set of realistic or operational objectives can be formulated. Costing projects is important in setting operational objectives. Aspects which would need to be assessed include staff costs, capital costs (machinery, equipment, materials), contracting costs (for specialist advice or plant operation for example), monitoring costs and ongoing maintenance costs of works.

Land Use

Current or future land use of a site should also be considered. Certain land uses can coexist with bog management for conservation purposes. Light grazing, for example, may have benefits (*see* 5.4). Due consideration should also be given to changing land use as a result of conservation management. Encouraging public access onto nature reserves, for example, is a desirable goal providing that this does not affect the nature conservation interest of the site. Bogs are, though, sensitive to trampling, so provision may need to be made for anticipated changes in visitor pressure (*see* 5.6).

Consultation

Given all these considerations, setting objectives is never as straightforward as one may imagine. Different people, groups or organisations have different views on what should be achieved. Differing wildlife, land-use and recreational interests may conflict. An effective solution is to form a working party so that all interested parties can give their views. The aim is to accommodate all or most of these views when setting out management objectives. This may not be possible, in which case objectives must be prioritised to solve conflicts.

3.2

3.3   ACTION PLAN (PRESCRIPTIONS), DAMAGING IMPACTS AND SOLUTIONS

3.3.1   Introduction

The next step in the production of a management plan is to devise a set of actions (prescriptions) which should achieve set objectives. In effect, an action plan is devised. For a given site, the types of actions that are necessary vary widely, and this handbook can only guide rather than dictate land managers towards appropriate actions to manage bogs.

The approach taken has been to assume that bog managers are attempting to switch a bog back to a more 'natural' state. In some cases, this may be impossible given the starting conditions, and objectives and associated actions should be tailored accordingly (*see* 3.2). However, for many bogs, the types and impacts of damage are common and, with management, a more 'natural' state can be achieved. This section relates to the damage that a bog sustains (*see* 1.8–1.14 and Appendix 3) and to the types of actions (and associated techniques) which could be pursued to ameliorate the effects of such damage. The following look-up tables are designed to couple commonly-encountered forms of damage with various options and associated remedial techniques.

3.3

3.3.2   Peat Extraction

Extraction method	Cross-link to damage	Management options	Cross-link to management	Comments
Traditional	1.8.2 A3.2.3	Maintain or reinstate traditional methods	–	Vegetation is often thrown back into the cutting (*shoeing*) which promotes recolonisation. The relatively slow extraction rate also helps this process.
		Relocate cutting	–	Where possible, cutting should be avoided in sensitive areas or those of particular conservation importance.
		Stop cutting and do nothing	–	Many abandoned peat fields show good signs of natural recolonisation. However, if drainage systems still operate, the site may continue to dry out.
		Rehabilitate cutting areas	5.1	If ombrotrophic peat still remains and there is a local population of bog species, all that may be required is to block existing drainage channels.
Sausage/ extrusion	1.8.3 A3.2.4	Maintain cutting	–	The impacts from this method of extraction relate partially to the scale of operation. It can range from small-scale domestic extraction to large commercial workings.
		Do nothing once cutting has stopped	–	The potential for natural rehabilitation is limited by sub-surface drainage, compaction from machines and shading from drying peats. During commercial operations, the surface maybe stripped to facilitate mechanised collection of the peats.
		Rehabilitate old cuttings	5.1	Sub-surface drains can be difficult to relocate and block effectively. If these are not blocked, the site may continue to dry out.
Baulk and hollow (sod)	1.8.4 A3.2.5	Maintain cutting	–	This practice has now been superseded by milling and sausage cutting for commercial operations.
		Do nothing once cutting has stopped	–	A system of raised baulks, flat fields and trenches is left when cutting stops. The drier raised baulks are frequently dominated by heath communities, whilst the trenches and fields, if wet, may still support an assemblage of bog species.
		Rehabilitate old cuttings	5.1 5.3	Recolonisation of bog species can be encouraged by raising and stabilising water levels. The water storage capacity of a functioning acrotelm is high in contrast to peat. Rehabilitation success rests on developing a high water storage capacity on cut-over peat – either by creating open water or by encouraging *Sphagnum* growth. Difficulties may arise on larger sites when the surfaces of the cutting fields are at different levels. To maintain a regular water level, a system of dams and sluices may need to be installed. The remaining raised baulks can be beneficial as retaining walls for impounded water and provide access routes. These may have to be reinforced with other materials. If the site has been abandoned for a number of years, tree removal may be necessary.
Milling	1.8.5 A.3.2.6	Maintain cutting	–	There is very little potential to maintain nature conservation interest during the extraction process. Before extraction (which can last for decades) begins, the surface is stripped and drains are installed. The water content of the peat is reduced by 80–90% prior to harvesting.
		Maintain cutting adjacent to intact areas	5.1.3 5.1.4	The extraction zone may draw down the water-table in the adjacent peat body. Considerable engineering works such as stepped edges and the construction of bunds may be required to help maintain water levels.
		Rehabilitate milled fields	5.1–5.3	The rehabilitation of milled fields can be a considerable financial undertaking. Where possible, rehabilitation works should be planned during the extraction programme, so as to optimise after-use conditions, site expertise and machinery. There may be very little ombrogenous peat remaining. If fen peat or mineral soils are exposed, there is very little opportunity to recreate ombrogenous conditions. The remaining peat may be dried and oxidised, lacking the physical properties required to develop a functioning acrotelm. Water levels within milled fields are characteristically low and subject to large fluctuations. The water storage capacity of a functioning acrotelm is high in contrast to peat. Rehabilitation success rests on developing a high water storage capacity on cut-over peat – either by creating open water or by encouraging *Sphagnum* growth. The maintenance of a stable, high water-table may be achieved through the construction of flooded lagoons. Unless local refugia for bog species exist, vegetation may have to be introduced from a donor site. Unless rewetting occurs soon after milling ceases, the site may be colonised by undesirable species, notably birch and bracken. Wheeler and Shaw (1995) provide considerable detail.

> **For all peat-cutting activities, ideally, an experienced archaeologist should monitor the work in case an archaeological find or other palaeoenvironmental information is unearthed.**

3.3.3   Agriculture

Activity	Cross-link to damage	Management options	Cross-link to management	Comments
Sheep grazing	1.9 A3.3.3	Heavy grazing over winter period	5.4	This type of approach is *not* recommended where bog forms the dominant grazing range of the animal. Water-tables are higher during the winter months and the wet ground is more prone to trampling damage. Also there is very little shelter from bad weather. The following effects are characteristic of this kind of regime: a decline in ling heather and subsequent dominance of hare tail's cotton grass alongside a decline in bryophyte cover from trampling and increased areas of bare peat. The creation of bare surfaces may lead to larger-scale erosion problems, particularly on upland slopes. Bogs offer a low-nutrient diet, so supplementary feeding may be necessary; this can lead to localised enrichment and nutrient-cycling through dung dispersal.
		Heavy grazing over summer period	5.4	Sheep selectively browse purple moor grass (and other grasses), deergrass and hare tail's cotton grass in early spring. Scrub species such as birch may also be selected when in leaf. However, the benefits of scrub control must be weighed against the potential damage caused by trampling.
		Light grazing over summer period	5.4	Damage from trampling is minimised as stocking levels are reduced.
Cattle grazing	1.9 A3.3.3	Grazing with cattle	5.4	The use of cattle is not recommended on wet bog because of excessive poaching. However, given a selective preference for grasses, shrubs and scrub (in leaf) by cattle, they may be beneficial for degraded sites (prior to rewetting) where the surface is less prone to poaching.
Wild grazing	1.9 A3.3.3	Unrestricted grazing from wild populations of deer and rabbits	5.4	Red deer may compete with sheep for grazing in winter and early spring. Supplementary winter feeding concentrates damage through trampling and nutrient enrichment. However, where natural populations of wild grazers have access to bogs (blanket and raised), there may be some benefit given selective browsing of scrub.
Burning	1.9 1.12 A3.3.5	Burning	5.5	Burning on wet bog areas (or those dominated by *Sphagnum* communities) should be avoided, as severe burns destroy vegetation and expose bare peat surfaces. Burning on peatlands should only be conducted in accordance with the muirburn code.
Moor-gripping	1.9 A3.3.2 (1.10)	Do nothing	–	Large areas of blanket bog have been drained by moor-gripping. These closely-spaced shallow drains quickly dry out the acrotelm to leave a vegetation dominated by dwarf shrubs. Even when they have naturally infilled, they continue to function as drains.
		Block with peat dams	5.1.2.6	Small peat dams can be installed either by hand or by machine; machines are usually quicker and cheaper. Ideally, dark peat should be used and the vehicle tracked or fitted with low-ground-pressure balloon tyres.
		Block with sheet dams	5.1.2.2 to 5.1.2.5	A drain can be effectively blocked with a dam made from plywood, plastic-coated corrugated iron or plastic sheet. Although these dams may be more effective than peat, they are more expensive.
		Infill with peat	5.1.5	On steeper slopes, it may be more appropriate to infill the drain along its entire length. The most practical way of doing this is to push back the spoil excavated when digging the ditch.

3.3

The term 'heavy' grazing relates in this instance to >1 sheep/ha. This figure is, however, relative to the starting conditions of the site. For instance, wet, *Sphagnum*-dominated bog would be damaged by a stocking density of less than half this value.

3.3.4 Drainage

Drain Size (depth x width)	Cross-link to damage	Management options	Cross-link to management	Comments
Small drains c. 0.5m x 0.5m	1.8 1.9 A3.2 A3.3.2 (1.10)	Do nothing	–	Shallow drains dry out the acrotelm, with a subsequent loss of peat-forming vegetation. Typically, this effect is localised and is shown by a band of shrub and scrub species colonising along the ditch line.
		Block drains with peat dams	5.1.2.6	Small peat dams can be installed either by hand or by machine; machines are usually quicker and cheaper. Ideally, dark peat should be used and the vehicle tracked or fitted with low-ground-pressure balloon tyres.
		Block drains with small sheet dams	5.1.2.3 5.1.2.5 4.2 A6.2.2.4	A drain can be effectively blocked with a dam made from plywood, plastic-coated corrugated iron or plastic sheet. Although these dams may be more effective than peat, they are more expensive. Correct positioning requires levelling.
Medium sized drains c. 1m × 1.5m	1.8, 1.9, 1.10 A3.2, A3.3.2	Do nothing	–	On sloping ground, these ditches can cause considerable erosion and ditch scour problems. Medium-sized drains cut into catotelmic peat, considerably altering bog hydrology.
		Block with peat dams	5.1.6	Peat dams of this size require an excavator for construction; the peat used should be of a high enough humification (see 4.5.5).
		Block with plastic sheets	5.1.2.4 4.2 A6.2.2.4	Drains this size can be blocked with plastic sheet. Although these dams may be more effective than peat, they are more expensive. Correct positioning requires levelling.
		Block with solid wooden planks	5.1.2.2	Plank or board dams have been used successfully to block ditches of this size and larger. Though time-consuming to install, they provide a long-term solution.
		Block with plastic piling	5.1.2.8	Plastic piling, though initially more expensive than some hardwoods, is durable. One of its advantages is that it can be quickly and easily installed either by machine or by hand.
		Block with a composite dam	5.1.2.7	A composite dam is constructed from a combination of peat and an impermeable membrane or sheet. The peat merely acts as a support to the impermeable sheet. Compacted peat sandwiched between two boards can act as a bridge for occasional pedestrian or stock access.
Large drains c.>1.5m × >2m	1.8, 1.9, 1.11 A3.2, A3.4 A3.5	Do nothing	–	Large drains are very damaging, especially where the drain cuts into the mineral soils beneath the peat. *Guidance from an engineer should be sought before attempting to block very large ditches.*
		Block with plastic piling dam	5.1.2.8	Plastic piling can be used to breach quite large ditches. It can be strengthened with vertical or horizontal battens if required. Large dams are best installed by machine. Plastic piling is particularly effective when used to block very wide but shallow ditches.
		Block with composite dams	5.1.2.7	A composite dam made from plastic piling and peat (to add support) is a quick and relatively cheap method of blocking large ditches.

3.3

3.3.5   Afforestation

Trees	Cross-link to damage	Management options	Cross-link to management	Comments
Self-sown trees	1.14 A3.7.2	Do nothing	–	Scrub and tree encroachment causes a decline in typical bog species.
		Kill trees in situ	5.3.3.5 5.3.4.2 5.3.4.4	In-situ killing of trees can be achieved through herbicide application to standing trees through notching or injection. Non-herbicide methods include ring-barking and flooding.
		Cut with no herbicide application	5.3 (5.1)	Tree cover should be tackled at its root cause. This usually means that a programme of hydrological management as well as tree clearance is necessary. Trees capable of coppicing require secondary treatment. Non-herbicide methods include flooding, pulling, cyclical cutting and grazing.
		Cut and apply herbicide	5.2.3	Herbicide can either be applied directly to the foliage by spraying or weedwiping or onto cut stumps.
Immature or open-canopy commercial plantation	1.10 A3.4	Do nothing	–	Initial damage is caused by drainage. As the trees develop, secondary drainage and the application of fertilisers further damage the bog. However, when the trees are immature (that is, not at closed canopy) some bog species are usually present. Ineffective drainage may cause the plantation to fail.
		Fell and remove trees	(5.1) 5.3.1 5.3.2	Trees can be felled with chainsaws and either removed by low-ground-pressure forwarders or netted and lifted off with helicopters. Hydrological management should follow tree removal.
		Fell and leave	5.3.1	Given suitable conditions, *Sphagnum* can grow over fallen timber. Blocking drainage ditches is difficult.
		Harvest by standard methods	–	Standard harvesting on deep peat is not amenable to conservation objectives. Disruption to the surface through vehicle pressure and brash may hamper re-establishment of a functioning acrotelm.
Closed-canopy mature plantation	1.10 A3.4	Harvest by alternative methods	5.3.1 5.3.2	Harvesting trees with a view to rehabilitation is at present experimental. There has been some experimentation with whole-tree harvesting by helicopter and low-ground-pressure forwarders. Both these methods aim to reduce disturbance to the surface and maintain optimum conditions for re-establishment of bog species.

3.3

51

3.3.6   Other Types of Damage

Description	Cross-link to damage	Management options	Cross-link to management	Comments
Occasional pedestrian access	1.12 A3.6.5	Do nothing	–	The site should be regularly assessed for signs of damage. If trampling damage becomes evident, access provision should be considered.
		Provide access facilities	5.6	Access provision is required if a bog has a low carrying capacity – itself determined by vegetation and peat characteristics. Wet, *Sphagnum*-rich bogs are more sensitive than degraded, heather-dominated sites. Permanent provision can take the form of raised or floating boardwalks and footpaths, whilst brashings, pallets and mesh can be used for temporary provision.
Frequent pedestrian access	1.12 A3.6.5	Do nothing	–	Even bogs with a high carrying capacity can become damaged from heavy pedestrian use. Peat is rapidly eroded once vegetation is trampled and the surface exposed. Where pedestrians are encouraged or expected, some kind of permanent provision should be offered or the access re-routed.
		Re-route access	–	For management or non-interpretative access, sensitive or wet areas should be avoided.
		Provide temporary access facilities	5.6.4 5.6.6	Access points come under considerable pressure during management operations. Damage can be limited by laying down netting, wooden pallets, duckboards or plastic paths.
		Provide permanent access facilities	5.6	Footpaths and boardwalks make access easier for the pedestrians and help to contain pressure to one point.
Use of vehicles	1.12 (1.10) A3.6.6 A3.5.2	Do nothing	–	Even low-ground-pressure vehicles can damage the bog surface as the shearing motion of tyres and tracks damages fragile vegetation. Tracks widen as they re-route around previously damaged areas.
		Re-route access	–	Where possible, vehicle routes should avoid wet or steeply sloping ground.
		Provide temporary facilities	5.6.8	Wooden boards and geogrids can be laid to provide temporary protection from vehicle damage.
		Provide permanent facilities	5.6.7	The construction of permanent roads and tracks should be a last resort, as their impact is considerable. However, where access cannot be re-routed, damage may be limited and confined by constructing a permanent track.
Peat erosion	1.14	Reduce recreational pressure	5.6	Re-route walkers away from eroded areas or provide access facilities.
		Change grazing regimes	5.4	Reduce grazing and trampling pressure.
		Change burning regime	5.5	Reduce frequency and intensity of burning.
		Re-vegetate bare peat	5.2	Whilst changing recreational, grazing and burning regimes prevents erosion, once erosion has occurred, the priority should be to revegetate eroded areas.
		Experimental methods		A variety of methods have been used to stabilise mineral soils such as geotextile grids, adding soil stabilisers and so on. Some of these could be adapted to peat soils.

3.4 REPORTING, MONITORING AND EVALUATION

3.4.1 Introduction

On completion of the plan, management work can begin, and too often this is where the planning process stops. Management works are carried out and never evaluated; some vital parts to the plan are never completed; opportunities are missed; records get lost under the pile of paper in the corner; monitoring equipment is vandalised and never replaced, and so on. For a host of reasons, management is often less effective than the plan envisaged. To avoid this, the planning process must be maintained through good reporting, survey, monitoring and evaluation.

3.4.2 Reporting

An essential part of site management is to monitor the quality and quantity of work done. A useful way of reporting is to use site reporting forms (see 4.1.2) and project recording forms. Projects, which make up each action to achieve desired management objectives, can be recorded by using standard forms. The NCC project recording form, for example, records: site, project, description, compartment, months active, priority, photographic record, recorder, labour, costs and notes. The information can be collated either on paper in a site management file or on computer. Database software is particularly appropriate for this type of information, and the *Countryside Management System* has been specifically designed for this type of operation.

Reporting and on-site monitoring should be carried out every time the site is visited. This may be just checking that all is in order, or it may be more formalised by filling in site recording forms (see 4.1.2).

3.4.3 Survey and Monitoring

As the plan proceeds, extra survey and monitoring activities should take place (indeed, it is often integral to the plan). This has two main purposes: enhancing baseline survey information and monitoring the effectiveness of management.

3.4.3.1 Enhancing Baseline Survey Information

In the initial plan, baseline survey information may be necessarily limited. The NCC's suggested minimum management plan suggests that a brief description of the site followed by an evaluation of site features is enough in many instances, although, as explained above, more detailed information is nearly always required for peatland management. However, extra baseline survey information may include: more information on specialised species such as invertebrates (see 4.7.3) and rare flora (see 4.6); more information on the hydrology of the site (see 4.3); greater information on the archaeology and history of the site (see 1.6, 3.1.7); or further important information relating to the likely success of management, such as peat properties (see 4.5.5) and chemistry (see 4.4).

3.4.3.2 Monitoring the Effectiveness of Management

Whilst monitoring need not be time-consuming or expensive, its application can be useful.

- It is important to monitor the effectiveness of management to enable an effective review of the plan (see 3.4.4).
- Monitoring discerns when systems deviate from an expected norm, allowing replanning of management activities or even emergency actions.
- Monitoring adds to the baseline survey information used for the site description. More effective site evaluations can be achieved as the quantity and quality of information increases.
- Monitoring is a research tool, and results can be applied more widely.

All sorts of monitoring can be applied to assess the effectiveness of management. Of prime importance is devising a scheme which can assess whether the objectives for site management are being obtained. However, there is always a trade-off with the resources available for achieving this. The various monitoring activities suggested should be planned into an integrated monitoring scheme. It is useful to follow the following format when devising a monitoring scheme:

1. Restate management objectives for site management.

2. Formulate a set of objectives which monitoring should achieve.
3. Set out a series of techniques and methods which could be used to achieve those monitoring objectives.
4. Set out the resource implications for these methods and techniques in terms of labour and cost.
5. (Optional: Modify monitoring objectives or methods/techniques if resource implications are too high, and return to step 3.)
6. Set out method for data collection and devise necessary recording forms.
7. Set out the way in which data is to be stored (devise spreadsheets if appropriate).
8. Set out the way in which data is to be analysed.

For example:

1	Management objectives	Raise water levels (through damming) to restore typical lowland raised bog communities to the mire.
2	Monitoring objectives	To assess the success of damming and to assess the rate of vegetation change.
3	Methods	Automatic water level recording; automatic rain gauge; whole site monitoring using random quadrat vegetation monitoring each year.
4	Resource implications	Capital cost: £2,000; labour: (for one skilled professional) data collection – 4 days per year, data storage and analysis – 4 days per year (= too much).
3	Modified methods	Four WaLRaGs, rain gauge and one permanent quadrat near a drain.
4	Resource implications	Capital cost: £200; labour: (for volunteers) 12½ days per year – reading WaLRaGs and rain gauge; (for skilled professional) one ½ day for quadrat survey and one day for analysis of data, per year.
5–7	Data collection and storage	On prepared Excel spreadsheets.
8	Data analysis	WaLRaG and rain data plotted on same graph showing minimum and maximum water levels and monthly rainfall. Assessing target of minimum water level not to drop below 20 cm. Quadrat data plotted as 3-D columns across the quadrat for each species and as summary percentages of all species. Assessing target of 90% ground cover by bog *Sphagnum* species.

Generally, monitoring schemes are designed to gauge the impact and degree of success of management works and to allow successful techniques to be highlighted for use elsewhere.

Monitoring also has the side-effect of allowing site managers to become more familiar with sites in a structured way.

On bogs, the success of conservation management nearly always relates to the way in which hydrological factors and vegetation respond (they are, of course, inextricably linked). Often, it is vegetation change or stability which is sought, although this may be underpinned by hydrological control. In these cases, it may only be necessary to monitor vegetation alone (*see* 4.6). Normally though, vegetation change is too slow to allow plans to be reviewed, so some form of hydrological monitoring is carried out (*see* 4.3). As a consequence, the best approach is to *integrate* both vegetation and hydrological monitoring. Monitor hydrology to directly assess the effectiveness of hydrological control works (*see* 5.1) and integrate this with vegetation monitoring to assess the effect that has on the site.

When planning monitoring schemes, bear the following points in mind:

- Always clearly state the reason for monitoring before embarking on any particular scheme. Whilst this may seem obvious, it is too easy to collect data without clearly understanding its use. As a rule, if you are not sure why the data is being collected then seek advice or stop collecting it!
- When monitoring the effectiveness of management, it is necessary to monitor before and after management works in order to provide a comparison. Monitoring after management only assesses the new situation, which may not have changed. This is not always possible, in which case a desired target should be set (for example, an average water level of 10 cm or less below the surface) and monitoring performed to *see* whether the target is achieved.
- Bear in mind what data exists before the new phase of monitoring. Ensure that any new data collected can be meaningfully compared with previous data.
- Consider whether the techniques are appropriate or sensitive enough to detect likely changes. Measuring vegetation change using a three-point scale, though easy, may not pick up subtle changes (*see* 4.6.3, A6.4.3.3).
- Consider the appropriate recording time-interval – a compromise between time resources and what is required is necessary. Fixed-point photographic monitoring of vegetation (*see* 4.1.3) on fairly stable sites may only need to be done every

five years. Dipwell monitoring (*see* 4.3.3.2) require weekly readings to be meaningful.

- Consider the quality and quantity of data. It is too easy to collect lots of information which is of little use due to poor monitoring planning or because the data may be difficult to analyse.
- Consider how the data should be stored. It is useful to set up spreadsheets on a PC which enable the data to be easily analysed. Blank forms, mirroring the spreadsheet, can then be printed out (on waterproof paper if necessary) to be used in the field. This helps to minimise recording mistakes.
- Consider how the data is likely to be analysed – this helps in setting up recording forms and spreadsheets.
- If water levels are monitored to assess the effect of management (a damming programme, for example), always measure some climate variables (rainfall in particular) to check whether the rise in water level is not simply the result of wet weather (*see* 4.3) rather than because of management works. Alternatively, arrange to receive the same data from a nearby meteorological station.

3.4.4   Evaluation and Updating

Good reporting and well-planned and executed monitoring schemes should leave the manager of a site in a much better position to update the plan. Management plans are normally written for a five-year period, although this can vary according to the complexity of the site. Plans for new, complex or poorly-understood sites may have to be revised after two or three years as rapid changes take place or a greater understanding of the site is gauged from survey and monitoring programmes. For a reasonably undamaged bog, a plan may only need revision once every ten or twenty years.

Revisions are likely to stem from the following:

- Greater survey information reveals factors which had not been taken into account previously. These might be the presence of rare species, a better understanding of hydrology and so on.
- New methods and techniques for management are devised which change one's approach to a particular management problem.
- Monitoring reveals the success or failure of particular management schemes.
- Constraints on management approaches change.

Note that the management plan should be a concise document which is easy to use. Any necessary supporting material should be added to appendices. These may include detailed habitat survey or technical annexes, for example.

3.4

MONITORING AND SITE ASSESSMENT

Part 4 is laid out in the following sections:

Monitoring and Site Assessment

In Part 3, much was made of the need to plan conservation management in order for it to be effective in achieving the desired objectives within set costs. This process (see 3 – Deriving a Management Plan) follows four stages: (1) description, (2) evaluation and setting objectives, (3) action planning and (4) reporting (including monitoring and evaluation). In Part 4, a series of methods and techniques which are likely to be used in the implementation of stages 1 and 4 of the management planning process are outlined. The descriptive part of the process mainly concerns site assessment, whilst stage 4 requires monitoring of management operations as well as the progress of the plan itself. It is particularly important to check whether the plan is being adhered to and whether any agreements (with other people or organisations) are abided by.

In practice, the methods used for both stages 1 and 4 are often the same. For example, a site assessment of the general condition of a bog and its vegetation may be conducted using aerial photograph interpretation (API – *see* 4.6.4). This information could then be used as part of the site description. However, after conservation management has taken place, a resurvey may be used to assess the effectiveness of management. Exactly the same techniques could be employed, this time collecting information for stage 4.

The methods and techniques for site assessment and monitoring of bogs vary considerably in their complexity and cost. Simple subjective and qualitative field assessment (*see* 4.1.2) can yield extremely valuable information such as the impending failure of a major dam. The usefulness and ease of such monitoring means that it is usually conducted as a matter of course by site managers. Other methods are more complex and costly, often requiring the services of a specialist. For example, using lysimeters (*see* 4.3.5) is a complicated endeavour although it is essential if a bog's water-balance equation is to be calculated (*see* 2.5.2).

Whatever methods and techniques are used at a particular site, note that monitoring may be costly in terms of time and money. It is, therefore, particularly important to plan monitoring schemes carefully (*see* 3.4.3). Having urged caution, conservation management suffers from poor evaluation and reporting (*see* Introduction). Further, monitoring and evaluation are an integral part of the management planning process and should always be incorporated into management schemes. Good evaluation allows the management planning cycle to be completed (*see* 3 – Devising a Management Plan).

In Part 4, the main methods and techniques used for monitoring and site assessment are outlined. Methods and techniques which are directly related to bogs are covered.

For those methods/techniques which are used on many different habitats, including bogs, the reader is advised to refer to more specialist texts. However, for some of these common methods, summaries are provided and more detailed accounts given in Appendix 6.

MONITORING AND SITE ASSESSMENT

4.1 GENERAL SITE MONITORING

4.1.1 Introduction

Most of Part 4 discusses the monitoring of specific variables. This section addresses less technical approaches for more general site monitoring. The main aim of these schemes is to record the following:

- management operations;
- site structures, such as dams, boardwalks and bunds;
- associated habitats, such as woodlands, grasslands;
- habitat boundaries; and
- other types of information such as visitor numbers.

Proper planning is required even though this type of monitoring does not involve complex scientific methods or sophisticated analysis techniques. The aims and objectives of a scheme should be defined and all resources identified (*see* 3.4.3). The type of information generated (mainly descriptive and pictorial) is not readily quantified, although it does form an informed basis for evaluating management work and assessing whether management objectives are being reached.

4.1.2 Field Assessment

Field assessment involves recording major site features through standardised recording of observations and planned and unplanned events. A standard recording form is useful. Possible applications include:

- a visual assessment of water levels in ditches, for example, comparing summer and winter levels;
- an inspection of management structures such as dams, bunds and boardwalks;
- an inspection of natural site features such as pools and rare plant communities; and
- a record of unplanned events and observations.

The information is best kept as a paper record of site development, management and observations. An example of a standard recording form is shown in Figure 4.1. This is easily customised and can be stored as a paper copy or entered onto a computer database to allow fast access to and analysis of the information.

Alternatively, a computer-based recording system, such as the *Countryside Management System*, can be used (*see* 3.4.2) where the record is complex and sophisticated.

4.1.3 Fixed Point Photograph Monitoring

Taking a series of photographs of the same view or object from the same point at different times provides a visual history of change. As with any monitoring scheme, it is important that it is well planned (*see* 3.4.3). This type of approach is a valuable way of monitoring sites that are visited infrequently or where resources are limited.

4.1.3.1 Planning

When setting up a monitoring scheme using photographs, consider the following:

- Diversity of habitats: try to include each habitat that is important to the management of the site.
- Resource implications: time taken to collect and collate data and all relevant costs.
- Purpose: critically assess what can be gained from each shot (avoid similar views).
- Flexibility: points may be added or deleted over time. Note that presently accessible positions may become less accessible as a result of management, for example, flooding operations.
- Frequency: the time between taking photographs should be assessed in relation to likely changes on the site. For rapidly-changing sites, photographs should be taken often; where sites are stable, photographs need only to be taken once every five or even ten years. Examples are given below:

Site Recording Form

Site name   *Bankhead Moss*   **Date** *10/I/96*   **Time**   *10.04*

Recorder   *Pete Matthews*   **Weather conditions** *Raining*

Purpose of visit

> *Check condition of dams and record dipwells*

Condition check list: Specify condition and any relevant information

Dams

> *Installed for one month. Holding water back well with no sign of leakage. Dam number three (see attached map) not working as well as others - could be in the wrong place. All other dams on site working well.*

Boardwalk

> *Three pieces of decking need replacing (see map)*

Dipwells

> *Dipwell number 15 has been pushed down into the peat. All dipwells have been recorded.*

Observations

> *One short-eared owl hunting over the grassland near the northern boundary.*

Action Required

> *Replace dipwell 15 before February.*
>
> *Replace boardwalk decking immediately.*

Figure 4.1   An example of a site recording form.

Landscape views showing limited
    detail of vegetation and structures   5+ yrs
Scrub encroachment   2–5 yrs
Management features, such as dams
    and bunds   1–5 yrs
Detailed vegetation features
    (close-ups) on stable sites   5 yrs
Detailed vegetation features
    (close-ups) on changing sites   2 yrs

- Integration: photographic monitoring should be integrated with other site monitoring as part of an integrated plan (see 3.4.3).
- Location: select locations that can be used for more than one view; this not only saves time in the field but also reduces the number of markers required. Consider also the following:

   - Repetitive shots of large areas of 'homogenous' vegetation are not particularly useful when recording vegetation cover. Aerial photography (see 4.6.4) is better for showing shifting vegetation boundaries.
   - Any elevated vantage point, on or more usually off the bog, can prove useful.

- Time of year: take photographs at the same time of year, as areas of open water change during the year and vegetation dies back during winter. Winter weather is unpredictable and can prevent monitoring (for example, snow or fog).
- Displays/talks: photographs are useful for displays and talks, although colour slides soon deteriorate if they are viewed through a projector too often. Panoramic views of overlapping shots are popular.

An example of a fixed-point photograph monitoring scheme is shown in Figure 4.2.

4.1

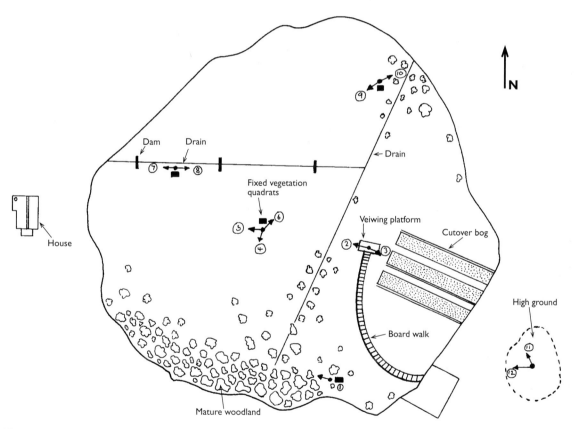

Figure 4.2   An example of fixed-point photograph locations.

Key to fixed point locations: 1. Woodland edge and encroaching scrub. 2. Centre of bog and fixed quadrat location. 3. Cutover bog area and east boundary. 4. Mature woodland. 5. Open bog and western boundary. 6. Open bog and drain lines with encroaching trees. 7. Dam, drain and western boundary. 8. Dam and drain. 9. Open bog. 10. Encroaching scrub. 11. Site overview. 12. Site overview.

4.1.3.2 Marking Fixed Points

Photographic positions should be marked in the field and on a site map to allow positions to be relocated – particularly important given that different people will probably be involved. It is recommended that each position is marked with a letter (A, B, C) and each subsequent shot taken from the same position given a number (A1, A2, A3). If more than one site is being recorded, a unique site identification letter(s) should be added (for Flanders Moss – FMA1, FMA2 and so on). As photographic monitoring is a long-term programme, it is important to use field markers that are not easily lost or moved. Several options exist:

- *Reference to permanent structures on and off site* (taking bearings and distances – *see* 4.2): this option, though time-consuming, is a useful back-up if field markers are lost or moved.
- *Wooden post:* (untreated softwood may need to be replaced every 4–8 years depending on species): posts should be pushed at least 1m into the peat to prevent vandalism. Mark posts with painted, etched or stamped code.
- *Metal posts*: old scaffolding poles are a good alternative to wood. They are very robust and difficult to vandalise. Mark poles with painted, etched or stamped code.
- *Bamboo canes*: not suitable as a long-term marker. They are easily removed or lost and difficult to mark effectively.
- *Electronic markers:* relocation devices planted beneath the surface can be relocated by sweeping a transceiver over the surface; deters vandalism, although expensive.

> **Any posts protruding above the surface may attract curious visitors and perching birds.**
> **Take one or two photographs of the fixed point itself to help relocation.**

4.1.3.3 Taking the Photograph

The detail of a photograph can be significantly enhanced if it is taken by the *stereographic* method. By taking two shots of the same view from slightly different angles, they can be viewed under a stereoscope as a 3 D image. The procedure for taking a stereo image is very simple:

- Stand with feet slightly apart (approximately 40 cm).
- Frame the image centrally in the viewfinder.

- Keeping the image central, move your weight onto your left foot (i.e. move the camera slightly to the left), making sure that the camera stays at a horizontal angle (Figure 4.3).
- Take one frame.
- Shifting your weight onto your right foot, repeat the previous two stages.

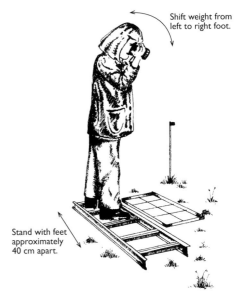

Shift weight from left to right foot.

Stand with feet approximately 40 cm apart.

Figure 4.3   Taking a stereo-photograph of a vegetation quadrat.

4.1.3.4 Keeping a Record

Each image should be recorded on a standard recording form. This form can either be incorporated into the site recording form (Figure 4.1) or be a separate form. An example is given in Figure 4.4.

4.1.3.5 Photographic Advice

A 35mm single lens reflex (SLR) or good-quality 35mm compact camera gives best results. If the focal length is changed, it must be noted on the recording form. When using an SLR, aim to maximise the depth of field by using a small aperture (higher f stop). This may necessitate the use of slower shutter speeds, so a tripod and cable shutter may be required. If the camera has an automatic exposure setting, do not include too much sky in the frame, as this leads to the ground coming out too dark. The best weather conditions for photographing vegetation are bright with

Site Name	Drury Moss	Site Code	DR	Date	26/8/95
Recorder	Pete Matthews	Equipment	Olympus A10 with 35mm auto focus lens. Kodachrome 100 ASA slide film.		
Weather	Overcast with sunny intervals	Comments	Could not locate marker post for point D1. Marker post C2 in need of replacement.		

Photo Point	Film and Frame Number	Right or Left Foot	Bearing	Time	Details
A1	1/1	L	320°	11.00am	Edge of woodland-barn in right hand side of frame
A1	1/2	R	320°	11.00am	
A2	1/3	L	110°	11.05am	Edge of woodland towards boardwalk section.
A2	1/4	R	110°	11.05am	
etc					
etc					

Figure 4.4   A example of a basic photographic recording form.

4.1

some cloud (not bright sunshine). Evening and winter shadows obscure too much detail.

There are three main film formats to choose from; each has its relative merits and disadvantages, as shown in Table 4.1.

The introduction of digital images and storage systems is likely to change the present approach to photographic recording. It is now possible to store good-quality colour and black and white images digitally with the important advantage of maintaining the image quality.

> **It is useful to use the same media over time.**

Table 4.1:   Format for Photographic Monitoring

Format	Advantages	Disadvantages
Colour Print Film	• Can be viewed anywhere • Easy to compare a series of photographs • Cheap and easily obtained • Tolerant of bad exposure • Useful for interpretative or public liaison work • Reprints from negatives easy	• Quality of image variable • Durability over time questionable • If not stored correctly colours may fade
Colour Slide Film	• Gives good-quality colour saturation, accuracy and detail • Cheap and easily obtained • Useful for public talks	• Difficulty in viewing and comparing slides • Requires light box for stereo viewing • Durability over time questionable • Archive processing expensive
Black and White Print Film	• If processed to archive standard – excellent longevity of image • Good-quality image – high contrast	• Requires reasonably skilled photographer • Interpretation of image more difficult • Not as useful for interpretative or public use

4.1.3.6   Camera Platforms

Bogs are flat and sometimes rather monotonous; photography is sometimes required at a scale between that possible on the ground and the scale used in aerial photography (see 4.6.4). For this, alternative camera platforms can be used. These include: fixed tower, 'cherry-picker' (commonly used for repairing street lights in the UK!), telescopic boom arm, model aircraft, balloons and kites.

There is greater control of viewing geometry with the first three types. It is also worthwhile considering the use of medium-format aerial photography obtained from light aircraft. With all these platforms, remember to ensure an adequate framework of ground reference points.

> The use of aerial photography is discussed in section 4.6.4.

4.2   TOPOGRAPHY

The morphology of a bog is a key determinant of hydrology and vegetation. In many cases, management decisions can only be made given a detailed knowledge of topography (see 3.1.4). The methods and techniques used for topographic survey are generally common for most habitats, and standard survey texts should be consulted, although more detail is provided in Appendix 6.

Note that independent reference markers should be sought when levelling. Independent reference points enable survey data to be related to a fixed datum which can be used as a reference point for future or additional surveys. An independent reference point can be provided by a peat anchor (see 4.5.3). The most appropriate independent reference points, however, are those that are long-term or permanent features such as large boulders, bedrock exposures and benchmarks (UK Ordnance Survey reference marks).

For ground survey, common techniques used include the following:

Levelling Frame

These are suitable for surveying small features (microtopography) less than 1m across to produce precise maps – usually only required for research purposes (see A6.2.2.2).

Plane Table

This is a simple and inexpensive survey method which allows detailed mapping of small-scale topographic features (see A6.2.2.6).

Hand Levels (Abney Level and Stadia)

These are pocket-sized instruments which can be used to measure height only (stadia) or height and slope (Abney levels). They are useful for precise 'levelling' (topographic survey) over a few metres or less detailed but rapid survey over greater distances such as drains (see A6.2.2.3).

Dumpy and Quick-set Levels

These levels can be used for longer distance (1–2 km) levelling and are very precise although rather time-consuming. The instruments are generally composed of a scope mounted on rotating scale. The scope contains a graticule with three horizontal lines. Readings for the upper and lower lines are used to calculate distance. These are useful for levelling drains. If the instrument is set up at one end of the drain, a colleague can be instructed to walk along the drain placing bamboo canes to mark dam locations every 10-30 cm elevation or declination (see 5.1.2; A6.2.2.4).

Theodolites

Trained surveyors use theodolites, which are both accurate and versatile, allowing measurements to be made over long distances. (see A6.2.2.5).

Electronic Equipment

Many of the surveying techniques described above have now been superseded by newer electronic equipment, of these the most useful are Electronic Distance Measurers (EDMs) and Geographic Positioning Systems (GPS). EDMs use reflective plates which reflect light back at the instrument to record exact distances. Measurements can be downloaded directly into computer software allowing much quicker survey. GPS relies on satellites. Instruments search and fix on a series of satellites orbiting above. GPS is becoming more and more accurate with positions now being fixed to within a few metres – usually

4.2

good enough for the survey requirements of conservation management.

Aerial Photogrammetric Survey

The other method of obtaining detailed contour maps is to use aerial photogrammetric survey. These surveys use stereo-images to construct topographical maps. This is specialist work and should be contracted out. The costs are around £5,000 per site (1996). Bear in mind that the method maps the top of the vegetation, not necessarily the ground surface. This is fine for *Sphagnum* dominated bogs but is inaccurate for woodland.

4.3   HYDROLOGY AND RAINFALL

4.3.1   Introduction

Bog management is invariably concerned with water (*see* 2.5, 3.1.3). Effective management, therefore, requires an understanding of the hydrology of a site, and some form of hydrological monitoring to assess the effectiveness of management may be required. However, before embarking on hydrological monitoring, remember that results should always be compared to climate data. The main hydrological parameters (Table 4.2) measured are:

- Rainfall (4.3.2): measured using a rain-gauge or data collected from a local meteorological station.
- Water levels (4.3.3): levels can be mapped using ground survey or using instruments which measure the actual level such as dipwells, WaLRaGs, chart recorders, automatic level recorders, remote sensing and stage boards.
- Discharge (4.3.4): this gives an idea of the seepage emanating from a site, although it is only really useful on highly-drained sites where water is lost at discrete points. V-notch weirs and tipping bucket flow gauges can also be used. The rate and direction of seepage may be measured by using piezometers.
- Evapotranspiration (4.3.5): this is almost impossible to measure directly but can be measured using a lysimeter.

4.3.2   Rainfall

This can be measured directly using a rain-gauge, or data can be sought from a local meteorological station. The simplest rain-gauges consist of a funnel set into a sharp-rimmed metal or plastic cylindrical container (Figure 4.5). Gauges cost between £30 and £180 or can be made for about £12. Snowfall is more difficult to measure, although car-battery-powered heated bucket gauges can be used. More sophisticated designs – tilting siphon gauges (£1,600) and tipping bucket

Table 4.2:   A summary of the variables measured and how easy it is to collect the data.

Variable	Method	Section	Easy?	Cost (1996)
Rainfall	Collecting rain-gauge	4.3.2	Yes	£12–£180
	Recording rain-gauge	4.3.2	No	£1,600–£2,700
Water level	Site wetness mapping	4.3.3.1	Yes	None
	Dipwells	4.3.3.2	Yes	£60 per 20
	WaLRaGs	4.3.3.3	Yes	£55 each
	Water-level logger	4.3.3.4	No	£900
	Aerial infra-red	4.3.3.5	No	Not applicable
Pool water level	Stage board	4.3.3.6	Yes	£10 each
Evapotranspiration	Lysimeter	4.3.5 A6.3.3	No	£1,500–£2,500
Ditch or streamflow	Tipping bucket gauge	4.3.4.2 A6.3.2	No	£1,250–£2,000
	V-notch weir	4.3.4.1 A6.3.2	No	£1,000–£3,500
Seepage	Piezometers	4.3.4.3	No	From £150 a set

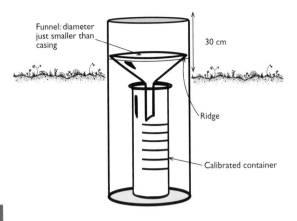

Funnel: diameter just smaller than casing

30 cm

Ridge

Calibrated container

Figure 4.5   A design for a simple collecting rain-gauge.

a plastic funnel cut to size and sealed inside with bath sealant. A two-litre plastic bottle should be adequate for monthly readings at lowland sites, though perhaps only for two weeks at an upland site (in Britain). The gauge should be sited in a typical part of the bog with its rim protruding 30 cm above ground. Pack the gauge firmly into the ground. Place duckboard near the gauge to stop poaching, and cut away any overhanging vegetation. The catch is measured using a measuring cylinder. Calibrated cylinders can be bought for standard rain-gauge in diameters of 127mm (5 inches) and 203mm (8 inches). Otherwise, use the following equation:

$$R = c / 0.0785(rd)^2$$

where R = rainfall (in mm), c = the catch (ml/cc) and rd = the rim diameter of the rain-gauge (in cm).

gauges (£2,000) – can be used if the gauge cannot be regularly visited.

Straightforward gauges can be made from 40 cm lengths of 10 cm diameter PVC soil drainage pipe, with a joining collar. A disc, cut from 3mm PVC sheet, should be glued onto the bottom and

The data can be displayed as a bar chart alongside water level fluctuations (for example, Figure 4.6).

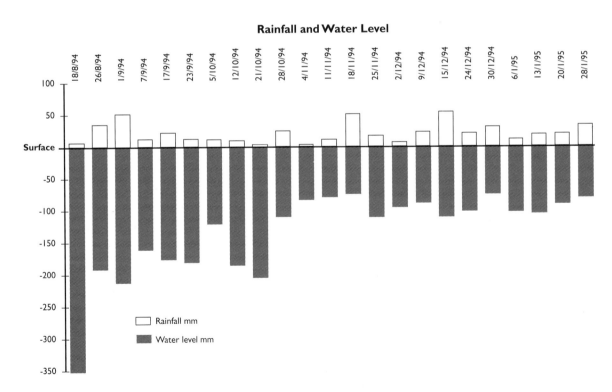

Figure 4.6   Data analysis can be made easier if rainfall and dipwell data are displayed on the same graph.

4.3.3   Water Levels

4.3.3.1   Ground Wetness

A map of site wetness is a surprisingly useful description allowing, for example, al- terrain vehicle (ATV) access to be devised and ditch-damming programmes to be targeted. Assessing whole site wetness patterns can be achieved using the following technique:

- Use a method to select a series of points for survey across the site, such as, a grid.
- Put in a short post or stake to mark each observation point. Observation points should be accurately recorded so that the survey can be easily repeated.
- Survey the bog once during summer and once in winter.
- During a survey, judge the wetness at each observation point by recording:
  - surface water (yes/no),
  - a quaking surface on jumping (yes/no),
  - adjacent pools (within 20m) (yes/no),
  - *Sphagnum*-dominated vegetation (yes/no).

- At points which are not particularly wet, judge the dryness by observing:
  - sloping ground (slope more than 2°) (yes/no),
  - rabbit holes (within 20 m) (yes/no),
  - tree- or heather-dominated vegetation (yes/no),
  - adjacent ditches (within 20 m) (yes/no).

This type of approach has not been extensively tested, and similar maps can be prepared by simply recording areas of open water in summer and winter. These are particularly useful for planning ditch-blocking programmes and for assessing safety hazards on the bog (*see* 6.1).

4.3.3.2   Dipwells

The commonest and easiest way to measure water levels is to use dipwells. These are simply perforated plastic tubes pushed into a hole in the ground. Dipwell diameters range from 8 mm (microbore) to 5 cm and can be constructed from perforated plastic pipe or solid-walled pipe with holes drilled in. A cap should be fitted over both ends: on the base to stop peat from upwelling into the dipwell (these are not always fitted and are not necessary for firm peats and microbore dipwells) and on the top to keep out snow, mice and insects. The dipwell can be fixed to the surface

by adding a flanged collar (Figure 4.7); this is useful as dipwells should not be moved once recording starts.

The duration and frequency of monitoring should be chosen to suit particular circumstances. Note the importance of monitoring before as well as after management operations so that any resulting changes in water level can be demonstrated by comparing the averages before and after. Since the water level is affected by the

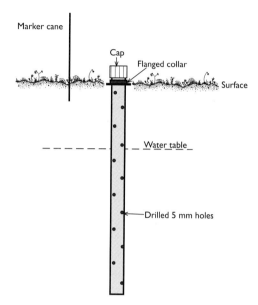

Figure 4.7   A design for a dipwell with a flanged collar. The cap aids visibility as well as keeping out snow, mice and insects.

weather, take enough readings to get an average uninfluenced by weather. Six readings, at least a week apart, are sufficient provided that they are taken during the winter and not more than two are taken on days when the weekly rain-gauge catch is less than 5 mm. For example, if monitoring is undertaken to find out how successful a ditch-damming programme is in raising the water-table, readings may be taken at weekly intervals for 6–10 weeks before the damming and the same afterwards. For short-term monitoring of this type, it is best to avoid summer and early autumn because the water level is usually drawn down by warmer and drier weather. For longer-term monitoring, the frequency can be reduced to monthly intervals especially if the dipwell data is supplemented by WaLRaG data (*see* 4.3.3.3) to measure the range of water-table fluctuation between monthly readings.

Locate the dipwells in positions of average ground level (carpets, flats and so on), avoiding hummocks and hollows. For ease of location, it is useful to align dipwells into straight transects, although this may not be the most informative arrangement. A grid system may provide more useful information. It is also important to consider what, exactly, is hoped to be discovered. For example, dipwells should be placed within the management area if the measurements are to assess the direct effects of management. Whole site effects can be gauged by siting dipwells away from the main management areas.

For groundwater modelling or when the absolute water level is required, dipwells should be anchored to the substrate and levelled to a fixed level (such as ordnance datum). If it is simply the case of ascertaining the relative distance from the peat surface to the water level, dipwells need not be anchored.

Once constructed, dipwells are placed in the peat either by pushing in or, preferably, taking out a core of peat so that the peat is not disturbed too much. It is useful to place a post marked with a piece of fluorescent tape (deters birds and makes it easier to find) close to the dipwell.

The depth to the water-table (DWT) is calculated by measuring from the top of the dipwell to the ground surface and subtracting that from the top of the dipwell to the water level. Steel measuring tape can be used, though specially-made dipsticks which buzz or light up when the end reaches the water are more practical. For microbore dipwells, a fine plastic tube connected to a stethoscope is used. By blowing down the tube, bubbles are heard when the end touches the water (Figure 4.8).

Dipwell data is usually simply graphed against time (Figure 4.6) whilst transect data is plotted against distance. Grid data is usually plotted as isolines on a map.

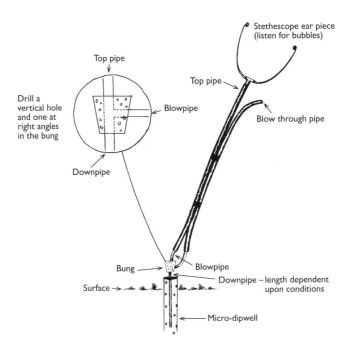

Figure 4.8   A stethoscope measuring device used to measure water levels in microbore dipwells.

4.3.3.3   WaLRaGs

The WaLRaG (Water Level Range Gauge) is a dipwell which gives the current depth to water-table (DWT) and also shows the highest and lowest DWT since the previous reading. Lower extremes are particularly useful to know because this is a limiting factor for many typical bog species. WaLRaGs have also been used for archaeological monitoring – a particularly useful application.

Various designs of maximum and minimum recording wells have been used in the past with varying degrees of success. Most have been home-made, but at least one type (Figure 4.9), which works well, is now commercially available in Britain (*see* Appendix 7), and other designs are also available.

If the recording interval for measuring water-tables using conventional dipwells is long, it is useful to supplement this data with information derived from WaLRaGs.

WaLRaG installation is as follows:

- The pipe is installed by pushing it into a hole made with a suitable sized auger. Alternatively, you can use a knife. Make sure the hole is deep enough for the float to fall in dry weather.
- Push the pipe down the hole and, with one foam block in the channel, lower the float down inside it, fitting the roller bearing into the channel.
- Push the other foam block down inside the channel before screwing on the top cap.
- Move the foam blocks so that they both touch the roller bearing. A week or so later, check that the bottle is afloat and decide whether the hole needs to be deepened to prevent the pointer from going off the bottom of the scale.
- Once you have made any necessary adjustments, ensure that the pipe cannot slip or get pushed further into the ground, by attaching a flanged collar fixed at ground level with two screws or a (treated) timber batten fixed in place with an angle bracket. Again move the foam blocks to touch the bearing.
- Start reading the following week or month.
- Ensure that the foam blocks move freely and, if necessary, trim the blocks slightly to reduce friction.

The pointer shows the current reading while the upper block shows the maximum reading and the lower one shows the minimum reading since they were last reset. It is important to remember

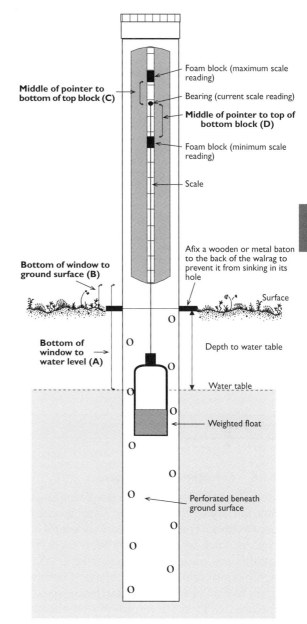

Figure 4.9   A WaLRaG or Water Level Range Gauge, used to record maximum and minimum water-levels.

to reset the instrument by pushing the foam blocks back to touch the pointer after taking readings.

Store the readings on paper or on a computer spreadsheet. The following technique for taking readings effectively allows for movement of the WaLRaG in the peat. Other methods have been used; *see* Bragg et al. (1994) and Ninnes and Keay (1994).

- With the float in place, use a dipstick or a tape measure to measure the distance from the bottom of the window down to the water level (Figure 4.9 A).
- Measure the distance from the bottom of the window to the ground surface (Figure 4.9 B). Subtract B from A to give the current DWT.
- Measure from the middle of the pointer to the bottom of the top block (Figure 4.9 C). Subtract this figure from the DWT, to give minimum DWT (that is, the highest water level in the recording period).
- Measure from the middle of the pointer to the top of the bottom block (Figure 4.9 D). Add this figure to DWT to give the maximum DWT (that is, the lowest water level in the recording period).

When you have calculated the true DWTs, look for any maximum or minimum values which seem markedly different from the rest. Look at the previous set of readings and decide whether the person reading them that day had forgotten to move the blocks back to touch the bearing. If so, discard the unreliable readings.

> **When using WaLRaGs, refer to Bragg et al. (1994).**

4.3.3.4 Automatic Data Loggers

Automatic data loggers can be used to measure a whole variety of variables. For water levels, two types have been commonly used. Clockwork chart recorders, such as R-16s, have been used. They provide continuous paper water-level charts. Machines are usually set to chart water-level variations for a one-month period before the chart is replaced. Continuous records of water level can be extremely useful, especially when addressing the pattern of water-level movement – a key determinant of a 'healthy' site (*see* 2.5.5). However, the data produced by R-16s is difficult to handle. To explore the data thoroughly, either the chart is read off manually and input into a computer or the line digitised allowing easier data manipulation usually in spreadsheet software.

Increasingly, clockwork machines are being replaced by battery-powered data loggers, as clockwork machines are difficult to maintain.

These use sensors to record water levels on computer chips. General-purpose loggers can be adapted to suit many purposes, although expertise is required to choose the appropriate sensors and link them with the logger.

More usually, a specially-designed data logger is used (such as the Chambers Logger – *see* Appendix 7). These allow water levels to be recorded every few seconds to every few days. The logger often only needs to be visited once every six months, and the data can be downloaded straight into computer spreadsheets. The time saved by visiting the logger infrequently and not having to input any data normally outweighs the capital cost of the equipment (between £500 and £5,000 in 1996). However, before embarking on the use of data loggers, consider the following:

- the property to be measured;
- precision of readings;
- reading interval;
- site visits to download readings;
- getting equipment out onto the bog;
- vandalism or theft;
- keeping the logger dry;
- site temperature range required;
- requirement for a portable computer to download readings;
- mains power supply to monitoring equipment;
- battery power, life, changes and cost;
- use of solar or wind power to charge batteries;
- need for an unbroken run of data;
- tolerable gaps in the dataset;
- ease of maintenance and operation;
- the necessary equipment: sensors, cables, data logger, batteries (with charging system if necessary), data storage and transfer medium (data cards, cartridges, EPROMs or suchlike and appropriate readers) or portable computer, PC with software for storing, analysing and displaying data;
- the logger's data storage capacity and battery life dictate the schedule of downloading/battery-changing/general maintenance visits; and
- insurance of equipment.

4.3.3.5 Remote Sensing

Water levels can be mapped by using remote sensing. Infra-red and multi-spectral sensors have been tried. These methods are still being researched. However, in the next few years, aerial techniques should become easier and cheaper and may become a practical option. For now, such techniques are only appropriate for one-off assessments and may be useful when dealing with complex topography and remote terrain.

4.3.3.6 Stage Boards

Stage boards are used to measure water levels of standing water bodies. Measurements allow long-term trends to be distinguished from seasonal fluctuations. They can also be used as a crude indicator of stream or ditch flow if situated in a place with a stable cross-section and a slow current.

The board simply consists of a board capable of withstanding constantly wet conditions, with a scale painted on it with numbers large enough to be read from a few metres away (Figure 4.10). A home-made stage board can be made for about

The board can be fixed onto a post hammered into the peat. If the peat is too soft to get the post in firmly, fix the board onto a timber rail with the 1.0m mark level with the lower edge of the rail. Nail the ends of the rail onto wooden posts hammered in almost to ground level on two sides of the water body so that the board is partially submerged in the water and it can be clearly seen from firm ground. The lower edge of the rail should lie along the ground surface. Try to keep the structure as discrete as possible. Use a duckboard to reduce trampling at the place from which you intend to read the stage board.

Data is used graphed against time; it is useful to show rainfall on the same graph. By plotting the relationship between the stage reading and the discharge, a stage reading can also be used as a surrogate for discharge.

4.3

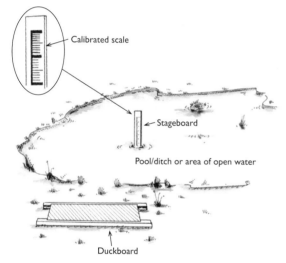

Figure 4.10 A stage-board. The board shows the water-level in standing water features such as a pool. The duck boarding is used to prevent damage to the bog surface.

Labels in figure: Calibrated scale; Stageboard; Pool/ditch or area of open water; Duckboard

£10. It is useful to use binoculars to read it if the nearest accessible place is some distance away.

Use an oak or elm board or a length of plastic piling to make a stage board. Paint the board white or black and use the contrasting colour for the scale. Start with zero at the lower end and mark off every centimetre, using a longer mark every 5 cm, and label each 10 cm mark.

4.3.4 Seepage/Discharge

4.3.4.1 V-Notch Weir

The V-notch weir is a specialist piece of equipment widely used by the water industry and for research. The disarmingly simple design – a V-notch in the top edge of a weir – hides considerable complexity in its use. The level of water backed up on the upstream side of the 'V' is related to discharge, thus representing lateral seepage from a bog (see 2.5.1). Details of using a V-notch weir can be found, for example, in the British Standard 3680, and more information is contained within Appendix 6.3.1.

4.3.4.2 Tipping Bucket Flow Gauge

Another method of measuring discharge is by using a tipping bucket flow gauge. This is used for measuring smaller rates of discharge, from lysimeters (see 4.3.5, A6.3.3) for example. Essentially, the gauge is a divided container set on a pivot. Water pours into one half of the bucket until it is full and causes the bucket to tilt and tip out its contents, at which point the other side of the bucket fills until it is full. Each bucket tip is counted. The number of tips relates to the discharge. More details are shown in Appendix 6.3.2.

4.3.4.3 *Piezometers*

Stage boards, V-notch weirs and tipping bucket flow gauges all measure discharge in discrete ditches or streams. Measuring seepage through the peat is achieved by using piezometers. Piezometers are similar to dipwells except that water only enters through the base of the tube. They can be bought or made easily from 52mm internal diameter PVC pipe or 2″ plastic waste pipe. To stop peat filling up the pipe from the base, cover the base with ladies' tights (or gauze) and affix with tape.

To measure the rate and direction of seepage towards a cut face, an array of piezometers is required.

- Mark out a line at right angles to the face and mark two points on this line, 1m and 5m from the face.
- At both of these points, install a group of piezometers at 0.5m depth intervals down to the level of the base of the cutting. Within a group, install the individual pipes 20 cm apart in a line parallel with the cutting.
- The pipe must be a tight fit with no gaps along the outside. To achieve this, push the piezometer straight into the ground, rather than into a ready-made hole. A 10 cm length protruding above ground and a coloured cap on top will make it more visible.
- The piezometers are read with a dipstick and the depths to water recorded.
- At some time during the monitoring period, measure the height of the ground surface at each piezometer relative to a fixed datum point, such as the top of a firm post, using an automatic level, if available, or by careful use of a straight edge, a spirit level, a plumb line and a tape measure.

Calculating seepage rates and exact directions from piezometer measurements is complicated and should be done by an expert. However, a rough idea of the direction of water movement can be obtained by using the rule of thumb that water moves from areas with a high pore water pressure towards places with a lower pressure. For example, water is likely to move from an area with a nest of piezometers showing high water levels to an area with a nest showing lower water levels.

4.3.5 Evapotranspiration – Lysimeters

Evapotranspiration is a difficult variable to measure but can be assessed indirectly by using a lysimeter. Basically, a lysimeter consists of an area of vegetation and peat which is isolated by a waterproof barrier to prevent seepage. A dipwell in the lysimeter measures changes in storage, a rain-gauge measures rainfall whilst the discharge from an outlet pipe is also measured. Using the water-balance equation (*see* 2.5.2), evapotranspiration can then be calculated. More detail is shown in Appendix 6.3.3.

4.4 CHEMISTRY

4.4.1 Introduction and Sampling

The acidic and nutrient-poor nature of bogs makes them very sensitive to pollution of any sort (*see* 2.6, 1.13, A3.7.1). Chemical analyses should be considered when, for example,

- pollution is suspected;
- water is being directed or redirected onto the bog surface;
- the potential of restoring cut-over bog is being examined.

Hydrological changes also bring about chemical change by oxidation and mineralisation of dry peat.

A bog's chemical environment is partly indicated by measuring acidity (pH) and conductivity, for which cheap and easy-to-use hand-held measuring devices are available. The pH of bog waters is generally between 3 and 4.5 whilst conductivity is generally less than 100 µS. Different figures would suggest that there may be a problem. A more definitive description of bog chemistry is derived by measuring other variables: cations, anions, dissolved organic matter and redox potential; these are more difficult to analyse and often have to be carried out in a laboratory. Nitrogen and phosphorus are useful variables to measure, as they indicate soil fertility.

If samples are to be sent to a laboratory, they have to be collected carefully. Chemical data expressed by dry weight (gravimetric samples) are easy to collect, as compaction and/or expansion is not a problem. Where analyses are expressed by volume (volumetric samples), the samples need to be collected and stored so as not to affect its bulk density. Samples collected for mineral or gross organic determination (for example, calcium, carbon, nitrogen or sulphur) can be stored in metal or plastic bags, tubes or boxes. If organic components are to be analysed (for example, pesticide residues), only metal or glass containers can be used.

For surface water analyses, waters should be stored in completely filled 300 ml polypropylene bottles to avoid oxidation, and stored at 2–5°C in a refrigerator (never frozen).

4.4.2 pH

pH is simply a measure of how acid or alkaline a sample is. Technically, pH = $-\log_{10}[H^+]$, where $[H^+]$ is the concentration of hydrogen ion in aqueous solution. It is commonly measured using electro-chemical meters. The meter probe is inserted into the sample, into wet peat or into peat mixed with de-ionised water. Remember to calibrate the meter using standard solutions before use. The literature accompanying the pH meter and the standard buffer media explain the procedure in detail.

Water samples should be measured with a temperature compensation allowance, that is, with the solution temperature-compensated by measuring the pH of a standard at the same temperature (carry your field standards *externally* in a polythene bag, if using battery-powered equipment), or by the inclusion of automatic temperature compensation within the pH meter. Modern portable and laboratory pH meters are fully temperature-compensated with a temperature thermistor included in the electrode array. This feature can be useful in determining sample temperatures and electrode performance (*see* ion-selective electrodes below).

> Watch the readings and be aware of slowly downward-drifting results when analysing samples which are likely to contain a lot of iron or aluminium. Try to read samples more quickly.
> Glass electrodes are usually designed to measure pH in solutions of conductivity of >100 S cm^{-1}, but certain water samples, such as, rainwaters or upland waters, may be below this limit. Low-conductivity electrodes are available, and *must* be used if these low conductivities are encountered and an accurate pH measurement is required.

Soil pH values (or soil reaction) are normally measured by mixing soil and de-ionised or distilled water in 1:4 proportions for air-dried organic soils such as peats. Since dried peat is usually difficult to rewet, measurement of pH is best made using field-moist peat samples, in a moist peat:water ratio of 1:2.

Note that pH values in intact peat cores may be up to 0.5 – 1.0 units less than those seen in suspensions. This is due to the dilution effect of mixing a sample with water.

4.4.3 Conductivity

The measurement of electrical conductivity in water samples gives a measure of their content of ions and can be performed in the field using equipment similar to pH meters. In peat surface and drainage waters, this determination can give indications of the incursion of unwanted inorganic components perhaps derived from adjacent agricultural land, of mineral groundwater or sea-salt contributions. The determination is simple and is usually performed in conjunction with pH measurements. Conductivity is temperature-dependent, so, if conductivity measurements are required, buy a combination pH, conductivity and temperature metre.

Several field meters are available for the simultaneous measurement of pH, temperature and conductivity; these also usually have a mV mode which allows the measurement of redox potential and ionic strengths (for selective ion determinations). These are very useful meters in situations which require detailed monitoring of water quality. Redox potential, for example, is considered to be an important variable when monitoring the burial environment of in-situ archaeological remains since it gives an indication of aerobic/anaerobic conditions.

4.4.4 Laboratory Techniques

There are many techniques used for analysing chemical constituents. A few are shown below:

Technique	Analyses	Cost (1996)
X-ray fluorescence	Ca, Na, K, Mg, Fe, Al, Si, Mn, S, P, Cl in a single analysis	£10/sample
Total nitrogen by digestion	N	£5.50/sample

Gas chromatography	C, H, N	£9/sample
Plasma spectrometer	Ca, Na, K, Mg, Cu, Zn, Mn, Fe, Al, Si, S, P in a single analysis	£9/sample
Ion-exchange chromatography	Cl, NO_3, SO_4	£6.50/sample
Flow-injection analysis	NH_4, PO_4	£3/sample
Oxidation/ combustion	Dissolved organic carbon	£2.50/sample

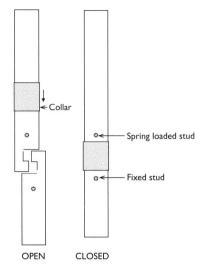

OPEN   CLOSED

Figure 4.11 Metal rods can be used to measure the depth of peat. The rods can be inter-locked using bayonet connections.

4.5   PEAT

4.5.1   Introduction

The inextricable links between the peat, water and the vegetation often mean that it is important to look at the peat itself. A knowledge of peat depth, peat surface level changes and some idea of the peat properties can be useful supplementary information for managers. Such information, for example, would be important to assess the likely success of rewetting peat fields. Shallow depths of poorly-humified peat could lead to high vertical seepage losses making rewetting schemes impossible.

This section describes how to gauge peat depths (4.5.2), assess changes to surface levels (4.5.3) and sample peats (4.5.4). In addition, a brief description of the main methods for assessing seven of the most important peat properties is given (4.5.5). This can be specialised work, and land managers are advised to consult more specialist texts or seek advice from specialists.

Methods for monitoring peat erosion are also briefly mentioned. This widespread phenomenon (see 1.14) has yet to be managed successfully (for example, Phillips et al., 1981), although there has been much research work. The types of methods used in this research are mentioned here (4.5.6).

4.5.2   Peat Depth

Where peat overlies mineral ground directly, peat depth is easy to assess. Interlocking rods (linked with bayonet connections (Figure 4.11) or screwed together) are simply forced through the peat until the underlying firmer mineral ground is reached. For peats overlying lake basins (many raised bogs for example), the peat/sub-surface boundary is more difficult to gauge. With experience, the 'feel'

of rods pushing through the sediment can indicate when a different material from peat has been reached. However, to be really sure, peat should be sampled (see 4.5.3). Difficulties are also encountered where the peat is woody. In these cases, it is useful to attach a screw auger to wind through soft wood.

Ideally, augering positions should be levelled (see 4.2/A6.2.2) to allow absolute sub-surface heights to be plotted.

In some situations (where the underlying sediments and the peat are very different), peat depth can be ascertained using radar and seismology. Techniques are still partly experimental and expensive.

4.5.3   Surface Level Changes

The surface level of a peat bog can change. This is because peat is mostly water, so changes in water content affect the height of the column of peat. Effective drainage schemes can, for example, cause a peat surface to drop by half. Commonly, the surface levels change between winter and summer – a phenomenon known as *Mooratmung* or 'bog-breathing'.

Peat anchors are used to detect changes in the fall or rise of the bog surface or to detect peat

> It is sometimes confusing to work out exactly where to measure to the surface. Measuring to the top of a *Sphagnum* carpet (where available) is probably best.

accumulation over many years. Wood or metal (such as gas pipe) can be used, but wood is suitable only for shallow peat and is more easily dislodged by frost and animals. Metal conduit pipe is generally suitable:

- Prime and paint (for example, Hammerite) metal conduit pipe to protect it from corroding or to protect the bog from zinc pollution if the pipe is galvanised (non-galvanised pipe is available).
- Determine peat depth using depthing rods (*see* 4.5.2).
- Cut an appropriate length of conduit.
- Push through peat until the underlying mineral ground is reached, then with a sledgehammer, or similar, drive into mineral ground until the pipe is secure.

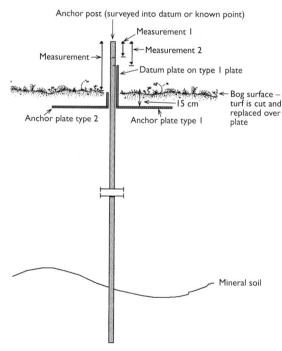

Anchor post (surveyed into datum or known point)

Measurement 1

Measurement 2

Measurement →

Datum plate on type 1 plate

15 cm — Bog surface – turf is cut and replaced over plate

Anchor plate type 2

Anchor plate type 1

Mineral soil

Rise and fall of bog is measured in two ways:–
1. By measuring from the top of the anchor post to the top of the anchor plate post
2. By making a saw cut in the anchor post at the top of the anchor plate

Figure 4.12 Design details of the anchor posts used to measure the rise and fall of a bog (adapted from a design by J.Davis, CCW).

- The pipe protruding above the surface of the bog can be protected with a capped length of uPVC fall pipe. A protrusion of 30 to 50 cm is adequate.
- Measure from top of conduit to bog surface, using a ruler or a collar and ruler.

A slightly more sophisticated version, used at Cors Caron (*see* 6.13) and the South Solway Mosses (*see* 6.3), is shown in Figure 4.12.

4.5.4 Sampling Peat

Before peat's properties can be assessed, it needs to be sampled. To sample peat at depth, there are a variety of coring devices available. Shallow peat can be sampled with a spade or a section of drainage pipe. The commonest devices are shown in Figures 4.13, 4.14 and 4.15.

Peat cores from these corers provide a rich and neatly stacked archive of cultural and environmental information (*see* 1.6) and are commonly used; they can often be borrowed from university environmental departments. Alternatively, they can be specially made or bought commercially (*see* Appendix 7).

Figure 4.13 A Russian corer provides a half cylinder of peat. Compaction is minimal and the sampler is easy to use. Russian corers are usually quite thin, although wider 9cm corers have been designed (see Figure 4.15 and Barber, 1984). (Rob Stoneman)

Figure 4.14   A box corer is simple to use for collecting surface samples. The front face of the corer has been removed to show the sample. (Stuart Brooks)

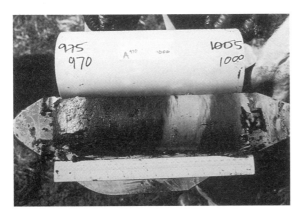

Figure 4.15   A core from the basal sediments of Bolton Fell Moss, Cumbria taken with a wide gauge Russian corer. (Rob Stoneman)

4.5.5   Peat Properties

4.5.5.1 Degree of Decomposition or Humification

The level to which plant material decomposes, during peat formation, affects other properties such as bulk density, water storage capacity and hydraulic conductivity. In ombrotrophic peats, the degree of decomposition or humification also relates to how wet the bog was during peat formation and hence the prevailing climatic conditions (Barber, 1981). Various methods are used to assess humification.

The first is the Von Post method, which assesses a humification or H-scale running from H1, undecomposed peat, to H10, completely decomposed peat, based on a number of diagnostic features and criteria (*see* Table 4.3). The steps required for Von Post assessment are as follows (with reference to Table 4.3):

- Sample the peat (using a Russian-type, gouge or box sampler, grabbing a handful and so on).
- Inspect peat for changes in colour, texture and so on, and note or mark the depths at which changes occur.
- Take a piece of peat, break and inspect the fresh surface to confirm above observations and observe the nature and proportion of identifiable plant remains (Table A3, column 3).
- Squeeze the peat slowly and gently and observe whether water is extruded out and the colour of the water (Table A3, column 1).
- Squeeze firmly and observe whether peat is extruded between fingers and the proportion of the sample that is extruded (Table A3, column 2).
- Rub a small amount between forefinger and thumb to determine the texture (Table A3, column 4).
- Compare the proportion of identifiable plant remains before and after the peat is squeezed and rubbed (Table A3, columns 3 and 5).
- With reference to Table 4.3, assign an H-value to the sample.

4.5.5.2   Fibre Content Method

A number of methods have been devised for assessing the degree of decomposition in terms of the fibre content of peat. The fibre content is expressed as a percentage of volume or of dry weight of peat. The system devised for the US Department of Agriculture (Lynn et al., 1974) and is summarised below:

- Sample peat using an appropriate sampler.
- If peat has dried in the field, soak samples for twenty-four hours.
- Remove excess water by rolling in paper towels.
- Pack a 5 ml syringe, that has been cut in half longitudinally, with the peat. Compact sample just enough to force air, but not water, out of the sample.
- Transfer sample to a 100 mm mesh sieve and wash under running tap water until effluent appears clear.
- Blot sample and repack in the syringe.

Table 4.3   Assessment of degrees of decomposition based on the Von Post scale.

Degree of decomposition	**Principal diagnostic features**					
	1. Nature of water expressed on initial squeezing	2. Proportion of peat extruded between fingers on further squeezing	3. Nature of plant remains	4. Texture	Description	5. Comments
H1	Clear, colourless	None	Unaltered	Very rough and very spongy	Undecomposed	Living or recently dead
H2	Almost clear, very pale yellow-brown		Little altered, entire structures	Very rough and spongy	Almost undecomposed	
H3	Slightly turbid, brown		Broken in pieces but easily identified	Moderately rough and slightly spongy; somewhat moulded residue when squeezed	Very slightly decomposed	
H4	Turbid, brown		Broken into component fragments, for example, leaves are easily identified	Very slight soapy feel; moulded residue	Slightly decomposed	
H5	Strongly turbid brown, contains a little peat in suspension	Very little	Many difficult to identify	Slightly soapy feel. Moulded residue	Moderately decomposed	Unsqueezed peat may appear to have greater proportion of identifiable remains than expected, some or all of which on squeezing or rubbing become amorphous
H6	Dark brown, much peat in suspension	One third	Many unidentifiable	Moderately pasty; moulded residue	Well decomposed	
H7	Very little water, dark brown	One half	Few remains identifiable	Very pasty; moulded residue	Strongly decomposed	
H8	Little or none	Two thirds	Only resistant fibres, roots, bark etc. identifiable		Very strongly decomposed	
H9	None	Almost all	Practically no identifiable structures	Feels greasy	Almost completely decomposed	
H10		All (unless too dry)	Completely amorphous	Feels very greasy	Completely decomposed except for microscopic structures. e.g. pollen	

4.5

- Read the residue volume and record as a percentage of unrubbed fibre.
- Return residue to the sieve and rub between thumb and forefinger in running tap water until the effluent is clear.
- Repeat blotting and repacking process and record volume as a percentage of rubbed fibre.

4.5.5.3 Calorimetric Method

The colour intensity of an extract of an aqueous alkaline solution of a peat sample relates to humification (Aaby and Tauber, 1974). The simplest method is used by the US Department of Agriculture:

- Take a 2.5 ml sample (fibre content method).
- Add 1g of NaP_2O_7 crystals to 4 ml of water, add peat and stir.
- Stand for one day.
- Restir and insert one end of a strip of chromatography paper (0.5 cm x 3.0 cm) until all of the strip is moistened.
- Compare colour of the paper with a standard Munsell colour chart.

More complex quantitative methods are described by, for example, Aaby and Tauber (1974).

Humification values are often plotted against depth forming proxy-climatic curves (for example, Blackford, 1993).

4.5.5.4 Water Content

Water-level readings can be supplemented by calculating the water content of peat. In natural catotelmic peat (lower, saturated peat), water content is commonly 90–96% of fresh weight of peat. Occasionally, water content is expressed as a percentage of dry weight, in which case values of 1,800–2,400% are typical. The assessment procedure is as follows:

- Remove a core of peat from the site (see 4.5.4).
- Place the full sampler horizontally on the bog surface before opening the chamber to minimise water loss.
- While peat is still in the chamber, cut samples into appropriate depth increments and place in sample cans or polythene bags. Use at least two bags, as welds can fail.
- Press air from bags and seal (fold top over and wrap an elastic band around folded top, or if bags are large enough close with a knot).
- Keep sample as cool as possible.

- Weigh sample as soon as possible.
- Oven-dry at 90°C until weight is constant.
- Weigh sample.
- Calculate water content:

$$\% \text{ fresh weight} = \frac{\text{Fresh weight} - \text{Dry weight}}{\text{Fresh weight}} \times 100$$

$$\% \text{ dry weight} = \frac{\text{Fresh weight}}{\text{Dry weight}} \times 100$$

4.5.5.5 Bulk Density

Bulk density is a measure of the dry weight per unit volume of fresh peat. Shrinkage of peat in response to drainage or erosion increases its bulk density. The procedure for determination is as follows:

- Cut peat, while in sampler chamber, into incremental lengths and place in sample cans or polythene bags (see water content methods).
- Weigh fresh peat samples.
- Oven-dry samples to a constant weight.
- Bulk density = $\dfrac{\text{Dry weight (grams)}}{\text{Volume of sample (l, ml or cm}^3)}$

4.5.5.6 Ash Content

The ash content is the mineral residue that remains when peat is combusted. It consists of atmospheric and groundwater-borne mineral inputs and the mineral components of plants. Bog peat has a low ash content which mostly ranges from less than 2% to about 5%. The value can be affected by the degree of decomposition of the peat, but high values generally indicate a groundwater input at the time of deposition. The procedure for estimation is as follows:

- Oven-dry and mill or grind sample (use a coffee grinder).
- Redry sample and place a weighed (weigh to two or three decimal places) sub-sample of approximately 0.2g in a crucible.
- Place in a furnace at 500°C to 600°C and leave for 24 hours.
- Weigh residue.
- Calculate ash content as a percentage of oven-dry peat:
- Ash content = $\dfrac{\text{Weight of ash residue}}{\text{Weight of oven-dried sample}} \times 100$

4.5.5.7 Botanical Composition

It can be useful to study the composition of the peat – the semi-decomposed remains of the plants which formed the peat. These remains reveal much of the site's past history: its development, the pre-interference vegetation and the effects of certain events, for example. In bog peats, there are few different types of vegetation: *Sphagnum*, sedges and ericoids are most common. The main components are shown in Table 4.4.

Table 4.4   Description of principal botanical components.

Sphagnum	In peat of low H-value, almost entire, clearly observable plants may occur. In moderately decomposed peat, stems and leaves are usually separated. *Sphagnum* leaves (Figure 4.16) are characteristically boat-shaped.
Mosses (excluding *Sphagnum*)	In bog peat, very few mosses besides *Sphagnum* are identifiable in the field. The commonest are *Polytrichum* (*P. commune* and *P. alpestre*) and *Racomitrium lanuginosum* (wavy-hair moss). *Polytrichum* remains usually occur as thin mats of dark stems on which at least a few leaves of several mm length remain. In the northern maritime and high-altitude bogs of Scotland, *R. lanuginosum* can be a peat-former. In such situations, *R. lanuginosum* is usually abundant in the present vegetation. In the peat, it appears as a crushed or compacted mid-brown version of the living plant. A hand lens clearly reveals this resemblance.
Sedges and grasses	Two species of cotton grass are commonly found in peat, namely *E. angustifolium* (common cotton grass) and *E. vaginatum* (hare's tail cotton grass). Both shoot bases and roots can be identified. The shoot bases are fibrous, but those of common cotton grass mostly occur singly whereas those of hare's tail cotton grass are generally clumped. The shoot bases of the latter species are generally stronger and more resistant to breakage when handled. Some of the roots of common cotton grass and hare's tail cotton grass are pink and black respectively in freshly, exposed peat samples. *Scirpus cespitosus* (deer sedge) bases and rhizomes are occasionally found but are difficult to distinguish from undifferentiated sedge

remains. Of the grasses, only purple moor grass (*Molinia caerulea*) is a feature of bog peat and then usually only in very high-rainfall areas. It has a characteristic swollen leaf base and an irregularly-shaped rhizome with leaf-base scars. The roots are twisted, pale-coloured and up to 2 mm broad.

Woody structures	Small quantities of fine twigs and roots occur in most bog peat samples. They are mostly the remains of ericaceous plants and particularly ling heather. Cross-leaved heath and cranberry may also occur. A somewhat twisted, irregularly and sparsely-pitted and striated twig is characteristic of ling heather. Cross-leaved heath twigs are generally straight, and the rings of leaf scars may be visible. Cranberry twigs are fine (approximately 1–2 mm diameter) and wiry. Roots are rarely distinguished and are generally categorised as ericaceous roots. Birch twigs and roots may occur. They have a smooth and shiny bark. Occasionally alder, willow and pine is found. The bark of alder and willow may also be shiny and hence difficult to distinguish from the commoner birch.
Fruits and seeds	These are only occasionally found. Those that are 1–2 mm long, trigonous or elliptical with a break are usually Cyperaceae (sedge family) fruits or seeds. *Carex* (sedge), *Eriophorum*, *Scirpus* and *Rhynchospora* are the main genera found. Elongated bean-shaped *Potentilla erecta* seeds up to 2 mm long with undulating ridges are occasionally found. More frequently, rounded bean-shaped *Menyanthes* seeds up to 3 mm across occur in peat deposited in or around former wet hollows.

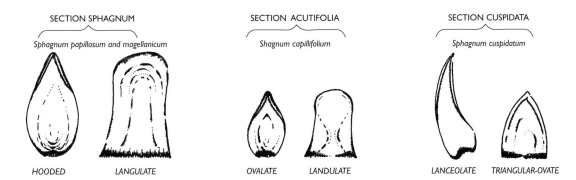

Figure 4.16   Identifiable *sphagnum* leaves from moderately decomposed peat can be identified to section level on the basis of their shape. For more details see Daniels and Eddy (1990) and Hill (1992).

4.5.6 Peat Erosion

4.5.6.1 Introduction

To date, most erosion investigations have been carried out to determine the rate of surface lowering and to find out how rapidly peat erosion features develop. This has yielded useful insight into the age and persistence of erosion features. For example, Birnie (1993) found that peat erosion was progressing at the rate of 1–4 cm per year, suggesting that the peat landforms in Shetland would persist for between 30 and 150 years depending on peat depths. However, from a management perspective, it is probably more critical that a monitoring programme is linked to a programme for assessing the effectiveness of alternative management regimes for reinstating damaged peatlands or for controlling further erosion (for example, exclusion of large herbivores).

4.5.6.2 Methods

Assessing quantity and rates of peat erosion can be approached through the use of reference markers, mapping and estimating the sediment resulting from erosion.

The use of reference markers involves pushing thin (1–10 mm) erosion pins or rods into the peat or, in shallow peats, through to the mineral ground. The pins should be surveyed and then the amount protruding above the ground measured at appropriate time intervals. Another way to achieve similar results is to bridge two pegs with a point quadrat frame (see A6.4.3.3) and measure the distance between inserted needles and the peat.

The area of erosion or differing erosion patterns can also be mapped. This data can be used in conjunction with reference markers to assess the quantity of peat eroded and provide information about the rate of spread/retreat or lateral expansion of erosion systems. Of the methods outlined in Appendix 6, plane table mapping (see A6.2.2.6) and a simple line survey (measuring along tape measures the distances where erosion occurs) are most appropriate. Aerial photography (see 4.6.4) can also be used to map erosion features and systems. Tallis (1981) describes a method to calculate the rate of peat erosion by comparing aerial photographs taken on different dates.

A proxy method of measuring erosion rates is to measure the amount of sediment arising from erosion (bearing in mind that wind and oxidation also remove peat). Sediment can be trapped using screens of different mesh sizes (for example, Tallis, 1973) and then dried and weighed. The quantity of sediment trapped by reservoirs in upland catchments have also been examined (Ledger et al., 1974; Tallis, 1981) to determine peat erosion rates.

4.6 VEGETATION

4.6.1 Introduction

Conservation management of bogs is often undertaken to change vegetation composition and structure. This is achieved by direct methods of vegetation management (see 5.3–5.5) or indirectly by modifying hydrology (see 5.1). Whatever, the effects of such management can be ascertained by monitoring vegetation. The techniques are common to many habitats, so only a summary is provided here. A more detailed account can be found in Appendix 6.4.

Prior to embarking on vegetation monitoring schemes, the study area should be defined. It may be the whole bog, or a representative part of a bog, in which management is to take place, or has taken place. Whole site assessment can be achieved through the use of aerial photographs (see 4.6.4), although this approach is not necessary on small areas or small sites. A different approach uses representative plots chosen for monitoring.

Important considerations include:

- Should the plot be unfenced or fenced to stop monitoring equipment getting damaged by animals and/or to monitor the effect of grazing?
- Plots often need to be relocated – reference markers or obvious features are used for guidance.
- Monitoring itself may affect the plot, confusing the results.
- What species should be monitored – all or a representative set of indicators?
- If representative plots are chosen (usually quadrats), do they need to be permanent? There has been a tendency to use targeted permanent quadrats for monitoring bogs in the UK (for example, Lindsay and Ross, 1994) despite the fact that the resulting data is not amenable to multivariate analysis.

4.6.2 Marking Monitoring Positions

Whatever methods are chosen for vegetation monitoring, the monitoring positions often need marking. They can be marked in a variety of ways. Bamboo garden canes are generally suitable; they are inexpensive, light to carry, easy to install and easy to find, last for about four years and are easy to replace when necessary. However, on sites grazed by large herbivores such as sheep and deer or where vandalism is a realistic threat, canes can easily be broken or pulled out and more substantial markers, such as stakes, may be necessary. Buried metal markers can be used in addition to, or as an alternative to, stakes and canes. For precise location, a 1 cm x 30 cm steel rod can be pushed vertically into the peat; or for less precise location, a polythene-wrapped 10 × 10 cm aluminium plate can be buried horizontally just below the surface. Buried metal markers can be relocated using a metal detector.

Canes or posts marking the general location can be allied to buried metal markers which enable precise repositioning for future recording, for example, metal rods protruding at the two opposing corners of an area quadrat or at the ends of a point quadrat frame.

4.6.3 Using Quadrats

The most common way of monitoring vegetation is to use a quadrat. These are simply areas of space of any size or shape, although often $1/2$ m × $1/2$ m or 1m × 1m squares. Four quadrat positioning systems are used:

- *Random* – statistically the most objective method of sampling, although relatively large numbers are required for an adequate characterisation.
- *Stratified random* – though less objective, by using some existing knowledge of the site (for example, hummocks or hollows, intact or damaged areas; land uses), the number of quadrats can be reduced and comparisons are easier.
- *Grids or transects* – useful for monitoring relatively uniform areas.
- *Targeted quadrats* – used where particular features only are monitored.

Bear in mind that analysis is often concerned with comparing two sets of data. Resurvey can be undertaken on the same quadrats, in which case they should all be marked (*see* 4.6.2) and

remonitored or a new set of quadrats surveyed. If new quadrats are monitored, observed variation may relate only to sample differences rather than to actual vegetation change.

Different types of quadrat can also be used (A6.4.3.3):

- *Area quadrats* – These range in size from 10 cm × 10 cm to 10m × 10m. For bogs, rectangular quadrats less than 45 cm deep (and any distance long: 50–900 cm is common) is preferable, as the surveyor can lean all the way across the quadrat without trampling on any of the vegetation. Quadrats are often divided into smaller squares for which abundance of differing species is assessed.
- *Point quadrats* – Although very intensive and time-consuming, this method is considered to be the most objective and quantitative means of estimating species composition. The method works by recording all contacts made between a frame of needles and the vegetation: 100–200 contacts should be recorded on bogs to allow calculation of percentage cover and relative frequency.
- *Line quadrats* – This method is useful for recording vegetation mosaics. A line/tape is laid across the vegetation and species contact is recorded at regular intervals or the distance of species contact is measured along the whole length of tape.

Data is best stored on computer spreadsheet and processed to give cover as a percentage or as a relative frequency (*see* A6.4.4). Data runs (over a number of years) or a number of quadrats can be compared graphically or numerically using various statistical packages.

4.6.4 Aerial Photograph Interpretation

Aerial photograph interpretation (API) allied to ground survey is particularly useful for assessing vegetation variation across a whole site. The precision of API depends on the quality and scale of the photograph. False colour, 1:250 photographs have been used to map patterns as small as individual hummocks and pools. Such intensive and detailed survey is achieved by etching boundaries onto the photograph itself. The lines are then digitised for use in a geographical information system (GIS).

Rarely is this level of detail required for conservation management as opposed to pure

4.6

research. More usually, standard 1:24,000 aerial photographs are used in the following manner:

- View the image under a magnifying (× 10) stereoscopic viewer.
- Overlay acetate sheet or tracing paper onto a similar-scaled map (in the UK, 1:10,000 OS maps are ideal).
- Trace onto the overlay obvious vegetation compartments. At 1:24,000, compartments down to $^1/_4$ ha in size should be distinguishable.
- Use a coding system which indicates the type of vegetation likely to be found based upon the photograph (such as, *Sphagnum*, water, heather, scrub, trees, fen and so on).
- Take a photocopy of the resulting map out to the site to check, and if necessary correct, boundaries and to describe vegetation and other notable characteristics (*see* 3.1) including damage (*see* 1.8–1.14 and A3) in each compartment.

These maps can be digitised along with the compartment information to allow the data to be analysed and manipulated using GIS. An example of this approach is given by Parkyn and Stoneman (1996). Otherwise, maps can be drawn by hand providing the basis for the management plan's site description (*see* 3.1).

4.6.5 Remote Sensing

Remote sensing has the potential to map vegetation quickly across large areas. Images are collected from the air and from satellite. Essentially, different types of vegetation have their own spectral signature (reflection of radiation at different wavelengths). Once the signature is identified, it is then possible to map the same signature across the whole image. Unfortunately, most vegetation is composed of various hues of green so different vegetation types are difficult to tell apart. Nevertheless, vegetation mapping is possible using remote sensing (for example, Reid et al., 1996), and techniques are likely to become more effective and accessible.

4.7 FAUNA

4.7.1 Introduction

Many different types of fauna can be and are monitored on peat bogs. Rare species are often monitored to assess whether populations are stable or increasing. It would be too lengthy to include details of all types of faunal monitoring here, although some of the monitoring methods for birds and invertebrates are outlined. This is because these two groups often respond rapidly to management works and can be a useful guide to the success of management.

4.7.2 Birds

4.7.2.1 Introduction

Bird populations can change rapidly as a consequence of conservation management. Removal of large areas of scrub woodland and the creation of open water has a particularly strong impact. This allows the success of management to be monitored via bird recording as a surrogate measure for habitat change. Other objectives of bird monitoring programmes are:

- to provide baseline data for previously unrecorded sites;
- to provide information on species that have particular conservation interest;
- to complement interpretation of hydrological and botanical data;
- to provide information to non-specialist audiences; and
- to supplement national bird monitoring programmes.

There are several standard techniques used in Britain and elsewhere that can be adopted for monitoring birds on peatlands. These are:

- *Breeding Bird Survey* aimed at monitoring populations of widespread and abundant species in the UK (4.7.2.2).
- *Common Bird Census* designed to estimate national bird population changes through monitoring of sample survey sites (4.7.2.3).
- *Point counts* where all birds are recorded at a designated number of locations (4.7.2.4).
- *Transect counts* for large areas of uniform habitat (4.7.2.5).

Though each technique is designed for a specific purpose, they can be adapted to suit the requirements of individual sites. The point and transect count methods are most adaptable, as the other methods have been designed within a national framework. As with any form of monitoring, it is important to clearly define the objectives of the scheme and assess all resource requirements (*see* 3.4.3.2).

The following is a very brief description of the four methods mentioned. For more information, consult Bibby et al., 1992, or in the UK contact the BTO or RSPB at:

British Trust for Ornithology	RSPB
The Nunnery	The Lodge
Thetford	Sandy
Norfolk	Bedfordshire
IP24 2PU	SG19 2DL

4.7.2.2 Breeding Bird Survey

The Breeding Bird Survey (BBS) was designed and implemented by the British Trust for Ornithology (BTO) as a potential successor to the Common Bird Census (CBC).

One-kilometre grid squares are randomly chosen. Two transects are established, 1 km long and 500m apart. The habitats along the transects are described and coded (BTO methodology). Bird observations are recorded at two visits (all species) and divided according to distance from the transect: within 25m, 25–100m, greater than 100m and in-flight. An average visit takes approximately 1½ hrs depending on the habitat.

4.7.2.3 Common Bird Census

The Common Bird Census (CBC) was established by the BTO in 1962. Its principal aims were to measure the background variation in bird numbers and the extent of population changes due to pesticide use and habitat changes. A national picture is extrapolated from a series of sample sites (plots) which are recorded annually. Approximately 40,000 individual bird territories are mapped from 300 plots visited during March–July each year.

A total of ten visits per year are made to the plot. On each visit, all birds seen or heard are recorded on a 1:2,500 map. When all the visits are complete for the year, the information is transferred to a species map which, when analysed, shows the territories of individual birds. The result is a series of maps for each plot, species and season showing the number and position of each territory. These then form the basis for the extrapolated national picture. The fieldwork and mapping requires at least sixty hours of work, which inevitably limits the number of plots visited.

4.7.2.4 Point Counts

Point counts can be an efficient way of collecting species abundance data. They are particularly good in scrub habitats, as they avoid excessive disturbance to the birds. They are not particularly well suited to large areas of open bog, as birds are disturbed on open bog.

Points are selected either systematically or randomly within the study area. They should be spaced far enough apart to avoid duplication of individuals. Counts should last 5–10 minutes. On longer counts, individuals may be recorded more than once. If a distance estimate is given for each record, a crude estimate of population density can be expressed.

This method has no standard, national approach and could be readily adapted to suit individual needs and resource limitations.

4.7.2.5 Transect Counts

Transect counts are particularly useful in covering large areas of open habitat. There is no standard methodology although there are a certain number of guidelines which should be adhered to.

Transect lengths are variable; they are dependent upon habitat (longer for open habitats), ease of access and time limitations. They should be spaced widely enough to minimise the risk of duplicating sightings. The recorder walks the length of the transect at a steady pace and maps or records all sightings. Supplementary information on behaviour, sex and so on, can also be noted. A distance estimate (from perpendicular to the transect) is also noted.

This method may be particularly suited to bogs, as many species are flushed from cover as the recorder walks the transect route.

4.7.3 Invertebrates

4.7.3.1 Introduction

Monitoring invertebrates on a bog can be a time-consuming, methodologically difficult exercise which demands a great deal of expertise on behalf of the surveyor. Resources rarely allow for a detailed study. However, some invertebrate monitoring can be rewarding.

Where site comparisons are being made, the methodology should be consistent between sites. Where possible, surveys should be designed so that they can be easily repeated as part of longer-term monitoring projects (Fry and Lonsdale, 1991).

Another consideration is the range of habitats across the site. Surveys should be planned in a systematic manner to cover the main habitats on the site. This is important, as the greatest diversity of invertebrates are often found within marginal habitats (lagg fens, scrub and so on) which, though interesting, may not be representative of the whole site. As with any monitoring, it is important to set out the objectives of the scheme carefully (*see* 3.4.3.2).

Where possible, invertebrate monitoring should be linked as closely as possible with botanical and hydrological monitoring programmes on a site. Climatic records are also of importance in interpreting invertebrate monitoring data (Shaw and Wheeler, 1995).

4.7.3.2   Survey Types and Methods

Fry and Lonsdale (1991) identify five types of general invertebrate survey, all of which are applicable to bogs.

1. Inventory surveys where the aim is to find out what there is and if anything is of significance in terms of community size, community structure, species richness, species rarity and faunal assemblages and so on
2. Site invertebrate comparisons.
3. Evaluating the effects of management practices where the aim is to discover whether a certain management procedure is of benefit or detriment to the invertebrate fauna.
4. Impact assessment which requires predictions about the effects of certain proposed activities on the invertebrate fauna.
5. Rare species surveys in which specialists assess the present status of certain rare species on one site or a series of sites.

Most surveys involve some combination of the above. This list is useful in deciding exactly why the survey is required and to establish primary objectives (*see* 3.4.3.2).

Methods to achieve such surveys can be divided into trapping techniques and direct counting techniques. Trapping techniques include malaise (4.7.3.3), pitfall (4.7.3.4), water (4.7.3.5), light (4.7.3.6) and suction trapping (4.7.3.7). Direct counting techniques include transect walking, netting, hand searching and use of quadrats (4.7.3.8). Advantages and disadvantages are shown in Table 4.5.

4.7.3.3   Malaise Traps

Malaise traps are designed to sample large numbers of flying insects, especially flies (*Diptera*) and wasps (*Hymenoptera*), without the need of a power source. The standard Malaise trap (Figure 4.17) looks rather like a ridge tent made of netting, without sides but with a central vertical partition. The insects fly into the central partition and then move upwards towards the light, eventually reaching the apex of the trap where there is a plastic collecting bottle. Some type of killing agent (for example, Vapona) can be placed in the bottle.

Malaise traps are relatively inexpensive and have the advantage that they do not require any power source and can, therefore, be taken anywhere. The fact that malaise traps catch large quantities of insects is both an advantage and a disadvantage. If the time and expertise is available to identify all the invertebrates sampled, then malaise traps become a very useful tool for examining populations and communities of winged invertebrates. Under most circumstances, this will not be the case and many of the

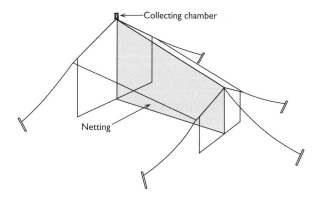

Figure 4.17   A malaise trap. Flying insects hit a vertical wall of netting. They move upwards towards the light and are funnelled through a small hole into a collecting chamber (from Kirby, 1992).

Table 4.5   Survey methods: advantages and disadvatages (survey types 1–5 refer to the list in Fry and Lonsdale, 1991).

Survey method	Survey type	Advantage	Disadvantage	Cost
TRAPPING				
Malaise	All	Samples large numbers. No power source.	Samples large numbers Kills large numbers. Standardisation difficult.	Cheap
Pitfall	All, 2, 3	Simple to use. Expertise not always required. No power source.	Methodologically unsound. Kills samples.	Very cheap
Water	All	Simple to use. No power source.	Kills samples. Standardisation difficult.	Very cheap
Light	All	Used at night. Traps sample alive.	Power source needed. Traps limited range of taxa.	Expensive
Suction	All, 1	Easily standardised. Comprehensive sampling.	Samples large numbers. Time consuming. Expertise essential. Poor in wet conditions.	Very expensive
DIRECT COUNTING				
Transect walking	2, 3, 4, 5	Simple. No expertise required.	Samples very limited range of taxa. Requires regular repetition.	Very cheap
Aquatic netting	2, 5	Simple.	Standardisation difficult.	Cheap
Sweep-netting	2, 3, 4, 5	Simple.	Standardisation difficult.	Cheap
Quadrat counting	3, 4	Simple.	Can be inaccurate.	Cheap
Sieving	1	Simple. Samples lesser known invertebrates.	Expertise required for ID of smaller taxa.	Cheap
Extraction funnels	All	Samples lesser known invertebrates.	Expertise required for ID of smaller taxa. Time consuming.	Moderate
Pooters	1	Simple. Can sample species not caught in traps.	No standardisation.	Cheap
Hand searching	1	Simple. Can sample species not caught in traps.	No standardisation.	Very cheap

4.7

invertebrates sampled will be discarded or will remain in perpetual storage. In these cases, the trap should be used sparingly or alternative sampling techniques used.

It is not recommended that malaise traps be used on small sites (a good example is a small lowland raised bog), as this could have a detrimental effect on local populations of invertebrates associated with, or adapted to, those sites. Similarly, malaise traps should not be used where an endangered species is known to occur.

A few useful guidelines when using a malaise trap are:

- Change the bottle at least every two days in the summer months, as sampled invertebrates soon begin to decompose. If the site cannot be visited every two days, use alcohol to delay decomposition for approximately one week.
- Where there is scrub or woodland on the bog, place the trap at 90° to the edge of a block of trees – this catches the invertebrates hawking along woodland edges.
- Loosely place some vegetation or tissue paper in the collecting bottle along with the killing agent – this helps to prevent antagonism between individuals and increases the surface area within the bottle.
- Malaise traps consisting of a collecting head, a spare collecting bottle, six metal tent pegs, two

jubilee clips for attaching the head to the main support post, six strong nylon cords as guy ropes and an instruction sheet cost about £95 (1996) – *see* Appendix 7.

4.7.3.4 Pitfall Traps

Pitfall trapping (Figure 4.18) is a relatively simple and useful technique for sampling certain groups of invertebrates, particularly errant species such as ground beetles (*Carabidae*), rove beetles (*Staphylinidae*) and spiders. Many authors (for example, Greenslade, 1964; Holopainen, 1990) have questioned the use of pitfall traps as a survey technique and discussed the relative attractiveness to invertebrates of the various solutions used in traps. It is argued that the 'catch' reflects invertebrate activity rather than abundance and that some species are always under-recorded. Despite these drawbacks, it remains a useful technique, with the bonus on bogs that traps can be easily sunk into the peat.

In a survey of the ground beetle fauna of Welsh peatland biotopes (Holmes et al., 1993), pitfall trapping was used as the primary method of sampling along with hand searching and water trapping (*see* 4.7.3.5). In that case, white plastic vending cups, 70 mm in diameter x 80 mm deep, with a preservative solution of 10% ethylene glycol, 10% formaldehyde plus detergent were used. The preservative was necessary because the traps were only checked once every two weeks and many insects decompose in a water/detergent mix over that time period. Each trapping station had a line of five traps, two metres apart. Any sort of cup or container can be used as a pitfall trap, but it is useful to follow these guidelines:

- All containers should be of standard size and colour and spaced evenly along a transect.
- All should contain the same solution.
- It is a good idea to have the trap the same colour as the ground or surrounding vegetation, as some insects may be repulsed or attracted by particularly bright or dark colours. In the summer months an uncovered, light-coloured trap may act like a water trap (*see* 4.7.3.5) for numerous flying insects, particularly flies, rapidly filling up the container.
- Always mark the site of the traps well; they are surprisingly difficult to find again.
- Use preservative in solution if the trap cannot be checked at least every two or three days. An anti-freeze can be used in the winter months.
- Pitfall traps are useful in survey and monitoring in conjunction with management where, for example, there are different grazing regimes on an extent of bog with the same hydrological regime or to monitor the change in invertebrate fauna before and after rewetting.

4.7.3.5 Water Traps

Water traps (Figure 4.19) are designed primarily to attract flying invertebrates. They consist of some sort of bowl or tray (metal baking trays are good) painted a bright colour and filled with water; a drop of washing-up liquid reduces the surface tension, enabling capture. White and yellow traps attract the greatest number of individuals, but other colours, particularly black,

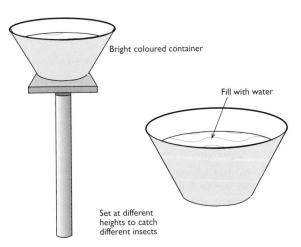

Bright coloured container

Fill with water

Set at different heights to catch different insects

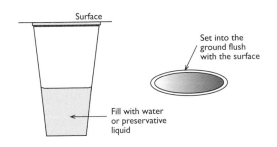

Surface

Set into the ground flush with the surface

Fill with water or preservative liquid

Figure 4.18   A pitfall trap. Set into the ground, these intercept ground-dwelling insects, they are particularly useful for catching active predators.

Figure 4.19   A water trap. Many insects will settle into a liquid-filled container. Bright yellow or white containers are best.

may attract different species. Water traps do not provide absolute population estimates, nor do they attract the full range of flying invertebrates. They are, however, very cheap and simple to use and can be useful in determining which are the most common species on the wing at any one time. For water traps to be of use in a monitoring programme, it is advisable to set the traps regularly through the spring and summer months in order to include a range of weather conditions. Setting the trap only once or twice a year and then repeating this on the same date in subsequent years may give misleading results, as the sample taken depends upon the weather on that particular day. The following guidelines are of use:

- When painting trays, use enamel paints as these tend to be resistant to water.
- Traps placed at different heights above ground level attract different insects – use a square board nailed onto cut off fence posts as a platform.
- When making site comparisons, ensure, the traps are placed in similar types and heights of vegetation and that the survey is carried out at the same time.
- Empty the traps daily if possible. Check the weather forecast – remember that on hot days, water evaporates whilst in wet weather water overflows.
- Store specimens in alcohol, for example, isopropanol.

4.7.3.6 Light Traps

Light traps are designed to sample night flying insects, primarily moths, although many other groups of insects may also be attracted to the trap. The trap usually consists of a powerful lamp set at the centre of a shallow funnel which leads into a closed box into which the moths are drawn (Figure 4.20). Once inside the box, the moths cannot escape and usually settle in among open egg-boxes which are used to give the insects a resting place. Light traps have the advantage of catching insects alive and unharmed and are, therefore, ideal for survey work. Light traps can be useful for monitoring changes in the population of night flying moths in conjunction with management practices. The following guidelines are of use:

- Be sure to use the same trap in the same place when monitoring population change from year to year.

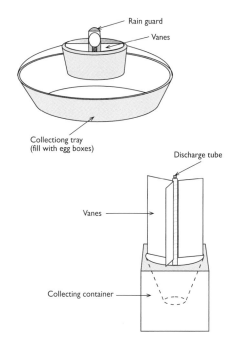

Figure 4.20 A light trap can be used to collect night-flying insects. There are a number of designs in common use, of varying power, size and portability.

- Always release the insects caught in the trap back to the same site. Scatter individuals over an area in and among undergrowth to prevent predation from birds.

Moth traps cost about £200 (*see* Appendix 7).

4.7.3.7 Suction Traps

Of the techniques for surveying airborne invertebrates, suction traps are the most accurate. They have been developed, standardised and their efficiency measured so precisely that aerial populations of invertebrates can now be assessed with a greater level of accuracy than those in most other habitats.

A basic suction trap consists of an electric fan that pulls air through a gauze cone. The insects are filtered out and collected in a tube or bottle beneath. Traps can be fitted with a segregating device which can be set to switch at a given time. The advantage is that information on the flight period of insects can also be obtained. Absolute population estimates and information on invertebrate community structure can be obtained using suction traps. The disadvantages are that they are relatively expensive and can generate large samples which require arduous sorting and identification.

Suction traps cost about £2,000 (*see* Appendix 7).

4.7.3.8 Direct Counting

There are a number of direct counting techniques to estimate populations of given taxa.

Transect counting: More conspicuous invertebrate groups, for example dragonflies and butterflies, can be monitored using the simple technique of walking a defined transect at a steady pace and counting all the individuals encountered. Once chosen, the route should not be altered. Annual comparisons are dependent on continuity from year to year, and an annual index is dependent on weekly/monthly continuity.

Sweep-netting: For less conspicuous invertebrates dwelling within vegetation, sweep-netting is a useful technique. The surveyor need not count the entire 'catch' from every sweep but can concentrate on counting a few key taxa. Sweepnetting, when standardised over a given transect, is a useful and inexpensive monitoring technique. The same criteria also apply to aquatic netting, which is a useful technique for monitoring aquatic invertebrates in bog pools and deeper hollows.

Hand searching: This is another method of direct counting which, although almost impossible to standardise, can be useful for finding those species which defy other trapping efforts. It is particularly useful for finding ground-dwelling Heteropteran bugs and invertebrates within vegetation tussocks (Kirby, 1992).

Quadrats: Counting the number of an invertebrate species within a fixed quadrat is also a useful method. The quadrat should be surrounded by a perspex, or similar, shield before counting begins to prevent individuals from escaping. This method becomes more difficult when the vegetation is tall and/or dense but could, for example, be of use on ground where bare peat is revegetating.

Other methods: Invertebrates can also be extracted from vegetation, soil and air using a variety of other apparatus including extraction funnels, sieves, pooters and beating trays.

METHODS AND TECHNIQUES FOR MANAGEMENT

Many sites have been damaged in varying ways (see Part 1). In Part 3 (see 3.3), types of damage were related to possible methods and techniques which may ameliorate the effects of that damage. These methods and techniques are laid out in the following sections. Note that some of the methods are well tried and tested, do not require great expertise to undertake and, taking a 'do it yourself' (DIY) approach, can be achieved rather cheaply. In contrast, other methods require specialist input and are expensive.

5.1   Hydrology

5.2   Revegetating Peat Surfaces

5.3   Managing Scrub and Trees

5.4   Grazing

5.5   Burning

5.6   Access Provision

METHODS AND TECHNIQUES FOR MANAGEMENT

5.1 HYDROLOGY

5.1.1 Introduction

Most activities which damage bogs cause direct or indirect changes to hydrology (*see* 1.8–1.14 and A3). Consequently, work to raise and stabilise water levels, through the installation of dams (5.1.2), bunds (5.1.4) and sluices (5.1.3), along with ditch-filling (5.1.5) and pumping (5.1.6), is one of the commonest forms of bog conservation management.

5.1.2 Dams

5.1.2.1 Introduction

Blocking open ditches requires the insertion of a series of impermeable (or nearly so) barriers. Initially, barriers (dams) raise water levels within the ditch back to the surface (Figure 5.1). Water still requires an exit over the barrier, so most dams should include a spillway or weir within their design, although remember that the purpose of a dam is to bring water levels back to the surface, so spillways should be shallow. With the water level back to the surface, the next priority is to revegetate resulting open water to effectively fill in the ditch. The time-scales involved are varied, dependent upon the prevailing ditch conditions and their suitability for *Sphagnum* growth. The intention should be that the ditch infills during the lifetime of the dam.

There are many different dam designs appropriate to different ditches, the resources available to the manager and the overall site management objectives. In most cases, however, it is the size of the ditch that dictates techniques and materials adopted for damming. Table 5.1 gives guidelines to the most appropriate dam types for varying sizes of ditch. There is still great potential for experimentation to increase

Table 5.1 Damming guidelines.

Width	Depth	Material	Section
<1m	<1m	Peat (by hand)	5.1.2.6
		Polyethylene sheet and peat	5.1.2.6
		Ply sheet	5.1.2.3
		Corrugated steel	5.1.2.5
<2m	1m	Peat (by machine)	5.1.2.6
		Ply sheet	5.1.2.3
		Plastic sheet (unsupported)	5.1.2.4
		Plastic piling	5.1.2.8
>2m	1m	Peat (by machine)	5.1.2.6
		Plastic sheet (supported)	5.1.2.4
		Solid plank	5.1.2.2
		Composite	5.1.2.7
		Plastic piling	5.1.2.8
>3m	>1.5m	Peat (by machine)	5.1.2.6
		Plastic piling	5.1.2.8
		Composite	5.1.2.7

damming efficacy and reduce resource requirements.

Resources also have a bearing on the technique selected. A small peat dam (*see* 5.1.2.6) is inexpensive if labour is in ready supply. Plywood dams (*see* 5.1.2.3) are less expensive than plastic-coated corrugated steel (*see* 5.1.2.5), and both require similar labour resources. Large plastic dams (*see* 5.1.2.4) have several advantages over solid plank dams (*see* 5.1.2.2); generally they are less expensive and are quicker and easier to install. Both large peat dams (*see* 5.1.2.6) and large composite dams (*see* 5.1.2.7) require the use of plant machinery and an experienced operator, as they are too big to construct by hand. Consideration should also be given to vehicle

> When blocking ditches over 1.5m deep, it is recommended that a suitably qualified engineer be consulted at the planning phase.

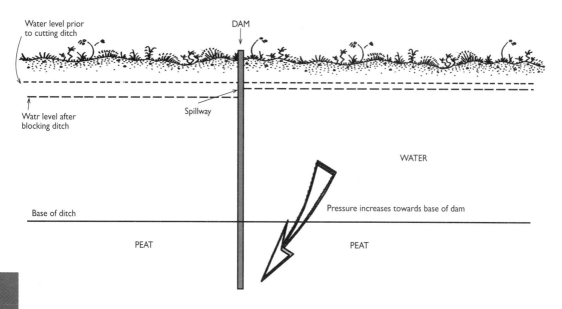

Water level prior to cutting ditch

DAM

Spillway

Watr level after blocking ditch

WATER

Base of ditch

Pressure increases towards base of dam

PEAT

PEAT

5.1

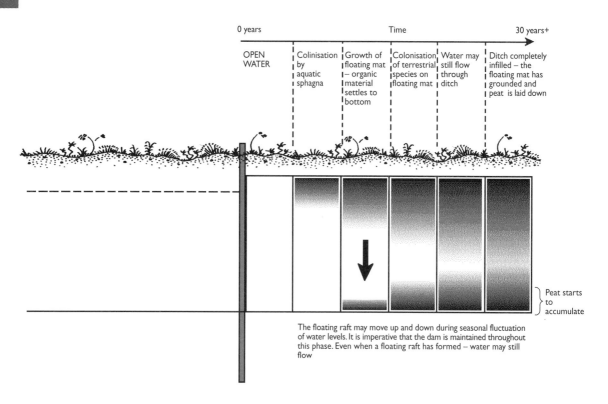

0 years

Time

30 years+

OPEN WATER

Colinisation by aquatic sphagna

Growth of floating mat – organic material settles to bottom

Colonisation of terrestrial species on floating mat

Water may still flow through ditch

Ditch completely infilled – the floating mat has grounded and peat is laid down

Peat starts to accumulate

The floating raft may move up and down during seasonal fluctuation of water levels. It is imperative that the dam is maintained throughout this phase. Even when a floating raft has formed – water may still flow

Figure 5.1   The main principles of dam installation.

access and the damage to the bog surface caused during construction (*see* 5.6).

Whatever material is used, it is important that dam spacing and positioning are planned correctly.

Judging the correct spacing of dams is important to a scheme's success. Given an ultimate aim to raise water levels to the surface, water, backed up behind a dam, should reach the next dam just below its spillway (Figure 5.2).

In Figure 5.2i, the dams have been spaced too far apart. This has two consequences:

- The speed of water falling from the spillway is increased, which may cause scouring of the ditch base immediately in front of the dam. As the main pressure point for any dam is the base, failure is likely to occur there.
- Away from the dam, the surface of the water is well below the bog surface and the management objective is not attained.

By inserting two more dams (C and D between dams A and B), the water level is maintained nearer the bog surface along its entire length (Figure 5.2ii). As the water level in front of each dam is higher, the speed of flow falling from the spillway is reduced and potential scouring is minimised.

The most accurate method for determining dam spacing is by surveying the ditch gradient with a theodolite or optical level (*see* 4.2 and A6.2.2). A profile of the ditch can then be drawn up and the number of dams determined. Alternatively, dam positions can be marked directly in the field by a person holding a staff. The levelling device is set up at the end of the ditch, and readings are taken at regular intervals. When the correct drop in slope (usually 10–20 cm) is reached, the point is marked with a cane. Ditch gradients are rarely constant – rising and falling over short distances. This means that readings should be taken at several intervals along the ditch. As a guideline, a reading should be taken at least every 15m (more if the ditch obviously undulates).

If the intention is to expend considerable resources on a damming scheme, appropriate planning at this level is necessary. The cost of contracting a survey or hiring equipment is justified if the dams are eventually located in the correct positions. This type of survey can also be used to estimate the number of dams required – enabling better costing and organisation.

Only the approximate location for the dam can be determined through levelling. The exact position depends on local factors. As a guide, avoid:

- Large vegetation tussocks when installing sheet dams: they are difficult to cut through with a spade.
- Trees: their roots are difficult to cut through and may also provide a conduit for water seepage.
- Small depressions or rises along the ditch profile; similarly be aware of the topography immediately adjacent to the proposed dam site and avoid obvious gullies exiting the ditch.
- Cracked, oxidised and eroded peat banks where possible. Water that backs up behind a dam may soon find its way through such cracks and pass around the barrier.

5.1

5.1.2.2　Plank Dams

Introduction

Solid wooden plank dams (sometimes referred to as palisade dams) have been used very successfully on many sites in the past (*see* 6.6). Properly-located and carefully-installed dams can be used to block drains of a considerable size (over 1m deep and 2m wide). The installation of these dams can be carried out using non-specialist labour (under experienced supervision).

Practical Considerations

- The construction of solid plank dams is labour-intensive.
- Until further investigations are conducted on the effects of using chemically-treated timber on bogs, it is recommended that untreated hardwood be used. However, such untreated wood is prone to rotting, especially at the air/water interface. The most common woods used are oak, elm and larch.
- The volume of timber required can be considerable. Timber may have to be transported to remote areas of bog over difficult terrain. Transport methods should be considered with regard to costs, practicality and potential damage to the bog surface (*see* A3.6.5, A3.6.6 and 5.6).
- Prevent large groups of people from congregating around the construction site; the peat will quickly become 'puddled' and this may lead to eventual dam failure.

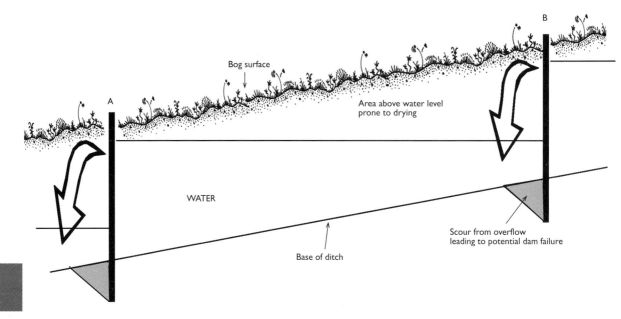

5.2i Incorrect dam spacing along ditch

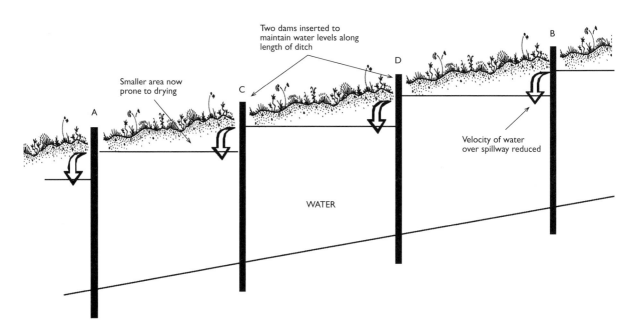

5.2ii Correct dam spacing along ditch

Figure 5.2   Incorrect (i) and correct (ii) spacing of dams along a ditch.

Construction Method

- *Step 1* Lay a solid board across the top of the ditch overlapping the bank on either side by at least 50 cm. This can either be used as a stringer or as a platform to work from. At this stage, it is best to secure the board in place temporarily with wooden stakes at either end.
- *Step 2* Hammer in (using a heavy rubber maul or steel mell) the centre board in the middle of the ditch, making sure that the board stays vertical at all times. The centre board only is chamfered on both sides. The board should be hammered in until its top is just proud of the immediate bog surface (Figure 5.3).
- *Step 3* Alternating installation on either side of the centre, hammer in the other boards. To the right (facing the dam), all boards should have a right chamfer, and to the left a left chamfer. This means that when the plank is hammered in, it is pushed tightly against the adjoining plank. Be certain to extend the dam well into the sides of the ditch (Figure 5.5).

> If the ditch is old and the peat in the immediate area shows signs of cracking, extend the dam into the ditch sides by at least 75 cm. Also be aware of secondary cracks running parallel to the ditch line. These cracks will act as very effective drains if not blocked at the same time (Figure 5.6).

> If several dams are to being constructed, make a metal cap to fit over the ends of the planks to protect them during installation (Figure 5.4).

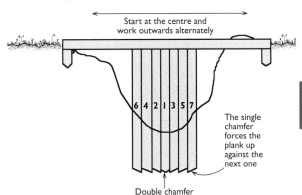

Figure 5.5 Vertical planks should be inserted in sequence with the chamfer helping to force the planks together.

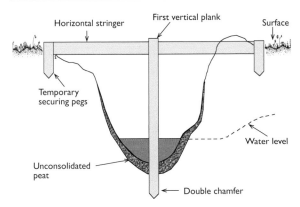

Figure 5.3 The first step in constructing a plank dam.

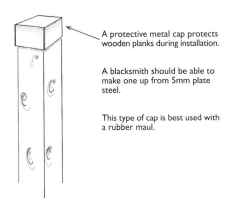

Figure 5.4 A protective metal cap used to stop planks splitting and cracking when they are hammered into the peat.

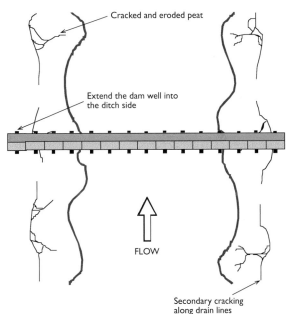

Figure 5.6 Old ditches often have parallel secondary cracks which also require blocking.

- *Step 4*   When all the vertical boards are in place, the horizontal stringer can be firmly secured to each board with a heavy-duty nut and bolt (Figure 5.7). Alternatively, a second stringer can be added to sandwich the vertical planks in place, reducing the need to secure each plank with a nut and bolt. Every third or fourth plank should be sufficient.

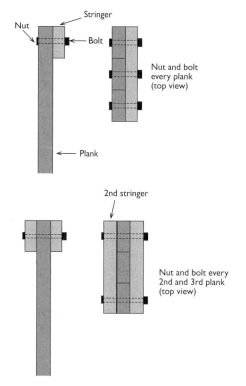

Figure 5.7   The vertical planks can be secured with nuts and bolts to a single or double stringer arrangement.

- *Step 5*   If a spillway is required, knock the central two or three planks down by the appropriate level (3 cm is usually sufficient) – this level should now correspond to the bog surface. If the water level has to be controlled, sluice boards can be added to the front of the spillway (*see* 5.1.3).
- *Step 6*   Immediately after construction, small gaps may be evident between planks. As the wood swells, these usually disappear, but to speed up the process wet peat can be forced into the gaps. The dam is now complete (Figure 5.8).

Figure 5.8   A completed and working plank dam at Flanders Moss, Scotland. (Julian Anderson)

5.1.2.3   Plywood Dams

Introduction

Exterior-grade or marine plywood sheets have been extensively used (*see* 6.9) to block small surface ditches. Inserted across the ditch, they act as impermeable membranes. They are quick and easy to install and require few specialist tools; they can prove very cost-effective.

Practical Considerations

- Potential problems of rotting arise at the air/ water/peat interface (below the water or bog surface, little rotting occurs in the anaerobic environment). The situation is exacerbated by water levels fluctuating, promoting increased weathering from continual wetting and drying (Figure 5.9). However, dams have been in place in the Border Mires, Northumberland, since 1985 and, as yet (1996), show few signs of rotting. If the top of the board is damaged (during installation), the layers of plywood may open up and rot more quickly (Figure 5.10).
- Plywood sheets can be obtained from most timber merchants. The standard size is 2,440 × 1,220 × 12 mm (8′ × 4′ × ½"), but they can be cut to any size either by the retailer or in the field with a panel saw. Large sheets need greater strength – 24mm thickness.

5.1

Figure 5.9   A plyboard dam is prone to rotting at the air/water/peat interface. If the water level can be maintained at the bog surface and *Sphagnum* quickly re-colonised, rotting is reduced. (see also Figure 5.10). (Stuart Brooks)

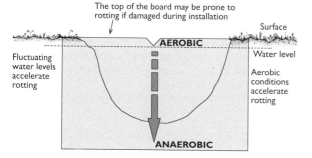

Figure 5.10   Damaged boards can rot quicker.

- Boards should be carried on site by two people.
- As with any dams, the correct spacing along the ditch line is critical (*see* 5.1.1).
- To protect the top of the dam during installation, a protective 'C' bar should be used, in conjunction with a heavy rubber maul (Figure 5.11).

Installation

- *Step 1*   Site dams correctly (*see* 5.1.2.1).
- *Step 2*   Cut a starter slot with a spade across the ditch. If using a normal spade, only push it down to the bend in the shaft to ensure that the gap is not too big; otherwise, once the dam is in

> When storing large sheets on site prior to installation, lay them as flat as possible on a plastic sheet to help prevent warping.

Figure 5.11   Hammering in a ply-sheet dam. Note the C-bar and the use of the rubber maul. (Stuart Brooks)

place, water may find its way through and potentially wash out the dam (Figure 5.12).

> Traditional peat-digging spades (straight-shafted) are ideal for this job, as they can create a thin deep slot. A deeper slot means less hammering in. Specialist toolsmiths can make up a straight-shafted spade (Figure 5.13).

- *Step 3*   With the slot created, the board is pushed firmly in and held as vertical as possible. Now place the 'C' bar on top of the board and hammer it in using the rubber maul. If a large board is being installed, two 'C' bars can be used, one at each end of the board requiring a person at each end to hammer. The board should be hammered in until it is just above the bog surface (by 2–3 cm).

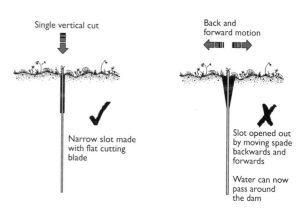

Figure 5.12   Water can pass around the side of the dam if the slot is opened out.

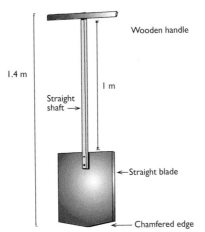

Figure 5.13 A basic design for a straight shafted peat spade, ideal for installing plywood or plastic dams.

> **Concentrate the hammering at the ends of the board in alternate sequence. The maximum force is then placed on a smaller area and the board will go in much quicker.**

- *Step 4* To allow excess water to pass over the dam rather than forcing its way around the sides (leading to erosion and dam failure), it is necessary to add a small spillway. Cut a 'V' notch with a saw in the middle of the board. To be effective the spillway need only be approximately 6 cm wide and 3 cm deep. The bottom of the spillway should always be *just* below the surface of the bog.

5.1.2.4 Plastic Sheet Dams

Introduction

Plastic sheets, usually comprising an ultra-violet stable polyethylene base, can be used in a similar way to impermeable sheet dams. In Germany, they have been used extensively and successfully for over a decade. Plastic sheets and piling (*see* 5.1.2.8) have also been used recently in the UK (*see* 6.11).

Depending on the application, the advantages of plastic sheets are:

- 100% impermeable;
- inert; ultra-violet stable – should not break down or leach out chemicals into the bog;
- very sturdy – capable of being hammered/driven in;
- light and therefore easy to transport;

- available in large sizes and thickness and can be joined together;
- long field life (100 yrs+); and
- made from recycled materials.

Practical Considerations

- The costs of using plastic dams are higher than plywood, but they are likely to last longer.
- A 'C' bar (*see* 5.1.2.3) should always be used when driving in the sheets with a heavy rubber maul. As plastic sheets tend to be thin (approximately 6 mm), a tight-fitting bar, with elongated sides (20 cm), should be used to stop cracking along the top edge.
- When installing larger sheets, it may be appropriate to fit a hardwood or plastic stringer (horizontal beam) across the sheet prior to installation.
- The sizes of the sheets are limited by three factors:

  1. Rigidity across an open ditch. Large unsupported sheets have the tendency to bow under pressure. This can be countered by incorporating structural supports (Figure 5.14).
  2. Installation problems. Manual installation restricts the depth to the height that a person can safely hammer from (that is, below shoulder height).
  3. Large sheets are difficult to manoeuvre, especially in the wind.

- Excavation of an open slot for installing the sheet should be avoided where possible as this could lead to problems of water seeping around the sides of the dam. However, a large board (>2m high) is difficult to hammer in without a slot. Therefore, a very narrow slot should be cut with a specialist tool or a traditional straight-shafted peat spade.

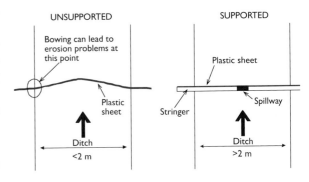

Figure 5.14 Large plastic sheets can be strengthened by incorporating a horizontal stringer.

Installation

- *Step 1*   Site the dam correctly (*see* 5.1.2.1).
- *Step 2*   When the exact position has been determined, lay the board across the ditch. If absolutely necessary, use a spade, or specialist tool (Figure 5.15), to cut a starter slot across the ditch. To avoid erosion problems, take care not to open up the slot by pushing the spade backwards and forwards (Figure 5.12).
- *Step 3*   Push the sheet into the starter slot, keeping it vertical. Place the protective 'C' bar (Figure 5.11) on top of the plastic sheet. This prevents any damage to the top of the sheet during installation.

Figure 5.15   A plastic sheet dam installed at Flanders Moss, Scotland. (Stuart Brooks)

> Try to minimise the gap between the 'C' bar and the sheet to prevent any cracking along its top edge. If a gap does exist, small branches or wooden blocks can be wedged in to secure it in place. Ideally, the 'C' bar should be specifically designed to fit the plastic sheet.

- *Step 4*   Hammer the sheet slowly into the peat with a rubber maul. Work from side to side until the board is fully inserted into the ditch. The top of the dam should be just proud of the bog surface.

> On small dams (<1.5m x <1m), a team of 3–4 people per dam is ideal. This allows each member of the team to circulate jobs and prevents too much fatigue!

- *Step 5*   When the dam is in place, cut a very shallow spillway at the centre.

5.1.2.5   Metal Sheet Dams

Introduction

Corrugated metal sheet dams have proved very successful in blocking small surface ditches (*see* 6.5).

Practical Considerations

- The most commonly-used type of metal sheet dam is made from double-sided plastic-coated corrugated steel (Figure 5.16). It is essential to use an appropriate 'C' bar when installing the dam.
- It is difficult to obtain sheets in widths of over 1m. Sheets can be joined with pop rivets, though this may cause leakage along the join. Sheets are best used in narrow ditches (<1m wide).

Installation

- *Step 1*   Site the dam correctly (*see* 5.1.2.1).
- *Step 2*   Cut a starter slot with a spade.
- *Step 3*   Push the sheet into the starter slot and keep it vertical. Place the 'C' bar across the sheet and hammer it in with the rubber maul. The sheet should be knocked down until its top is just proud of the bog surface.
- *Step 4*   To deter water forcing its way around the side of the dam and washing it out, a channel should be created in the centre of the dam. A jab from the spade or a heavy blow with the 'C' bar should be enough to make a sufficient dent to act as a spillway.

> If two sheets need to be joined together, sandwich a thin piece of rubber (such as roof sealing strips) between the two and rivet in place.

Figure 5.16   A plastic coated corrugated sheet dam. (Stuart Brooks)

5.1

5.1.2.6 Peat Dams

Introduction

An obvious dam-building material on bogs is peat, given its low permeability, ready availability and no cost. However, the use of peat to build dams has many limitations and several factors should be considered prior to its selection.

Practical considerations

- Highly-humified peat (Von Post H6–H8) is of low permeability and is suitable for use as a dam material (*see* 2.3, 4.5.5.1). Lower-permeability peats (humification of Von Post H3 and below) are unsuitable for use in dams, as are very well-humified peats (>H8).
- When peat has been dried and exposed to air, it loses its ability to retain water (*see* 2.6.2). This process is irreversible, so highly-oxidised peats should never be used for dam-building.
- The size of the dam determines the technique adopted. Peat dams constructed by hand should be limited to ditch sizes less than 1m wide (Table 5.1). All other peat dams should be constructed using plant machinery.
- Wet peat is heavy; it is impractical to carry it by hand over long distances, and vehicle use can potentially cause damage to the surface (*see* 5.6). The best option, therefore, is to take peat from the immediate vicinity of the ditch or preferably from within the ditch itself.
- When constructing dams with plant machinery, adequate planning must be given to the movement of the machine across the bog during and after rewetting. Following dam construction, large areas can rapidly rewet to make conditions unsuitable for heavy machinery. This should also be considered when planning for future maintenance work.
- Peat is not completely impermeable, so in dry areas (continental Europe, or eastern Britain), it is better to use an impermeable membrane rather than peat to ensure maximum water retention.
- On steep gradients, peat dams are not suitable:

  1. It is difficult to incorporate an effective spillway within the design of a small peat dam. Plastic pipes will either block, or the peat around them will erode away. Without a spillway to control excess run-off, water eventually erodes away the top of the dam or finds a way around the sides.
  2. If the peat for the dam comes from the area adjacent to the ditch, a string of excavation hollows could act as a secondary parallel drain (Figure 5.17).

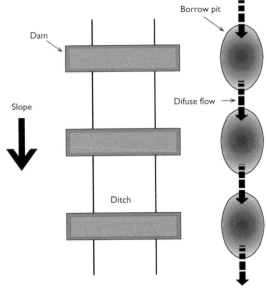

Figure 5.17 A string of excavation hollows can act as a parallel drain, especially on a slope; a problem when blocking ditches on blanket bog.

Construction – Small Peat Dams

- *Step 1* Site the dams correctly (*see* 5.1.2.1).
- *Step 2* Mark out the position of the dam by cutting away the turf (top 20 cm) on either side of the ditch in the exact position of the proposed dam (Figure 5.18).
- *Step 3* Remove the peat from the sides and base of the ditch (indent up to 40 cm), leaving a clean, wet peat face. If removing peat from next to the ditch, create a shallow slope into the ditch to promote the recolonisation of *Sphagnum* (Figure 5.18).
- *Step 4* The peat used for the construction of the dam should be taken from either the ditch, upstream of the dam, or adjacent to the ditch (avoiding dried-out or unconsolidated peat).

> **If excavating hollows adjacent to the ditch, do not unintentionally create another drain by leaving holes in a line spaced closely together (Figure 5.17).**

- *Step 5* Fill in across the ditch with wet peat, compacting all the time to reduce permeability of the peat. If possible, use large blocks of peat cut with traditional hand tools instead of small amounts. If peat is handled too much, it loses its structure, becoming a sloppy soup and making it impossible to work into a solid dam. Build up the dam until it is above the bog surface by approximately 30 cm. This allows for any settlement or shrinkage (Figure 5.19).

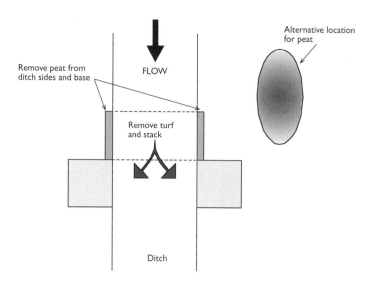

Alternative location for peat

Remove peat from ditch sides and base

FLOW

Remove turf and stack

Ditch

5.1

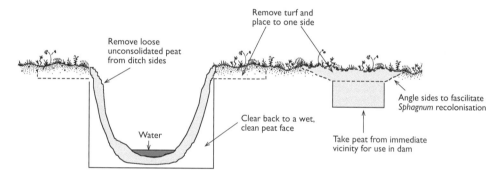

Remove turf and place to one side

Remove loose unconsolidated peat from ditch sides

Angle sides to fascilitate *Sphagnum* recolonisation

Water

Clear back to a wet, clean peat face

Take peat from immediate vicinity for use in dam

Figure 5.18   Plan view and cross-section of a small peat dam.

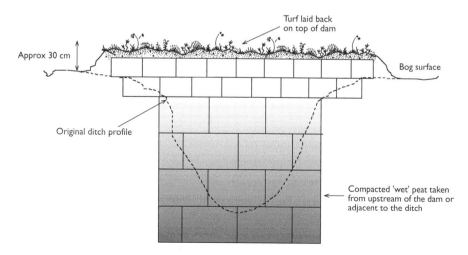

Turf laid back on top of dam

Approx 30 cm

Bog surface

Original ditch profile

Compacted 'wet' peat taken from upstream of the dam or adjacent to the ditch

Figure 5.19   A completed peat dam standing proud of the surface by about 30cm.

Figure 5.20 A small peat dam constructed on Liffey Head Bog, Ireland. (Rob Stoneman)

- *Step 6* The original turfs should now be laid back on top of the newly constructed dam. This will help prevent erosion of the bare peat face at the top of the dam (*see* Figure 5.20).

> There is not normally provision for a spillway within a peat dam. On shallow gradients, this should not be a problem, as water flows diffusely around or over the top of the dam without causing erosion. However, if gradients are steeper and flows are strong, erosion across the top or the sides of the dam may be a problem. In this instance, it would be better to construct another type of dam that could incorporate a spillway.

Construction – Large Peat Dams

Ditches of considerable size can be effectively blocked if an appropriate peat-type is used in conjunction with a low-ground-pressure excavator.

> The reach of the excavator must be sufficient to work the ditch from one side only, as crossing the ditch may be hazardous or impractical.

- *Step 1* Site the dams correctly (*see* 5.1.2.1).

- *Step 2* The machine operator should be experienced at working on deep peat sites and be aware of the potential risks and the management objectives of the particular task.
- *Step 3* Start by excavating the vegetation in turfs (top 20 cm) from the area designated for the dam. The dimensions of the dam are determined partly by the properties of the peat (Table 5.2).

> As ditch size increases, all dam dimensions should increase to counter increased pressure.

- *Step 4* Clean out any unconsolidated or oxidised peat within the ditch to leave a fresh peat face. Indent into the banks on either side by approximately 50 cm to key the dam into the side (Figure 5.21).
- *Step 5* The peat used to build up the dam can be excavated either from the zone in front (upstream) of the proposed dam or from a borrow pit behind the working arc of the excavator. In both instances, the top turf should not be used but skimmed off and placed to one side. Also, all oxidised or unconsolidated peat should be avoided, as it is not suitable for dam construction. If a borrow pit is excavated, it should be deep enough to hold water throughout the year to enable *Sphagnum* recolonisation.
- *Step 6* Excavate wet peat and place it against a fresh cut face within the drain, making sure that adequate compaction seals the two surfaces together. Continue to build up the dam, compacting with the back of the excavator bucket at regular intervals.

> Do not overwork the peat, as this results in loss of structure and leads to dam failure.

- *Step 7* When the peat dam is approximately 50 cm above the surface of the immediate bog, the original vegetation turfs should be placed back across the top of the dam (Figure 5.22). A dam left unsurfaced erodes and may fail.

Table 5.2: Large peat dam dimensions (for ditch 3m wide).

H-value (4.5.5.1)	Dam length (<½m deep)	Dam length (1–1½m deep)	Indent	Height over surface
Low (H3–H5)	2m	4m	1m	30 cm
High (H6–H8)	1–1½m	2–3m	1–1½m	50 cm

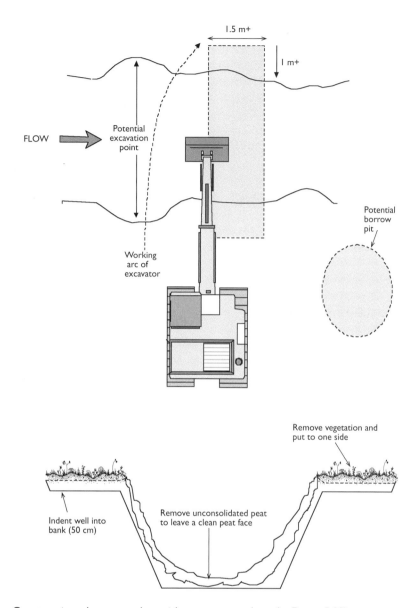

Figure 5.21 Constructing a large peat dam with an excavator (*see also* Figure 5.22).

5.1.2.7 *Composite Dams*

Introduction

A composite dam (Figures 5.23 and 5.24) is made of two impermeable sheets infilled with peat. In this instance, the peat merely provides the structural support for the dam, and so peat of any quality can be used.

A composite dam can also be used as a bridge for either vehicle or pedestrian access over a drain.

Construction Procedure

- *Step 1* If dams are to be constructed along the entire length of the drain, determine their location by levelling (*see* 5.1.2.1). Access dams should be placed where convenient and preferably where the ditch is narrow.
- *Step 2* The impermeable barrier can be constructed from either plywood (5.1.2.3), plastic (5.1.2.4/5.1.2.8) or corrugated sheet metal (5.1.2.5), and the appropriate methods for

Figure 5.22 A large peat dam constructed by excavator working from wooden bog mats, Swinabbey Moss, Scotland. (Stuart Brooks)

Figure 5.24 A composite dam made from hardwood boards and peat, Bell Crag Flow, England. (Stuart Brooks)

5.1

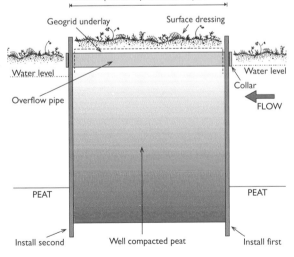

Figure 5.23 Construction principles of a composite dam.

installation should be followed in each instance. Start with the sheet nearest to the upstream side (Figure 5.23), as this stops water, making construction easier. The sheet should be pushed in, leaving 10 cm above the surface.

- *Step 3* Install the second sheet about 50 cm to 1m from the first. A bridge for vehicles should be wider than for people.
- *Step 4* Remove any unconsolidated peat or vegetation from the inside of the two sheets, to leave a fresh, wet peat face. Turves should be placed to one side to be used to vegetate the surface of the infilled section.
- *Step 5* Infill between the two sheets, compacting the peat down as work progresses. It is not necessary to use well-humified peat, as the sheets act as an impermeable barrier.
- *Step 6* If the dam is to be used as a bridge for either pedestrian or vehicle access, a layer of geogrid or geotextile (*see* 5.6.5) should be laid above the overflow pipe, which in this instance should be enclosed.

> If the dam is not to be used as a regular bridge, a half-pipe can be used as a spillway. If necessary, cover with a piece of board to prevent peat from falling in and blocking it up.

- *Step 7* With the overflow and matting in place, finish off with vegetated turves.

> To stop the boards splaying out whilst compacting infilled peat, insert four vertical stobs, one at each corner, in front of the boards. Added strength can be gained by fitting horizontal cross-members underneath terram matting affixed to both boards.

5.1.2.8   Plastic Piling Dams.

Introduction

Pre-formed recycled plastic piling takes its design from metal piling used in the construction industry. So far, its use to block drains on peat bogs has been limited to just a few sites (*see* 6.23, 6.3, 6.11) and, therefore, the technique is experimental.

Results so far have been favourable, and it appears that the material has considerable advantages over standard peat dams (5.1.2.6) and plank dams (5.1.2.2). The material is light (making transport easier), durable (at least a 150-year life expectancy) and easy to work with (dams can be constructed very quickly).

Practical considerations.

There are two types of plastic piling in the UK (*see* Appendix 7). The main differences concern the joining mechanisms and the final configurations (Figure 5.25). Choosing between the two systems depends upon individual requirements and personal preference.

Installation procedure (to 5m wide)

The piling sections should be driven into the ditch, starting at the centre, and working progressively outwards. They can either be driven in with the hydraulic arm of an excavator or manually installed with a heavy rubber maul. Sections can be cut or ordered to any length (max. 8m).

- *Step 1*   Insert the central pile first. The central piles will usually be the longest and, if installing

by hand, the most difficult. Piling with lengths greater than 3m cannot be easily or safely installed by hand.

> Place a solid plank across the ditch and use this to work from. This makes installation easier and safer (by reducing the distances one has to stretch). To keep the piles in a straight line, run a taut line across the ditch and use as a guide.

- *Step 2*   The join acts as a guide for the next section. It should be possible to push the section the first 30 cm into the unconsolidated peat. It is important to keep the piling as vertical as possible at the start.

> To increase the effectiveness of the seal, flex each section against the next whilst hammering in. This should produce a watertight seal when the water backs up behind the dam. It is important to flex the sections in the direction of flow (Figure 5.26).

- *Step 3*   Work progressively towards the banks (Figure 5.27). Sections may be trimmed with a panel saw.

> The dam may initially leak through the joins. These soon seal as peat particles plug the gaps. To aid this process, a few handfuls of unconsolidated peat can be tossed into the upstream side of the dam.

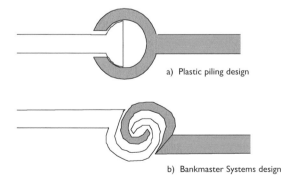

Figure 5.25   Joint mechanism for two types of plastic piling. Both materials provide a reasonably watertight seal if the dam is constructed correctly.

a) Plastic piling design

b) Bankmaster Systems design

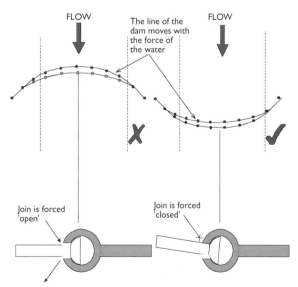

Figure 5.26   Flexing the dam, during installation, in the direction of flow increases the strength of the seal.

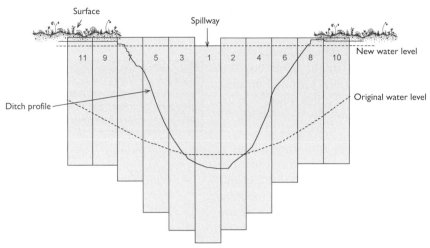

Figure 5.27 Plastic piling dams are best constructed in the following sequence, starting from the centre and working outwards towards the sides of the ditch .

- *Step 4*   When the correct height of the dam is reached, that is, level with the surface of the bog, knock down the central pile about 3 cm to form a spillway (Figure 5.28). Note that the design of the dam requires a fairly high water pressure to help seal the joins by 'bowing', so a top stringer should not be added.

A second configuration of the plastic piling sections is possible by inverting every other pile. This will form a 'box' section, as opposed to the standard 'deep-V' (Figure 5.29). The box section is technically a stronger design but forms a weaker seal (due to opposing forces) and is also more expensive (more sections are required per metre).

Installation procedure (over 5m wide)

To impound large volumes of water, it may be necessary to construct the dam in a 'box' sectioned format (Figure 5.29). However, from the experiences gained with smaller dams in box section, it appears that opposing forces on the seals open the joins and the dam leaks. In this instance, a 'hydro-seal' or an expanding polymer can be inserted into the gap (contact suppliers for advice). With the hydro-seal added, horizontal strength can be gained through the addition of backing stringers. These can be made from hardwood or recycled plastic (*see* 6.11) and bolted

Figure 5.28   A completed plastic piling dam, Langlands Moss, Scotland. (Stuart Brooks)

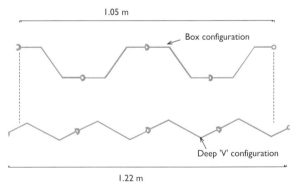

Figure 5.29   Plastic piling dams can be constructed in two configurations, the deep 'V' minimises costs and is usually adequate for most situations but where the ditch is very large the dam may be best constructed in box configuration.

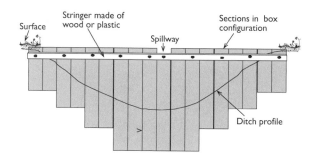

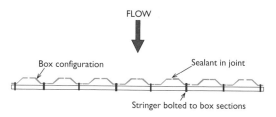

Figure 5.30   A long plastic piling dam, constructed in box configuration, can be strengthened using stringers and made watertight by inserting sealant or hydro-seal into the gaps.

onto the back of the dam across its top edge (Figure 5.30).

5.1.3   Sluices and Weirs

5.1.3.1   Introduction

Sluices are channels or pipes used to regulate the flow or level of water and can be used to measure flow (see 4.3.4). They can either be part of a larger structure, such as an angled pipe within a bund (see 5.1.3.2, 5.1.4), or they can act as dams in their own right (see 5.1.3.3, 5.1.3.4).

Water-level management is essential in many bog conservation schemes (see 2.5). Cut-over bogs, in particular, require careful management, as natural hydrological processes have been considerably modified. Inundation of fields connected by sluices is a common form of cut-over bog restoration.

Water levels on any bog are governed by the level of input from precipitation (see 2.5.1). In periods of high rainfall, surface run-off increases as the acrotelm saturates. Excess run-off may, therefore, needs to be controlled to alleviate flooding of neighbouring land from arterial drainage systems. If a weir is used, discharge can be measured (see 4.3.4).

Measuring water discharge past a specific point has several advantages:
- Discharge data can be used as evidence to counter claims of flooding by neighbouring landowners/occupiers.
- Data can be used as part of a more extensive hydrological monitoring scheme; especially run-off/discharge/storage calculations (see 4.3.4).
- Discharge data can also be used as an indicator of management success or failure.

5.1.3.2   Angled Pipe Sluices

An angled pipe sluice (Figure 5.31) is a hollow pipe with one or both ends attached to a swivelling right-angled join. This allows the level of two water bodies, separated by an embankment, to be controlled. This type of sluice is extensively used on large rehabilitation projects where water-level control within enclosed water bodies is desired.

In most situations, an angled pipe sluice is incorporated into a peat bund or embankment (see 5.1.4).

Practical Considerations
- The diameter of the pipe should be large enough to cope with storm events.

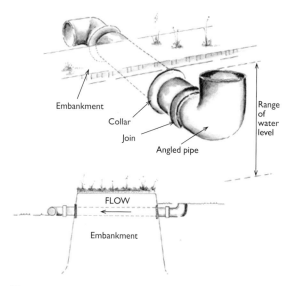

Figure 5.31   An angled pipe sluice and its use in an embankment to control waterlevels in two separate water bodies.

- Vandalism is a threat in many locations. It is difficult to build into such a simple design vandal-proof measures. Housing the assembly within a lockable enclosure can be difficult and expensive. If a threat does exist, an alternative sluice design may be required (*see* 5.1.3.3, 5.1.3.4).
- The pipe must be made from a suitable material capable of withstanding exposure and a regime of wetting and drying. Ultra-violet stable plastic pipes are the most suitable; these are available from local agricultural suppliers or specialist pipe stockists.

Installation

- *Step 1* – The sluice may be incorporated either into an already existing structure (for example, a raised baulk between old peat fields) or into a newly-constructed bund or embankment. When inserting the sluice into an existing baulk or bund, levelling gradients should precede any work. The sluice should be placed at the lowest point of the bank and have the capacity to raise water to the optimum level required. Often, more than one sluice may be required.

> A stage board (commercial or home-made) can be located at the ends of the pipe. This allows greater precision when setting water levels (see 4.3.3.6).

- *Step 2* Pipes should be buried at least 35 cm below the surface to protect against trampling. Peat should be packed around the pipe to prevent seepage.

> Collars attached to the pipe help to prevent movement of the pipe within the peat and deter water from channelling around the outside. These can either be bought commercially or made from plastic sheeting.

- *Step 3* With the pipe inserted, peat should be laid back over and compacted. Re-lay the peat with vegetation turves to help prevent erosion of bare peat.
- *Step 4* The swivelling right angled end(s) can now be set to the desired height (Figure 5.32).

5.1.3.3 *Wooden Plank Sluice*

Introduction

This commonly-used design consists of hardwood planks fitted into metal or concrete channels which are keyed into the banks and base of the ditch. The height of the water is controlled by adding or removing boards.

Figure 5.32   An adjustable angled pipe sluice in place, Bargerveen, Netherlands. (Lucy Parkyn)

Practical Considerations

- Unless a locking device is fitted, or the boards are set away from the bank, they can be easily lifted out and are prone to vandalism.
- Unless properly machined, or fitted as a double layer, most plank sluices leak.
- A firm foundation is important. Wet peat is not always stable enough to hold pressure built up behind the sluice, and dry peat leaks and causes the sluice to fail.
- Standard plank dams (*see* 5.1.2.2) can be readily modified to make a sluice (Figure 5.33), or the sluice can be constructed between concrete pillars and foundations.

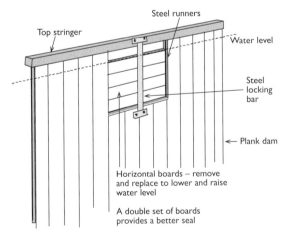

Figure 5.33   Plank dams can be modified to incorporate an adjustable sluice at the spillway to give a greater degree of water level control.

Sluice Adaptation of Plank Dam

Plank dams can be modified by adding steel (preferably) runners set into the upstream side of the planks to act as a guide for the horizontal planks. Wooden guides could be used but are less durable. A locking device can be added to the sluice boards to deter tampering.

Specialist Plank Sluices

Ready-made sluices are available as whole units that slot into place. The body of the sluice is constructed from glass-fibre reinforced concrete (*see* Appendix 7). This material is light, durable and virtually vandal-proof. The design of the body includes a splashpan and moveable side rails. Boards are slotted into grooves in the side rails and bolted down with a locking bracket (Figure 5.34).

> It may be necessary to extend the sides of the sluice so that it is keyed further into the peat banks. This helps to prevent seepage and erosion around the sides of the sluice.

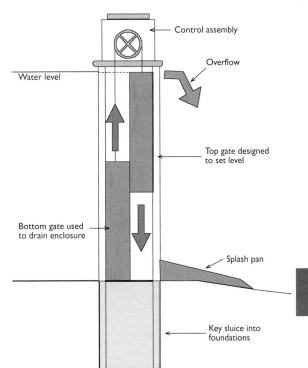

Figure 5.35   A design for a double gate sluice.

5.1

5.1.3.4   Sheet Sluices (Gates)

Sheet sluices have a limited application on peatland sites but can be adapted to allow variable levels to be set (Figure 5.35). The design

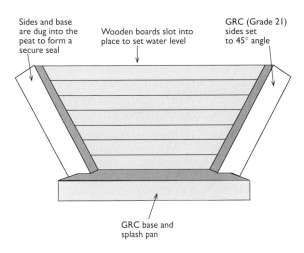

Figure 5.34   Plank sluices can be purchased ready made from BCM Contracts Ltd. (see Appendix 7). They are constructed from glass reinforced concrete and have horizontal wooden planks which can be added or taken away to set the desired water level.

incorporates double gates: at the base to allow complete drainage, and at the top to set a variable water level.

5.1.4   Bunds

5.1.4.1   Introduction

A bund is an impermeable embankment or barrier. It may be used to restrict water losses or to impound open water. Materials used include peat (*see* 5.1.4.2), peat and plastic (*see* 5.1.4.3) or impermeable mineral materials – often clay – (*see* 5.1.4.4).

There are two types of bund. The first is raised above the peat surface to impound water (Figure 5.36). The second reduces lateral seepage with an impermeable barrier (Figure 5.37), for example, at the margin of a bog or adjacent to active peat workings.

The volume of water impounded by a bund is a product of the depth of water impounded and its area. This volume is also affected by the amount of incoming water, the efficacy of the bund and the permeability of the peat itself.

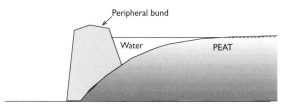

i) Peripheral bund at bog margin, designed to minimise seepage and run-off and raise water level above bog surface

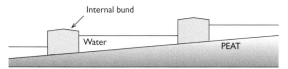

ii) Internal bunds designed to raise water levels across large areas of cut-over bog

Figure 5.36 Raised bunds designed to inundate the surface of the bog.

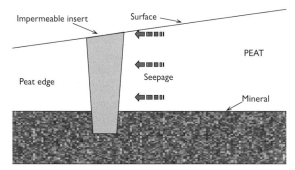

Figure 5.37 Internal bund designed to seal off sub-surface flow at the bog margin.

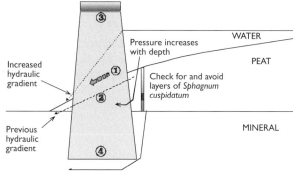

1. The main pressure and failure point of the bund is at the base of the peat (1). If an appropriate binding is not made with the surface, or if it is not keyed into the mineral substrate (4) the bund may be pushed outwards by the pressure of water behind.

2. With a high enough pressure water may be forced underneath the bund (4).

3. If water levels fluctuate, drying may lead to cracking. As water levels subsequently rise, leakage and failure may ensue.

Figure 5.38 Likely stresses and failure points on a typical raised peat bund.

In the UK, impoundment of large volumes of water (>25,000 m³ above the natural level of adjoining land) is regulated under the 1975 Reservoirs Act; it requires planning permission and must be planned under the guidance and supervision of a qualified civil engineer. It is also recommended that advice should be sought for smaller-scale operations, particularly where adjoining land is outside the conservation area. Where water is impounded behind a structure, particular consideration should be given to the following:

- the resilience of the structure to wetting and/or drying;
- the likely high pressure and failure points (Figure 5.38);
- the maintenance requirements and subsequent access provision for future management; and
- provision for control of levels during particularly wet or dry periods (*see* 5.1.6, 5.1.3).

For small bunds, internal baulks and sub-surface impermeable barriers, the risk of flooding adjacent landownings is small. Internal bunds are often obscured by water and peat, so weaknesses are difficult to detect. However, every effort should be made to monitor the condition of the bund to detect any defects before they result in large-scale failure.

Whilst peat for bund construction may have to be brought in, it is best to use a local source to obviate transportation problems:

- it may be costly if contract hauliers are required;
- overhandling wet peat causes it to lose its structure, turning it into a runny, soupy mess;
- access to the bunded area may be difficult if little infrastructure exists; and
- it may be difficult to find an alternative site.

5.1.4.2 Peat Bunds

Introduction

Peat bunding is widely practised in the Netherlands (*see* 6.15) and Germany (*see* 6.14). On cut-over sites, where both the acrotelm and catotelm have been destroyed, peat bunding has proved useful for rewetting. Its use has now been extended onto more intact sites (*see* 6.13, 6.16) both on the periphery of the bog and on raised bog domes themselves.

Not all peat is suitable for bund construction. Well humified black peat (H 6 – 8; *see* 4.5.5.1) is more appropriate for peripheral bunds. Less-humified white peats may be utilised on internal bunding or reinforced with an impermeable membrane (*see* 5.1.4.3). Fen peats are variable in composition and should be examined carefully before deciding on their suitability for bund construction.

Peripheral Bunding

Peripheral bunds are constructed to minimise water loss via drainage and seepage at the edge of the bog, and to counter drying of the dome due to cracking and slumping at unnatural edges (Figure 5.39).

The peat used for bund construction should ideally come from close by. Extraction of peat could have archaeological implications (*see* 1.6, 3.2). It is suggested that an archaeologist be consulted prior to the start of work.

The bund foundation may be either on mineral soils or on well-humified peat (ideally of similar properties to the construction material). If the bund is built over weakly-humified peat, it may sink and, therefore, must be built to a higher level than is ultimately required (*see* 4.5.5.1).

There must be a good seal between the bund and the peat face/foundation. To achieve this, the outer 30 cm (approximately) of peat should be

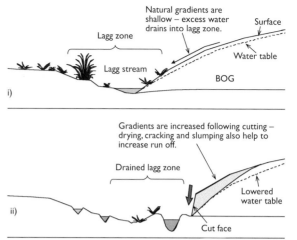

Figure 5.39 An unnatural edge (ii) causes cracking and shrinkage in contrast to an undisturbed edge (i) which generally has shallower gradients and a lagg fen.

stripped away to leave a fresh peat face and foundation.

If the peat used in construction is derived on-site, it should be excavated from the zone in front (bog-side) of the bund. The borrow pit may act as a reservoir for water storage and help maintain moisture levels within the peat bund (Rowell, 1988), preventing shrinkage and cracking. In an effort to deter erosion from wave action against the bund face, the borrow pit should not directly abut the bund face, but should be inset to leave a wave 'shelf'. This platform may also provide a convenient working location for the excavator (Figure 5.40) and act as a platform for rafting (*see* 5.2.5) vegetation (Wheeler and Shaw, 1995).

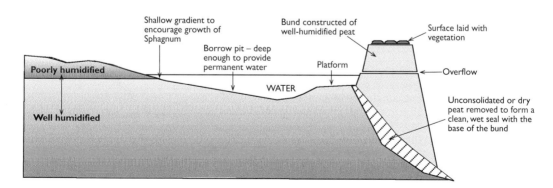

Figure 5.40   Bund construction showing the layout of the platform and borrow pit.

As the bund is built up, peat should be well compacted but not 'overworked'. The gradients of the bund edges are determined by the properties of the peat, but, as a guideline, 30–40° covers most situations. Where slopes are too steep, the bund may be prone to slumping as moisture content changes through wetting and drying; with shallow gradients, a larger volume of material is required to attain the same height. Streefkerk and Zandstra (1994) offer guidelines for bund dimensions based on experimentation at the Bargerveen (*see* 6.15; Table 5.3).

Table 5.3: Bund dimensions.

Water depth at inner side of bund (m)	Height of bund (m)	Width at top of bund (m)
0.50 – 0.75	1.50	3.00
0.75 – 1.00	2.00	4.00
1.00 – 1.50	2.50	5.00

> **Bunds should be constructed to allow for shrinkage and settlement if the peat is poorly humified or very wet (80%+ moisture content).**

To stop overtopping and erosion of the bund, provision for outflows should be made at convenient locations. Overflow levels can be altered by using adjustable 90° angle pipes on the inner face of the bund (*see* 5.1.3.2). Peat sods (containing vegetation) or poorly-humified peat should be layered over the finished construction to stimulate vegetation colonisation and deter erosion of the bare peat surface.

> **Scrub should be prevented from establishing on bunds, as it promotes drying and cracking.**

There are a number of potential problems which should be assessed at the planning stage:

- It is extremely important to determine accurately (*see* 4.2; A6.2) the correct height of the bund overflows to prevent inundation of areas of high conservation significance. Large bodies of open deep water are not conducive to *Sphagnum* recolonisation (Wheeler and Shaw, 1995), and attract wild fowl and gulls which, through eutrophication, alters the chemical characteristics of impounded water.
- Large areas of impounded water may pose a flooding risk to surrounding land. Manipulation

of bog hydrology for conservation purposes may also affect areas which receive drainage, or run-off, from the bog. Landowners may be concerned about the possibility of flooding adjacent fields.

- The rewetting of the peat inside the bund may cause the bog to rise (if shrinkage had previously occurred), potentially altering gradients and water flow characteristics at or near the periphery (*see* 4.5.3, 4.3.3.4).
- A long-term commitment to maintenance of the bund must be established (*see* 4.1). Following rewetting, access to the inner face of the bund may no longer be possible; suitable alternative strategies must, therefore, be devised to maintain the bund (such as the provision of a sluice to drain the site completely should the need arise).

Internal Bunding

Internal bunding can increase water levels on over-steepened increased gradients (following extraction, drainage and/or slumping) or can truncate dense drainage networks (Figure 5.41).

To avoid damage during transportation, it is advisable to use a local peat supply. If local peat is inappropriate, provision should be made for temporary vehicle access (*see* 5.6.8). A low-ground-pressure excavator or an excavator working on bog mats is the most cost-effective machinery for bund construction.

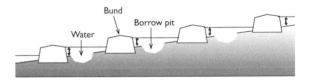

a)

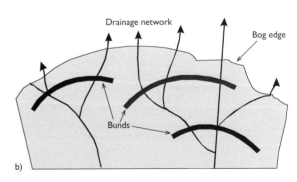

b)

Figure 5.41   Internal bunding designed to (a) increase water-levels on over-steepened gradients or (b) truncate drainage networks.

When creating open water, the bund must protrude above the surface and be constructed from well-humified peat or contain an impermeable insert. In this situation, the same principles for peripheral bunding apply (Figure 5.42). Seepage through the top layers of weakly humified peat can be retarded if an internal bund of well-humified peat is installed (*see* Figure 5.43).

5.1.4.3 Plastic and Peat Bund

A bund may require the insertion of a plastic membrane to decrease its permeability if only low-humification peat is available (<H5 – *see* 4.5.5.1). For this, non-toxic and non-biodegradable plastic or heavy-duty polythene sheeting (available from builders' merchants) can be buried within the bund.

At Raheenmore (*see* 6.16), internal bunding has been applied to a more or less intact peat dome. Streefkerk and Zandstra (1994) give the following guidelines:

- An assessment of peat depths and properties should precede any construction (*see* 4.5.2, 4.5.5). Bunds should not be constructed over unconsolidated *Sphagnum cuspidatum* layers.
- A plastic membrane is inserted vertically into the bog surface within a narrow slot (Figure 5.44a). It is not necessary to insert the membrane to the bottom of the peat body (Wheeler and Shaw, 1995), but it should penetrate to at least 1m. The plastic should be held in place as the slot closes against the sheet. Remember to leave a folded section of sheet to cope with the bog expanding as it rewets (Figure 5.44b).

- The top sod (vegetation layer) should be removed from the bog surface over the width of the bund base. This creates a good seal between the bund and the bog. To help stabilise the plastic screen, a small section of vegetated sod should be left on either side of the screen (Figure 5.44c).
- For long bunds (>20m), wooden posts should be hammered down to firm peat at the outside edge of the plastic screen. Posts should be spaced at every 5–10m to protrude above the bog surface by the desired water level height. A notch cut into the top of the pole is used to attach a plank to the top of the plastic screen. As the bog swells, following rewetting, the plastic screen can fold out.
- Peat can be excavated from a borrow pit 1–2m in front (bog-side) of the bund location (place the top sods to one side). The bund is built up around the plastic sheet and the wooden posts. It should be built to at least 50 cm above the desired water level (top of the wooden posts) and eventually dressed with the top sods taken from the base and borrow pit (Figure 5.44d).
- At regular intervals, provision should be made for overflows. The easiest method is to incorporate plastic drainage pipes just above the horizontal planks.

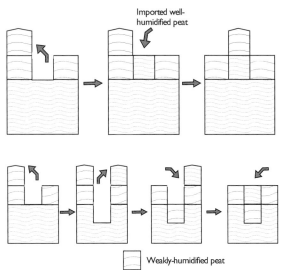

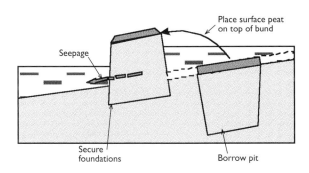

Figure 5.42 A basic design for the construction of an internal bund designed to impound water above the surface level.

Figure 5.43 Internal bund construction using highly humified peat; (I) by replacement of upper, weakly humified, peat with imported well-humified peat; (ii) by the interchange of well- and weakly- humified peat horizons in trenches (adapted from Wheeler and Shaw, 1995).

5.1

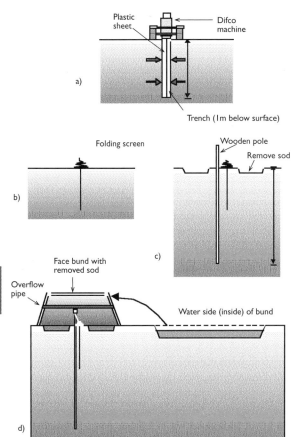

Figure 5.44 Construction of a plastic and peat bund: a) insertion of plastic sheeting with difco machine, b) surface concertina of plastic sheet, c) removal of peat sod, d) bund construction (after Streefkerk and Zandstra, 1994).

5.1.4.4 Clay Bunds

The use of clay as a bunding material on nutrient-poor bogs is generally not recommended for the following reasons:

- Drying causes clay to crack and leak. Excessive leakage may lead to pipe formation and an eventual large-scale failure (not specific to bogs).
- Clay alters the chemistry of bog waters (see 4.4) affecting the survival or recolonisation of desirable bog species as well as being detrimental to archaeological remains (see 1.6).
- Clay bunds have to be built onto mineral rather than peat substrates, as peat is too unstable to support the weight of a clay bund.

However, clay bunds can be used to seal a damaged edge to stop lateral seepage from the edge of a peat body. Note, though, that such constructions alter the natural functioning of a peat body since there would normally be constant lateral seepage (see 2.5; Figure 5.45).

Clay for bund construction should be wet, free from woody material and stones and impermeable. The bund is constructed by removing a narrow (1m) trench of peat (where necessary) down to and into the mineral substrate. Clay is then packed into the trench and compacted to force out any cracks or air gaps. Peat should then be added across the top of the clay bund in an attempt to seal in the mineral source (Figure 5.45).

It is important to maintain moisture levels within surrounding peat which, in turn, keeps the clay wet. Though revegetation of the peat cap should be encouraged, scrub should be prevented from establishing.

Additionally, clay bunds can be used to recreate the lagg fen system around a raised bog. Here, the bund is built some way from the bog edge to allow shallow flooding between the peat body and the clay bund. Enrichment of fen waters from the clay is fine provided that the water level is below the bog surface. Vegetation exploiting more nutrient-rich conditions within the fen, such as reed species, is not then able to colonise the peat dome. This approach appears to be working well at Cors Caron (see 6.13) where peat instead of clay was used.

5.1.5 Ditch infilling

The lowering of the water-table caused by drainage ditches can be reversed by installing a

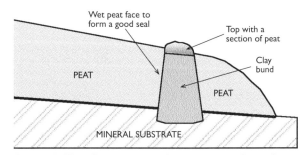

Figure 5.45 Cross-section of a clay bund used to reduce lateral seepage at a damaged bog margin.

series of dams (*see* 5.1.2). However, there may still be greater movement of water through dammed ditches (especially on steep gradients) than naturally within the upper layer of a bog. An alternative approach, therefore, is to infill the ditch completely. This technique has been used at a few sites (*see* 6.18, 6.17). From the experience gathered from these limited applications, several practical considerations should be borne in mind:

- Moving peat alters its physical structure; excessive handling turns peat into a sloppy soup. Consequently, although a ditch may be infilled, it may still act as a conduit for water.
- Material used to infill should be nutrient-poor and relatively impermeable. Dried, oxidised and mineralised peat is unsuitable.
- The volume of excavated peat needs to be greater than the volume of the ditch because of compression and structure loss. The method is limited, therefore, to sites where peat is readily available and its excavation does not compromise conservation objectives (archaeology, for example). Wet peat is very heavy and transportation is extremely labour-intensive. The use of machinery allows large volumes of peat to be excavated (with minimal disturbance to its structure) and moved with relative ease. As with any use of machinery on site, the impacts to the bog surface in terms of damage should be carefully considered (*see* 3.3.6, 5.6).

Ditches outside or at the edge of the peat boundary can be filled with materials other than peat (Figure 5.46), although nutrient enrichment problems should be considered. It is particularly important that nutrient-enriched water does not back up onto ombrogenous bog vegetation.

Bearing in mind the above problems of ditch infilling, the following guidelines are of use:

- Clean out the ditch, removing any unconsolidated peat or plant material.
- Pack the peat into the ditch- making sure that no cracks are left. Obvious weakness points are at the ditch walls and base.

> Only use a wheelbarrow fitted with a balloon tyre when carrying peat.
> Laying down temporary protection around the excavation point reduces levels of trampling damage. If duckboarding is not available, use wooden pallets. A temporary path between the excavation area and the ditch is useful.

5.1

- As the peat is packed into the ditch, it should be compacted down to decrease permeability. A flat 'tamper' should be used in preference to feet.
- Fill the ditch until the infill is slightly proud of the bog surface to allow for settling.
- To prevent erosion, the surface should be dressed with vegetation. This is best taken from the original excavation area(s) as sods (Figure 5.47).
- Plough-drained bogs have a ridge of excavation spoil parallel to the ditch. The spoil can be used as infill. Peat from older spoil is too oxidised (Figure 5.48).
- The use of other materials entails the same approach as above. However, the nutrient

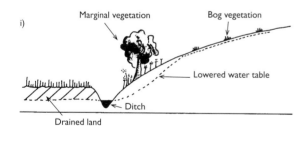

i)

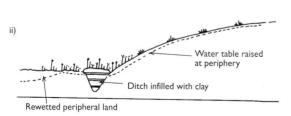

ii)

Figure 5.46 Infilling peripheral ditches with clay: (i) before works and (ii) after works.

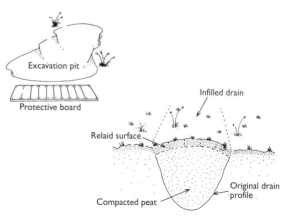

Figure 5.47 Infilling a ditch with peat taken from an adjacent borrow pit.

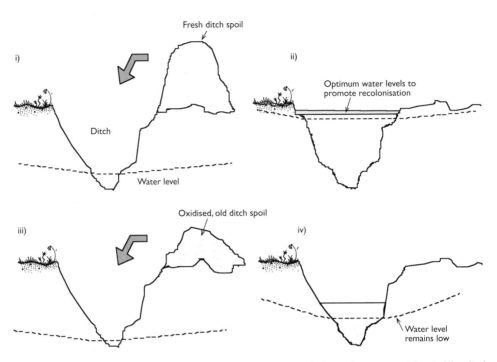

Figure 5.48 The comparative efficacy of fresh (i and ii) versus old (iii and iv) spoil as a material to infill a ditch.

component of the material should be carefully considered before infilling ditches on the open bog (*see* 4.4, 4.5). Even if a clay infill is capped with peat, enrichment may still occur, changing the vegetation within the immediate vicinity of the ditch.

> This technique is amenable to large-scale schemes using wide-track bulldozers to move the peat (see 6.17, 6.20).

5.1.6 Pumping

Water is vital to any peatland system (*see* 2.5, 3.1.3), and in special circumstances it may be necessary to supplement the natural supply (from precipitation) with an alternative source by pumping. To maintain or encourage rain-fed vegetation, the water must also be rain-fed (Wheeler and Shaw, 1995). The use of minerotrophic water generally promotes the development of fen flora. Circumstances in which pumping may be useful include:

- the preservation of archaeological artefacts or palaeoecological records (1.6, 6.4);

- the maintenance of water levels in open water bodies or ditches (this can be used to artificially raise water levels in peat remnants (Figure 5.49);
- temporary measures to kill off unwanted vegetation (usually scrub);
- temporary measures during periods of drought; and
- rewetting following major management operations.

As with all management techniques, pumping should be carefully considered within the overall management scheme for the site (*see* Part 3). Pumping water should be viewed as a short-term solution; it is not a sustainable management option. Pumping can usually only be targeted at rather small areas. Consideration should be given to the following:

Resources

The technical specification of the pump determines its output and often its price. Depending on specific situations, the pumping scheme may require supervision and staff time.

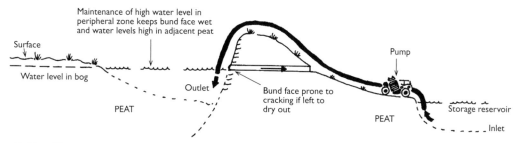

Figure 5.49 Using a pump to maintain high water-levels behind a bund.

Water Source

Given that, in most situations, the requirement is for rainwater, a suitable storage facility is necessary – the volume of water required dictates the size and characteristics of such a facility.

Water Quality

Even when meteoric water is used its movement through pumping increases oxygen levels and may lead to increased microbiological activity (Wheeler and Shaw, 1995) which may in turn stimulate the mineralisation of peat.

Application

Unless the water is pumped into another body of open water or a ditch system, problems may arise at the outflow point through local inundation, erosion or the creation of run-off gullies.

5.2 REVEGETATING PEAT SURFACES

5.2.1 Introduction

Bare peat surfaces are difficult to revegetate because of a variety of inhospitable conditions. The success of any revegetation scheme depends upon the following:

- Hydrological characteristics (see 2.5, 4.3).
- The microclimate of the peat surface. In summer, bare black peat can heat up to over 80°C (Maas and Poschold, 1991), and the exposed surface is highly susceptible to erosion from frost, wind and rain.
- The chemical conditions of the bare peat. High evaporation and an unnatural hydrological regime cause mineralisation and oxidation. Peat extraction may have exposed more mineral-rich sediments, further changing the surface chemical

properties (see 2.6, A3.2.2). The chemical and nutrient status of the peat surface affects the type of vegetation which can colonise it. Oligotrophic bog species are unable to colonise nutrient-rich fen peats, for example (Poschold, 1992), although this may be tolerable if the resulting fen acts as a transition to rain-fed bog vegetation in the longterm (Wheeler and Shaw, 1995). Figure 5.50 shows the differing characteristics before and after peat extraction.

- The distance from a suitable refugium of bog species and the vegetation composition of that refugium.
- The viability of a possible seed bank within the remaining peat.

Whatever the conditions of the bog surface to be revegetated, recolonisation may need to be accompanied by hydrological management (see 5.1) and must always be carefully planned (see Part 3). It is particularly important to carefully consider after-use conservation plans of sites currently under peat extraction (see 1.8, A3.2), as it is important to plan into extraction activities a safeguarded refugium of bog species to use as a harvesting source for direct reintroduction (see 5.2.3) or for seeds/spores (see 5.2.2). It is also particularly important, in terms of cost and expertise, to plan the final phases of extraction to leave (sculpt) bare peat surfaces which have the maximum potential for rewetting and revegetation (see Wheeler and Shaw (1995) for more detail).

Wheeler and Shaw (1995) consider renaturation of bare peat surfaces in some detail and should be consulted if these approaches are used. However, the main approaches are summarised here. These are natural recolonisation (5.2.2), transplanting whole plants (5.2.3), using seeds and spores (5.2.4) and rafting (5.2.5). The approach

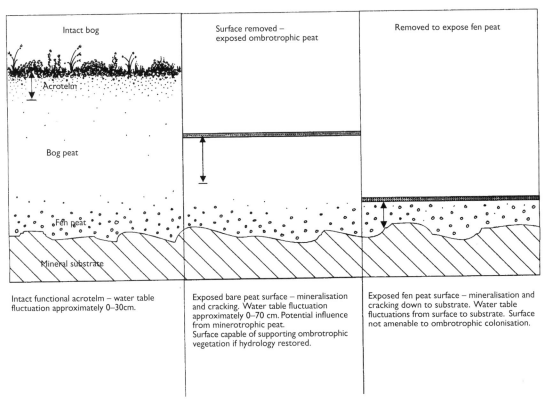

Figure 5.50 The changing environmental conditions at the peat surface following extraction dictates the type and range of species that may colonise the site.

used relates to different rewetting strategies (Table 5.4).

Table 5.4: Rewetting strategies and introducing vegetation

Rewetting strategy	Introducing vegetation
Construction of embankments/bunds, leading to continual inundation.	Rafting of aquatic *Sphagnum* – introduction of fragments and/or whole plants.
Initial inundation through sluice control of embankments. Fluctuation may be seasonal (governed by climate) or controlled (by sluices).	Rafting of *Sphagnum* coupled with 'tussock buffering' from cotton grasses and purple moor grass.
Strategy aimed at raising levels to surface for all or majority of year. Minimise fluctuation and inundation (mimic 'natural' levels).	Individual whole plant/fragments or within turves – seeding/spores of all desired species directly to surface.

5.2.2 Natural recolonisation

Natural recolonisation of a bare peat surface may occur from a viable seed bank stored within the uppermost layers of peat or from windborne spores/seed from adjacent refugia.

Ombrotrophic mire species have the capacity to store persistent seed banks (Wheeler and Shaw, 1995). On a small scale, peat samples can be cultivated in pots or trays to give an indication of the range and abundance of species that are still viable within the seed bank. However, at most peat-mining operations, the uppermost layers, which contain the greatest percentage of viable seed, have been removed, thereby reducing the potential for recolonisation from this source. Sometimes, the top layers of vegetation and peat are stored prior to commercial extraction to be spread over the bare peat surface, in a thick layer (approximately 30 cm), to help facilitate revegetation on cessation of mining. This material is known as *bunkerde* in Germany. Evidence to support the value of this approach is inconclusive (Wheeler and Shaw, 1995).

Another mechanism for natural recolonisation is from windborne spores or seeds derived from local refugia. Little is known about either the dispersal capabilities or the capacity of the seed to colonise onto bare peat surfaces. The success of natural recolonisation schemes depends upon the factors outlined above (5.2.1).

Open water can be colonised by encouraging aquatic *Sphagna* to colonise (rafting – *see* 5.2.5). Rafting is the establishment of an initial layer of vegetation onto which successional colonisation of other species takes place. Rafting schemes have taken place with some success (*see* 6.15), and recent palaeoecological histories (Joosten, 1995) would also suggest that the approach can work. The exact requirements for this type of successional development, however, are still unknown, and it remains an area for further research.

5.2.3   Transplanting

Transplanting whole plants onto bare peat surfaces has been tested at Kendlmühlfilzen (*see* 6.14), Gardrum Moss (*see* 6.26) and elsewhere. The following points should be noted:

- there may be difficulty in locating a suitable donor site;
- there may be unacceptable levels of damage to the donor sites from plant collection;
- pioneer or 'nurse' species may have to precede *Sphagnum* reintroduction because the microclimate is too extreme for *Sphagnum* recolonisation;
- procedures can be very labour-intensive;
- the technique is unsuitable for large-scale operations; and
- adequate investigation of hydrological and chemical parameters must precede plant introduction.

Whole plants used for colonisation may be either individual specimens or groups moved as turves. Individual plants are best transported and planted as a peat core; this should prevent excessive damage to roots. Tussock species such as hare's tail cotton grass are best transplanted as juvenile specimens or split into smaller parts from large tussocks. Hare's tail cotton grass seeds well

if it is burnt the year before. *Sphagnum* has the capability of growing from small fragments of whole plants. However, the success rate of scattering fragments onto bare peat is governed by the microclimatic characteristics at the surface. Small fragments or juvenile plants are very susceptible to drought and do not possess the water-retentive abilities of larger hummocks. If the surface is not initially suitable, *Sphagnum* should be introduced either in conjunction with 'nurse' species (Figure 5.51) or in larger peat turves (for example, Sliva et al., 1996).

The translocation of vegetation in turves is the most practical way of introducing whole plants onto a bare peat surface. This method has not been fully tested for bogs. However, on heaths, young heather stands have been successfully translocated using a turfing machine (Gimmingham, 1992). The turves are cut in 1m-wide sections to a minimum depth of 5 cm, rolled up and transported to the receptor site. Older heather stands have been moved in larger turves cut with an excavator. At the receptor site, the large turves are placed in shallow trenches and the gaps between the turves infilled with peat and heather cuttings (Gimmingham, 1992).

Other species can also be translocated in turves. Turves containing cotton grasses or purple moor grass should be cut to a depth of approximately 30 cm (Figure 5.51) or one spade's depth. This provides adequate protection to the rootstock and reduces stress during and after translocation. *Sphagnum* is probably best introduced by this method. There may be an advantage in incorporating 'nurse' species within a *Sphagnum* turf to ensure more amenable microclimatic conditions at the receptor site. However, this should be weighed up against the possibility that the 'nurse' species may out-compete the *Sphagnum*.

> The physical, hydrological and chemical conditions at the receptor site must suit the growing requirements of the translocated species.

An important benefit of transplanting species within turves is that soil micro-organisms and ground invertebrate communities are incorporated.

5.2

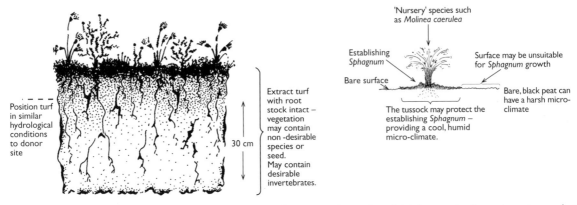

Figure 5.51   Species can be introduced in turves or directly to the surface. Initially growing 'nurse' species such as *Eriophorum vaginatum* can help to maintain a more suitable micro-climate for *Sphagnum* colonisation.

5.2.4   Seeds and Spores

Where local refugia exist (there is little knowledge about quite how local it should be) and prevailing conditions are appropriate (*see* 5.2.1), recolonisation from seeds and spores may be possible. Unfortunately, little is known about the capabilities of different *Sphagnum* species to colonise bare peat or open water from spores. However, dammed ditches are rapidly colonised.

Vascular species (for example, ling heather and hare's tail cotton grass) have been studied in more detail, and their colonisation of bare peat surfaces can be rapid but may not be desirable. Birch and bracken can be particularly difficult management problems should they colonise bare peat surfaces (*see* 6.19). In most cases, such colonisation is a reflection of the physical (hydrological and chemical) regime of the exposed peat surface (*see* 2.5, 2.6).

Areas may be deliberately seeded using seed from local sources. Seeds of local provenance are preferable, but care should be exercised as such stocks may also include unwanted or inappropriate species. Some species, such as heather, may be available as part of commercial seed mixes. Given the difficulties inherent in covering large areas, planting (*see* 5.2.3) or seeding numerous small areas to act as nuclei for natural recolonisation (*see* 5.2.2) is advisable.

5.2.5   Rafting

Rafting is usually associated with the revegetation of a post-extraction surface (that is, oxidising bare peat). Bunds are constructed (*see* 5.1.4), and the surface is flooded to encourage the colonisation of aquatic Sphagna (for example, *Sphagnum cuspidatum*) to form floating rafts. Eventually, successional colonisation by terrestrial *Sphagnum* species may take place. If the growing raft meets the surface, peat may start to accumulate and some of the functions of the acrotelm may be restored (*see* 2.5.4).

Practical considerations include:

- Maintaining a flooded surface all year round may require bunds or embankments (*see* 5.14).
- If the water level drops below the surface (*see* 4.3.3) for any considerable time, colonising vegetation may be prone to desiccation.
- Water chemistry must be suited to colonising species (*see* 2.6, 4.4). A settling period of at least twelve months should precede any vegetation introduction.
- Large, open water bodies may attract considerable numbers of wild fowl. This can lead to eutrophication and disturbance which are detrimental to *Sphagnum* growth.
- Large, open water bodies are affected by wave action which deters *Sphagnum* growth (Figure 5.52).
- There is no guarantee that terrestrial *Sphagnum* species will colonise a floating raft.
- Observations from a number of sites have shown that 'weed' species such as birch may colonise the floating raft.
- If *Sphagnum* does not already exist in wet hollows or ditches, it can be introduced as whole plants or fragments from a suitable donor site (*see* 5.2.3).
- Water levels should remain above the surface (maximum 50 cm) for the entire year (*see* 4.3.3).

Figure 5.52   Large open water bodies are unsuitable for *Sphagnum* recolonisation because of disturbance from wildfowl and wave action (Neustädtermoor, Germany). (Stuart Brooks)

Sphagnum communities, which existed in wet hollows prior to inundation, may float up to the surface with any loose material and start to grow. If, however, *Sphagnum* was not found before inundation, it may need to be introduced. The most successful coloniser of open water is *Sphagnum cuspidatum* which can be introduced as whole plants or mashed up and introduced as fragments (Money, 1994). Other aquatic species, *Sphagnum recurvum* and *Sphagnum auriculatum*, do not regenerate so well, and it may be more prudent to introduce these species as whole plants (Wheeler and Shaw, 1995).

> A food blender can be used to thoroughly mix up fragments prior to dispersal. A soup of different species can be made, depending on prevailing conditions and availability.

To aid initial colonisation, scrub brashings or similar can be thrown into the open water. These may then act as a protective and binding framework for *Sphagnum* to colonise over. This technique can also be useful in minimising wave action (Figure 5.53).

Rates of colonisation are variable. If the conditions are amenable to *Sphagnum* growth, colonisation can be rapid, although successional colonisation of other *Sphagnum* species, such as *Sphagnum magellanicum* or *S. papillosum*, appears to be slow (*see* 6.15). At Bargerveen, successional colonisation has been very slow even though a thick (> 50 cm) skin of *S. cuspidatum* and *Sphagnum recurvum* has already established. Conversely, other sites such as Wieninger Filz in Germany demonstrate rapid successional ombrotrophic revegetation (Figure 5.54). Variation in the rate and success of succession relates to:

* distance from refugia;
* inability of species to colonise over aquatic *Sphagnum*;
* nutrient status of either rainfall or groundwater; and
* fluctuating water levels or prolonged grounding, and therefore drying, of the *Sphagnum* raft.

5.2

Figure 5.53   Scrub thrown into open water acts as a wave break and a framework for *Sphagnum* growth, Neustädtermoor, Germany. (Stuart Brooks)

Figure 5.54   Successional colonisation of hummock Sphagna onto a floating raft demonstrates the potential of re-vegetating bare peat surfaces by inundation, Wieninger Filz, Germany. (Lucy Parkyn)

5.3 MANAGING SCRUB AND TREES

5.3.1 Introduction

Where the climate is dry enough – central Europe for example – trees are a natural element of bog flora. Even in oceanic Britain, studies have shown that, in the past, trees have grown naturally on bogs (for example, Chambers, 1996) during climatic warm periods which allow trees to become established (Barber et al., 1994). Today, many sites are subject to scrub or tree invasion because of various human-related activities (*see* 1.14). Often, scrub is controlled through grazing and burning (Smout, 1996), leading some writers to suggest that trees are unnaturally absent from some British bogs (Ingram, 1995).

Scrub invasion, once initiated, tends to succeed towards woodland because:

- Established scrub and mature trees intercept rainfall in the canopy before it reaches the bog surface. A proportion of this rainfall is then lost to the atmosphere through direct evaporation. Scrub and trees also have higher transpiration rates than bog vegetation. Hence total evapotranspiration is enhanced considerably.
- Drying of the peat surface stimulates the release of nutrients locked in the peat, which encourages the process further.

The pattern of encroachment shown in Figure 5.55 is typical. Note that, whilst succession to closed-canopy woodland is not uncommon, the ground flora often indicates the sites' boggy past – still dominated by *Sphagnum* mosses (especially *S. palustre*) – as the substrate is still peat. Impacts of scrub encroachment are shown in Table 5.5.

To control scrub, it is necessary to establish the root cause of the problem (Rowell, 1988). There is little point in expending considerable resources on scrub removal to find that the problem simply recurs. If trees have established in response to a lowered water-table, efforts should be made to rewet the site. Any scrub clearance measures should be incorporated into a comprehensive site management programme (*see* Part 3). Methods for removal include:

- hand pulling (5.3.2.1) for seedlings and saplings;
- cutting with bow saws (5.3.2.2) or brush-cutters (5.3.2.3) for young trees; and
- chainsawing (5.3.2.3) for mature trees.

It is important to clear scrub and trees as quickly and safely as possible, minimising disturbance to the bog surface. Some species coppice when cut and require secondary treatments such as recutting (5.3.3.3), flooding (5.3.3.4), grazing (5.4) or chemical applications through spraying (5.3.4.2), weedwiping (5.3.4.3) of the new growth or painting of the cut stumps (5.3.4.4). Once scrub is cut, it is often removed – difficult on large sites and/or with large volumes of material (5.3.5).

5.3.2 Cutting and Felling

5.3.2.1 Hand Pulling

For small saplings and seedlings, hand pulling is an effective method of control although it is labour-intensive. Disturbance of the ground is the biggest problem associated with this technique. It is useful to adhere to the following guidelines:

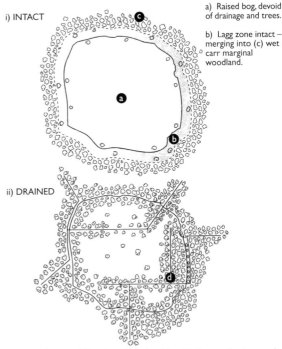

i) INTACT

a) Raised bog, devoid of drainage and trees.

b) Lagg zone intact – merging into (c) wet carr marginal woodland.

ii) DRAINED

Following drainage of (b) and creation of peripheral drains, woodland encroaches initially along drainage lines (d). Peripheral cutting also stimulates this encroachment. The site may eventually turn to woodland.

Figure 5.55 A typical pattern of scrub encroachment on a drained and cut raised bog.

Table 5.5: Impacts of Scrub Encroachment

Species	Conditions for establishment	Sapling	→ Light scrub	Impacts with age Established scrub	→ Dense scrub	Mature trees
Silver birch (*Betula pendula*) and **Downy birch** (*Betula pubescens*). Seeds ripen between July and August – shed between September and November – germination in the field between April and June. Good coloniser of open, bare ground – coppices when cut.	Lowered water-table, disturbance of bog surface creating open areas of bare peat. Nutrient enrichment or flushing. Seed source. Lack of grazing.	Impacts are minimal when trees are < 20 cm tall, though root system may already be extensive.	Five-year-old trees affect immediate area around the base of the tree by drying and shading. Increases seed source.	Vegetation change across a larger area due to increased evaporation and interception losses. Shading and nutrient enrichment increases. Invertebrate and bird populations change.	Physical changes in peat due to compaction and disturbance from root systems around the base of the tree. Impacts from nutrient release and shading limited to immediate area. Large seed source.	Majority of vegetation shaded out. Bare, oxidised peat surface. Cracking around base and roots. Shrinkage of peat. Invertebrate and bird populations now solely woodland communities.
Scots pine (*Pinus sylvestris*) Seeds take three years to mature on tree – released in March–April. Tolerant of wide range of habitat. Does not coppice when cut.	Lowered water-table, disturbance of bog surface creating open areas of bare peat. Seed source.	Impacts are minimal when trees are less than 20 cm tall. Roots still shallow.	Vegetation change to drier communities around individual trees.	Vegetation change across larger areas, switch to *Calluna*-dominated communities. Invertebrate and bird communities change.	*Sphagnum* may still be present in open areas. Physical changes in peat due to compaction and disturbance from root systems around base of tree. Increased seed source.	*Sphagnum recurvum*-dominant species in wet, open areas, dry areas; dominated by heath communities. Oxidation, shrinkage and cracking of peat. Woodland invertebrate and bird communities.
Rhododendron ponticum. Prolific seed production – establishes well on bogs – shade tolerant with potential for rapid growth. Ability to coppice when cut.	Even a small decrease in water-table makes a habitat suitable for establishment. May establish quickly from local seed source.	Impacts minimal although growth may be rapid.	Quickly forms dense shading over ground flora to reduce cover of shade-sensitive *Sphagnum* species.	Shades out bog species entirely from dense growth of bushes – may increase acidification of surface from leaf litter. Prolific seed production: 2m x 10m bush can produce over 1 million seeds.	Tends to cover ground entirely from many separate root stocks. Shades out all other species to leave bare peat – surface may remain wet.	

5.3

- The best time to pull young trees is when the ground is least susceptible to trampling damage – during summer when water levels are low or in winter during mild frosts. Resulting disturbed ground may be seeded by neighbouring trees at certain times of the year (September–October for birch and February–March for rhododendron).
- Areas for scrub clearance should be specified within the management plan (or annexes) for the site (*see* Part 3). It is useful to mark areas out with canes and tackle in an orderly manner – a 'police-type' sweeping line is useful to ensure that areas of scrub are not missed and to help accurate record-keeping (Figure 5.56).
- When pulling seedlings, reduce damage to the surface by placing the feet as close as possible on either side. This prevents *Sphagnum*

hummocks from being pulled up with the root systems (Figure 5.57).
- Seedlings can be either left on site or collected in sacks. Remove the plants more carefully if they are to be used elsewhere or sold.
- If there is a possibility of disturbing archaeological remains, then do not pull.

5.3.2.2   Hand Sawing

Hand sawing of trees is common – *see* Brooks (1980) for a detailed account. On bogs, consider the following when sawing:

- Trees that coppice require after-treatment (herbicides) following felling. To relocate cut stumps, it may be useful to cut the tree high, leave

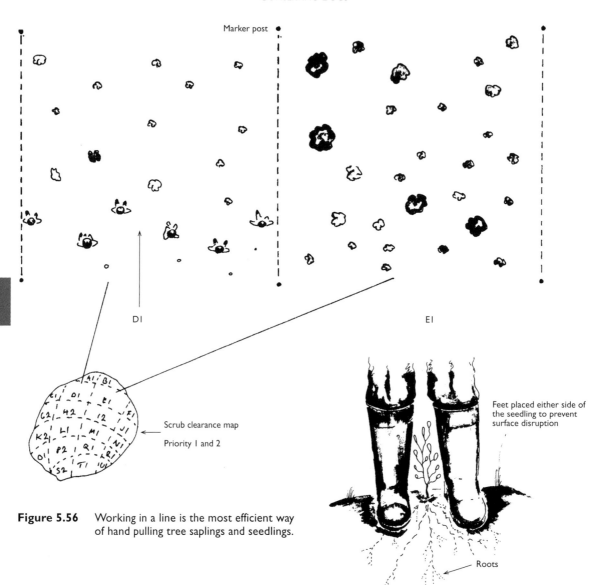

Figure 5.56 Working in a line is the most efficient way of hand pulling tree saplings and seedlings.

Marker post

D1

E1

Scrub clearance map

Priority 1 and 2

Feet placed either side of the seedling to prevent surface disruption

Roots

Figure 5.57 Placing your feet on either side of a tree seedling before pulling it up helps to reduce damage to the bog surface. This is important as disturbed surfaces can readily colonise with new seedlings.

the stump visible, then come back on another day, cut to groundlevel and treat.

- For non-coppicing trees (pine), cut as low as possible to allow *Sphagnum* to grow over the stump. Birds use stumps for perching, which can enhance local enrichment.

5.3.2.3   Brush-cutter and Chainsaw Felling

For larger trees, chainsaws are the best option, although these instruments should not be used without adequate training – *see* Brooks (1974) for full details. The Forestry Safety Council has produced leaflets (*see* Appendix 7) which highlight the safety issues inherent in chainsaw use.

Poor terrain and difficult access on many bogs accentuates the need to follow strictly all health and safety guidelines.

5.3.3 Scrub Control without Herbicides

5.3.3.1 Introduction

The use of herbicides should be avoided where possible in line with precautionary principles – the long-term effects of substances like herbicides are not yet known. There are a number of techniques that can be employed to control scrub without resorting to herbicides. These are ring-barking (5.3.3.2), cyclical cutting (5.3.3.3) and flooding (5.3.3.4).

5.3.3.2 Ring-barking.

Ring-barking can be used to kill a tree in situ. A section of bark is cut away with a bill-hook around the whole circumference of the trunk. This severs the vessels in the cambium and xylem which are responsible for growth and the transport of nutrients between the leaves and the roots. The process is simple and, when conducted properly at the appropriate time of year, effective. There are, however, several factors to consider:

- To secure the death of the tree, a section of at least 12 cm (for birch and pine species) must be removed down to solid wood. Smaller sections of 3–5 cm can heal over, and the tree may eventually recover.
- The timing of ring barking is important. The tree should be cut immediately after it has set seed (*see* Table 5.4); cutting before this induces the tree to produce more seed.

5.3.3.3 Cyclical Cutting

Once a tree is felled, continued cutting of regrowth eventually kills it. Though effective, this method is labour-intensive and is not really suited to large areas or quantities of scrub.

- Strip the newly-grown shoots with a bill-hook or similar bladed tool. The more damage to the stump the better, as this encourages infection and further stress. It is important to cut back all regrowth, including any basal buds which are starting to form.
- The same treatment should follow in subsequent years. Most species die after approximately five years from this kind of treatment. Given the difficulties in relocating cut stumps, one should expect a lower-percentage kill rate than would be expected using chemicals.

5.3.3.4 Controlling Scrub by Flooding

Depending on the species, soil and water conditions, scrub can be killed by raising water levels.

Some species can tolerate wet conditions, and raising water levels back to the surface (that is, approaching natural conditions) may only slow down growth (Figure 5.58). Birch and willow, in particular, are capable of surviving waterlogged conditions for most of the year.

Flooding for the entire year is more effective. This may necessitate the construction of bunds to impound water (*see* 5.1.4). Where water levels can be controlled, through the manipulation of sluice gates (*see* 5.1.3) within bunds (*see* 6.13), levels can be dropped after the scrub has been killed. An advantage of killing scrub by this method is that when the tree eventually falls (into the open water), it acts as a temporary framework for establishing aquatic *Sphagnum*. Dead wood also decreases wave action which in turn aids *Sphagnum* development (*see* 5.3.1).

Flooding can also be employed to control regrowth by diminishing a tree's chance of recovery through coppicing.

5.3.4 Scrub Control with Herbicides

5.3.4.1 Introduction

The control of invasive species may require herbicides. These can be applied directly to the leaves (5.3.4.2, 5.3.4.3), applied to the trunk (5.3.4.5) or painted onto the cut stump (5.3.4.4). Their use should be carefully controlled both for health and safety reasons and so as not to affect non-target species. Herbicides should only be used if absolutely necessary (*see* 5.3.3), as the fate of these herbicides in peat is unknown.

5.3.4.2 Chemical Spraying

As the long-term effects of spray drift on vegetation and invertebrates are unknown, large-scale spraying should be avoided as a means of controlling scrub.

However, studies on drier heath communities suggest that foliage spraying of either saplings or regrowth of cut stumps is effective and the effects on non-target species are comparatively minor.

5.3

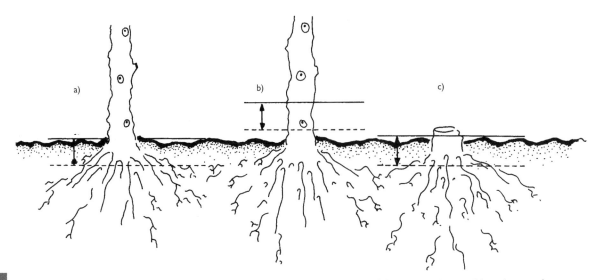

5.3

a) Water level fluctuation from surface (max) to at least 15 cm below surface. Fluctuation is seasonal (maximum in winter – minimum in summer).

b) Water level fluctuations by similar level to a) but minimum level is at last 15 cm above surface – maximum level approximately 30 cm above surface. Fluctuations still seasonal.

c) Water level fluctuations similar to a) but minimum level is approximately 0–5 cm above surface and maximum level is 15–20 cm above surface. Tree has been cut prior to hydrological management but water levels raised in winter period.

Figure 5.58   Some trees may be able to survive when water levels have been raised through hydrological management. Kill rates are improved when water levels are raised above the surface and can be maintained throughout the year.

Krenite (fosamine ammonium) appears to have limited effects on ling heather (Marrs, 1985). Glyphosate, if administered in weak solution in May–June, also appears to have a limited influence on non-target species (Gimingham, 1992). In these studies, however, non-target species are defined as dwarf shrubs rather than mosses.

The use of a drench–gun to administer a measured dose of herbicide to a small surface area reduces the risk of large-scale overspray. Alternatively, weedwiping (*see* 5.3.4.3) can be used. Both fosamine ammonium and glyphosate have British government approval for use with drench-guns.

Using a drench gun to treat cut stump regrowth with fosamine ammonium: Fosamine ammonium should be applied to all visible foliage two months before leaf fall. The herbicide is absorbed through the foliage, stems and buds of treated plants and effectively prevents bud formation the following year. Spraying should take place in dry weather, allowing six rainfall-free hours before and twenty-four rainfall-free hours after application (Marrs, 1985). A non-ionic wetting agent (for example, Agral) mixed with the standard fosamine ammonium and water solution (follow product label guidelines) may enhance herbicide performance on birch. A kill rate of up to 90% has been recorded for this method (Marrs, 1985). Note that fosamine is difficult to obtain and is costly – £29 per litre (1996).

Using glyphosate to treat cut stumps with a drench gun: Treatment must be during dry weather, otherwise the herbicide may wash off before being absorbed. Always spray systematically by following a predetermined route, preferably using a marked grid. This ensures that all areas are covered and helps to evaluate management; grid references can be recorded with dates, times, weather conditions, herbicide solutions, and so on. June and July are the best months for treatment. Not all the regrowth from individual trunks needs to be covered, as the herbicide is systemic. If treating rhododendron, the additive High Trees Mixture B (at 2% of spray volume) should be incorporated within the solution (mixed to labelled guidelines).

5.3.4.3   Chemical Application by Weedwiping

A weedwiper consists of a rope wick attached to a reservoir handle (Figure 5.59). Herbicide solution, in the handle, impregnates the wick which is then brushed over the target vegetation. Calibration of the weedwiper depends upon herbicide solution concentration (follow manufacturer's recommendations on the label), and the flow rate from the handle to the wick can be adjusted. It is important that a constant flow to the wick is maintained.

This method is particularly useful on peatland sites where it is still unclear what effects non-selective herbicides have on the specialist flora and fauna. Glyphosate is recommended for use with weedwipers.

The procedure is as follows:

- Work out a systematic pattern to work across the bog. Treat each area thoroughly before moving onto the next area.
- Use glyphosate (Roundup) in a solution of 12–18% in water (Cooke, 1986) with an appropriate colour dye.

> Food colouring can be used as a cheap alternative to specialist dyes. Change the colour of the dye each year to help determine success rates over time.

- Apply herbicide whilst target species are actively growing and in leaf.
- It is not necessary to cover all of the plant, as glyphosate is systemic; partial coverage effectively kills regrowth from cut birch stumps.
- *Avoid contamination of non-target species*; glyphosate is non-selective and affects all contaminated vegetation.
- Ensure that the wick remains wet throughout application.
- Follow manufacturers' guidelines for the safe use of the chemical and its disposal.

5.3.4.4   Herbicide Application by Painting Cut Stumps

This method of herbicide application is favoured on peatland sites, as the risk of contaminating surrounding vegetation is low. British government approval has been given to application of glyphosate (Roundup) and triclopyr (Garlon) by painting. The technique is not always effective, especially where treatment does not immediately follow cutting and/or it has rained before, during or after treatment. However, provided that suitable conditions exist, kill rates for birch and rhododendron can be up to 90%. A good success rate has been reported if the regrowth is treated in the spring following cutting (that is, just as the dormant buds are sprouting).

It is important that adequate planning is undertaken before any practical work starts. The areas to be treated should be identified on a site map and preferably marked on the ground with canes. Establishing a grid system is the most common method for dividing up a site. By doing this, work is concentrated in small zones rather than dispersed across the whole site, and recording management operations is easier. Figure 5.60 shows the procedure for use, although bear in mind the following points.

5.3

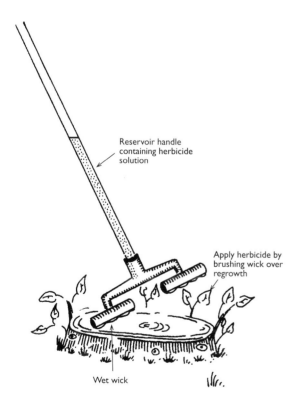

Reservoir handle containing herbicide solution

Apply herbicide by brushing wick over regrowth

Wet wick

Figure 5.59   A weed wiper, used to apply herbicide to leaves and re-growth.

1.

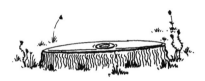

Mark out the area to be treated with canes

2.

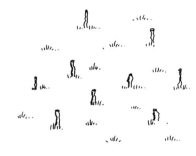

If cutting and treatment is not planned for the same day – leave stumps high to aid relocation above surrounding vegetation

5.3

3.

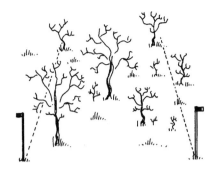

The stump should then be cut as low to the ground as possible on the same day as treatment

4.

Cut notches across the face to aid take-up by chemicals

5.

Add a colour dye to the solution and paint the whole cut face wearing appropriate protective clothing

6.

If stumps regrow – repeat treatment

Figure 5.60   When applying herbicide to cut stumps, follow a standard procedure.

- Avoid treating a tree when its 'sap is rising' (that is, just before and whilst the tree is in leaf) – this deters absorption of the herbicide into the cut face.
- Cutting and treatment should be done on the same day. If this is not possible (for example, it starts to rain), then cut the stems high above the surrounding vegetation, return, cut low and treat.

> Preferably, do not separate the cutting process from the painting. Work in teams of three or four, with one person painting whilst the others cut. Even though this method is labour-intensive, it is more efficient as it reduces the number of stumps that are cut and left untreated.

- Treatment should always take place during dry weather and, to allow the solution to be taken up, a dry spell of at least twenty-four hours should follow.

5.3.4.5 Application of Herbicide to Standing Trees

Spraying (see 5.3.4.2), weedwiping (see 5.3.4.3) and painting of cut stumps (see 5.3.4.3) deal effectively with the problems of regrowth following cutting. However, where the objective is to kill a standing tree, other methods are employed. Ring-barking (see 5.3.3.2) and flooding (see 5.3.3.4) are useful approaches though not always successful. Herbicide application may be necessary, in which case frill-girdling, notching and drilling are used. Note the following advantages and disadvantages:

Advantages
- Problems associated with disposal of cut material from remote or difficult locations are avoided.
- Waste disposal damage (see 5.3.5) is avoided.
- Dead trees provide an excellent habitat for invertebrates and birds.

Disadvantages
- Dead trees are potentially hazardous and should be felled where there is public access.
- Large or particularly dense areas of dying trees may alter the nutrient status as they decay.
- If trees are stressed, they produce a larger number of seeds.

A *frill girdle* is prepared by making a series of overlapping downward sloping cuts at the base of the trunk with either a light axe or a bill-hook (Figure 5.61). The cuts should be deep enough to

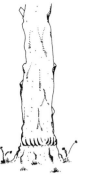

1) Overlapping cuts to creat a frill girdle – cuts should penetrate the cambium.

2) Downward sloping notches in a series around the entire circumference of the tree. Notches should not be spread any further than 10 cm apart.

3) Holes can be drilled into stumps or standing trees and filled with herbicide crystals.

Figure 5.61 Standing trees can be killed by frill-girdling, notching and drilling.

penetrate the cambium, allowing effective absorption of the herbicide.

Ammonium sulphate (Amcide) crystals at 15g per 25mm trunk diameter (Cooke, 1986) should be packed into the cuts. It is important that herbicide application should immediately follow cutting. Best results are obtained from applications made between June and August. Application must be during dry weather, as crystals dissolve in water and wash out of the cuts.

Notching is similar in principle to frill-girdling and is the recommended method for dealing with large trees in situ. A series of evenly-spaced pairs of downward sloping cuts are made around the full circumference of the tree as close to the ground as possible (Figure 5.61).

Ammonium sulphate crystals (15g/notch) should then be packed into each notch. Application should only occur during periods of dry weather, as crystals dissolve in rain and wash out of the notches. The best time for application is between June and September. On larger trees, a second application may be necessary.

An alternative to notching is *drilling* (Figure 5.61). Holes should be at least 25mm diameter and penetrate into the trunk by up to 75mm. Ammonium sulphate crystals are packed into the holes.

> Once the crystals have been packed into the holes, plug the hole with stones, bark, tape, and so on, to prevent the crystals from dissolving and washing out in the rain.

5.3.5   Waste Disposal

5.3.5.1   Introduction

Removing scrub and cut timber waste from bogs presents numerous difficulties and is a common management problem, especially where large volumes of material are involved. Leaving the brash on site can lead to localised enrichment and shading-out of intolerant species and also represent a significant fire hazard. Table 5.6 details some of the techniques that have been employed.

The effects of enrichment from leaving cut material on site have yet to be fully determined. Impacts from shading are clearer. Heavy localised shading from a wood pile, for instance, kills many species, in particular *Sphagnum* mosses. Therefore, where large volumes of material are being cut, it is advised that the majority of it be removed from the bog surface. Many of the techniques detailed require material to be dragged either off the bog or to a central point for burning, chipping or stacking. Dragging heavy branches and trampling by people soon damage *Sphagnum*-rich areas (*see* A3.6.5). At their most severe, trampling and dragging lead to bare peat surfaces ideal for colonising birch (Atkinson, 1992). When birch is in seed (June–October), well-intentioned but unplanned scrub removal may worsen the situation by encouraging rapid birch colonisation. If these approaches are used, temporary tracks should be laid to help protect the bog surface.

5.3.5.2   On-site Disposal

The effect of leaving waste on site is now being explored using permanent plots incorporating a number of different species within a broad range of environmental variables (Scottish Wildlife Trust, 1994); this has provided some useful information on short-term vegetation changes. Initial findings have shown that dead wood is rapidly covered by vegetation when it is predominantly in contact with the bog surface and *Sphagnum* is the main constituent of the vegetation. Where the material is piled up (that is, not in contact with the surface) or the surface is dry, there is little opportunity for colonisation.

The best locations for disposing of scrub on site are blocked drainage ditches or open water bodies (man-made, not natural pool systems). The brash acts as a framework for *Sphagnum* to grow over and is particularly useful in deeper water bodies where *Sphagnum* is slow to colonise. Semi-submerged brash may also suppress wave action across large open water bodies (Figure 5.62).

5.3.5.3   Burning Waste

A common method of disposing of woody material on non-peat habitats is to burn it on site (Brooks, 1980).

On peatland sites, the following *risks* should be considered:

- Always plan emergency measures before burning – contact the local fire-brigade, for example (*see* 3.16).
- Consider burning in frosty weather so that, should the fire spread, the damage is curtailed, or in wet weather to reduce the chance of a fire getting out of control.
- Avoid burning directly on the bog surface itself. As well as burning off original vegetation and enriching the area with potash, there is a possibility of igniting the peat itself. Once alight,

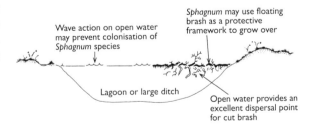

Wave action on open water may prevent colonisation of *Sphagnum* species

Sphagnum may use floating brash as a protective framework to grow over

Lagoon or large ditch

Open water provides an excellent dispersal point for cut brash

Figure 5.62   Throwing scrub into open water suppresses wave action and can act as a framework for *Sphagnum* growth.

Table 5.6   Methods of felled tree and scrub (waste) disposal.

Approach	Resource requirements	Site requirements	Comments
Leave on site (stacked). 5.3.5.2	No direct costs other than labour.	Best suited to large sites with zones of dense scrub and where options for disposal are limited	Could be a fire risk and also lead to localised enrichment. Best to stack material as it is cut. Avoid dragging scrub long distances.
Leave on site (unstacked). 5.3.5.2	No direct costs – other than those associated with felling.	Best suited to large wet sites where scrub is distributed widely in low densities.	Where wood is in full contact with the surface of the bog, *Sphagnum* quickly covers it. Minimal extraction damage.
Leave on site in ditches. 5.3.5.2	Small cost implication; labour-intensive if large volumes of waste are to be disposed of.	Open ditches or flooded lagoons.	Scrub can act as a framework for *Sphagnum* growth in ditches; scrub also impedes flow (but does not act as a dam). This is the best option for on-site disposal.
Drag to the edge of the bog. 5.3.5.2	Small cost implication; can be very labour intensive. May require temporary boardwalk sections.	Inappropriate on large sites due to dragging distances.	Can cause damage to sites from trampling and dragging over sensitive areas. This can be reduced by laying temporary boardwalks.
Burning on site. 5.3.5.3	Relatively small cost implications; labour dependent on scale of operation.	Best suited to larger sites.	Risk of fire, local enrichment and scorching of bog surface.
Chipping on site. 5.3.5.4	Cost of purchase/hire of chipper and means of moving chipper. Labour resources dependent on scale of operation. Possible revenue from sale of chips.	Can be utilised on large and small sites. Chippings may still have to be removed.	Chipping waste reduces volume. It still requires the chippings to be disposed of. Unadequate provision for transporting chipper may lead to damage of bog surface.
Helicopter off site. 5.3.5.6	Extremely expensive to hire helicopter. Labour required to prepare waste for uplift. Possible revenue from sale of timber.	Appropriate for large sites or sites with very poor access.	Due to associated expense, adequate planning should be used. Only an option in limited circumstances due to excessive costs.
ATV extraction. 5.6.9	High labour requirement for preparation of material. Cost of purchase or hire of suitable ATV.	Best suited to drier sites capable of sustaining vehicle use. The relatively small payload means that many journeys are required.	Where dragging by hand is the only alternative, the use of ATVs may actually reduce damage to the bog surface. Ideally, temporary tracks should be laid down for the duration of the operation.
Winch off site. 5.3.5.7	Cost of winch/block and tackle. Labour resources reasonably small. Possible revenue from sale of timber.	Not appropriate on large sites.	Risk of damage to bog surface from dragging. Dependent on skilled labour to operate winches and pulleys safely.
Standard commercial forestry equipment.	High cost and skill demand, although output is considerable.	Only suitable on damaged sites or those under commercial forestry.	Standard machines (forwarders and harvesters) are too big and heavy to work on bog surfaces without causing extensive damage or jeopardising the safety of the machine. Standard practice on deep peat is to work over a brash mat laid down by the harvester.
Specialist machines, such as, Vimek Minimaster 101. 5.3, 5.8	Initial purchase or hire costs significant, although, as with a helicopter or standard extraction machines, a high output can be achieved. A trained operator is required.	Can be utilised on a broad range of sites. Low-ground-pressure vehicles are specifically designed to work on wet sites.	These types of machines offer good potential for effective removal of timber with minimal damage to the bog surface. Even though ground testing has been very limited, this approach does appear to address many common problems associated with timber extraction from bogs.

5.3

peat is difficult to extinguish. Fires can smoulder for months, burning slowly beneath the surface, resurfacing considerable distances from the original source.

> **Dig a temporary circular ditch, or mow a firebreak, around the fire to isolate it and stop it spreading (Rowell, 1988).**

- Some damage to the bog surface, from ash enrichment and especially trampling, is bound to occur even if protection (*see* below) is used.
- Ash is a concentrated fertiliser on a bog and must be removed from the bog.
- Surface burning may be deleterious to surface and near-surface archaeology.
- Always have beaters at hand in case the fire gets out of control.

A useful technique for avoiding some of the problems of burning is to employ a raised burning bin. The bin is raised above the surface to counter scorching, can be moved around the site and the ash can be left to cool down safely before removal. A burning bin is used in the following way:

- Locate the bin in the centre of the cleared area close to the wood piles. Choose a position where the bog surface has already been damaged. Areas immediately around large stumps are ideal. Avoid wet areas that would be quickly damaged by trampling (Figure 5.63).
- Protect the surface of the bog by placing fire blankets or corrugated sheeting on an area which is 40 cm wider than the bin base on all sides.
- The base of a semi-portable bin should not exceed 3m x 2m (larger bins become too heavy to lift).
- Using one large sheet, or several smaller sheets riveted together, prepare the bin base. Drill 3–5mm holes, 2 cm in from the edge, at regular intervals around all sides of the bin (Figure 5.64).

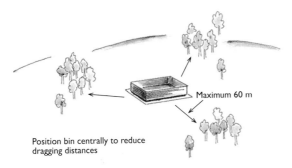

Position bin centrally to reduce dragging distances

Maximum 60 m

Figure 5.63 Position the bin centrally within the working area. Avoid wet areas which are more susceptible to trampling damage.

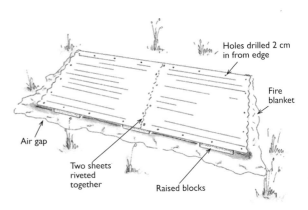

Holes drilled 2 cm in from edge

Fire blanket

Air gap

Two sheets riveted together

Raised blocks

Figure 5.64 Corrugated metal sheets or fire blankets should be laid directly onto the bog surface.

- Construct a platform for the bin base on top of the fire blanket (metal buckets and log sections have both been used successfully in the past). This creates an air gap beneath the bin base to further reduce scorching of the bog surface (Figure 5.65).
- The next stage is to construct the sides of the bin. These contain the fire and stop it and the ash spilling over onto the bog. The sides should fit just inside the bin base (directly in front of the base holes) giving a 2–3 cm overlap. Drill 3–5 mm holes to line up with the holes on the base. Holes should also be drilled up the side of the sheets to allow them to be joined together. Join the corners of the sides and the sides to the base by threading pieces of wire through the pre-drilled holes and twisting the ends together (Figure 5.66).

> **Lay duckboarding or metal sheets up to and around the bin to protect the most heavily trampled areas.**

- Once the fire is established (the gaps between the base and sides should provide an adequate draught), designate one person to manage the bin. Do not let the fire rage uncontrollably. Always have a spade available (to dig a trench if the peat catches fire) and a fire beater. Allow at least one hour for the fire to die down. Never leave the fire burning in the bin unattended.
- When the fire is 'safe' place a lid, constructed in a similar fashion to the base, on top of the bin. This can be weighted down with heavy logs to stop it from blowing off with the wind. Left overnight, the ashes are warm the next day. A fire can easily be restarted on the embers. Collect the ashes for disposal (the ashes can be used as garden fertiliser) once they have cooled before moving the bin. The bin can be moved by sliding

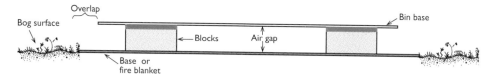

Figure 5.65 An air gap, created by raising the bin on blocks, helps to reduce scorching of the surface.

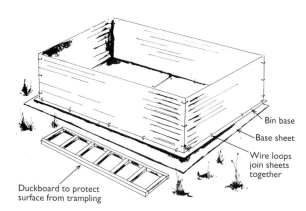

Figure 5.66 The finished burning bin. It is important to protect the immediate area around the bin from trampling.

Figure 5.67 The burning bin in use, Flanders Moss, Scotland. (Julia Keleman)

two or three long lengths of wood underneath to provide a platform. A 1.5m x 2.5m bin can be easily moved by between four and six people. Alternatively, the bin can be constructed with handles on the sides or attached to the base. Instead of joining the sheets with wire, a system of hinges or brackets can be used enabling the bin to be collapsed for transportation.

5.3.5.4 Chipping Waste

Chipping reduces the volume of timber waste produced by scrub clearance operations, thus reducing impacts to the surface from dragging (*see* A3.6.5) and trampling. An associated benefit of chipping timber is that it produces a useable or saleable commodity. Wood chippings are used as a horticultural mulch or top dressing for footpaths. Alternatively, shredded material (including leaves) is used as a basis for an organic compost (a good peat alternative). Equipment used for chipping is given in Appendix 7.

Consider the following:

- Access to and on the site is important. Larger chippers require a vehicle, preferably an all-terrain vehicle (ATV – *see* 5.6.9), to tow and manoeuvre them around the site. Some sites may have steep slopes or wooded fringes which hamper access.
- Impacts to the surface increase with the size and weight of the machine. Balloon tyres can be fitted to reduce impacts (but may require specialist customisation of wheels and axles). Temporary tracks or roads (*see* 5.6.8) can be laid down to allow the chipper to be easily towed with minimal impact to the surface of the bog. Relatively short sections of track can be laid down, either directly onto the surface or on top of a brash carpet. The track is moved forward as required (Figure 5.68).
- Once the brash has been chipped there still remains the problem of disposal. Options are to remove by vehicle (preferably along temporary access routes – *see* 5.6.9), by helicopter in bags (*see* 5.3.5.6) or to leave on site (*see* 5.3.5.2).
- All the chippers mentioned are fitted with a rotating discharge chute. If the chippings are

5.3

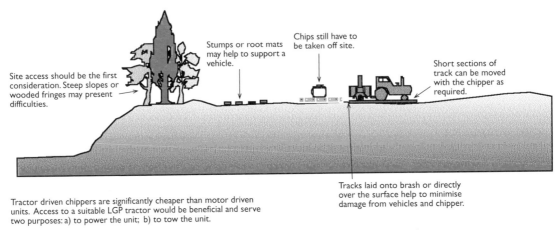

Site access should be the first consideration. Steep slopes or wooded fringes may present difficulties.

Stumps or root mats may help to support a vehicle.

Chips still have to be taken off site.

Short sections of track can be moved with the chipper as required.

Tracks laid onto brash or directly over the surface help to minimise damage from vehicles and chipper.

Tractor driven chippers are significantly cheaper than motor driven units. Access to a suitable LGP tractor would be beneficial and serve two purposes: a) to power the unit; b) to tow the unit.

Figure 5.68   Particularly on very large sites, it may be appropriate to chip cut material on-site.

being bagged, an extension to the chute may be required to feed chips directly into the bag.

- Chipping off site is an option where access is restricted, potential damage to the surface is unacceptable or the material is derived from the edge of the bog.
- Short-term hire or lease of the machine is probably more cost-effective than purchase where volumes are low to moderate.

5.3.5.5   Dragging Scrub Off-site

Dragging scrub off site is cheap (when using voluntary labour) though labour-intensive, and can significantly damage the bog surface. The following guidelines should be considered:

- Dragging distances should be kept to a minimum. People soon become bored and tired if distances are over 40m.
- An appropriate disposal point is required. The best place to dump cut scrub is in open ditches, either on site (see 5.3.5.2) or at the edge. If there are no ditches on site, scrub should be stacked off the bog, avoiding other areas of conservation interest.
- To reduce trampling, distribute the scrub around the periphery rather than dumping at one spot.
- Avoid dragging over wet areas.
- Reduce damage from dragging by bundling scrub waste within a heavy tarpaulin sack (Figure 5.69). The tarpaulin is dragged over the surface by two to four people.

5.3.5.6   Removing Trees by Helicopter

Introduction

Despite the high cost of helicopter hire (c. £700 per hour), it can be cost-effective to remove large

Figure 5.69   A large sheet or tarpaulin can be used to drag scrub over a site. Using this method more material can be moved in one go, which in turn, minimises damage from trampling.

volumes of trees (see 6.23) and scrub (see 6.21). The following guidelines are of use:

- Cut material should be stacked and packed before uplift and in accordance with the capabilities of the helicopter.
- Know the operational limitations of the helicopter: its payload and refuelling requirements. An initial site visit with the helicopter pilot is essential. The dumping zone and refuelling area should be inspected.
- The number of ground-workers should be kept to a minimum when the helicopter is in the air. Those that are present should be suitably briefed on the necessary safety procedures.
- Local residents should be informed of the intended scheme.

- Choose a dumping zone as close to the uplift area as possible to reduce helicopter time.
- Operational difficulties such as dropped loads, refuelling and so on are bound to occur. Before commencing work, assess likely difficulties and incorporate contingencies into the wording of any contract with the helicopter company.
- Weather conditions dictate helicopter use, so it is important to make contingency plans to account for any bad weather.
- Using helicopters to remove scrub or trees off bogs is a newsworthy event – contact local media.

Removing Scrub and Brash

Prepare forestry nets, such as those used to lift Christmas trees, before cutting scrub. Special attention should be given to the attachment points. There should be at least four on every net with one at each corner. Loops are directly attached to the helicopter or used to hold a long strop which is then attached to the helicopter remote release mechanism (Figure 5.70).

A strop (looped at both ends) is fed through the net loops and then the other loop of the strop. The strop loop is then attached to the remote release. The strop is released with the net at the drop-off point. There needs to be enough strops to cover all the nets or enough to allow the helicopter to fly continually (until it requires refuelling). The added expense of the extra strops

is justified by reducing helicopter waiting time during loading and unloading.

To remove the maximum amount of scrub in the minimum number of nets, scrub should be cut up into small sections. Time spent on compacting the scrub into the nets is well spent given the subsequent reduction in helicopter flying time. However, care should be taken not to overpack nets either by volume (preventing the loops from being drawn together) or by weight.

All strops should be attached to the nets prior to the arrival of the helicopter. Ground crews should be briefed and stationed at locations around the nets and at the drop zone (in case the release mechanism snags the strop). Commonly, nets or strops break, discharging the contents onto the bog; so beware of this risk.

Removing Chipped Timber

The volume of material that can be packed into a net or sack can be increased by chipping on site prior to removal, hence reducing the number of helicopter journeys, although the resulting cost reduction may be outweighed by the extra cost of chipping (*see* 5.3.5.4). Also, the reduction in volume of material means that each sack or net is considerably heavier, possibly requiring a larger helicopter at greater expense.

The removal of the chippings is quite straightforward once a system of hooking and releasing the bags is devised. Large sacks used to transport animal feed or building materials are ideal for this purpose. The handles on the sacks should be reinforced and able to withstand a full load of wood chips weighing approximately one tonne. These can be purchased from specialist sack manufacturers (in 1996, £11 each).

Some costs can be recouped through the sale of the wood chips for horticultural mulch or dressings for footpaths.

Removing Whole Trees

For mature plantations, the damage caused by standard tree-removal methods can be reduced by whole-tree harvesting and removal by helicopter (*see* 6.23; Brooks and Stoneman, 1996). To ensure that the operation is as economic and effective as possible, effort should be made to minimise lost time through operational failures.

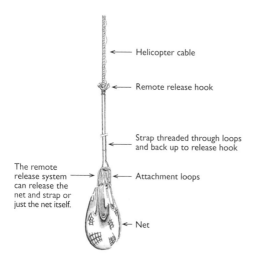

Helicopter cable

Remote release hook

Strap threaded through loops and back up to release hook

The remote release system can release the net and strap or just the net itself.

Attachment loops

Net

Figure 5.70   A system of fixed and remote release hooks can be used to maximise efficiency in the field and thus reduce costs.

5.3

The speed of the operation is dictated by the slowest component, which is not necessarily the most expensive. Further research into plantation harvesting on peatlands is required before this method can be adequately assessed.

5.3.2.7 Removing Trees by Tractor and Winch

Trees can be winched off the site without causing too much damage to the bog surface. As a small tractor or 4 × 4 vehicle is required to drive the winch, access to the site is a critical factor. The method is best suited to smaller sites or to the removal of peripheral trees. At Muckle Moss, Northumberland, a team of four people removed 3ha of dense Scots pine and birch in five weeks. A Norse 5500 forestry winch was used to remove up to four medium-sized trees per pull from distances in excess of 100m (Figure 5.71).

5.3.5.8 Specialist Extraction Machinery

Technology developed for Swedish forests has now been introduced in the UK in the form of the Vimek Minimaster 101. This is a low-ground-pressure tractor and powered trailer unit capable of extracting 2,000kg of timber per run. Initial tests have been favourable, and it appears that this type of machine has potential for scrub and tree removal from wet peatland sites. Similar technology has been utilised in the forested peatlands of Switzerland for a number of years and has proved equally successful.

For a full account of the Vimek Minimaster 101 in operation, *see* Bacon and Lord (1996).

5.4 GRAZING

Grazing of domestic and wild herbivores has had a significant influence on the historical development of peatland habitats (Thompson et al., 1995; Clarke et al., 1995; Welch, 1996), although the effect of grazing is difficult to separate from often-associated burning and drainage. Indeed, the cessation of traditional grazing practices on raised bog nature reserves may be responsible for the increase in scrub and shrub communities (Ingram, 1995; Chambers, 1996); this is enhanced when sites are fenced off, also reducing natural grazing pressure. Re-establishing light grazing on raised bogs may have a positive effect on the vegetation by reducing shrubs and scrub and favouring *Sphagnum* communities.

Grazing for conservation management may be used for:

- control of scrub encroachment – new seedlings or regrowth from cut stumps;
- control of ling heather – short-term strategy linked to hydrological management;
- control of ling heather – long-term strategy where there is little potential to raise water levels ;and
- maintenance of specific habitats created by grazing (for details, *see* Rowell, 1988).

Overgrazing can lead to serious environmental problems (*see* 1.9 and A3.3.3). In this section, some of the factors relating to changing or initiating grazing regimes are outlined; however, research and practical experimentation are still required. It is therefore recommended that any grazing initiatives be supplemented by detailed monitoring (*see* Part 4).

Initiating new grazing regimes in order to fulfil conservation objections should be carefully considered before enacting. Factors to consider include the following:

Foraging behaviour

Several large herbivores are found on bogs. Most common are sheep, red deer, cattle, rabbits and mountain and brown hares. All have differing preferences and requirements (*see* A3.3.3), producing differing vegetation communities in terms of composition and structure. Of these, most is known about the foraging behaviour of sheep, for example, the MLURI hill grazing management model which can be used to set stocking rates on heather moor (Armstrong, 1993).

Only certain breeds of sheep can cope with the poor grazing provided by bog vegetation. These include Blackface, Swaledale, Welsh Mountain, Soay, Hebridean and Moorschnucke. The German Moorschnucke sheep have been used specifically for bog conservation objectives (*see* 6.27).

Sheep have a narrow bite and preferentially select certain plant parts, such as, growing buds and shoot tips. In contrast, cattle browse by wrapping their tongues around clumps of vegetation to pull them up. This results in an uneven vegetation structure, and a comparatively larger amount of dead material is consumed.

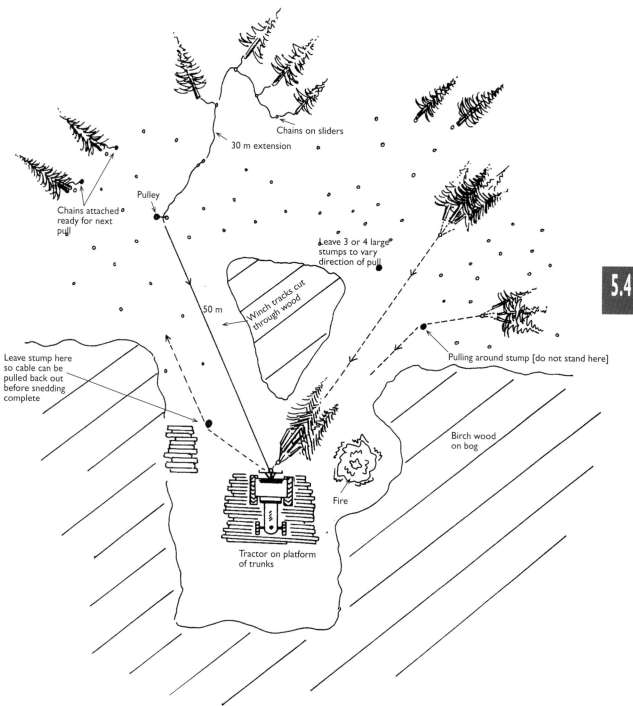

5.4

Figure 5.71 Using a winch to remove trees from the open bog.

Thus, cattle may be used to restore old, degenerate heather stands on drier heathland sites. However, only beef cattle can cope with the low-nutrient status of bogs (*see* Rowell (1988) for relative grazing values of bog communities). Hardy breeds such as the Galloway or Highland are most appropriate.

Pre-existing vegetation

Bogs provide poor grazing, and ditches can be dangerous for livestock. Digestibility varies according to the plant species and according to the time of year. The main edible species on bogs are ling heather, deer grass and purple moor grass. If heather is growing in discrete clumps, sheep often eat grasses and sedges growing between it rather than eating the heather itself. On species-poor sites, cattle favour purple moor grass (often associated with past burning and overgrazing by sheep). Short-term grazing programmes involving cattle, or cattle and sheep, can be utilised to control the initial development and subsequent spread of these species. Cattle may also select other species not particularly favoured by sheep, such as mat grass and heath rush.

Time of year

Different species become more or less palatable as the seasons change. In spring, cotton grasses provide an early 'bite', whilst purple moor grass is more palatable in summer. Heather is most palatable in the summer but may also be grazed in the winter when grasses become less available. As animals are likely to graze the most palatable plants, introducing grazing at different times of the year can be used to control different species. For example, to control birch scrub, grazing should be introduced in late spring when its leaves are most palatable.

The time of year strongly influences the negative effects of grazing. Winter rains inevitably make bogs more susceptible to poaching. Poor winter grazing may only be maintained through supplementary feeding. If extra feed is used, a bog may suffer from eutrophication as animals defecate on the bog surface (*see* A3.3.3).

Stocking levels

Low stocking levels (for example, less than 1 sheep per ha) allow sheep to graze selectively. In summer, more palatable grasses and sedges are grazed in preference to heather, for example. If stocking levels are increased, vegetation types with a higher standing biomass are grazed earlier in the year even if they are less digestible than other available species. Thus, the stocking level can be adjusted to ensure control (via grazing) of certain species or groups of species. However, an increase in stocking density may lead to a complete loss of species through overgrazing, trampling damage and enrichment (*see* A3.3.3).

There are few long-term studies relating to grazing levels on wet bog (both blanket and raised), so guidelines for setting stocking levels are rather vague. Most studies relate to grazing to maintain heather moorland (for example, Armstrong and Milne, 1995; Armstrong, 1993; Gimmingham, 1992; Grant et al.,1976; Grant et al. 1987; Hudson and Newborn, 1995; Rowell, 1988; Welch, 1984; Yalden 1981). For example, one study sets stocking levels at less than 2.7 sheep per ha to maintain a healthy heather cover (Welch, 1984). However, on more waterlogged ground (bogs), stocking levels should be reduced considerably (Welch, 1996). Welch and Rawes (1996), for example, found that a stocking level as low as 0.6 sheep per ha was checking heather growth on a north Pennine blanket bog. It is assumed that stocking levels set to maintain a healthy heather cover would be damaging to more sensitive communities and should be reduced accordingly (*see* Table 5.7).

Table 5.7 suggests appropriate sheep stocking levels for conservation management based on a variety of studies. The suggested stocking levels should only be used as a rough guide. Local conditions, differing management objectives and the other factors outlined in this discussion must also be considered. A monitoring scheme should be implemented where grazing is introduced. Stocking levels should be reassessed on appraisal of the monitoring data.

A moderately heavy grazing regime (for example, >2.5 sheep per ha) reduces the cover of ericoid species, hence promoting an increase in graminoids. Graminoids withstand defoliation

Table 5.7:   Suggested stocking levels.

Habitat	Levels (sheep/ha)	Comments
Dry heath	1.5–3	Conservation management of dry heath through grazing usually focuses upon maintenance of heather stands.
Wet heath	1–1.5	As for above. Other communities may become more important and sheep may have to be restricted to drier areas.
Degraded bog	0.25–0.37	As a means of controlling scrub and shrub invasion, light seasonal grazing may prove effective as either a short- or long-term policy. Shepherding may be required.
Wet Bog	<0.25	Large variability in habitat means that levels are difficult to assess. Light grazing may be beneficial. Natural grazing pressure may be adequate and can be altered with appropriate fencing.

better as they grow from the shoot base rather than the shoot tip (Welch, 1996).

Reducing stocking levels also has an effect. An increase in cover and height of heather is a common outcome (Marrs and Welch, 1991). There may also be an increased build-up of dead woody material. Chapman and Rose (1991) reported a build-up of heather, cotton grass, purple moor grass and wavy-hair grass litter following the cessation of light grazing at Coom Rigg Moss. This appeared to be responsible for a decline in both *Sphagnum* spp. and bog rosemary.

Supplementary feed

Paradoxically, small amounts of supplementary feed increase the overall digestibility of sheep's diet, resulting in a greater forage consumption. Sufficient supplementary feed, on the other hand, does reduce grazing. Grazing impact can thus be partly controlled by supplementary feeding.

Accessibility

The vegetation growing close to the preferred grazing area, for example, the edge of a bog, is more heavily grazed than that growing towards the centre of large patches of unpalatable vegetation.

Burning

Sheep prefer to graze newly-burnt heather, possibly because of easy access, new grass growth and/or the higher nitrogen content of pioneer heather. Small-patch burning (*see* 5.5) can help to spread grazing pressure across a peatland.

Wetness

Sheep do not like very wet ground and are likely to concentrate in drier areas. Cattle and red deer are particularly damaging on wet areas through poaching.

Archaeology

Excessive poaching and enrichment may affect sub-surface archaeological remains (known or unknown) and can disturb the most recent part of the peat profile (*see* 1.6).

5.5

5.5   BURNING

Upland landscapes which often include blanket bog (in Britain and Ireland) have traditionally been managed using fire (*see* A3.3.5). In particular, heather burning is used to create long (20–30m wide and hundreds of metres long) strips of different aged heather stands for red grouse. In these situations, the vegetation communities developed through careful and controlled burning – heather moorland (Figure 5.72) in the main – are often considered to be desirable in nature conservation terms. However, these communities are not 'naturally'- occurring bog communities so management objectives should be clearly defined before considering the use of fire (*see* 3.2). For bog conservation, burning is rarely used. There may be a temptation to control heather or scrub on bogs by burning. However, without hydrological management, burning is likely to stimulate heather and scrub regrowth; burning to control heather and scrub is unsustainable. As a general rule, when conserving bogs – *if in doubt, do not burn.*

The following principles are taken from *The Manual of Grouse and Moorland Management* (Hudson and Newborn, 1995) which should be consulted for more detailed information:

Figure 5.72   Patchwork of burnt and unburnt moorland. (Barry Scames)

- Burning removes degenerate heather, dead woody material and litter, stimulating growth of the stand. It provides a patchwork of uneven aged heather, utilised for breeding, nesting and feeding of red grouse (*Lagopus lagopus*).
- Following fire, the principal regeneration method of young stands is from the rootstock, whereas old stands regenerate better from seed. For twelve-year-old heather, 58% of stems regenerate whereas only 10% regenerate from twenty-five-year-old stands.
- Seeds germinate after exposure to heat (40–100°C) for less than one minute.
- As little as 30% of vegetation is burnt in a cool fire and 90% in a hot fire.

There are numerous problems associated with burning on a regular basis, although most of these can be overcome by following the guidelines laid down in *A Muirburn Code* (Scottish Natural Heritage, 1994) and Chapter 2 of Hudson and Newborn (1995). They both stress the need for a rigorous burning plan and its careful implementation with regard to the variety of habitat, aspect, season and adjacent land use.

Statutory regulations (*Hill Farming Act*, 1946; *Wildlife and Countryside Act*, 1981; *Wildlife and Countryside Act (Amendment)*, 1985; *Highways Act*, 1980; *Clean Air Act*, 1956; and *Health and Safety at Work Act*, 1974) governing burning on peatlands (refers to UK only) are:

- Heather-burning is only allowed between 1 October and 15 April (30 March in lowland areas).
- Burning between 1 October and 30 April is allowed on the authority of a proprietor or of the relevant Agricultural Department (SOAFD, MAFF, WOAD) above 450m (1,500 feet), extendible with permission to 15 May.
- Tenants must give landlords twenty-eight days written notice.
- Notify neighbours with twenty-four hours written notice of the date, place and intended burning area.
- Burn only at night between one hour after sunset and one hour before sunrise.
- Never leave a fire unattended – you must ensure all fires are out.
- Never let the fire get out of control; or at least satisfy authorities that all reasonable steps were taken for its proper control.
- Do not damage woodland or neighbouring property with fire.
- Always keep to the stated prescriptions of heather-burning on a Site of Special Scientific Interest.

5.5

These regulations apply to the burning of all types of moorland vegetation and not just heather. Contravention of these regulations may, on conviction, entail a fine of up to £1,000, or £2,500 if appropriate procedures were not adopted on a SSSI (SNH, 1994).

5.6   ACCESS PROVISION

5.6.1   Introduction

Peatlands are susceptible to damage from both pedestrian and vehicular traffic (Slater and Agnew, 1977; Habron, 1994); the most severe impacts relate to heavy and localised traffic over wet, *Sphagnum*-dominated bog (Emanuelsson, 1985). Dry, often degraded bogs have a greater carrying capacity due to more resistant woody shrub vegetation and a firmer surface, yet are still sensitive to repeated trampling by vehicular traffic.

Provision of access facilities is usually designed to restrict surface damage, although the access provision itself may have an influence on vegetation or on the physical properties of the peat. Larger, more permanent structures have more effect. As a rule, it is better not to over-cater, taking a minimum approach and modifying as necessary.

The type of access provision is also determined by its intended use. For public access and special-needs requirements, safety and finish should always be considered. Access for management does not require the same level of sophistication but may have different demands.

This section outlines the different types of access provision commonly used on bogs. Table 5.8 suggests appropriate provision according to the type of use and its characteristics.

5.6.2   Raised Boardwalks

5.6.2.1   Introduction

The most common and effective way of encouraging visitors on to wet bogs is to use a

Table 5.8   Access provision

Hydrological characteristics (uncut or cutover bogs)	Botanical characteristics	Peat characteristics	Timescale	Traffic pressure and ensuing damage	Pedestrian access provision	Low-ground-pressure vehicle provision
Wet: water levels at or close to the surface; pool systems.	Dominated by *Sphagnum* and other wet bryophyte communities or bare peat.	High water content; *Sphagnum* peat.	Permanent	Serious damage can result from even light use.	Raised boardwalk (5.6.2); floating boardwalk (5.6.3).	Permanent road or track (5.6.5); reroute where possible.
			Temporary	The wettest and most heavily-used areas are most prone to damage.	Sections of boardwalk over wet areas (5.6.6).	Floating track sections (5.6.3).
Seasonal or spatial variations; wet and dry areas.	Broad species mix; wet *Sphagnum* dominated areas and dry shrub zones.	Variable.	Permanent	Localised damage; dry zones may sustain moderate use.	Sections of boardwalk over wet areas (5.6.6). If heavy use is predicted, a permanent boardwalk may be required.	Reroute around wet areas.
			Temporary	Temporary use for management or monitoring access	Temporary paths (5.6.4) or boardwalk sections (5.6.6).	Temporary tracks (5.6.4).
Dry; water levels low; seasonally wet.	Dominated by dwarf shrub and scrub species.	Dry and compacted with continuous vegetation cover.	Permanent	Permanent use; damage to vegetation may lead to exposure of surface and erosion.	Permanent paths: terram matting/woodchip (5.6.5).	Temporary tracks (5.6.4).
			Temporary	The surface should withstand light or temporary traffic.	No provision required.	No provision required.

boardwalk. It fulfils two main functions: to protect the bog surface from the damaging effects of regular or heavy pedestrian trampling (*see* 1.12 and A3.6.5) and to protect the pedestrian from the difficult wet terrain of the bog. The boardwalk also serves to encourage visitors to stay on the route of the boardwalk and not walk over dangerous and/or sensitive areas of bog (Figure 5.73).

Figure 5.73   A boardwalk made from untreated timber, Peatlands Park, N. Ireland. (Lucy Parkyn)

5.6.2.2   *Materials*

Boardwalks have been successfully constructed from both treated (*see* 6.20) and untreated timber (*see* 6.28). It is essential that treated timber be left to 'weather' before installation so that any excess chemicals are leached out before they can damage the bog. There have been one or two cases reported where treated timber has leached chemicals into the surrounding peat and killed off the vegetation. There is not enough published information to give firm recommendations for specific chemicals, treatment processes and weathering times. There are advantages in using treated timber: its increased life expectancy, its price and general availability. However, until further information emerges, it is recommended that treated timber be used with great care. Untreated hardwoods may be more appropriate; suggested British hardwoods for maximum durability are oak and chestnut. Elm is also commonly used, but its availability is now quite restricted in the UK. For more information on qualities and suitability of different wood, *see* Agate (1983).

Pre-formed recycled plastic can be used as an alternative material to wood (*see* Appendix 7).

Plastic 'wood' is hard-wearing, non-corrosive, non-toxic and non-slip, it requires no pre-treatment and has the 'appearance' of timber. Its durability and low-maintenance requirement make it ideal for wetland boardwalks although, as yet, it has had limited application on peatlands. Initial costs may be slightly higher than for hardwoods, although these should be recouped in lower maintenance and replacement costs. There should also be scope to mix the two materials in the same construction, perhaps by installing wooden decking over plastic stobs.

5.6.2.3   *Construction*

Where possible, the boardwalk should avoid wet areas or those areas that are particularly sensitive to visitor pressure, that is, bird nesting sites. Also, avoid constructing in non-aesthetic, long, straight lines. Provision should be made to protect the bog during installation; this may require temporary paths (*see* 5.6.4) over particularly sensitive areas, site entry and exit points.

Raised boardwalks provide an excellent opportunity to increase accessibility to the countryside for those people with special needs. If this is intended, consultation with local special-needs groups prior to construction is recommended.

Boardwalk dimensions depend largely on the intended use. For heavy use, a width of at least 900mm should be used, and for one-way, occasional use, about 750mm. Different dimensions are required for disabled access. Passing places and information points may require wider sections. Detailed boardwalk specifications can be found in Agate (1983) and Countryside Commission for Scotland (1989).

Most raised boardwalk designs work on the principle of horizontal decking attached in sections to vertical stobs (Figure 5.74). Care should be taken to minimise slippery surfaces; rough wood decking or wire coating can be used to reduce this hazard (Agate, 1983).

It is important on peatland sites to make sure that stobs are sufficiently large to stop sinking in waterlogged conditions. Stobs should be sunk at least 750mm below the surface level and have a minimum surface area of 100mm². The vertical stob is prone to rotting at the peat/air/water

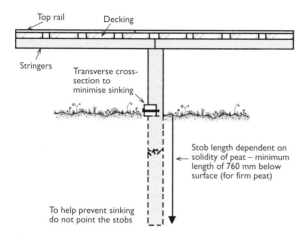

Figure 5.74 A typical raised boardwalk design. The length of vertical stob below the surface is dependent on the nature of the peat.

interface, so special attention should be given to the durability of materials at that point. Areas of mature scrub are problematic, as roots make it difficult to insert the vertical stops into the peat.

> **When working in particularly soft peat, do not cut a point on the stob ends. A flat end provides a firmer support for the boardwalk and prevents sinking.**

5.6.3 Floating Boardwalk

5.6.3.1 Introduction

Alternatives to raised boardwalks (*see* 5.6.2) are simpler 'floating' boardwalks which are suited to flatter, drier situations. Heavy wooden blocks or logs sit directly on the bog surface and support various designs of top planks or decking (Figure 5.75).

5.6.3.2 Materials

Railway sleepers have been used extensively for floating boardwalks either longitudinally or in horizontal section (Figure 5.75). They are easy to work with as they are of uniform shape and size, have excellent durability and provide safe, strong support. Availability and prices are variable.

Rough-sawn wood may provide an alternative to sleepers if they are either too expensive or not available. However, when using wood derived from the site, problems may be encountered in

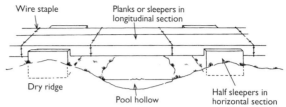

Figure 5.75 If available, an effective and durable boardwalk can be made from railway sleepers.

obtaining enough material of even proportions. The durability and finish may also be inappropriate.

5.6.3.3 Construction Principles

There are various designs currently employed for floating boardwalks (*see* 6.20), although they all tend to follow basic principles.

- Ground supports should be spaced along the length of the boardwalk, spreading the weight of surface decking and people. Place ground supports on drier ridges to span the boardwalk over wet hollows. Sleepers can be placed either longitudinally or in horizontal section.
- The top decking can be constructed from sleepers (laid longitudinally) or sawn timber.
- Sleepers can be placed horizontally directly over the ground (with no support), in which case the vegetation immediately underneath the boardwalk may die and the decking may consequently sink. If such horizontal decking is used, wire should be stapled across sections to deter vandalism or movement.
- If the surface becomes slippery when wet, chicken wire or similar can be stapled on for better grip.

5.6.4 Temporary Paths

5.6.4.1 Introduction

There may be situations where sections of bog are intensively used over short periods of time, such as:

- during management operations, especially at site entry and exit points; and
- during low-intensity monitoring of fixed installations, again including entrances and exits where pedestrian pressure is greatest.

5.6

In these situations, a solid-construction boardwalk is unnecessary; temporary paths can be built instead.

5.6.4.2 Brash Paths

As a by-product of scrub clearance, whole saplings and brashings can be laid over wet or bare peat areas. The brashings should be well packed down with larger material at the base and finer brashings at the surface. This protects the surface from irreparable damage, although it may cause localised enrichment as the wood rots. Brash can either be taken back up or left as a semi-permanent path (topped up when necessary).

5.6.4.3 Plastic mesh

Polythene and polypropylene mesh (often termed geogrids) can be used as either a temporary surface path or a permanent footpath base (see 5.6.5). Choose a material that is light (easy to transport), UV stable, acid-resistant and non-toxic to plants. Mesh sizes in the range of 20–35mm are most suited to peatland sites. If the mesh is left on the ground, holes should be large enough to allow plants to grow through, hence binding the mesh to the surface and increasing the path's durability. It is also necessary to fix the mesh in place with stakes or by digging it into the peat along the length of both sides. If the path is infrequently used, the mesh can be rolled up and taken off site.

5.6.4.4 Inflatable Path

Developed for the emergency services to be used over ice, mud, shallow water or unstable ground, the inflatable path is made from rot- and chemical-resistant Alcryn-coated nylon. Its use has never been tested on peatlands, although in situations where access is needed to seasonally-inundated monitoring equipment, or where areas of very unstable peat need to be crossed, this portable (packs down to 787 × 533 × 406mm) platform may be useful (see Appendix 7).

5.6.4.5 Plastic Path

A cheaper alternative to an inflatable path is a plastic path – Portapath. This is a lightweight sectioned plastic path manufactured for use in the garden. It comes in 3m and 6m lengths and can be joined either lengthways or sideways. The Portapath costs £20 for 3m and is available from garden or horticultural suppliers.

5.6.5 Permanent Footpaths

5.6.5.1 Introduction

Sites that experience heavy pedestrian pressure may require permanent access provision, either as a boardwalk (see 5.6.2) over wet, deep peat or as a footpath over more durable terrain (that is, cut-over bogs or thin blanket peat). A permanent footpath deters the formation of casual walkways (desire lines) and reduces erosion and trampling associated with people's avoidance of eroded wet patches. A wide variety of materials and methods are discussed in Agate (1983), which is recommended as a reference before deciding on, or implementing, any footpath work.

5.6.5.2 Materials

The materials used depend upon the site characteristics. Deep peat requires a firm sub-base to support a top dressing such as geotextile and woodchips whilst thinner peat may already lie over a firm mineral base that can support stone blocks. Materials used include:

- *Geogrid/textile and stone*: Geogrids are specially-engineered plastic meshes. They form an effective base beneath stone on peatland sites. This type of path is best used on degraded sites where pedestrian traffic is particularly heavy.
- *Geotextile and woodchips*: Geotextile materials (such as, Autoway 120) are designed to act as a reinforcing base. Woodchips can be derived on site from scrub clearance operations or purchased from timber merchants.
- *Stone*: Where locally available, large stones can be used to reinforce footpath sections on thin blanket peat. If they are used on deep peat sites, they may sink. On deep blanket peats in the Cheviots, the Pennine Way has been strengthened successfully by using large, flat paving slabs taken from disused Lancashire cotton mills. These slabs are very heavy (they have to be brought in by helicopter) and yet, remarkably, float on the peat.
- *Log sections or chestnut palings*: Laid directly onto wet peat, wooden pathways tend to sink as their movement stirs up the supporting peat into a soupy mess. On drier peats, on thin blanket peat or over a suitable sub-base, these pathways may offer a durable surface and provide a suitable use

for waste derived from scrub and tree clearances. Over areas of deep peat, log sections can be hammered in vertically.

5.6.5.3 Construction

Geogrid and Stone

- All scrub and large shrubs should be removed from the line of the path.
- Dig a tray (a shallow flat trench) to a minimum depth of 18 cm below the surface. Cut the geogrid to the desired width and lay it in the base of the tray. Pegs should not be required, as the weight of the stone should keep it in place.
- Cover to a depth of about 16 cm with a layer of aggregate (type one or equivalent). This should be adequately compacted before a final 1–2 cm of fines is added as a surface dressing.
- To avoid enrichment, limestone or other alkaline rocks should not be used for such construction.

Geotextile and Woodchip

- Clear the intended route of obstacles such as roots and stones and create a level surface. Bushy vegetation should be flattened down (or cut) but not removed. Wet hollows are best avoided.
- Lay the geotextile in long lengths (>20m at a time), digging the edges down into the peat. These can be staked if necessary. It is important that the material should sit as flat to the surface as possible. On very dry sites, it may be possible to scour the surface and remove any obtrusive vegetation.
- Face the geotextile with a good coating of woodchips, approximately 12–15 cm depth. These settle over time and become compacted, so an annual top-up is usually necessary (Figure 5.76).

> Decomposition of the woodchips may enrich areas at the edge of the path.

Stone Paths

- Test the depth of peat along the required route; it should be no deeper than the vertical axis of the stone blocks.

- Hammer the block into the peat with a heavy rubber mallet (paviour). The stone should sit with its flattest face upwards to provide a reasonably smooth walking surface. It should also be wide enough at the base to prevent the stone from toppling over.
- Space the stones along the path to act as 'stepping-stones', rather than packing them closely together. If the stones are able to move around freely in the peat, it quickly loses its structure.
- If the stones do not rest on the substrate comfortably, larger flat slabs can be placed on the bog surface. This is only appropriate on very heavily-used sections of firm peat (Figure 5.77).

5.6.6 Short, Temporary Boardwalks

These are used mainly for protection of monitoring installations and entry/exit points during management operations. Duckboarding and ladders are often used.

Duckboards are usually narrow (approximately 50 cm), short (approximately 1m) lengths of boardwalk decking attached to two lateral stringers (Figure 5.78). They are portable, cheap and easy to construct, making them ideal for temporary access provision. Where access over difficult or wet terrain is required (for example, during dam construction) or protection around monitoring installations is necessary, duckboarding can protect the surface well. Duckboards can be constructed from any material, as long as it is reasonably hard-wearing and does not leach any harmful chemicals into the bog. Wooden pallets can also be used.

Aluminium ladder sections are a good alternative to wooden duckboards. They are very light, strong and non-corrosive. They can be purchased for about £15 (1996).

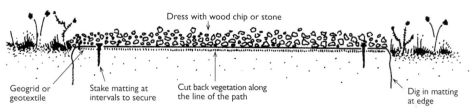

Figure 5.76   Paths can be underlain by a membrane of geotextile or geogrid. They can be surfaced with stone or wood-chips, depending on pedestrian pressure.

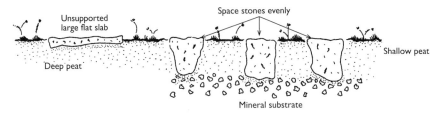

Figure 5.77   With care, large stones can be used to provide durable pedestrian access over deep and shallow peat.

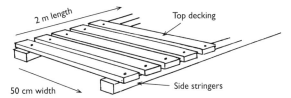

Figure 5.78   A basic design for a wooden duckboard. As a lighter and more durable alternative, aluminium ladder sections can be used.

5.6.7   Permanent Roads and Tracks

5.6.7.1   Introduction

Permanent vehicle routes across bogs should not be established as it is better to reroute around the bog to avoid serious hydrological and botanical damage. However, if there are no alternative routes, there are some options to alleviate erosion. Note that uncontrolled use of low-ground-pressure (LGP) vehicles (*see* 1.12, A3.6.6) over wet peat can cause extensive damage (*see* 6.29; Figure 5.79).

Where vehicle damage is limited to small areas of wet ground or is seasonal in nature, temporary short sections of track or surface reinforcement may be adequate, otherwise permanent tracks have to be constructed.

These specialised operations should be planned by engineers. The problems associated with building over deep peat are considerable. Subsidence, fluctuating water levels, wash-outs, cracking and structural loss may all cause road failure. Further, it is important to take into account archaeological considerations. Any major track or road construction, especially across peatland, should be assessed and evaluated with respect to archaeology. Regular maintenance may be necessary and provision should be made. Potentially non-aesthetic linear features also detract from the visual appeal of open landscapes.

If the peat is thin, it is advisable to excavate to the mineral substrate. This provides a better foundation for the track, although it modifies the hydrological character of a peat body (Figure 5.80). Flow characteristics above and below a

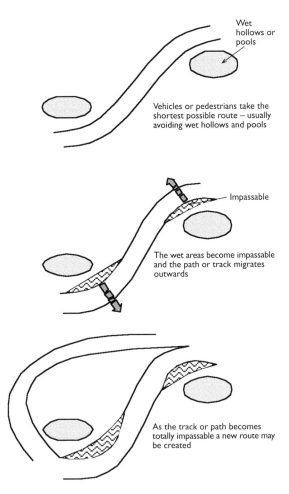

Figure 5.79   Damage caused by vehicles or pedestrians can quickly spread laterally if it is not contained and managed properly.

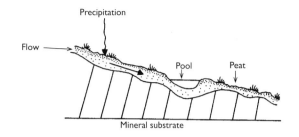

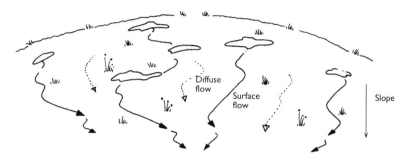

5.6

i) Before construction – water flows over the surface and through the peat

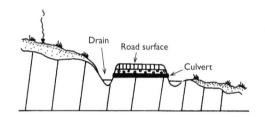

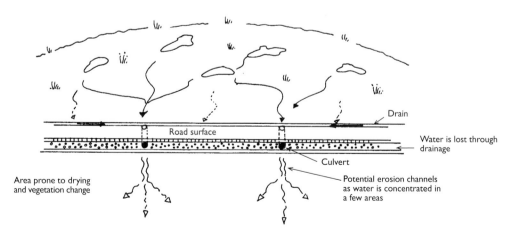

ii) After construction – roads act as a barrier to normal flow. To prevent flooding of the road water is channelled through culverts and exits into drains and at selected points down slope.

Figure 5.80 Hydrological flow characteristics of water through blanket bog - before and after road construction.

newly-constructed road are modified, possibly resulting in erosion by channelisation, or cause the drying of the adjacent peat. Imported material or exposure of the mineral substrate may also serve to change the chemical composition of the water flowing through the peat, resulting in local eutrophication and vegetation change.

5.6.7.2 Materials

Construction materials for deep peats often have to be imported from elsewhere, making access to main roads important. Upland sites offer better opportunities to use locally-derived materials than lowland bogs, reducing construction costs and possibly helping to reduce the visual impact on the landscape. The substrate and surface materials required ultimately depend on the types of vehicles which are likely to use the track (their ground pressure, tyres and the frequency of their intended use).

5.6.7.3 Construction

The two main techniques currently employed are:

* The floating road or 'on-top construction' favoured by the Forestry Commission over deep peat sites (Figure 5.81).
* The solid substrate road which sits directly on the underlying mineral ground usually in thin peat areas (Figure 5.82).

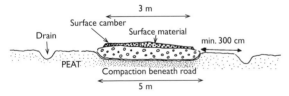

Figure 5.81 Roads can be floated across deep peat if predicted traffic is not expected to be heavy.

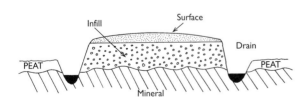

Figure 5.82 Road on mineral substrate through shallow peat.

One of the main problems associated with a floating road is the tendency for it to sink under its own weight. This is partially countered by the use of a brash and log substrate in the Morris design (Morris, 1990). The use of an artificial mesh, such as terram, laid underneath the brash or directly underneath the aggregate infill, may also serve to deter sinking. Note that wood should be laid below the water-table to prevent decomposition (Figure 5.83).

Provision must be made for road drainage, either by construction of a camber or cross-fall or by underground culverts. This helps to prevent both the washing-away of surface material and the loss of cohesion within the substrate infill (through saturation). Whatever method is employed, annual maintenance is usually necessary. Resurfacing and drain clearance are the most common tasks required.

5.6.8 Temporary Vehicle Tracks

Where possible, always reroute around wet, sensitive areas onto firmer terrain. If this is not possible and there are no alternatives to using vehicles, then the use of temporary protection or short sections of permanent reinforcement may be necessary.

Hinged hardwood boards laid as a double row offer excellent short-term protection from vehicle damage. The boards consist of approximately twenty hardwood strips joined by two transverse steel bars, looped at the end to allow fixing to consecutive boards. Boards can be purchased or hired (see Appendix 7).

Temporary reinforcement by heavy-duty plastic netting laid directly onto the surface may

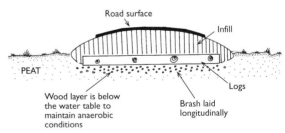

Figure 5.83 To prevent the road from sinking a wooden framework can be laid underneath the sub-surface (after Morris, 1990).

provide adequate protection from the shearing motion of ATV tyres. Plastic netting is particularly useful during management operations where people and materials need to be transported across difficult or wet terrain. The use of a vehicle and surface protection may cause less damage than unprotected pedestrian access (and may be cheaper by cutting labour costs).

5.6.9   Vehicles

Vehicle use over a wet peatland surface should be avoided, as extensive long-term damage results even through infrequent use (see A3.6.6). If vehicle use is envisaged, it is important to use a vehicle with low-ground-pressure tracks or tyres and to follow routes which avoid wet areas, steep inclines, *Sphagnum* lawns, pool systems or flushes. Firmer ground such as thin peats, mineral outcrops (on blanket bog) and areas dominated by less sensitive vegetation (dwarf shrub and scrub communities) should be used for vehicles if absolutely necessary. If damage occurs, then construct temporary or permanent trackways (see 5.6.8, 5.6.7).

Wide-tracked excavators working either on mats or directly on the surface have been utilised extensively on the Solway mosses (see 6.3, 6.10) with little damage to the bog surface.

Access problems are particularly acute on very large rehabilitation sites. In these situations, a small hovercraft could even be considered.

There are two main vehicle uses on peatlands:

- *Transportation of people*: Small ATVs such as quad bikes can be used for the transport of one or two people. On large areas of blanket bog, these machines have proved particularly useful. They are also useful on large, degraded raised bogs (raised baulks in particular offer good, firm access). The transportation of more people requires a vehicle such as an Argocat (see Appendix 7). This vehicle, fitted with between six and eight balloon tyres, can transport up to six people without causing too much damage.
- *Use for management work*: Materials for management work can be transported by hand (labour-intensive and impractical on large sites) or by helicopter (very expensive). An alternative is to use vehicles such as Glencoes (see Appendix 7), which have successfully been used on many peatland sites. More recently, timber extraction on bogs has been made more cost-effective by the use of specialised equipment such as the Vimek Minimaster 101 (see 5.3.5.8, Appendix 7). Most of the large engineering jobs, such as the construction of bunds and dams, requires the use of an excavator. Many of the manufacturers produce excavators with wide tracks which, with care, are capable of working safely and effectively on deep peat.

5.6

PART 6

PRACTICAL EXAMPLES OF BOG CONSERVATION

This section gives twenty-nine examples of actual bog conservation management across Europe (*see* Figure 6.1). The case-studies have been chosen so that virtually all the techniques and methods outlined in Part 5, and many of the methods/techniques detailed in Part 4, are highlighted by an example. The breadth of work undertaken at each site cannot, obviously, be detailed in this volume. Instead, the case-study gives a general overview and concentrates on a particular technique. The case-studies are laid out in order of their featured techniques, although some of the studies concentrate on more than one technique. The highlighted techniques are indicated below.

MONITORING

6.1	Fenns and Whixhall Mosses	Site survey	4.1
6.2	Balloch Moss	Data loggers and WaLRaGs	4.3.3
6.3	The South Solway Mosses	Invertebrate monitoring	4.7.3

MANAGEMENT
Hydrological Control

6.4	Shapwick Heath	Conserving archaeology, flooding	3.1.7, 5.1.6
6.5	Blawhorn Moss	Elmboard dams, steel sheet dams	5.1.2.2, 5.1.2.5
6.6	Felecia Moss	Elmboard dams, large-ply dams	5.1.2.2, 5.1.2.3
6.7	Wedges Rigg	Small-ply dams	5.1.2.3
6.8	Shielton	Plastic dams	5.1.2.4
6.9	Clara Bog	Small peat dams, piezometers	5.1.2.6, 4.3.4.3
6.10	Wedholme Flow	Large peat dams	5.1.2.6
6.11	Black Snib	Supported plastic piling dams	5.1.2.8
6.12	Engbertsdijksvenen	Angled pipe sluices	5.1.3.2
6.13	Cors Caron	Compression bunds, slat sluices	5.1.4.2
6.14	Kendlmühlfilzen	Bunds	5.1.4
6.15	Bargerveen	Bunds	5.1.4
6.16	Raheenmore	Peat and plastic bunds	5.1.4.3
6.17	Abernethy Forest	Infilling drainage ditches	5.1.5
6.18	Rothenthurm	Infilling drainage ditches	5.1.5
6.19	The Humberhead Peatlands	Flooding and pumping	5.1.6

Vegetation Control

6.20	Peatlands Park	Recontouring, boardwalks and terram matting	5.2, 5.6.3, 5.6.5
6.21	Flanders Moss Wildlife Reserve	Scrub removal	5.3
6.22	Roudsea Mosses	Rhododendron control	5.3
6.23	Langlands Moss	Tree removal by helicopter	5.3.5.6
6.24	Maol Donn	Tree removal	5.3
6.25	Bankhead Moss	Weedwiping, painting and spraying	5.3.4
6.26	Gardrum Moss	Recontouring and transplanting plants	5.2.3
6.27	Neustädter Moor	Burning and grazing	5.4, 5.5

Access

6.28	Red Moss of Balerno	Boardwalk	5.6.2
6.29	Gualin (Strath Dionnard)	Permanent tracks	5.6.7

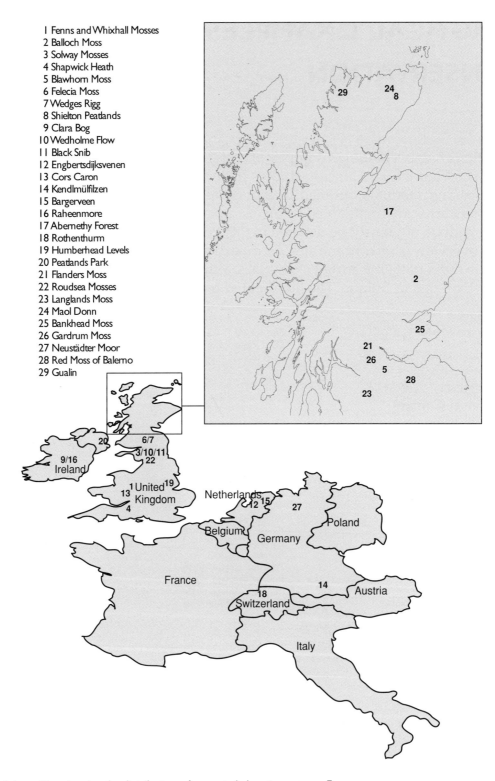

1 Fenns and Whixhall Mosses
2 Balloch Moss
3 Solway Mosses
4 Shapwick Heath
5 Blawhorn Moss
6 Felecia Moss
7 Wedges Rigg
8 Shielton Peatlands
9 Clara Bog
10 Wedholme Flow
11 Black Snib
12 Engbertsdijksvenen
13 Cors Caron
14 Kendlmülfilzen
15 Bargerveen
16 Raheenmore
17 Abernethy Forest
18 Rothenthurm
19 Humberhead Levels
20 Peatlands Park
21 Flanders Moss
22 Roudsea Mosses
23 Langlands Moss
24 Maol Donn
25 Bankhead Moss
26 Gardrum Moss
27 Neustädter Moor
28 Red Moss of Balerno
29 Gualin

Figure 6.1   Map showing the distribution of case study locations across Europe.

PRACTICAL EXAMPLES OF BOG CONSERVATION

6.1 FENNS AND WHIXHALL MOSSES

Featured technique	Integrated monitoring
Cross-reference	4.1
Location	Straddling the English-Welsh border between Shropshire and Clwyd, UK
GB Grid reference	SJ 490365
Contact address	Site Manager Fenns, Whixhall and Bettisfield Mosses Manor House Moss Lane Whixhall Shropshire SY13 2PD
Telephone	01948 880362
Area	966ha
Classification	Raised bog
Designations	SSSI, NNR
Date of featured Works	1991 onwards
Management objectives	Maintain areas of intact mire surface, re-establish the hydrological integrity of the site, provide conditions conducive to rehabilitation towards raised bog and collect a comprehensive baseline survey.

Site Description

There has been a long tradition of peat-cutting across this large site. At the turn of the century there was a switch from small-scale, domestic cutting to commercial extraction which became increasingly intensive until, in 1990, the site came under the ownership of the statutory nature conservation agencies. A large financial outlay by the conservation agencies in the first year of management (c. £1.6 million) financed purchase of the land and a range of plant machinery. A permanent workforce is now stationed at the site including a site manager and five estate workers.

Despite the previous extraction works, up to 4m of peat remains. The site had been cut by a rectangular network of drainage channels into which a rolling programme of dam insertion has been initiated. Working outwards from the areas of intact mire surface, a range of dam materials have been tried (see 5.1.2), including peat, corrugated iron and polythene-and-peat composites. All drain blocking is preceded, where necessary, by scrub removal (see 5.3). Eighty per cent of the birch on the southern section of the site has been removed, whilst the remaining 20% has been retained for its value as habitat for birds and invertebrates. Temporary crossing points (installed by the peat extractors) have been upgraded and clearly marked (see 5.6.8), however, due to the variety of safety hazards, public access to the site is currently by permit only.

To avoid alienating local residents, a blanket ban on peat extraction was not imposed by the conservation agencies; instead, an area to the north of the site – which had already been damaged – has been set aside for small-scale hand-cut extraction. The site is susceptible to nutrient enrichment from drains carrying effluent from adjacent housing developments and from the Shropshire and Union Canal which bisects the site (see 1.13). In addition, there is a threat of heavy metal pollution from lead bullets and smoke-bombs which fell into the peat during the First and Second World Wars.

The site supports an exceptionally diverse invertebrate community with 168 notable, and twenty-nine Red Data Book, species.

Background to the Featured Technique

Aspects requiring survey or data collection were identified. In decreasing order of priority these aspects were: health and safety audits of equipment and working practices (see 3.1.6 and A4), water levels (see 4.3.3), bog vegetation (see 4.6) and finally bog fauna (see 4.7).

6.1

Approach

Health and Safety Audits

Standard procedures and associated documents were designed to assess the safety and general condition of site hardware (such as paths, signs and route markers, dangerous trees and so on) and of plant and machinery (assessments being at designated intervals ranging from daily to annuals checks – see 3.1.6 and A4). A reserve Safety Statement and Risk Assessment forms (listing all hazards on the site) were prepared for circulation to all staff and casual visitors to the site. A Fire Plan and standard procedure was drawn up in consultation with the emergency services. This plan illustrates key features such as: areas of high fire risk, lines of firebreaks, telephone points and contact numbers, access points for fire tenders. It is intended that all visitors to the site carry this information.

Water Levels

A map of the ditches across the site was drawn up by the ex-foreman from the commercial works; this map was later extended to cover the adjacent pasture land.

The gradients of the main arterial drains were then levelled in to assess the implications of weir installation on back flooding. The extent of the peat body was also mapped (at 0.5m intervals) following a photogrammetric survey of the site and the adjacent land (see 4.2/A6.2.2.10); this enabled assessment of the wider ramifications of raising water levels. The level of water visible in the drains and over any flooded areas is recorded twice a year (in summer and winter) and keyed into a series of colour-coded maps (see 4.1.2).

80⅜" (2 cm) dipwells, anchored and levelled to Ordnance Datum, cut the site in four transects (forming two distinct crosses) and are currently read on a fortnightly basis. Following several years of data collation, it is intended to focus collection of the dipwell data at selected, key locations. Dipwell data is tabulated within a spreadsheet. Two continuous water-level recorders have also been installed: one on an intact section and one on a commercially cut area (see 4.3.3.4).

Water movement in the system is recorded in several ways. Rainfall, evaporation and evapotranspiration are monitored using two tipping bucket rain-gauges (see 4.3.2), an evaporation pan and two lysimeters (see 4.3.5) respectively. It is planned to monitor water-flow off the site by installing thin plate weirs allied to continuous water-level recorders (see 4.3.4). Peat movement, following rewetting, is assessed by the relative shift in metal plates laid adjacent to peat anchors at seven points across the site (see 4.5.3). These stations have yielded little significant change and, with hindsight, may have been over-provided for.

Habitat/Flora

The percentage cover of the major vegetation components was assessed on a largely subjective basis and recorded on colour-coded maps which were later used to assist management decisions. Various photographic records were consulted to interpret gross habitat distribution across the site:

- Vertical black-and-white images (1:10,000)
- Fixed point stereo photographs and pairs of colour transparencies
- Oblique colour aerial photographs (which proved particularly informative given the highly visible and systematic grid of drainlines which traverses the site).

All aerial photo interpretation was subsequently ground-truthed (see 4.6.4).

Two 1m² permanent quadrats (see 4.6.3) were installed in representatives of each of the different cutting fields (uncut, handcut, recent commercial cut and old commercial cut); the quadrats were located in different topographical areas (for example, ditch and peat baulk and so on). Species recording across these quadrats requires two person-months. 0.5m² quadrats were deemed unsuitable given the type of existing vegetation (for example, birch, purple moor grass). Stereo photographs are regularly taken of every quadrat although these records have not yet been analysed (see 4.1.3). This quadrat data provided a baseline data set prior to management works although it should be noted that, in certain flooded areas, repeat monitoring may not be possible for many years (see 4.1.3).

6.1

Due to the expertise required to identify mosses and liverworts, specialists are periodically contracted to perform such surveys at predefined locations across the site.

Fauna

Invertebrates: A team of university experts were contracted to carry out a desk review of historical accounts of invertebrate sightings on the site; this review was then used as a basis for current surveys (carried out by eight entomologists at specified locations). Ground and flying invertebrates were monitored over three seasons using standard pitfall (*see* 4.7.3.4) and water traps (*see* 4.7.3.5) (with two replicates in each type of cutting field) although, due to a combination of limited money and limited access to relevant expertise, problems were encountered with the identification of the samples collected. Three transects are annually surveyed (standard methodology – *see* 4.7.3.8) for butterflies and dragonflies (with emphasis being placed upon sightings of large heath butterfly and white-faced darter). The identification of Red Data Book species relies upon periodic assessments made by visiting experts.

Birds: A breeding bird survey was conducted in 1988 and repeated in 1995 (*see* 4.7.2.2). A wader survey has also been carried out at 200m intervals along defined transects (*see* 4.7.2.5).

Appraisal

This site provides a good example of a wide-ranging, yet targeted, monitoring programme devised to aid management decisions over a large and complex site.

The experience of the site gained by the previous employees of the peat extraction company was usefully exploited by those now managing the site for nature conservation (for example, location of ditches). Student placements are frequently used to assist with collection and analysis of the monitoring data. Site mapping, and its division into clear sub-units, also enables casual visitors to contribute to species monitoring by noting, accurately, the location of any species they encounter whilst visiting the site.

The initial survey work, continued monitoring and selected management works on this site are all geared towards achieving a balance between rehabilitating the bog versus maintaining the existing, sometimes rare, fauna and flora which have established on the site.

Due to the potential for litigation and possible compensation to adjacent landowners following any flooding, emphasis has been placed upon collation of hydrological data to assess the effect of water management works. The incorporation of such survey information onto colour-coded maps eases the interpretation of site-wide data, thus aiding management decisions.

The combination of visiting members of the public, a large workforce, extensive range of equipment and a complex and potentially hazardous site warranted the time commitment required for the production of such detailed health and safety procedures.

6.2   BALLOCH MOSS

6.2

Featured technique	Data loggers, WaLRaGs (Water Level Range Gauges) and peat anchors
Cross-reference	4.3.3, 4.5.3
Location	5km north-west of Kirriemuir, Scotland, UK
GB Grid reference	NO 353576
Contact address	Area Officer Scottish Natural Heritage West Lodge Airlie Angus DD8 5NP
Telephone	01575 530333
Area	16ha
Classification	Raised bog
Designation	SSSI. Access by appointment.
Date of featured works	1994 onwards
Monitoring objectives	Monitoring was initiated in anticipation of restoring higher water levels through management. Research development was also an important consideration.

Site Description

Balloch Moss is a good example of a largely intact raised mire with a natural lagg. The dome supports distinct 'hummock and hollow' microtopography although the bog vegetation is degraded. The site has been extensively drained with both peripheral and surface drains. An adjacent plantation may also have impacted upon the hydrology of the site.

Background to the Featured Technique

The monitoring programme was established prior to management to ensure that a comprehensive baseline data set was collected (*see* 3.1). The potential for experimentation and research development was recognised. Balloch Moss was particularly suitable for such works due to its near-natural state and easy accessibility. A working partnership between the owner and Scottish Natural Heritage was formed.

Approach

Water levels over the site are monitored using WaLRaGs (*see* 4.3.3.3) and Chambers Automatic Watertable Loggers (*see* 4.3.3.4). Rainfall data from a nearby automatic gauge is also obtained (from the Scottish Environment Protection Agency).

Twenty-four WaLRaGs were installed (Figure 6.2) and recordings are taken on a fortnightly basis. Once installed the WaLRaGs were surveyed and anchored to the mineral substrate (*see* 4.5.3). The anchors (3.8 cm (1.5″) diameter gas pipe) enabled absolute changes in the watertable to be estimated by measurement of movement of the mire surface (*Mooratmung*).

The raw data is being stored in a spreadsheet (Quattro Pro) and relevant graphs have been plotted although their interpretation has yet to be undertaken. In addition to the WaLRaGs, two Chambers automatic watertable loggers (Figure 6.3) were installed adjacent to WaLRaGs 8 and 15 (*see* 4.3.3.4). The probes for each logger were inserted into a dipwell which was anchored to the moss surface and the top covered with a protective turf. The loggers were set to record watertable movement every 4.8 hours (five times a day). Information was downloaded three times between 19 June 1994 and 8 October 1994, a process which took less than ten minutes in the field. Loggers are now downloaded every six months.

Monitoring of Management Success

Instruments were periodically assessed to check they were working normally. Both instruments were tested in the field to detect any obvious 'teething' problems.

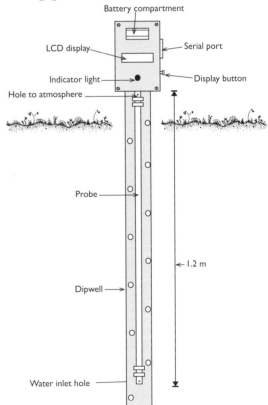

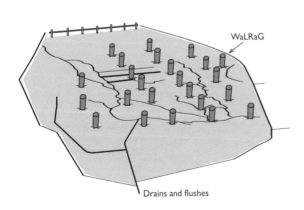

Figure 6.2 Sketch map showing the distribution of WaLRaGs on Balloch Moss (after Ninnes & Keay, 1994). (Not to scale)

Figure 6.3 A chambers automatic water-table logger (after Ninnes & Keay, 1994).

Appraisal

WaLRaGs were shown to record to a precision of ±2 cm when compared to automatic data loggers. Several problems were encountered with the WaLRaGs: the sliding scales occasionally under-recorded water-table fluctuation and, because some of the WaLRaGs had been set too low into the surface, the maximum was pushed to the top of the slider during wetter, winter months. The WaLRaG slides (which were plastic) have been changed to high density foam to remove the problem of sticking. Further problems were found in the exceptionally dry summer of 1995 when water levels were too low to fully float the bottle within the WaLRaG. Data loggers are expensive (£800) although simplicity of installation, ease of use and comprehensive data recording makes them an attractive option when measuring bog water levels.

Comparisons between the two methods showed a slight discrepancy, possibly because the loggers were not fully anchored to the mineral substrate. The dataset provides good comparative information showing that both instruments are generally acceptable.

6.3   THE SOUTH SOLWAY MOSSES

Featured technique	Invertebrate monitoring
Cross-reference	4.7.3
Location	North Cumbria, England, UK
GB Grid reference	NY 238603
Contact address	Site Manager English Nature Wayside Kirkbride Carlisle Cumbria CA5 5JR
Telephone	016973 51517
Area	NNR covers 94ha
Classification	Raised bogs
Designations	SSSI, NNR, NCR
Date of featured works	1993/94 with anticipated repeat in 1998/99
Monitoring objectives	Main aims are to determine whether the important invertebrate fauna of uncut bog are responding to the rehabilitation of cut-over bog.

Site Description

Glasson Moss and Wedholme Flow are part of a series of raised bogs on the south side of the Solway Estuary. The majority of both sites have been modified by peat-cutting, drainage and past burning, although there are areas within both which are among the best examples of intact bog found in England. The main management works since 1986 have been the damming of drains and peat cuttings to raise the water-table (Figure 6.4), birch scrub control and firebreak maintenance.

Background to the Featured Technique

The response of invertebrates to raised bog management is a relatively under-researched area (*see* 4.7.3). The study at Glasson Moss and Wedholme Flow aims to provide relevant information to raised bog conservation throughout the UK.

Approach

The invertebrate groups chosen for specific study were spiders, plant hoppers, and Dolichopid flies; carabid beetles were added later. Species were monitored though the installation of pitfall traps (plastic cups) and water traps (*see* 4.7.3.4 and 4.7.3.5). The pitfall traps were set up in 4m squares of nine traps (three rows of traps at 2m spacing). The cups were inserted to the level of the bog/*Sphagnum* surface and covered to prevent flooding. The water traps (plastic trays) were painted fluorescent yellow (to attract the insects)

Figure 6.4   A nine tonne excavator blocking ditches on Wedholme Flow. (Frank Mawby)

and installed at the corners and middle of each station. All the traps contained a small amount of preservative. Species were collected every three or four days from the water traps and once a month from the pitfall traps. Five stations were installed across a variety of locations, including areas of primary bog, recent damming and unmanaged areas of cut-over bog.

Monitoring commenced in 1993 and will be repeated at five-yearly intervals between May and September. In addition to general invertebrate monitoring, specific rare species have been sampled and studied on Glasson. The large heath butterfly (*Coenonympha tullia* – Figure 6.5) has been monitored using a 'standard' butterfly transect method (Institute of Terrestrial Ecology). Sightings of the species are recorded within a 10–15m band along the transect (*see* 4.7.3.8). The transect is located on the uncut bog and recordings are taken on an annual basis. Monitoring commenced in 1981, with the last recording taken in 1991.

Appraisal

Presently, the results for the general species monitoring form baseline data only (*see* 3.1). Other species, such as the Carabids, were collected and the samples preserved for future identification. Collecting the invertebrates is cheap and straightforward, although sorting and identification is expensive and time-consuming. However, the use of a standard methodology encourages the comparison of data collected from other raised bog sites. Monitoring data for the large heath butterfly have been analysed to compare trends between years. The data was summarised in 1986 and a short report has been written every year since.

The large heath butterfly has the potential to be used as an indicator species as its habitat range is generally confined to areas of primary bog (*see* 4.7.3.1). Population expansion into 'rehabilitated areas' could be assessed by extending such monitoring into these areas.

6.4   SHAPWICK HEATH

Featured Technique	Conserving archaeological remains
Cross-reference	3.1.7, 5.1.4.4, 5.1.6
Location	Close to Glastonbury, Somerset in the Brue Valley, England
GB Grid reference	ST 4340
Contacts	Site Manager English Nature Dowell's Farm Street Bridgewater Somerset TA5 2PX
Telephone	01278 652426
Area	350ha
Classification	Degraded raised bog; cut-over bog and woodland.
Designation	NNR, SSSI
Management objectives	Conservation of the natural, archaeological and historical interest of the site.

Site Description

Shapwick Heath is part of an extensive area wetland and drained land known as the Somerset Levels. Formerly, the whole area was composed of fen and raised bog. Since early medieval times, the land has been progressively drained and converted to pasture and arable fields. Peat has long been extracted from raised bogs, although in recent times this has been increasingly conducted by large, commercial organisations. Today, very little raised peat remains.

Figure 6.5   The large heath butterfly (*Coenonympha tullia*). (F. G. Rodway)

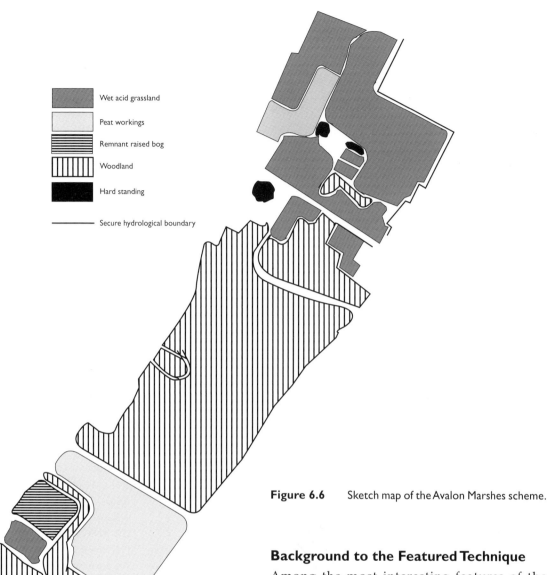

Legend:

- Wet acid grassland
- Peat workings
- Remnant raised bog
- Woodland
- Hard standing
- Secure hydrological boundary

Figure 6.6   Sketch map of the Avalon Marshes scheme.

6.4

Part of the Levels is now being managed to recreate its former wetland character. The Avalon Marshes scheme (Figure 6.6) incorporates EN, Somerset Wildlife Trust and RSPB nature reserves; intensive management of Fison's former peat-cutting areas; and utilises environmental incentive schemes (through designation as an Environmentally Sensitive Area) to aid management works.

Background to the Featured Technique

Among the most interesting features of the Somerset Levels are their archaeological remains. A long history of traditional peat-cutting has unearthed a variety of inorganic and organic remains. Of the most significance is the Glastonbury Lake Village and wooden trackways. In 1970, Ray Sweet, a local peat cutter, uncovered a wooden trackway deep in the fen peats (Figure 6.7). A multi-disciplinary investigation of the track, pollen, plant remains, beetles, spiders, associated flint and pottery finds allowed a remarkably good environmental and cultural reconstruction. Tree-ring analysis was used to date the construction of the track to 3806 BC. It was

Figure 6.7 The Sweet Track preserved in the peat at Shapwick Heath. (Margaret Cox)

demonstrated that the track was used for only 12–15 years before being engulfed by, and preserved in, the peat.

A short section of the trackway remains where it crosses the Shapwick Heath reserve; the remainder was destroyed by peat extraction. Investigations of the remains in the 1980s revealed that the trackway was beginning to deteriorate as summer water levels, in the remnant peat block, fell below the trackway.

Approach

To prevent the trackway from drying, the remnant block was enclosed with a clay bund (*see* 5.1.4.4) and water pumped (*see* 5.1.6) from drainage ditches running through the reserve (part of the Levels drainage system) into the remnant block. Although, the pump feeding the Sweet Track has a capacity of 60,000 gallons per hour, friction along the 800m feedpipe causes a 50% drop in capacity. Pumping takes place at night to take advantage of cheaper-rate electricity.

Monitoring

Water quality is gauged monthly for pH (*see* 4.4.2), temperature, oxygen content and conductivity (*see* 4.4.3). Dipwells, installed along the trackway, are used to observe water levels (*see* 4.3.3.2) frequently. Pumping rates are adjusted according to observations of the water level.

Appraisal

Pumping ensures that water levels now stay above the trackway. However, the capital cost of

this scheme was high (£35,000), with running costs of about £4,000 per year. It is hoped that, with management of the neighbouring land, water level management will be easier and pumping could be transferred to a wind-powered system. One problem of this approach is that the remnant block is now flooded with relatively eutrophic waters (*see* 4.4). Consequently, bog vegetation communities cannot be re-established. In this case, the archaeological interest is greater than the floral interest. However, the species mix on the eutrophic peat surface is of interest in its own right, and ombrotrophic vegetation is being encouraged on another part of the reserve. For a full discussion, *see* Cox et al. (1996).

6.5   BLAWHORN MOSS

Featured technique	Plank dam, PVC-coated steel sheeting dam.
Cross references	5.1.2.2, 5.1.2.5
Location	West Lothian, Scotland, UK
GB Grid reference	NS 886684
Contact address	Area Officer Scottish Natural Heritage Laundry House Dalkeith Country Park Dalkeith EH22 2NA
Telephone	0131 654 2466
Area	109ha
Classification	Raised bog
Designations	SSSI, NNR
Date of featured works	1987 onwards
Management objectives	The damming programme aimed to raise the water-table across the site to conserve the site as a raised bog.

Site Description

Blawhorn Moss is one of the largest remaining intact raised bogs in the central lowlands of Scotland (Figure 6.8). The site was extensively drained after 1945. Where the drains converge at the periphery, they have either created or exacerbated erosion gullies. These gullies are variable in profile, shape and size and, prior to management, were continuing to erode headwards into the bog (*see* 1.14).

Figure 6.8   Blawhorn Moss, one of the largest remaining intact bogs in the central lowlands of Scotland. (J. Hughes)

Background to the Featured Technique

Management was initiated in response to the bog reaching a 'critical point' in relation to both erosion and desiccation through drainage. The actions taken were principally aimed at raising water-levels whilst timber dams were installed to prevent further erosion, thus alleviating the ongoing degradation of the site. Work was planned and carried out by the Nature Conservancy Council.

Approach

In 1987, the majority of the small drains (c. 40 cm deep x 40 cm wide) were dammed using sheets of PVC-coated corrugated steel sheeting (*see* 5.1.2.5). Locations were determined by analysing gradients on the bog to determine distances between each dam. This ensured that water levels, once backed up, retained a depth of at least one half the dam height on the downstream side. To date, 2,400 sheets have been inserted at a cost of £6,000. This sum includes the cost of contract labour.

In 1988, fifty-eight elm board dams (*see* 5.1.2.2) were inserted along the main erosion gullies. 750 x 1,500mm section chamfered elm beams were driven in (central post first) across the gullies. Once installed, the vertical posts were stabilised with a crossbeam, and sluices were cut. The dams did not include aprons. The total cost of this operation (including contract labour) was £22,000.

Monitoring of Management Success

Two dipwell transects (approximately 100m long, composed of twelve dipwells each) run from the peripheral ditches into the centre of the bog (*see* 4.3.3.2). Additionally, there are several paired dipwells adjacent to smaller drains. Dipwell measurements are taken relative to fixed datum posts which were placed adjacent to dipwells and driven through to the mineral substrate (*see* 4.5.3). Vegetation is monitored via thirty randomly-placed permanent quadrats recording species percentage cover (*see* 4.6.3); stereo photography (*see* 4.1.3) is employed (although the dataset is incomplete). The monitoring programme was not initiated prior to the rewetting operations, making it difficult to evaluate the success of operations (*see* 3.4.3.2).

Appraisal

Initial water accumulation occurred in small ditches and dammed erosion gullies, with water levels rising significantly across the whole moss. After two years, however, several of the larger dams failed (Figure 6.9) for a variety of reasons:

- Lateral slumping became a problem in the larger gullies, particularly where the peat mass had become desiccated. Subsequent cracking resulted in alternative routes for water, enabling it to bypass the dams which were in situ.
- The head of pressure occasionally became so great that gaps were created beneath the dams.

Figure 6.9   Some of the large board dams at Blawhorn Moss failed due to excessive pressures building up on the up-stream side. (Stuart Brooks)

6.5

This enabled water to flow under the dams and upwell on the other side.
- Where water was held up to the spillway, the force of the water was so great as to 'heave' the dams forward. During periods of low-level flow, the dams moved back, leaving gaps between the peat and the dam.

It appears that the gullies are simply too large for this type of dam (*see* 5.1.2.1). In the light of this experience, it is considered that any dam over 2m wide and 50–75 cm depth has a higher risk of failure, although this depends upon the initial condition of the bog – amount of desiccation, presence of peat pipes and so on

The failed dams were subsequently sealed with butyl sheets with some success, and a further contract was let to extend the dams and intercept secondary cracking. Metal compression bands were installed to try to hold piles together, and additional piles have been inserted upstream from some dams. Even where dams are still leaking, they are stopping erosion and causing gullies to revegetate as material collects on the upstream side of the dam. In retrospect, it may have been more useful and cost-effective to leave these peripheral areas dry and concentrate on stopping erosion using a plug of peat at the gully head or brash piles (which act as sediment traps). Peat is not a suitable substrate for large dams.

6.6   FELECIA MOSS

Featured technique	Elmboard/large-ply sheet dams
Cross-references	5.1.2.2, 5.1.2.3
Location	Wark Forest, Kielder, Northumberland, England, UK
GB Grid reference	NY 721775
Contact addresses	Environment Forester FE Bellingham Northumberland / Reserves Warden NWT St Nicholas' Park Newcastle
Telephone	01434 220242 / 0191-284 6884
Area	33ha
Classification	Raised mire within blanket mire
Designations	SSSI, NCR site (Ratcliffe, 1977), one of six Irthinghead mires selected as RAMSAR wetlands (1985)
Dates of featured works	1990 onwards

Management objectives	To elevate and maintain the water table in order to promote the growth of bog vegetation and prevent erosion at the site margins.

Site Description

Felecia Moss is an island of wet bog within the large coniferous plantations of Wark Forest and arguably survives relatively undamaged. No serious attempt has been made to drain the mire, and the mature plantations are largely confined to surrounding mineral/shallow peat slopes. The mire has a varied micro-topography (hummock-hollow-lawn) and flora supporting, for example, an unusual abundance of lichens, notably *Cladonia* spp.

Felecia Moss is managed by the Border Mires Committee, a joint management committee involving FE, EN, Northumberland Wildlife Trust and Northumberland National Park.

Background to the Featured Technique

Workers interested in the Border Mires noticed that Felecia Moss appeared to be drying in the late 1980s. Forest boundary drains which had been fed into natural erosion complexes were also starting to cause concern as erosion channels began to incise back into the bog (Figure 6.10).

Approach

Channels between 1.5m and 3m wide coupled with steep gradients meant that any dams had to

Figure 6.10   Large plywood sheets were used to block drains towards the edge of Felecia Moss. (Stuart Brooks)

6.6

be large and solid. Elm board (*see* 5.1.2.2) was chosen as an appropriate material, as North-umberland National Park already had experience of this method at Hangingshields Rigg. The boards were taken to the edge of the site by tractor and carried to the drains by hand. Some of the installations (average cost of £100 each) support enormous volumes of water and are most impressive. This has necessitated the use of splashboards, which, as well as preventing erosion of the ditch bed, provide additional structural support (Figure 6.11).

Towards the edge of the bog, where the ditches are narrower and more incised, it was thought practicable to use 2.5 × 1.3m (8ft × 4ft) exterior-grade ply sheet dams (*see* 5.1.2.3) (experimentation has shown that they are cheaper, at £40 per board, and just as effective as elm plank dams). Transporting such large boards is hard work, and a method of dragging the boards was devised by drilling holes at one edge, through which rope could be threaded. One person can then drag the board whilst another guides the rear across the bog terrain.

When dealing with large boards, it is necessary to use a traditional peat spade to create a closed starter slot for the board. It was also found to be advisable to use two C-bars, one on top to protect the board whilst hammering, and one at the side to maintain rigidity.

Monitoring of Management Success

Four permanent quadrats were set up in 1993 to monitor vegetation changes resulting from damming. These are belt transects (*see* 4.6.3) located at each edge of the site, close to drains, and in the middle of the site. They will be recorded annually and were due to be reviewed in 1996. Each quadrat is associated with a WaLRaG (*see* 4.3.3.3) for max-min recording of the water-table. Forest Enterprise and the Northumberland Wildlife Trust jointly undertake the assessment of dams: visiting the site and noting leaks/signs of erosion and so on, carrying out repairs and installing additional boards (*see* 4.1). This is done at least annually.

6.6

Appraisal

Elmboard dams are labour-intensive to install and difficult to transport, although they have been successful. Installation of large ply dams is also arduous but still comparatively quicker and cheaper than the elmboard versions. Although Harvey (1993) finds no direct evidence to suggest that the dams have raised the water-table at Felecia, the site does appear to be wetter: heather *is* dying off (which may be the result of a less variable water-table). The dams are actively contributing to the reduction of erosion at the margins of the site.

Though having a good overall effect, elm dams require regular checking for leakage and large ply sheet dams require extra care during installation (i.e. ensure closed starter slot and install V-notch spillway). This experience shows that, when dealing with large plyboards (and hence large volumes of water), bowing and attendant problems can be prevented by ensuring that the sheets are at least 2.5 cm (1″) thick.

Figure 6.11 Elm board dams were installed in the larger, central erosion gullies at Felecia Moss. (Bill Burlton)

6.7   WEDGES RIGG

Featured technique	Small-ply sheet dams
Cross-references	5.1.2.3
Location	Wark Forest, Kielder, Northumberland, England, UK
GB Grid reference	NY 713743
Contact addresses	Environment Forester FE Bellingham Northumberland / Reserves Warden NWT St Nicholas' Park Newcastle
Telephone	01434 220242 / 0191-284 6884
Area	25ha
Classification	Saddle watershed mire (Lowe, 1993)
Designation	SSSI
Date of featured works	1992 onwards
Management objectives	To raise a very low water-table in order to re-establish *Sphagnum*-rich vegetation communities and encourage renewed formation of peat.

Figure 6.13   Looking north towards the area of felled plantation from the centre of Wedges Rigg. (Stuart Brooks.)

Site Description

Like Felecia Moss (*see* 6.6), Wedges Rigg is an island of moss within the large coniferous plantations of Kielder Forest (Figures 6.12, 6.13). Unlike Felecia, however, Wedges Rigg was extensively drained from east to west with parallel drains approximately 25m apart. Recently, slopes to the north and south of the site have been felled. These slopes have been identified by the Border Mires Committee (a joint management committee involving FE, EN, NWT and Northumberland National Park) as part of the bog's 'Conservation Unit' and will not be restocked. Large piles of brashings remain on the slopes. A mature forest compartment is present on a western section of the main mire.

Background to the Featured Technique

In 1992, the bog was dry, dominated by ling heather and purple moor grass, with no standing water. Plyboard was chosen as a suitable material for damming because the ditches, measuring 50×50 cm, would recolonise well within the lifetime of the plyboard and because previous experience with wood dams had been good (*see* 5.1.2.3). Damming began using c. $61 \times 122 \times 1.5$ cm (2ft $\times$ 4ft $\times$ ½″) exterior-grade plywood. Some 122×122 cm (4ft $\times$ 4ft) boards were also used for larger boundary ditches).

Approach

With small sheet dams, installation is fairly simple and the ditches to the south of the site were quickly completed with an approximate spacing of 20m. However, difficulties were encountered due to the large numbers of dams required and the poor access to the north of the site – boards had to be carried long distances over rough terrain. Forest Enterprise provided an ATV to transport boards across adjoining mineral ground

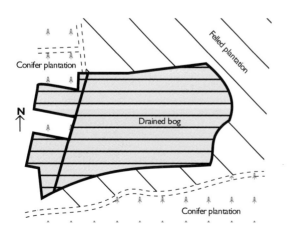

Figure 6.12   Sketch map of Wedges Rigg. (Scale 1:13000)

to stockpile them at a more convenient pick-up point.

Monitoring of Management Success

Regular visits by the Reserves Manager and other members of the Northumberland Wildlife Trust have ensured continuous assessment of the condition of dams and of site hydrology (*see* 4.1). Additional dams are installed if water levels are too low in a ditch. Fixed points have been set up and a stereo-photographic monitoring programme initiated (*see* 4.1.3).

Appraisal

An appraisal of the Border Mires in 1976 suggested that Wedges Rigg was irrecoverable given such heavy damage. However, water levels were usually less than 50 cm below the surface, and damming has elicited a rapid response, reflecting how intact the site remained despite the drainage. Recent observations have shown heather dying off and an increase in *Sphagnum* cover. Small plyboard dams are cheap, simple to install and effective. At a cost of £2.50 per dam, Wedges Rigg has been comprehensively dammed for under £1,000, resulting in a dramatic improvement in the water-table at the site within just two years. However, the work required a considerable amount of voluntary labour, provided by the Northumberland Wildlife Trust.

Little practical management now remains to be done at Wedges Rigg, showing how quickly and cheaply acrotelmic (surface) damage to mires can be rectified.

6.8   SHIELTON

Featured technique	Perspex dams
Cross-reference	5.1.2.4
Location	East-central Caithness, Scotland, UK
GB Grid reference	ND 2049
Contact address	Area Officer
	Scottish Natural Heritage
	NW Region Area Office
	Main Street
	Golspie
	Sutherland
	KW10 6TG

Telephone	01408 633602
Area	5,593ha
Classification	Blanket bog
Designation	SSSI
Date of featured works	1990
Management objectives	To dam agricultural drainage ditches and hence raise water-levels.

Site Description

Shielton is an example of an eastern (Scotland) watershed blanket bog and lies at the eastern extremity of the Flow Country. This type of peatland is characterised by a patterning of deep, widely-spaced pools (dubh lochans) – ranging from seasonal pools to concentric and eccentric flarks (elongated depressions) (Figure 6.14). The peat body is low-lying (gradually rising from 50m to 150m above sea level) and is largely ombrotrophic with only localised nutrient-flushing and few mineral outcrops. The site is designated as a SSSI for its blanket bog habitat and its breeding bird assemblage.

6.8

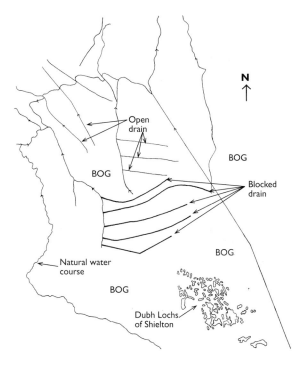

Figure 6.14   Sketch map of the Shielton Peatlands. (Scale 1:10000)

Background to the Featured Technique

In the 1960s, the site was cut by parallel drains (c. 1m wide by 2m deep) as a result of financial incentives for agricultural development. More recently, agreement has been reached between the farmer/landowner and the statutory nature conservation agency, to limit traditional muirburning and reduce sheep stocking levels. In 1990, this voluntary management agreement was allied to positive management works and a programme of dam insertion (April 1990) was initiated in an attempt to alleviate the effects of artificial drainage.

Approach

110 perspex dams (*see* 5.1.2.4) were inserted along selected drain lines across a 28ha section of the site (Figure 6.14). The dams were constructed from corrugated roofing material supported by horizontal wooden struts (Figure 6.15). The spacing of the dams was assessed by eye and varied in order to cater for the shallow surface incline. Each dam was inserted following five basic steps:

- A garden spade was used to cut a starter slot across the ditch.
- The sheet of corrugated perspex (1.5 × 2.5m) was inserted into the slot and pushed into the peat (by hand or maul).

- A wooden slat (15 cm × 2.5 cm) was inserted across the ditch flush with, but downstream of, the plastic sheeting. This slat was then tamped to the base of the dam.
- A second wooden slat was inserted to lie across the top of the dam.
- A V-notch spillway was cut into the dam.

Monitoring of Management Success

Prior to management works, a series of dipwells (*see* 4.3.3.2) (anchored to the underlying mineral ground) were installed in a transect running across the drains. An initial research project headed by MLURI visited the site at monthly intervals from March 1989 to October 1991, and then SNH timetabled biannual dipwell data collection (April and October) for two years to March 1993. Problems with funding resulted in transfer of this project wholly over to SNH who, due to limited staff time, could only commit to visiting the site 'whenever possible' (usually when water levels peak). The existing dipwell data has not yet been computerised, nor has any analysis been undertaken.

A methodology has recently been devised to link data from vegetation quadrats to that from the dipwells. It is intended to locate quadrats along two transects – one parallel and one perpendicular to the slope; it is estimated that survey of these quadrats will require four-person days per year.

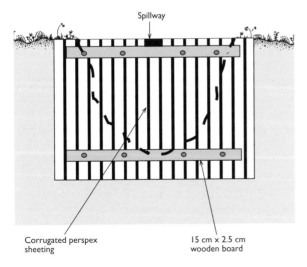

Corrugated perspex sheeting

15 cm × 2.5 cm wooden board

Figure 6.15 The design of the corrugated plastic dam used at the Shielton Peatlands.

Appraisal

Analysis of the dipwell data is under way (Hulme, pers. comm.) and will quantify the effect of ditch blocking. Preliminary results show that there has been a marked increase in water levels in the immediate vicinity of the ditch. Further away from the ditches, there has been little impact. This may be due to the high humification of the peat. At Rumster (also in the Flow Country), ditches had an immediate and widespread effect, causing water levels to fall across a large area. The peat at Rumster is poorly humified (little decomposed), in contrast to the peat at Shielton. This suggests that ditches, in peats of high humification (> Von Post 6), have only a limited effect. For sites where

6.8

upper layers of peat are poorly humified (raised bogs, for example), ditch blocking is more important.

A visual assessment shows that the undammed drains remain free-flowing with no *Sphagnum* growth and dense *Calluna* growth along the dry spoil heaps adjacent to the ditch. Those ditches which were dammed are now displaying limited recolonisation by *S. cuspidatum* (Figure 6.16).

Perspex sheeting was used as it is lightweight (aiding transport onto the site) and already in

Figure 6.16 Dammed ditches colonising with *Sphagnum cuspidatum*, Shielton Peatlands, Scotland. (SNH)

stock. Approximate costs for materials were £750 (1990 prices). The perspex proved to be sturdy enough for dam construction, although some breakages occurred during installation. Damage from weathering (UV, frost) does not seem to be a problem.

A site inspection in 1995 revealed varying degrees of lateral erosion around the edges of some of the dams. Although an *ad hoc* solution to the problem would be lowering of spillways, subsequent works should address the cause of this failure. It can be assumed that the erosive flow is following a line of weakness within the peat, and this might be attributed to two factors:

- the dam sheets might not cut far enough into the sides of the ditch;
- the insertion of the 'supporting' wooden slats might have disturbed the peat. It is possible that, given the small dimensions of these ditchlines, additional support is superfluous provided that the plastic sheeting is firmly embedded.

6.9 CLARA BOG

Featured technique	Small peat dams, piezometers
Cross-references	5.1.2.6, 4.3.4.3
Location	Off N80, County Offaly, Republic of Ireland
Irish Grid reference	N25 30
Contact address	National Parks and Wildlife Service Office of Public Works (OPW) 51 St Stephen's Green Dublin 2 Republic of Ireland
Telephone	01 661 3111
Area	665ha
Classification	Raised bog
Designation	Area of Scientific Importance, NNR – 465ha
Date of featured works	1988
Management objectives	Halt desiccation of the existing acrotelm and sustain and spread the conditions required for peat formation by damming water within 10 cm of the bog surface across the site.

6.9

Site Description

Clara is the largest relatively intact raised bog left in Ireland. Clara consists of several bogs which, although formed in separate basins, subsequently coalesced. The site has a well-developed soak system consisting of a series of interconnected lakes.

The Famine Road was cut across the centre of Clara Bog in 1838 and, in subsequent years, several limestone tracks were constructed leading away from the road and onto the bog. Peat subsidence of c. 5m (over ninety years) prompted relevelling of the road in 1910; since this time, a drop of a further 1m has been recorded. Peripheral peat-cuttings and arterial drains to the north and south have also promoted further desiccation, radically altering the shape of the bog such that its centre is now lower than its margins.

In 1983, Bord na Móna purchased a 440ha section of the site for £1 million. In preparation for peat extraction, the plot was cut with parallel drains and a car park installed. However, in 1986, the OPW bought the plot from Bord na Móna and management for conservation began.

Background to the Featured Technique

In 1989, a large five-year Dutch–Irish study into the ecohydrology of both Clara bog and Raheenmore (*see* 6.16) began. The main conclusion of the work on Clara bog was that the scientific interest of the site could only be retained if steps were taken to combat subsidence and high rates of surface run-off. During their ownership, Bord na Móna cut c. 400km of parallel ditches (50 cm wide × 40–60 cm deep) at a spacing of 18–20m. Due to political considerations, blocking every drain and rewetting peripheral lands was discounted; instead, management work has been concentrated upon the central high bog with the systematic insertion of c. 6,000 small peat dams (*see* 5.1.2.6).

Approach

Before dam construction, the surface contours and drainage network were mapped (*see* 3.1.3, 3.1.4) and data regarding the composition, percentage humification and water content of the peat was recorded. A 100m × 100m grid was superimposed onto the bog and marked; the level of each point on the grid was recorded and its height assessed with respect to all adjacent points. From this, the direction of water movement was determined and the gradient used to calculate the ideal number of dams. An average spacing for the dams of 4–5m was calculated to maintain water within 10 cm of the surface. Following consultation with an expert from Bord na Móna, it was decided to minimise surface disturbance by constructing dams manually. The management work commenced in the driest season, moving outwards from a central point.

Each dam was constructed by cutting a 60 cm long by 30 cm deep slot into the side of the ditch. This was then packed with wet peat extracted from the upstream edge of the drain. The top 30 cm of peat were deemed too permeable for dam construction and were stripped and retained as a vegetated turf. To allow for settling and avoid overtopping, the dams were built to stand 20–25 cm proud of the bog surface. Finally, the peat was compacted by foot and the vegetated turves laid over the top to add stability (Figure 6.17). Any turves which were not used to build the dam were

Figure 6.17   A completed peat dam at Clara bog, Ireland. *Sphagnum cuspidatum* can be seen beginning to colonise the open water. (Stuart Brooks)

thrown into the ditch to act as a substrate for *Sphagnum* recolonisation.

By cutting the damp peat from the ditch, recolonisation by aquatic *Sphagnum* was encouraged. Where alternative peat sources were used, peat was dug deep enough to ensure standing water in the resulting hole.

Where possible, dams were built into hummocks whilst hollows were avoided (due to their tendency to interlink and hence undermine the effectiveness of the dam). The purpose of damming was to restore the natural flow of surface water through the hollows; this flow may be impeded by the ridges of dry peat discarded during the original ditch construction. To overcome this, where such levées sat in hollows, the peat was removed and placed back into the ditches.

Monitoring of Management Success

Vegetation surveys are regularly carried out. Piezometer stations have been set up in transects across the bog.

Appraisal

At a rate of c. ½ hour per dam, it took a team of two, one year to successfully dam 130–150km of ditch. A superficial evaluation indicates that these works were successful; water has backed up behind the dams and *Sphagnum cuspidatum* is gradually recolonising the ditches.

6.10 WEDHOLME FLOW

Featured technique	Large peat dams
Cross-reference	5.1.2.6
Location	Near Carlisle, Cumbria, England, UK
GB Grid reference	NY 220530
Contact address	Site Manager
	English Nature
	Wayside
	Kirkbride
	Carlisle
	Cumbria
	CA5 5JR
Telephone	016973 51517
Area	779.5ha
Classification	Raised bog
Designations	NNR, SSSI
Date of featured works	1991–2
Management objectives	The main objective of rehabilitation work is to retain water, to encourage regeneration of the raised mire vegetation in the peat cuttings whilst maintaining and enhancing the existing mire vegetation.

Site Description

Wedholme Flow is one of the largest raised mires of the South Solway Mosses (*see* 6.3). Extensive damage has occurred over the site following drainage, peat-cutting and burning. Active commercial peat cuttings are now confined to 160ha in the eastern area. Two areas of the site remain uncut, and these retain characteristic raised bog flora.

Background to the Featured Technique

Wedholme Flow has been continuously cut since 1948. In 1990, in a bid to save the uncut areas and rehabilitate the cut-over areas, English Nature purchased 168ha of the moss. To prevent further degradation of the site, a programme of damming drains and cuttings was initiated to control water loss and stimulate *Sphagnum* growth. This large-scale work (150ha on Wedholme) is largely experimental and was aimed at developing new techniques.

Approach

Simple peat dams (*see* 5.1.2.6) were constructed to dam the network of drains (various dimensions) over the site. Due to wet and unstable conditions, a light (four tonne) Kubota KH18 excavator was used with specially-fitted wide tracks (Figure 6.18). As an extra precaution, the machine was used in conjunction with bog mats.

Vegetation was cleared from the drains and placed to one side. Peat was then excavated from the drains to build up the dams. Peat was taken from both upstream and downstream side of dams to form shallow (< 0.5m deep) 'borrow pits'. To ensure an effective seal, only black peat (i.e. highly humified) (*see* 4.5.5.1) was used. The dams varied in length, according to ditch dimensions (c. 3–5m long) and were built proud of the surface of the bog by at least 0.3m.

Once positioned, each consecutive sod was compressed with the back of the bucket to ensure that there were no cracks or lines of weakness. On completion of the dam, the stripped vegetation was replaced in the borrow pit. In larger drains,

6.10

Figure 6.18 A 4 tonne excavator constructing peat dams on Wedholme Flow. (Frank Mawby)

which were aligned in an east–west direction, 5m long plugs were inserted every 50m to counteract damaging wave action caused by prevailing westerly winds. The other dam locations were gauged by the Project Officer in the field.

The work was completed by a contractor between December 1991 and March 1992 at a total cost of £15,000. This included the machine, driver and a support vehicle to ferry fuel and be available to winch the Kubota KH18 out of danger if the need arose. The tender was based on an hourly rate of £15.50 over an 8.5-hour day.

Monitoring of Management Success

The water-table is monitored through three dipwell transects (*see* 4.3.3.2) installed in 1990. The transects run from the intact areas into the cuttings. A photographic record has also been made and the colonisation rate of *S. cuspidatum* is recorded.

Appraisal

Water is being retained in the ditch lines and *S. cuspidatum* is colonising the wetter areas. Analysis of the dipwell data shows that a large fluctuation in the water-table remains (Figure 6.19). There have been some problems with wave action in open water behind the larger dams. This has been partially alleviated by placing birch in the pools to break up the surface and provide a framework for *Sphagnum* growth (*see* 5.3.5.2).

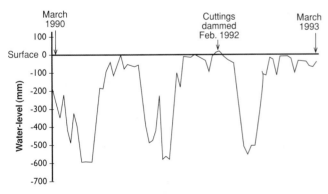

Figure 6.19 Graph showing water table fluctuations before and after management work on Wedholme Flow (readings taken every 2 weeks).

6.11 BLACK SNIB

Featured technique	Plastic piling dams (supported)
Cross-references	5.1.2.8
Location	Longtown, Cumbria, England, UK
GB Grid reference	NY 422676
Contact address	Site Manager — English Nature, Wayside, Kirkbride, Carlisle, Cumbria, CA5 5JR. Area Officer — English Nature, Blackwell, Bowness-on-Windermere, Cumbria, LA23 3JR
Telephone	01697 351517
Area	30ha
Classification	Raised bog
Designation	SSSI
Date of featured works	January 1995
Management objectives	Create conditions suitable for the regeneration of a natural raised-bog community on the deep peat and conserve an uncut peat surface. Create conditions suitable for development of fen communities on formerly afforested shallow peat.

Site Description

Black Snib was previously owned and managed by the Forestry Commission. The site was moor-gripped and planted with trees in 1954/55. The plantation was clearfelled in 1989 due to increasing risk of windthrow and rapidly-declining annual increment. The felling operation resulted in a large volume of brash left on the site. However, the site retains a good cover of *Sphagnum* species and also supports bog rosemary, which is regionally rare. Active management was required on the site to control scrub encroachment and reduce the volume of water leaving the site through the drainage network.

Background to the Featured Technique

Black Snib was notified as a SSSI in 1993 by English Nature after a public inquiry following a planning application for peat extraction. Planning permission was not granted, allowing English Nature to negotiate a management agreement with the landowner to facilitate the management work required to rehabilitate the site. The site

Figure 6.20 At Black Snib, waste material from scrub clearance operations was thrown into recently blocked ditches. (Frank Mawby)

Figure 6.21 A supported plastic piling dam at Black Snib. (Frank Mawby)

retains 12ha which has not been cut. This area has peat up to 5.4m in depth but has been drained with shallow forestry drains. The remaining area is cut-over with peat depths ranging from 20 cm to 2m. These drains were dammed following an extensive (£13,000) scrub clearance operation. Cut scrub was chipped and placed in drains (Figure 6.20).

Approach

The site was surveyed to produce a contour map (*see* 4.2) as well as allowing the incline of the drains to be determined. Rehabilitation has been undertaken through damming (*see* 5.1.2) and scrub clearance (*see* 5.3). Peat from the site was considered too desiccated to be a suitable material for dams, and plastic piling was chosen instead. In January 1995, 100 supported plastic piling dams were inserted at a cost of approximately £400 per dam. The interlocking sections (each 0.33m wide) were pushed in using the bucket of a nine tonne excavator. The sections were pushed in at least 1m below the bottom of the drainage channel to reduce the potential problems of water escaping under the dam. The machine was not used in conjunction with bog mats as sufficient support was gained from tree roots present in the peat.

The piling, once inserted, was supported with a 3m × 100mm × 100mm plastic cross-beam bolted across the top edge of the dam. Additional support was gained by backfilling these dams with peat (Figure 6.21). The peat used to backfill

the drains was excavated from the drainage channels. The peat was cleared of any vegetation and/or brash and was compacted with the machine to reduce leakage.

Monitoring of Management Success

At present (1996), there is no monitoring on Black Snib. Several vegetation quadrats were recorded to provide information for the public inquiry, and these may be incorporated into a monitoring programme. If this information is not available, a photographic record will provide the only method of management evaluation (*see* 4.1.3). No water-table recordings are envisaged due to restrictions of ground staff time and money.

Appraisal

In general, the dams have worked well, with large volumes of water backing up, even in the summer months. *Sphagnum* recolonisation has yet to occur in these pools. There has been some water seepage through the piling, probably because crossbeams hold the dam too rigid. If the dam could 'give' slightly with the direction of flow, the joins should be pushed tighter together. However, seepage is minimal and is decreasing as the seams become clogged with peat. The high cost (£400) of the dams is due to their large dimensions. The dams were constructed to be wide (at least 1m into each bank) to cope with potential problems of lateral seepage around the dams.

6.11

6.12   ENGBERTSDIJKSVENEN

Featured technique	Bunds, angled pipe sluices
Cross-references	5.14, 5.1.3.2
Location	Province of Overijssel, the Netherlands
Grid reference	52°28'N, 6°40'E
Contact address	Cor Beets Staatsbosbeheer Princenhof Park 1 PO Box 1300 3970 BH Driebergen The Netherlands
Telephone	+ 310 6926111
Fax	+ 310 6922978
Area	860ha
Classification	Raised bog
Designation	None
Date of featured works	1986
Management objectives	Rehabilitation of the peatland to enable growth of oligotrophic bog vegetation and hence reinitiate peat formation. Maintenance of areas of open water for their ornithological value.

6.12

Site Description

Engbertsdijksvenen is a remnant of a bog complex (original area c. 16 000ha) about 30km south-west of the once extensive Bourtangermoor peatland complex. It is now surrounded by fertile agricultural land reclaimed from peatland via a system of deep drainage which has a profound hydrological impact upon the site today. Although large, only 15ha of Engbertsdijksvenen remains

Figure 6.22   Engbertsdijksvenen has been cut-over for fuel and horticultural peat, large areas have also been used for buckwheat cultivation. (Stuart Brooks)

uncut (Figure 6.22). The remainder of the site has been cut-over – originally by traditional methods for fuel and, later, commercially for horticultural peat. Different mining concessions ceased at Engbertsdijksvenen between 1953 and 1983. In addition, before peat extraction, the whole of the site had been used for buckwheat cultivation (a common agricultural practice on such sites) and thus may have lost up to 1m of peat through burning.

The National Forestry Service (Staatsbosbeheer) purchased the semi-intact core of the site in the 1960s. Over subsequent years, the Staatsbosbeheer expanded their landholding to encompass the remaining peatland and some of the surrounding agricultural land. Until 1992, a sandy road and accompanying ditch ran across the site (east-to-west), hydrologically sealing the north and south sections of the bog; this division was removed when the road was bulldozed into the ditch and the new surface overlaid with a plastic liner followed by black peat (Figure 6.23). A number of cross-bunds were created at c. 50m intervals in order to create a series of pools and thus to minimise water loss from the adjacent peat. Prior to these works, agreement had to be reached with the rural community in order to channel the diverted agricultural water elsewhere.

Background to the Featured Technique

In the 1960s, the drains cutting the semi-intact core were blocked and infilled and the adjacent peat-cutting fields were flooded. Unfortunately, the remnant core stood too high above its surrounds for this flooding to drastically alter the hydrological gradient of the remnant. Accordingly, in the early 1990s, a circular bund was constructed around the core The bund was built from black peat into which 0.5mm-thick plastic sheeting was inserted. The top of the bund stood (after settling) level with the highest point of the 'core'. This bund has had a significant impact on the remnant core: after only a few years, the peat at the core edge had swollen, and today a *Sphagnum*-common cotton grass community exists adjacent to the bund (Figure 6.24).

The variety of extraction techniques used over the rest of the site had left a legacy of cutting fields

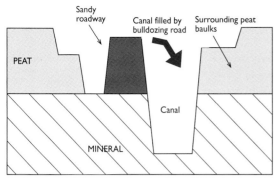

i) Road and canal prior to removal

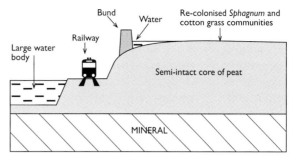

Figure 6.24 The bund around the semi-intact core.

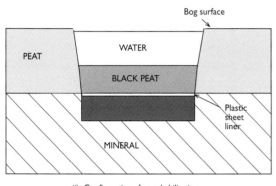

ii) Configuration after rehabilitation

Figure 6.23 The road and canal (i) prior to removal and (ii) after rehabilitation

with widely differing characteristics. The size and shape of these fields and the depth of peat remaining were recognised as crucial variables with respect to rehabilitation prospects. Bunding, incorporating sluices made from angled pipes, was used to inundate land.

Two different inundation strategies were tested:

- Deep inundation (i.e. > 0.5m) leading to permanent flooding to encourage colonisation by aquatic Sphagna (provided that wave action could be minimised). Drawing on previous Dutch studies, a maximum field diameter of 20m was adhered to and dried peat was thrown into the cuttings prior to flooding (forming floating mats onto which *Sphagnum* could later colonise).
- Shallow inundation, just sufficient to maintain the water level at the surface during the summer (c. 20 cm), enables Sphagna to colonise directly

onto the peat surface. The absence of significant wave action makes larger plot sizes viable.

To facilitate these extensive management measures, a railway line was built (Figure 6.24)

Approach

1,100m of bunds were constructed across the site. The bunds were built out of, and over, black peat (removing overlying white peat where necessary and possible). Where it was not possible to use black peat, white peat was used incorporating a plastic sheet (c. 2.5m deep) which was inserted into the constructed bund and then packed in with further peat. Right-angled pipes were built into each of the bunds in order to act as sluices and hence control impounded water levels (Figure 6.25).

6.12

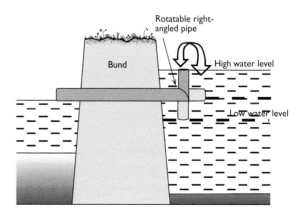

Figure 6.25 Rotatable right-angled pipe shines through a peat bund

Monitoring of Management Success

No systematic monitoring has taken place. However, in those areas which have been permanently flooded, floating mats of *S. cuspidatum* have replaced *S. recurvum* and purple moor grass. In contrast, due to the low humidity and high temperatures associated with seasonally bare peat, *Sphagnum* colonisation in the shallowly-inundated fields is often restricted to tussocks of dead purple moor grass or cotton grass.

Appraisal

Construction of the bunds cost c. 120 Dutch guilders (DG) per metre using Staatsbosbeheer labour. It is possible that further works will have to be carried out to elevate these bunds should the enclosed peat begin to swell. Although not a problem on this remote site, the basic angled pipe sluice is open to vandalism, and other site managers might be wise to incorporate some form of locking device to deter tampering.

For dams constructed from white peat, the plastic sheeting must be punctured in order to accommodate the angled pipe, and the resultant hole might act as a conduit for water. However, in fifteen years, few problems have ensued.

Wind impact (and hence wave action) on the permanently-flooded fields could be reduced by encouraging the growth of vascular species (for example, purple moor grass, cotton grass or birch) prior to flooding. This additional shelter might allow flooding of larger fields, hence reducing the number and length of bunds required (and enabling a reduced financial outlay). In contrast, in the shallowly-flooded fields, purple moor grass or birch might colonise during exceptionally dry summers (hence increasing evaporative losses and disfavouring *Sphagnum* colonisation).

Prior to management, certain peat fields had been cut down to the underlying sands. Despite bund construction, water initially failed to collect in these fields (where the sand acted as a plughole). However, after around eight years, organic matter began to collect over the sand, forming a less permeable layer and encouraging impoundment.

6.13 CORS CARON

Featured technique	Wooden plank sluices, compression bunds, automatic data loggers
Cross-references	5.1.3.3, 5.1.4, 4.3.3.4
Location	Dyfed, Wales, UK
GB Grid reference	SN 740775
Contact address	Site Manager CCW Minawel Ffair Rhos Ystrad Meurig Dyfed SY25 6BN
Telephone	01970 828551
Area	816ha
Classification	Raised bog
Designations	SSSI, NNR, NCR Grade 1, Ramsar site, pSAC
Date of featured works	1988 onwards
Management objectives	The main objective is to rewet the peat cuttings and reduce the hydraulic gradient between the centre and margins of the bog. The long-term aim is to reduce the cover of purple moor grass and encourage the spread of typical bog vegetation.

Site Description

Cors Caron comprises three raised bogs of which large areas remain uncut (Figure 6.26). On the cut-over areas, up to 4–5m of peat were extracted to leave a level surface surrounding the intact domes. Purple moor grass encroachment succeeding to willow carr is the predominant vegetation type in these areas. The intact areas of bog are affected indirectly through increased water loss from the artificially-steepened rand slopes. This loss has resulted in a transition from bog pool and hummock vegetation to a sward which is rich in ericaceous species.

Background to the Featured Technique

Management to reduce the impact of peat-cutting is a long-term initiative. The current areas of primary bog are of principal concern, and management is geared towards their conservation and long-term enhancement. Raising water levels within cut-over bog areas will have a dramatic effect in those compartments. There may also be a knock-on effect on the remaining intact areas of

Figure 6.26   Cors Caron contains three large areas of intact peatland. Water levels within these area have been intensively monitored since 1979 using R16 water level recorders (centre right). (Olivia Bragg)

bog. Raising surrounding water levels may, theoretically, cause the groundwater mound of the bog to rise also. To achieve this objective, a series of bunds were constructed enclosing the intact remnant.

Approach

Compression bunds

Since 1988, a total of 4,000m of pressure bund (*see* 5.1.4) and 300 peat dams (*see* 5.1.2.6) have been constructed on two of the three raised bogs. Peat is excavated using a Poclain Bogmaster excavator to create a finished bund 2–3m high, 5m wide at the base and 3m wide at the top (Figure 6.27). At least 1m of peat was left undisturbed at the bottom of the excavation. The use of black peat was not deemed necessary, as the weight of the bund

Figure 6.27   Constructing peat bunds on Cors Caron. (Margaret Cox)

compresses the underlying peat, providing an effectively waterproof seal. The cost of building pressure bunds as described, using a Poclain Bogmaster excavator, is around £5 per metre. Peat dams cost around £10 each.

Following the success of this trial bund, further sections of bund were constructed. A 600m embankment (£2,600) was built in 1990 to enclose 10.4ha around the south-east bog. This was extended by 1,000m in 1991 (£5,400). In 1992, the west side was sealed with a 200m section (£490) whilst, in the north, water was impounded with a 550m section. In 1993, a similar approach was followed for the north-eastern bog. These new bunds are constructed 7m wide at the base and 2m wide at the top, enabling access by an Argocat. Some problems were encountered: thick layers of peat ash (a result of steam engines sparking off fires) occurred within the profile and proved useless for construction purposes.

Wooden Plank Sluices

This type of sluice (*see* 5.1.3.3) was incorporated into the most recent bunds being installed prior to construction of the embankment. The sluice consists of 5 cm (2˝) stress-graded (no knots), treated planks. A rectangular framework constructed with galvanised bolts forms the main body of the sluice. The 'dam' is simply planks slotted on top of each other, on runners. The remainder of the frame acts as a spillway (Figure 6.28). The sluice is initially constructed out of the

6.13

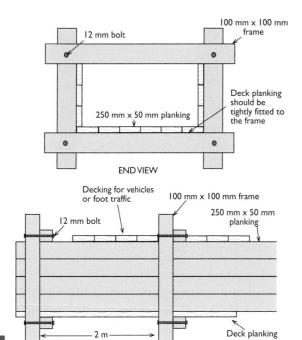

END VIEW

SIDE VIEW

All timber treated and all metal fittings galvanised – sluice can be made to any size required.

Figure 6.28   The design for the wooden plank sluice used at Cors Caron.

areas is monitored with R16 continuous water-level recorders (*see* 4.3.3.4) (since 1979) and lysimeters (*see* 4.3.5) (since 1986). Data is collected twice a month. Recently, the R16 chart recorder data has been digitised to allow for easier manipulation of the data.

Analysis of this data has shown water levels to remain constantly high (within 6–8 cm of the surface) in the flooded areas. Over the whole site, water levels rise rapidly in response to rainfall events and have then dropped increasingly gradually. This pattern is now consistent with a relatively healthy bog (*see* 2.5.3). Several practical problems have been encountered with the R16 chart recorders: for example, inaccurate clock speeds, which can result in inconsistent and/or non-useable data.

Appraisal

The compression bunds have proved successful in the flooded areas, raising water levels to a consistently high level throughout the year. The sluiced outlets provide control over the water levels, enabling consistently high levels to remain. There has been some purple moor grass and birch 'die-back', and recolonisation by bog bean is prolific. Monitoring is intensive, and the programme is currently under review. The data from the R16 chart recorders is particularly interesting given that the west bog is considered to be the most intact raised bog in Great Britain. Comparative water-level data is, therefore, immensely important for bog managers everywhere.

field, dismantled and reconstructed in the field. Due to the wet climate in mid-Wales, water levels rarely drop below the set spillway level.

Rewetting the Periphery

At Cors Caron, bunding of the cut-over bog areas is having a direct and dramatic effect in those compartments. Additionally, in conformance with the 'Groundwater Mound Theory' (Ingram, 1982 – *see* 2.5), rises in the surrounding water level should result in a rise of the whole groundwater mound including that within the remaining uncut core. This is, however, theoretical conjecture, and the bunding operations at Cors Caron were not planned to achieve this particular objective.

Monitoring of Management Success

Monitoring over the site has been relatively intense. Permanent vegetation quadrats (*see* 4.6.3) were installed in the flooded areas to record botanical changes. Hydrology on all the intact

6.14   KENDLMÜHLFILZEN

Featured technique	Recontouring milled fields, peat bunds; sowing and transplanting whole plants, *Sphagnum* transplanting.
Cross-references	5.1.4, 5.2
Location	Equidistant from Munich and Salzburg, 3km south of lake Chiemsee, Bavaria, Germany
German Grid reference	(4533 0000, 5296 0000)
Contact address	Prof. Dr J. Pfadenhauer Technische Universität München Lehrstuhl für Vegetationsökologie D-85350 Freising Germany

E-mail	pfladenha@pollux.edv.agrar.tu-muenchen.de
Telephone	+49 8161 713498
Area	900ha
Classification	Raised bog (component of the Chiemsee bog region- area c. 20km²)
Designation	None
Date of featured works	1985–6 (recontouring), 1986–7 (sowing and transplanting flowering plants), 1992 (*Sphagnum* transplanting, fertiliser experiments).
Management objectives	Maintain the water-table at, or just below, the surface throughout the year. Determine the success of vegetation establishment following different transplantation techniques.

Site Description

Kendlmühlfilzen has been under Bavarian State ownership since 1824. The tradition of domestic peat cutting was replaced by commercial block cutting around 1910, initially by hand and later using heavy excavating machines. To facilitate vehicular access, the area was drained and the water level lowered by 1.5–2m. In 1971, three 45ha plots were leased to a private extraction company, which adopted peat milling techniques until, in 1985, all mining activities ceased. Consequently, this site is now composed of a mosaic of conditions (Figure 6.29).

The percentage distribution of different habitat conditions across Kendlmühlfilzen is as follows:

Partly handcut	30%
Partly cut, totally drained	45%
Intact	20%
Commercially milled	5%

The 'intact' southern section of the bog (c. 2 km²) is the only bog in southern Germany to have a complex of surface patterning. Reference to historical records and photographs indicates that this patterning is wholly natural. In contrast, the northern, extracted section of the bog has experienced heavy drainage which occasionally cuts down to the underlying bedrock.

Surface Recontouring and Bund Construction

Background: Following cessation of peat extraction, the milled surface was only 0.5m deep, cut by drainage ditches, and sloped east-to-west by 0.3%. Before attempting to re-establish surface vegetation, works began to eliminate the slope, to reduce erosion, and retain rainwater and encouraging ponding (up to 5 cm depth).

Approach: In 1985, a modified Snowcat was used to level an experimental area of 30ha (Figure 6.30). Given their experience, the peat mining firm were contracted to carry out this work. The levelled fields were sectioned into polders and divided by low peat bunds (c. 30–40 cm high × 3m wide). Each bund contained a single overflow, set at 2–5 cm above surface level, and leading into a main ditch flowing off site. The area of individual polders was inversely proportional to

6.14

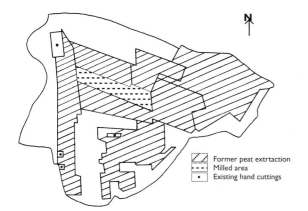

Figure 6.29 Habitat types found on Kendmühlfilzen. (Scale 1:58000)

Legend:
- Former peat extrraction
- Milled area
- Existing hand cuttings

Figure 6.30 Polders levelled and flooded for rehabilitation experiments at Kendmühlfilzen. (Lucy Parkyn)

the prevailing slope (avoiding large steps between adjacent levels) although average proportions were 100m × 50m.

Appraisal: Working the peat was hampered by relict tree trunks and by the plasticity of the peat (such that material was squeezed up within the adjacent polder by compaction of the bunds). The use of plant machinery already on site reduced the cost of the engineering works, although any works following rewetting of the peat relied upon slower, manual labour. At 1991 prices, the recontouring process cost £9,110 per hectare. In order for such a financial burden to be borne by the commercial developers, it would be advisable to incorporate such engineering works into the mitigation measures stipulated by planning authorities.

Such recontouring exercises have a negative impact upon the archive held within the peat stratigraphy.

6.14 Plant Reintroduction

Background: Initial experiments (1984–6) indicated that successful recolonisation by Sphagna hinges upon the presence of the correct microhabitat (*see* 5.2) rather than the re-introduction technique used. Accordingly, a project was devised to assess requirements for water level, water quality and the presence of a range of pioneer species.

Reintroduction of Flowering Plants

Approach: In order to accelerate the succession process, in 1986 and 1987, selected areas were planted up with key pioneer species (using both 'tillers' and seed).

Monitoring: The groundwater level (*see* 4.3.3) and nutrient dynamics (*see* 4.4) of the test areas were recorded and percentage vegetation cover estimated each year. Analysis of this data indicated that common and hare's tail cotton grass and *Carex rostrata* were the most responsive to such introductions. In 1994, an experiment began to assess the impact of phosphorus and/or potassium fertiliser upon the growth of these three species. Fertiliser application (Osmocote 3-4) improved the growth of common cotton grass and *C. rostrata* but not that of hare's tail cotton grass (Figure 6.31).

Figure 6.31 Vegetation recolonisation experiments - comparing the efficacy of fertiliser application on the growth of common and hares tail cottongrass and *Carex rostrata*, Kendmühlfilzen. (Stuart Brooks)

Reintroduction of Sphagna

Background: By 1992, no Sphagna had established among the vegetation. Transplants of *Sphagnum* were used to assess whether, and under which conditions, *Sphagnum* cover can be initiated or accelerated.

Approach: Within each plot (of the different flowering plants), sods of *Sphagnum* (*S. cuspidatum*, *magellanicum* and *capillifolium*) were planted at 50 cm intervals along 5m transects. The sods were inserted into 20–25 cm-deep holes (core sampler with 12 cm diameter used).

Monitoring: From 1992–5, the plots were monitored twice yearly assessing *Sphagnum* growth, ambient shade and soil moisture. Stable ombrotrophic conditions and a good cover of flowering plants gave the best results. It appears that a key role of the pioneer plants is to provide a physical support to encourage vertical development of the mosses.

Appraisal

Planting with vascular plants and *Sphagnum* sods costs about £100 per 100m² although the cost could rise if there are no suitable local supplies of *Sphagnum* and plants. This project emphasises that detailed survey, long-term planning and considerable financial resources are required to encourage vegetation back onto milled fields.

6.15   BARGERVEEN

Featured technique	Peat bunds
Cross-references	5.1.4
Location	Approximately 60km south of Groningen, South-East Drenthe, on the Dutch-German border, the Netherlands
Contact address	Jan Streefkerk Staatsbosbeheer Drenthe-Zuid PO Box 1300 3970 BH Driebergen The Netherlands
Telephone	+ 31 34 04 26 358
Area	2,000ha
Classification	Raised bog
Management objectives	To halt progressive desiccation of the intact core of the site and to reinitiate growth of acidic vegetation across areas of relict peat extraction.

Site Description

Straddling the Dutch–German border, Bargerveen is a remnant of the once vast Bourtangermoor. It is the best remaining example of raised bog in the Netherlands. The whole site has been used for potato and buckwheat cultivation, whilst various sections of the bog have also been cut for fuel since the seventeenth century. Birch is uncommon – a characteristic attributed to historical clearance by local people (perhaps for firewood).

Background to the Featured Technique

The site subdivides into three sections: Meerstalblok, Amsterdamscheveld and Schoonbekerveld. The former is a 66ha core of uncut bog which, until the 1960s, included a large pool system at its centre. Drainage on and around the Meerstalblok gradually dried these pools. The Schoonbekerveld is characterised by baulks and hollows of relict block-cutting, whilst peat milling has been practised across the fields of the Amsterdamscheveld (stopped in 1995).

In 1968, the State Forest Service (Staatsbosbeheer) purchased the Meerstalblok and its surrounds. Since then, their land purchase has extended out across the rest of the bog. More recently, surrounding land has also been purchased, forming a 1–2km buffer strip with a view to raising water levels (to decrease the hydraulic gradient between the bog and surrounding land). This scheme has large financial implications as it involves the diversion of both a public road and a canal.

Staatsbosbeheer's prime motive for initiating management works on Bargerveen was to conserve the central, uncut block by rewetting. Despite removing scrub, to decrease surface evaporation, and blocking all of the 7m, spaced buckwheat drains across the Meerstalblok, the hydraulic gradient down to the surrounding cuttings (and reclaimed land) continued to drain the core, so it was decided to flood these adjacent cuttings to raise the ground-water level.

The construction of a bund (*see* 5.1.4) around the adjacent cut-over fields (Figure 6.32) had the secondary impact of providing the opportunity for the regeneration of acidic vegetation within these newly-flooded cuttings. In order to enhance this, low peat walls were built to divide the cuttings into polders (each of which retained water at a depth of c. 1m). It later became apparent that, despite water impoundment, the hydrological gradient off the Meerstalblok was still too great, and an additional bund was constructed directly encircling the intact cupola.

A further, less intensive, bunding strategy is being implemented across the old milling fields of Amsterdamscheveld. It is intended to encourage *Sphagnum* recolonisation into the water impounded within these blocks.

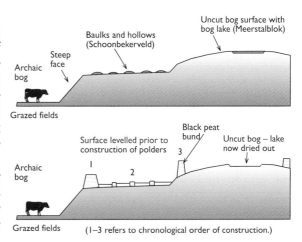

Figure 6.32   A schematic summary of bunding operations at the Bargerveen.

Approach

Where possible, the bunds were constructed from black peat keyed into black peat. Prior to construction, the existing vegetated layer was removed (being retained and replaced on top of the finished bund) and any overlying white peat was stripped away. The 5m-wide bunds were machine-built; the digger moved parallel to the bund using its bucket to compress the piled peat (and hence decrease its permeability). Where black peat was not readily available, bunds were built from white peat but incorporated plastic sheeting. Prior to such works, the white peat was left to dry for six to seven weeks in order to reduce its water content by 70–90%. Overflow pipes were incorporated into all of the bunds to protect them from the erosive pressure of overtopping.

Monitoring of Management Success

Monthly water table measurements are taken, whilst indicator species are recorded (using a DOMIN scale) on a rotational basis, once a year.

Appraisal

Meerstalblok: Construction of the bund around the core does appear to have halted desiccation of the cupola.

Schoonbekerveld: Although not their prime objective, the early bunds also initiated rehabilitation within the relict block cuttings. Aquatic Sphagna (for example, *S. cuspidatum*) have invaded the bunded pools colonising among tussocks of dead purple moor grass or onto floating mats of unconsolidated peat which have risen to the water's surface. Many floating mats are now around ten years old and show a succession from *S. cuspidatum* to *S. recurvum* (and on some of the drier mats, even purple moor grass or small birch). No hummock-building Sphagna (for example, *S. magellanicum*, *S. papillosum*) have yet established. Three theories have been proposed to explain this anomaly:

- Beyond a certain thickness, the mats become prone to summer grounding and hence greatly fluctuating water levels – this could be temporarily overcome by raising the bunds (and hence the impounded water levels). However,

such a course of action would simply perpetuate the situation – the mats must eventually be grounded to enable *Sphagnum* to spread out over the bog surface. Hence, the only long-term solution might be for the mats to have sufficient 'water storage capacity' to withstand these summer droughts – for this, a thickness of >1m has been postulated. However, it may transpire that such mats are inherently incapable of such water control and as such are not a valid means by which to rehabilitate bog surfaces.

- *S. cuspidatum* and *S. recurvum* are both capable of growing in mesotrophic conditions. The water chemistry of the Bargerveen pools (pH – 4.0; conductivity – 90–120 mS cm^{-2}) suggests a degree of nutrient enrichment (*see* 4.4); it may be that the chemistry of the water is unsuitable for other Sphagna.

- There may be no source from which these Sphagna can spread. Active introduction measures might be necessary.

Amsterdamscheveld: The effectiveness of water impoundment across the old milled fields has not yet been evaluated.

6.16   RAHEENMORE

Featured technique	Peat and plastic bunds
Cross-references	5.1.4.3
Location	County Offaly, Republic of Ireland
Irish Grid reference	N 4432
Contact address	National Parks and Wildlife Service The Office of Public Works (OPW) 51 St Stephen's Green Dublin 2 Republic of Ireland.
Telephone	+ 353 1 661 3111
Area	213ha
Classification	Raised bog
Date of featured works	1994
Management objectives	Halt the natural degradation of the site which is occurring as a result of historical drainage and peripheral peat-cutting.

Site Description

Raheenmore is still largely intact, although marginal peat-cutting and drainage ditches, cut between 1950 and 1970, have caused some degradation. The site still exhibits a well-developed carpet and hummock microtopography with the full range of *Sphagnum* species associated with Irish raised bogs (*Sphagnum fuscum* and *S. imbricatum* for example). However, pools have now dried out and an extensive system of arterial drainage works at the edge of the site has caused further degradation.

Background to Management Works

In 1989, a joint Irish–Dutch project into the ecology, hydrology and geology of Raheenmore concluded that – despite initial impressions – the bog vegetation over 50% of the site was dead or dying. This decline was attributed to subsidence at the margins (and consequent increased drainage) resulting from peripheral peat-cutting. The research team advised that, although the bog would naturally slump to fit a new ground-water mound (*see* 2.5.3), the remnant bog vegetation would perish before this process was complete. Hence, it was decided to raise the water level artificially in an attempt to re-swell the peat and restore the original gradient off the bog. The works at Raheenmore were regarded as an empirical test of an approach which, if successful, could be more widely applied.

Approach

An experimental area was selected which encompassed 4ha of cut-over, and 4.5ha of high uncut bog and whose vegetation communities ranged from dry (purple moor grass-gorse) through to a wet (*Sphagnum magellanicum*) vegetation communities.

Eight concentric bunds were constructed following the surface contours, moving progressively away from the centre of the bog, with the final bund standing off the bog. The distance between each bund was calculated to terrace the water level (and subsequently the peat surfaces) to produce a gradient of less than 30 cm per 100m. The precise location of each bund was then tailored to the surface topography. In an effort to avoid subsidence and/or slippage of the bunds, construction was preceded by core analysis (taken every 25m) to assess bulk density and stratigraphy of underlying peats (*see* 4.5.5.5,

4.5.5.7). Where possible, bunds were not built above uncompacted (low-density) peat nor where *S. cuspidatum* layers occurred within 4m of the surface.

The five bunds which were constructed on the intact dome were built from lighter, poorly-humified peat to avoid sinkage. Each of these bunds was keyed into fresh peat and built to stand 50 cm proud of the required water level (assuming 20 cm settling) with the walls sloping at 45°. Three of these five bunds had a sheet of polythene film incorporated into their design; the plastic was imbedded in a 1m-deep trench (excavated by a Difco), a surplus length concertinaed at the surface and the leading edge attached to a horizontal pole which should rise in line with any peat swelling.

The outer bunds were built on cut-over peat (Figure 6.33). These peripheral bunds were constructed of strongly-humified black peat and were again keyed into freshly-exposed wet peat. Significant subsidence was deemed unlikely given the increased stability of underlying ground, and these bunds were built to stand only 35 cm proud of the required water level. Different angles of slope were tested for each of these 'off-bog' bunds (2:1 and 4:1).

Twenty-one spillways were incorporated into each of the eight bunds in order to avoid erosion by overtopping. Finally each structure was faced

6.16

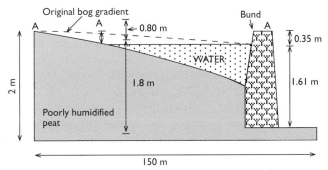

Dam height is calculated:
The sum of the height of the water level (1.61 m) inside the dam and the extra height required above the water level (0.35 m). The dam height at the facebank is then 1.96 m above the surface of the cut away.

Figure 6.33 Determination of water levels and dam height for bunds of poorly humified peat at Raheenmore.

with poorly decomposed moss peat to encourage recolonisation and prevent erosion.

Monitoring of Management Success

During their first winter, the bunds were examined for signs of erosion, subsidence or side seepage and any necessary repairs were made (N.B. the works contract was drawn up to incorporate a second phase of remedial works). For three years following management, it is intended to make fortnightly data collections. In order to monitor for adverse trends, the collected data will be analysed monthly throughout the first year.

The hydrology of the site is recorded via two automatic ground-water recorders (*see* 4.3.3.4), an automatic rain gauge (*see* 4.3.2) and dipwells (*see* 4.3.3.2) sunk into the peat on the inner side of each dam. A transect of peat anchors (*see* 4.5.3) and piezometers (*see* 4.3.4.3) runs perpendicular to the concentric bunding, enabling analysis of any swelling and consistency changes to the peat. The physical disturbance associated with the management works was felt to diminish the value of a transect for vegetation quadrats; instead, a series of 10 x 10m² relevées (with associated dipwells) will be recorded to assess vegetation change.

Appraisal

Raheenmore is still in relatively good condition, and this project was devised to forestall predicted vegetation degradation resulting from drainage damage.

The project relied upon a high level of research work, with the total cost of the works (including initial survey, planning, construction and foreseen maintenance) being approximately £100,000. The cost-effectiveness of this financial investment was maximised by the empirical nature of the project; preceding survey and post-works monitoring should enhance the more widespread applicability of the tested methods.

Should the peat swell as intended and the bog surface attain the required gradient, the 'natural run-off' might be impeded by any bunding remaining proud of the surface, and the site might benefit from the subsequent removal of these sections.

6.17   ABERNETHY FOREST

Featured technique	Infilling of drainage ditches
Cross-reference	5.1.5
Location	North-east of Aviemore, Scotland, UK
GB Grid reference	NJ 0213
Contact address	Site Manager Abernethy Forest Reserves RSPB Forest Lodge Nethybridge Inverness PH25 3EF
Telephone	01479 821409
Area	Reserve area 12,795ha, SSSI area 5,800ha
Classification	Blanket bog (valley mires)
Designations	SSSI, NCR (II) – Valley mires, NNR, SPA, RSPB Reserve, pSAC
Date of featured works	1981 onwards
Management objectives	Rehabilitation of valley mires through raising the water table in areas previously subjected to ploughing in preparation for afforestation.

Site Description

Abernethy forest SSSI encompasses a wide range of habitat types. Of most conservation interest are upland Arctic heaths, Caledonian pine forest and valley mires. However, many of the valley mires were recently drained in preparation for commercial forestry. The RSPB have now gained the management control over a large area of the forest through a series of land purchases. This enables the future management of the area to be sympathetic to its high conservation interest. Such management has been partly financed through woodland grant schemes and partly from the sale of smaller stock as Christmas trees. The revenue from the Christmas tree sales enabled the trees to be removed via a helicopter, hence reducing disturbance and damage to the bog surface.

Background to the featured technique

An extensive drainage network has contributed to a progressive decrease of typical bog species over the mire surfaces in response to a lowered water-table. The species lost are being replaced by heath. Without active management, continued water loss through the drainage system would result in the degradation of the conservation interest of the mire.

Approach

Forestry drains were blocked using Hymac diggers operated by skilled contract workers. The Hymacs were deemed appropriate machines due to their ability to work in very wet conditions. At Abernethy, they were used to excavate the original drainage channels.

Forestry drains were initially blocked with peat plugs (Figure 6.34). The peat was taken from borrow pits either adjacent to, or inside, the ditch. Prior to constructing the plug, all vegetation and dry humified peat was removed, leaving only wet peat to be placed upon wet peat. As it was built, the plug was progressively compacted to ensure

a watertight barrier. This method has been successful where the water-table is relatively high. In areas where the water-table is lower, leakage may occur when the peat plug dries and cracks to expose lines of weakness. Work has only been carried out on drainage channels thus far, leaving the plough lines unmanaged and active.

An alternative approach was taken in 1995 on a parcel of land which had been intensively drained in 1981. The plough ridges were bulldozed back into the channels to completely destroy the drainage network. In this drier area, the peat was pushed into the channels by a Hymac excavator. The peat was then tamped down with the machine's bucket to compress the material and reduce any lines of weakness through which water could flow (Figure 6.35).

6.17

Figure 6.34 Forestry ditches blocked by peat plugs, Abernethy. (Lucy Parkyn)

Figure 6.35 Forestry ditches have been infilled with peat to leave little trace of the original drainage channel, Abernethy. (Lucy Parkyn)

Monitoring of Management Technique

Presently, monitoring of the area is experimental and comprises field assessments (*see* 4.1) and air photograph interpretation (*see* 4.6.4) of the area before and after management work.

Evaluation

The complete infilling of the drainage network was undertaken in January 1995. Reports indicate that, by May, ling heather in the area had become senescent and the ground appeared much wetter. However, it is too early to comment on the overall success of the scheme. Complete infilling of ditches has several advantages over the peat plug method. It ensures that furrow lines, which act as effective drains, are also dealt with and it reduces the problem of communicating complicated instructions on dam construction to operators of varied skill.

6.18 ROTHENTHURM

Featured technique	Infilling drains
Cross-references	5.1.5
Location	Biber valley, between the Lakes of Lucerne and Zurich, Switzerland
Swiss Grid Reference	695 500, 223 400
Contact Aaddress	Andreas Grünig Advisory Service for Mire Conservation Swiss Federal Institute for Forestry Snow and Landscape Research CH-8903 Birmensdorf Switzerland
Telephone	+ 41 1739 2309
Fax	+ 41 1737 4080
E-mail	andreas.grunig@wsl.ch
Area	420ha
Classification	Blanket and raised bog
Designations	Mire and Mire Landscape of National Importance
Date of featured works	1992
Management objectives	Halt the artificial drainage of water off the site.

Site Description

The site has an uneven surface due to extensive peat cutting and evidence remains of small-scale horticultural activity (abandoned lazy beds). Harvesting of purple moor grass litter from the

site (past and present) has destroyed the natural microtopography and encouraged a predominance of sedges (*Carex nigra* and *C. rostrata*) within the sward. The impact of such harvesting is clearly visible when comparing managed areas with those which have not been mown for twenty years (Figures 6.36, 6.37)

Rothenthurm is a politically important site, considered to be a flagship for Swiss mire conservation. In 1983, the site was proposed for development as a military training ground. Following opposition by WWF, Switzerland, a document advocating the protection of all mire sites and known as the 'Rothenthurm Initiative' was submitted to the constitution. In 1987, the Initiative was passed by referendum, leading to an amendment to the Swiss Federal Constitution. According to the resulting *Inventory of Raised and*

Figure 6.36   The mown area at Rothenthurm, Switzerland. (Rob Stoneman)

Figure 6.37   An area left unmown for twenty years at Rothenthurm, Switzerland. (Rob Stoneman)

Transitional Bogs of National Importance, this 'mire landscape' is the largest surface of contiguous raised bog and fen vegetation within Switzerland.

Background to the Featured Technique

In the past, numerous narrow open drains were installed running parallel to the contour lines, to improve drainage at the site (and hence increase purple moor grass production for litter grazing). As the slope of the bog exceeds 2%, it was considered that dams were not appropriate, and that instead the drains should be completely infilled with peat.

Approach

Prior to infilling, the drains were opened up and any detritus removed. Wet peat was dug from an adjacent area. Peat was transported by a wheelbarrow to the ditch lines and the clean channels were infilled and compacted by hand. The infilled ditches were then topped with vegetated sods (in order to prevent erosion of the infilled peat and to encourage regeneration) (Figure 6.38).

Appraisal

Infilling by hand limits damage to the mire surface. However, this work was relatively labour-intensive, taking fifteen people one week to infill a 100m length of ditch. The works were carried out by a voluntary labour force. Permanent plots and a visual assessment both indicate that the

Figure 6.38 A ditch-line infilled with peat at Rothenthurm, Switzerland. (Rob Stoneman)

infilling has been successful – with ling heather decreasing and *Sphagnum* increasing along the drain lines. However, purple moor grass also appears to be increasing along the ditch lines; presumably this indicates that the drains still form lines of weakness for water flow. The source of peat for such infilling can prove problematic, and the hydrological impact of on-site extraction warrants careful assessment and if necessary post-extraction monitoring.

6.19   THE HUMBERHEAD PEATLANDS

Featured technique	Flooding and pumping
Cross-references	5.16, 5.3.3.4
Location	10km north-east of Doncaster, South Yorkshire, England, UK
GB Grid Reference	SE 730160
Contact address	Site Manager English Nature Don Farm Moor Road Crowle Scunthorpe DN17 4EZ
Telephone	01724 710595
Area	1,919ha
Classification	Raised bog (cut-over)
Designations	SSSI, NNR (1,174ha and expanding)
Date of featured works	1992
Management objectives	To encourage the development of raised bog vegetation in old peat workings by preventing water loss through drainage.

6.19

Site Description

Thorne, Goole and Crowle Moors, together with Hatfield Moors, are the remnants of a formerly more extensive area of wetland which occupied the flood plain of the Humberhead Levels several thousand years ago. They are the largest complex of lowland raised bog in Britain, covering an area of 3,318ha (Figure 6.39). A large area of abandoned peat workings are managed as a National Nature Reserve by English Nature. Parts of Crowle Moor are owned and managed by the Lincolnshire Trust for Nature Conservation.

Peat has been taken from the Moors for hundreds of years, firstly for domestic fuel, then as horse and cattle litter and currently for the

Figure 6.39 An aerial view of the Humberhead Peatlands showing the rewetted peat cuttings. (Peter Rowarth)

6.19

horticultural industry. This long history of use has given the Moors a chequerboard appearance of canals, peat fields, cuttings and baulks alongside the massive peat-milling fields. In some abandoned peat-cuttings, bog vegetation has returned alongside bracken, heather and birch on drier baulks. Areas of *Sphagnum* occur in the shallow canals. Old tramways are built up of lime-rich ballast and now support base-rich communities. The varied habitat of the Moors also supports a huge number of different invertebrates – over 3,000 species have been recorded.

The Moors are important for their breeding and wintering bird populations, for which regular surveys are carried out. This is particularly the case for the nightjar, whose numbers at Thorne exceed 1% of Britain's breeding population. Particular attention has been paid to monitoring breeding birds on the cut-over bog.

Background to the Featured Technique

Originally, English Nature controlled only 4% of the site as an NNR, and peat extraction on surrounding areas was significantly damaging the interests of the NNR. A nationally-negotiated agreement with Levingtons Horticulture (1992), signed in 1994, transferred all freehold peatland to English Nature on condition that a lease-back arrangement be upheld under which the company

could continue extraction where it was currently occurring. All sites would be left with a minimum 0.5m peat to allow restoration work. In total, 3,250ha of peatland has been transferred to English Nature of which 800ha, at Thorne, is available for immediate conservation management. Rehabilitation plans were quickly formulated.

Approach

A contract was let to install large peat dams (*see* 5.1.2.6) at the outlets from all main ditches and at 50m intervals along each ditch. This operation was then followed by the damming of minor drains and channels. In total, 2,000 peat dams have been installed.

This work was carried out by Levingtons Horticulture, who competitively tendered for the contract given their access to the necessary equipment and expertise. A specialised Hymac (type 14) was used with a modified chassis to support 1.2m-wide tracks, giving a working ground pressure of 1.5 pounds per square inch (psi). On the Humberhead Peatlands, there is not sufficient depth of peat to warrant the use of 'bog mats'. Costs came to about £25 per hour inclusive of driver.

Overflow pipes were installed to prevent overtopping and possible erosion. Peat dams were cheaper in comparison with the interlocking steel sheet pile dams which had to be used to flood the large boundary drains. The latter are driven into the substrate and require experienced labour to install. Even using second-hand materials, a single 4m-wide dam can cost as much as £2,000.

A dry period prior to 1992 had a very serious effect on the site, and so a pump was purchased to move water into the dammed area from the new cuttings to the south. This was first used to top up Old Mill Drain and then to wet the 1980s workings on Middle Moor East (Figure 6.40). The pump, a GPM100 Univac, purchased from Andrew Sykes Ltd, is powered by two diesel engines and was chosen for its robustness and ability to pump either clear or heavily-silted water. The pumping rate varies with the distance over which pumping is to take place (from 400 gallons/minute to 100 gallons/minute over 600m).

Figure 6.40 Pumping water into flooded areas on Thorne Moors. (Peter Rowarth)

Between July 1992 and August 1994, 22.9 million gallons of water were pumped over a maximum distance of 600m.

Costs were: GPM100 pump (two years old) – £4,500, 6,000 × 100mm suction pipe – £100, strainer for suction pipe – £40, 6,000 × 100mm delivery pipe – £40. The pump consumes an average of twenty litres of diesel every twelve hours.

Monitoring of Management Success

Dipwells (£5 prepared, £3 plain) coupled with a raingauge are used to monitor the water-table and help relate its height to precipitation (*see* 4.3). The site undergoes regular observation and study by the site manager and others (*see* 4.1) and is a popular location for local study and academic research.

Appraisal

Rapid rewetting is having a detrimental effect on birch, bracken and heather. The lower areas, which now remain wet all year round, are recolonising with cotton grasses and *Sphagnum fimbriatum*, *Sphagnum recurvum* and *Sphagnum cuspidatum*. Repairing severe catotelmic damage is a comparatively expensive and pioneering task. It is really too early to determine the effects of flooding and pumping, although preliminary observations are promising.

6.20 PEATLANDS PARK

Featured technique	Infilling (to recontour baulk and hollow), boardwalk and terram matting.
Cross-references	5.1.5, 5.6.3, 5.6.5
Location	South of Lough Neagh (just off the M1), Co. Armagh, Northern Ireland
Irish Grid reference	H900 610
Contact address	Site Warden Peatlands Park Environment Service – DoE Northern Ireland 33 Derryhubbert Road Dungannon Co. Tyrone Northern Ireland BT71 6NW
Telephone	01762 851102
Area	180ha (within a 263ha park)
Classification	Inter-drumlin raised bog
Designations	Two NNRs within the site: Annagariff (fen woodland) and Mullenakill (bog).
Date of featured works	Recontouring – 1984/85. Access provision – gravel paths: 1980; boardwalks and woodchip paths: 1986 (ongoing).
Management objectives	The main management priorities for this site are: conservation, education (specifically school-age) and recreation.

6.20

Site Description

Peatlands Park is one of a series of habitat-based country parks developed by the DoE (NI) in order to encourage access to the countryside within the province. The site is no further than fifty miles from any part of the province and is readily accessible by road.

Prior to 1900, the site was owned by a large estate and was used primarily for hunting. However, between 1900 and 1960, 140ha of the site was cut commercially by 200 men. Up to 3m of peat was removed. Consequently, when the site was purchased by the DoE, few areas of intact peat remained and the depth of peat ranged from 8–11m across the site.

An information centre (and shop) have been constructed on the site and in 1993 a customised education centre was opened. The narrow-gauge railway originally installed by the peat-extractors

Figure 6.41 A group being shown around Peatlands Park. The path is constructed by overlaying woodchips over a geotextile base. (Lucy Parkyn)

6.20

has since been restored to provide a 2.5km tour through bog and open woodland. A series of recommended routes are indicated by on-site waymarking posts, and guided tours are available (Figure 6.41). The channelling of resources into static signage has been limited to three interpretation boards. Cut-over sites are more robust than intact sites and can support large visitor numbers and the original target of 20,000 visitors per year is now exceeded by c. 100,000 per year.

The routine management programme includes scrub control (*see* 5.3). The cut stumps of rhododendron are either treated (with glyphosate) or upturned and removed, and the brash is burnt on tin sheets. Colonising birch are also cut and the timber removed, although no chemical treatment has been used to date. Heather is periodically cut using a field topper dragged by a low-ground-pressure bulldozer. An exotic invasive pitcher plant (*Sarracennia purpurea*) has been systematically removed from the site, and is now restricted to a showcase bog garden.

The majority of the 25 cm wide drains, which cut the site when purchased, have now been blocked by peat dams inserted by a low-ground-pressure bulldozer. Five fire-ponds have also been excavated at the edges of the peatland.

Baulk and Hollow Levelling

The remnant baulks and hollows were levelled in an attempt to bring the surface down to the water level and hence reinitiate the growth of peat-forming vegetation across the site (Figure 6.42).

Approach: A bulldozer was used to push the remnant baulks into the drains, effectively levelling the worked surface and blocking the ditches in one operation (ditches containing *S. cuspidatum* were left to act as refugia for the moss). This levelling technique was first tested on a 4ha block in 1984 before being extending in 1985 to cover c. 32ha of the main area of old commercial workings.

After four years, waterlevels in the test area had only increased on a localised basis (both spatially and temporally), and in 1988/89 a peat bund was constructed around the eastern edge. This bund resulted in a wide, 3 cm-deep pool, the water pressure from which eventually caused the bund to bow outwards. In January 1992, the ponded water disappeared overnight; as there was no evidence of downstream flooding, it has been postulated that the water flowed down into the peat mass. Ponding in subsequent years has been restricted to major rainfall events.

Monitoring: Permanent quadrats (*see* 4.6.3) were installed and surveyed in 1985; however, the survey has not yet been repeated. The need for resurvey has been emphasised in the site management plan.

Appraisal: Two months were required to level the main 32ha section. The water level has subsequently risen by 1–1.5m and is now at or near the surface of over 20% of the area for most of the year. *S. cuspidatum* appears to be spreading out from the remaining ditches and over hare's

Figure 6.42 Recontoured baulk and hollows at Peatlands Park, N. Ireland. (Rob Stoneman)

tail cotton grass hummocks. Small peat dams have since been constructed to hold water on the area. Within smaller fields, the majority of recolonisation occurred four to five years after the works (i.e. 1990/91). *S. cuspidatum* spread across ponded water to form floating carpets, and, despite wave action on the open water, *Sphagnum* coverage increased from <1% to >75%. The 1992 leak caused the *Sphagnum* carpet to drop to the peat surface where it continued to grow (cf. 6.15). Other species (for example, *S. magellanicum*, *S. papillosum*) are now beginning to colonise the more stable areas.

Provision of Access

Given the high visitor numbers, it was found that mown pathways were rapidly destroyed by trampling. Walkways which catered for constant use, casual footwear and wheelchair access were required. A system of woodchip and gravel paths was complemented by boardwalks (*see* Figure 6.41) (*see* 5.6.5).

Approach: Following experimentation with different wood sources, softwoods were rejected for chipping and rhododendron (cut and processed on site) was selected. A layer of semi-permeable sheeting (Terram – 4m-wide rolls) was placed between the ground and the chippings in order to stop the path from sinking into the peat. Given that the sub-surface woodchips remain damp, these pathways serve a secondary role as a firebreak during slow, winter fires. On arterial routes, the matting was laid over brash before being covered by up to 45 cm of gravel. This configuration can carry vehicles weighing up to four tonnes (*see* 5.6.7).

Two designs of floating boardwalk have been used at Peatlands Park (Figure 6.43). The boardwalks were constructed from tanalised wood which was stockpiled for several years to remove leachates. Movement of the second boardwalk design on drier areas was overcome by manually packing with peat.

Appraisal: There are currently c. $1\frac{1}{2}$ km of boardwalk, 4km of woodchip pathway and 10km of gravel pathway across the Peatlands Park site. Access provision is ongoing, being expanded on an annual basis. Construction of woodchip paths,

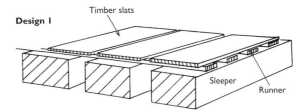

Design 1

Timber slats

Sleeper

Runner

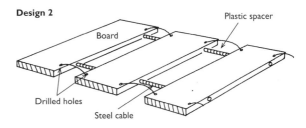

Design 2

Board

Plastic spacer

Drilled holes

Steel cable

Figure 6.43   Designs for two types of boardwalk used at Peatlands Park.

using an industrial chipper to process materials on site, costs c. £1.50m^{-2} (excluding labour) and is an efficient use for cleared scrub. The boardwalk design uses sleepers left on site after the commercial workings. Boardwalk costs were about £6 per metre.

6.21   FLANDERS MOSS WILDLIFE RESERVE

Featured technique	Hand-pulling/felling scrub; disposal of scrub
Cross-references	5.3.2.1, 5.3.2.3, 5.3.5
Location	16km west of Stirling, Scotland, UK
GB Grid reference	NS 636922
Contact address	Reserve Warden Scottish Wildlife Trust Cramond House Kirk Cramond Edinburgh EH4 6NS
Telephone	0131 312 7765
Area	732.5ha
Classification	Raised bog
Designations	SWT Reserve 45ha; SSSI, NNR, pSAC, pSPA, GCR site
Date of featured works	1987 onwards
Management objectives	To maintain and enhance the lowland raised mire habitat with particular regard to its hydrology and physical integrity.

Site Description

Though Flanders Moss is large, it represents a small part of a once extensive series of raised peat bogs which occupies the Carse of Stirling west of the Menteith Moraine. From 1767, many of these were reclaimed for agriculture, the peat was dug out and sods floated away down the Forth. Flanders managed to survive largely uncut, as it was used to impound water in reservoirs to assist in the clearance of the altitudinally lower Poldar Moss (Cadell, 1913).

The site provides some of the most detailed geomorphological/stratigraphical evidence in Scotland for the Loch Lomond Glaciation and the Late Glacial and Early Flandrian changes in sea level hence its GCR status. Francis Rose showed Flanders Moss to be an important site for *Cladonia* lichen species, and it is famous as a location for the rare northern acidophilous plant, *Ledum groenlandicum*. The Moss is a favourite site for overwintering pink-footed geese and hen harrier.

Background to Featured Technique

Bannister (1978) showed that birch woodland was actively colonising the site and stated that this was a threat to more ecologically important areas of mire to the south and west. Tree-removal, therefore, forms a major element of the management strategy at this site.

Approach

Firstly, drains were dammed in an attempt to tackle hydrological problems.

An area of the Moss was targeted and subdivided into a grid to organise scrub removal. Smaller seedlings were removed by hand and carried off site in fertiliser sacks (*see* 5.3.2.1). Larger saplings were not pulled because of disruption to the mire surface and because it was simply not feasible; instead these were felled with bow saws (*see* 5.3.2.2). Disposal of brash presented a problem. Removal by dragging trees off site was tried and considered undesirable due to physical damage to the bog surface and the potential for seed dispersal (*see* 5.3.5.5). This situation was improved by placing logs and brashings on large polythene sheets for dragging; however,

trampling damage remained a problem. Carrying and dragging trees is a feasible method of removal at the bog margins, but the distances involved at a site like Flanders make it unrealistic to consider manual removal for more central areas.

Burning brash on site was attempted. This involved constructing a burning bin from scrap materials (*see* 5.3.5.3). This was an effective method of disposal (*see* 6.22), although the original bin, which was constructed from scrap metal, has since been replaced with a better bin made from new sheets.

In October 1993, a helicopter was used to remove previously cut scrub from more remote areas of the bog (Figure 6.44) (*see* 5.3.5.6). It was a pioneering experiment, and many problems were encountered. Christmas-tree nets were borrowed from the Forestry Commission, and eighty volunteers packed 75–80 nets in one day. The nets did not have enough attachment points, and another twenty person-days were spent providing these (two were missed out and could not be used on the day). Poor advice from the helicopter company meant that the first helicopter brought

Figure 6.44   Helicopter lifting off scrub from Flanders Moss, Scotland. (N Wilcox)

6.21

in was too small to lift the weight of the nets, and so a larger 'Lama' was used, costing £535 per hour.

The helicopter has a fixed and a remote hook to allow the nets to be released over a drop site. The net loops were too small to allow attachment to the hooks, and so they were threaded onto a strop which was itself attached to the hooks. This allowed two nets at a time to be lifted, though the strops had to be removed manually from the helicopter which added time to the operation. The helicopter operated between two ground crews to ensure continuous lifting, and the whole operation took 1 hour 55 minutes or $1\frac{1}{2}$ minutes per net (including a refuelling stop).

Monitoring of Management Success

Some photographs exist from the period before scrub removal began in earnest and these have now been expanded to a full photographic monitoring programme which began in 1991 (*see* 4.1.3). All monitoring is based on the management grid system.

Hydrological monitoring equipment (four WaLRaGs, eighteen dipwells, ten piezometer nests – *see* 4.3.3.3, 4.3.3.2, 4.3.4.3) is recorded once a month. Seven permanent belt transects (*see* 4.6.3) have been set up at key points. The transects are recorded every six months for three years. The situation will then be reviewed based on an analysis of the dataset. Research has also been carried out to shed light on the cause of the scrub problem (Keleman, 1996). This is highly relevant to the future management of the site.

Appraisal

Since 1990, considerable effort has been put in to clear Flanders Moss Wildlife Reserve of scrub (Figure 6.45). Between September 1993 and April 1994, 33.5ha were cleared and treated.

Dragging is fine at the margins of a site like Flanders Moss, but the helicopter removal and burning on site must be considered for remoter areas. The use of voluntary labour substantially reduces the costs of such operations. A well-planned lifting exercise can be very effective, if expensive. It was suggested that the efficacy of the burning bin could be increased by spending around £100 on materials.

A report of the helicopter exercise was produced giving several hints for future use:

- Take care when packing nets to fit maximum loads into them.
- Check that nets have sufficient attachment points to hold their load on lifting (three nets collapsed during this exercise, catapulting their contents across the Moss).
- After packing, run a sturdy rope through the loops tying the ends to use as an attachment to the helicopter hook. This will speed up the operation and thus reduce the cost.
- A period of twenty days passed between the packing and lifting of the nets, during which time a considerable amount of leaf litter had fallen on the bog. A maximum of fourteen days between the two operations is recommended.

6.22 ROUDSEA MOSSES

Featured technique	Rhododendron control
Cross-reference	5.3.4.2
Location	4km south-west of Newby Bridge, South Cumbria, England, UK
GB Grid references	SD 335823 and SD 348805
Contact address	Site Manager 7 The Croft Flookburgh Grange over Sands Cumbria LA11 7NF
Telephone	015395 58588
Area	476ha
Classification	Composite raised mire
Designations	(Roudsea Wood and Mosses) SSSI and NNR
Date of featured works	Rolling programme beginning 1982
Management objectives	To remove all invasive trees and scrub as part of a conservation management programme aimed at the restoration of active raised mire conditions at the site.

6.22

Site Description

Roudsea is a large reserve consisting of several small raised bogs and diverse woodland on a complex mineral area.

Although the bog surface is mostly intact, an extensive drainage system has been in place for approximately 200 years. Restoration works have been ongoing for the past thirteen years, during

Figure 6.45 A great deal of effort and resources have gone into clearing Flanders Moss of scrub. The cut tree in the foreground has been left high and will be re-cut and treated with herbicide at a later date. (Julian Anderson)

Figure 6.46 Rhododendron can quickly colonise damaged bogs. (Peter Singleton)

6.22

which time over 2,000 dams have been installed. Mowing trials have taken place at the site (to control heather) which have proved largely successful and to which some *Sphagnum* species have responded favourably.

Background to the Featured Technique

The traditional drainage system at the site (drains spaced 'half a chain' or 11 yards (about 11m) apart) has lowered the overall water-table. Subsequent invasion of birch, pine, rhododendron and rank ling heather resulted, although significant scrub invasion has only occurred since the 1950s. Notoriously difficult to control, the shade from rhododendron's extensive foliage completely destroys bog vegetation (Figure 6.46).

Approach

The two-stage programme at Roudsea involves felling the rhododendron bushes and burning the brashings on site in year one. To prevent damage to the bog surface, the brash is burnt on galvanised corrugated sheeting sitting on blocks to create an air gap (*see* 5.3.5.3). Ash is removed from the site.

The following year, regrowth from the cut stumps is sprayed using *No-mix Chipman Formula*

(Glyphosate). Spraying is undertaken in sunlight in summer whilst the foliage is actively photosynthesising; this can result in 100% kill (*see* 5.3.4.2). For foliage more than a year old (hardened off), *mixture B* is used with Roundup to improve adhesion (although at Roudsea it is thought more economical to recut and treat the following year). As an example, it took three men approximately four months and cost £20,000 to clear 5–6ha of the site.

Monitoring of Management Success

The immediate results of scrub clearance are very obvious, and fixed-point stereo-photography (*see* 4.1.3) provides a record of this. Regular site inspections have been carried out by the site manager during the entire thirteen year period (*see* 4.1). Hydrological/botanical monitoring is not carried out due to lack of time and resources.

Appraisal

Rhododendron is rhizomatous, so the most effective removal technique involves 'grubbing out' the roots. This is not an appropriate method to use on raised bog due to the degree of damage caused to the acrotelm. Spraying with herbicide gives rapid coverage on large sites, and evidence to date, suggests that Glyphosate exerts limited influence on non-target species (*see* 5.3.4.1). Use of the *No-mix* concentrated formula simplifies the operation as it involves a much lighter pack than usual, and also leaves a white residue so that completed areas are easily identified. It was found best to advise contractors to quote for their time rather than for area completed, as the time taken to cover a hectare is highly variable.

At the commencement of the project, little similar work had been attempted in the UK. The technique has proved very successful, and since 1982 (121ha) of bog have been cleared of scrub. Recolonisation of poisoned ground has been variable, and raking up the ground surface has been considered as a possible solution. However, the site manager notes that, in general, the removal of rhododendron at Roudsea has had dramatic results leading to the return of ground-covering species such as *Sphagnum tenellum* and *Sphagnum papillosum* within just two years. Many original bog species have responded well, growing from incoming propagules and fragments within the moribund peat surface.

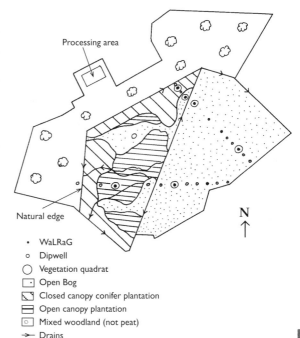

- • WaLRaG
- ○ Dipwell
- ◯ Vegetation quadrat
- ⊡ Open Bog
- ◺ Closed canopy conifer plantation
- ⊟ Open canopy plantation
- ◙ Mixed woodland (not peat)
- ➤ Drains

Figure 6.47   A sketch map of Langlands Moss showing the distribution of monitoring equipment. (Scale 1:10000)

6.23   LANGLANDS MOSS

Featured technique	Commercial forestry removal, plastic piling dams (unsupported), permanent vegetation quadrats
Cross-references	5.3.2.3, 5.3.5.6, 5.1.2.8, 4.6.3
Location	East Kilbride, Scotland, UK
GB Grid reference	NS 635511
Contact address	The Senior Ranger Calderglen Country Park Strathaven Road East Kilbride G75 0QZ
Telephone	01355 236644
Area	20ha
Classification	Raised bog
Designations	Local Nature Reserve (designated in 1996)
Date of featured works	1994 onwards
Management objectives	Rehabilitation of the moss through the removal of plantation forestry.

Site Description

Langlands Moss is small, though still largely intact, exhibiting a marked domed appearance. The western half of the site supported a commercial conifer plantation until March 1995 when it was felled (Figure 6.48). The bog is surrounded by agricultural fields, a golf course and light industry. There has been some marginal peat-cutting in the past and drainage has also occurred, leading to the loss of pool and lawn communities. The open bog surface is hummocky and, despite being dominated by ling heather remains relatively rich in *Sphagnum*. On the marginal slopes, erosion runnels have developed, possibly encouraged by previous fire damage. The main damage to the site, however, relates to the previously forested area and associated drains.

Background to the Featured Technique

A partnership of four organisations, Scottish Wildlife Trust, East Kilbride District Council, East Kilbride Development Corporation and Scottish Natural Heritage was developed to turn Langlands Moss into a new Local Nature Reserve. Resources became available through the 'Woodland Regeneration Project' of the East Kilbride Development Corporation. As part of this initiative, plans to sensitively remove the plantation were implemented. The Scottish Raised Bog Conservation Project (Scottish Wildlife Trust) oversaw the research, monitoring and management initiatives.

Approach

The established monitoring programme comprises two transects running from east to west across the site. The transects crossed areas of open bog and afforested land. Baseline data-collection was initiated prior to management to ensure that extensive 'before and after' information was obtained.

Dipwells were spaced every 30m, with seven WaLRaGs (*see* 4.3.3.3) placed at regular intervals along the two transects. Five permanent vegetation quadrats were also incorporated into the transects (Figure 6.47). These quadrats (*see* 4.6.3) are located in a variety of different habitats to monitor response to the management. 'Indicator' species are recorded using a simple percentage cover scale to monitor changes in species abundance and distribution. Initially, quadrat recording, accompanied by stereo-photography (*see* 4.1.3), was relatively intensive (once every six months) both prior to, and immediately following, felling.

A contractor undertook 'whole tree' removal to reduce damage to the bog surface from scarification and deposition of brash (Figure 6.48). The plantation was felled in its entirety and a helicopter utilised to airlift felled whole trees from the bog. Several trees were lifted at a time with rope chokers and carried to a processing plant

(Figure 6.49) at the nearby Curlingmyres farm (about 200m away but off the bog). Here, trees were brashed and processed. Brashings and low-grade small-diameter wood were chipped for use as footpath material; good-quality timber was transported away for saw logs and pulp.

Immediately after harvesting, rigid vinyl sheet piling dams were installed in the larger (> 2m wide x 1m deep) drainage ditches, to retain water within the system and raise the water-table (Figure 6.50). Plastic piling was chosen as it can be used on ditches of varying widths. The interlocking sheets can be made as wide as required and the sections can be bought in a variety of lengths. The sections were driven in by hand with a rubber maul. The sheets were

Figure 6.49 The processing yard adjacent to Langlands Moss. This is now the car park for the nature reserve. The felled plantation and open bog can be seen in the background. (East Kilbride Development Corporation)

Figure 6.48 Felled conifer plantation at Langlands Moss with minimal residual brash or disturbance to the surface. (Stuart Brooks)

6.23

Figure 6.50   One of the plastic piling dams installed at Langlands Moss. (Stuart Brooks)

installed in a bow shape pointing in the direction of flow. This deliberate positioning forced the section joins together to prevent seepage. The dams are self-supporting.

Appraisal

The trees were removed with almost no disturbance to the mire surface, and this approach left very little brash on the bog surface (Figure 6.48). Plastic dams are costly (at around £190 per dam, compared with £40 for plywood), but they are appropriate for ditches of larger dimensions as they are strong and durable. Unfortunately, at Langlands, the central spillway sections of the dams were set too low. Methods of rectifying this problem, through affixing additional sections of piling with waterproof seal, are currently being investigated (1996). The monitoring programme installed at the site is both comprehensive and practical (that is, the frequency and cost of recording are both low). Given that 30% of all Scotland's raised bogs are currently afforested, the management at this site provides valuable data on a topic which has important implications for

raised bog conservation in Scotland (Brooks and Stomeman, 1996).

6.24 MAOL DONN

Featured technique	Tree removal
Cross-reference	5.3
Location	Part of the 2,185ha Sletill Peatlands SSSI which straddles the Caithness-Sutherland border, Scotland, UK
GB Grid reference	NC 9845
Contact address	Area Officer Scottish Natural Heritage NW Region Area Office Golspie Sutherland KW10 6TG
Telephone	01408 633602
Area	277ha
Classification	Blanket bog
Designations	SSSI
Date of featured works	1994
Management objectives	Stop pool systems drying out by removing young commercial afforestation from the site.

6.24

Site Description

The Sletill Peatlands, of which Maol Donn is a constituent, form part of the pSAC known as the Flow Country. Sloping from 150–210m above sea level, the mire surface is patterned by a variety of pool complexes (dubh lochans, Figure 6.51). The ornithological interest of the site includes populations of golden plover, dunlin, and greenshank all at higher-than-average densities for the locality.

Figure 6.51   An oblique view of Maol Donn showing the adjacent forestry and dubh lochans. (Stuart Brooks)

Prior to SSSI notification (1985–1987), a total of 54ha of peatland (divided among five disparate blocks) had already undergone varying degrees of disturbance from forestry interests – ranging from preparatory ploughing to planting-up of a 3:3 Sitka:Lodgepole mix (occasionally accompanied by fertiliser application) – *see* Figure 6.52.

Background to the Featured Technique

Despite a lack of statistical data, anecdotal evidence suggested that the pool systems, adjacent to disturbed land, were gradually drying. A technique had to be developed which could be applied to large areas by a limited workforce (that is, without voluntary labour) and which did not rely upon removal of timber from the site (given that this was not deemed financially viable). A pilot contract was issued to evaluate the relative cost-effectiveness of two management techniques:

- Each tree was cut at ground level, the trunk pushed into an adjacent furrow, and peat spoil scraped over the exposed wood.
- A low-ground-pressure vehicle simply knocked the trees over into the furrows.

Although a certain degree of regrowth was predicted using the latter technique, this method was three times as quick as the alternative so, on this basis, the management operation was put out to contract specifying this technique.

Approach

A 'loose' contract was drawn up to provide the flexibility required for such an experimental approach; this meant that regular visits, by a SNH representative, to ensure suitable working practices were required. The management works were carried out from January to October 1994 (pausing during the bird breeding season). The contractor used a modified 360 Hymac (with extra-wide tracking) in order to push trees over into the plough furrows. In areas where water movement (drainage) was apparent, the weight of the vehicle was also used to compact peat around the felled trunk.

Monitoring of Management Success

A formal monitoring programme began in February 1996 which combines the use of fixed point photography with quadrat data (*see* 4.6.3).

Appraisal

This technique required 66 machine-days to clear 53ha of c. eight-year-old conifers. Total expenditure amounted to £26,900 including £2,900 for training. The vehicle hire rate was £21 per hour. Clearly, this is not suitable for organisations with limited financial resources. Despite provision of weekly guidance visits by an SNH representative (a costly investment in terms of staff time), problems of consistency were still encountered (with different subcontractors interpreting the contract in different fashions). Vehicular damage to the original peat surface was limited due to the experience of the contractors, combined with unusually dry conditions throughout 1994.

6.24

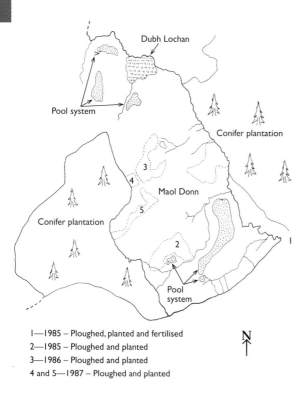

1—1985 – Ploughed, planted and fertilised
2—1985 – Ploughed and planted
3—1986 – Ploughed and planted
4 and 5—1987 – Ploughed and planted

Figure 6.52   Sketch map showing the main habitat features at Maol Donn. (Scale 1:45000)

Nevertheless, disturbance of the peat surface has encouraged colonisation by rosebay willowherb (and purple moor grass) and this, combined with the 'untidy' appearance of the flattened trees, might be a consideration for sites where public perception and landscape character are important factors.

In the year following the management works, some of the upturned trees were beginning to reshoot (Figure 6.53) (with up to 50% of the trees alive in certain areas). The ground is now too treacherous for renewed vehicular access; it is intended to rely upon winter weather to kill off new growth. If, after five years, regrowth remains a problem, a contractor may be required to cut back the new shoots.

Figure 6.53 Flattened trees beginning to re-shoot one year after management works, Maol Donn. (Lucy Parkyn)

6.25 BANKHEAD MOSS

Featured technique	Weed-wiping, painting, spraying
Cross-references	5.3.4.3, 5.3.4.4, 5.3.4.2
Location	8km south-west of St Andrews, west of Peat Inn, Scotland, UK
GB Grid reference:	NO 447103
Contact address	Reserve Manager Scottish Wildlife Trust Cramond House Kirk Cramond Edinburgh EH4 6NS
Telephone	0131 312 7765
Fax	0131 312 8065
Area	17ha
Classification	Raised bog
Designations	SWT Reserve, SSSI
Dates of featured works	1983 onwards
Management objectives	To provide conditions conducive to the maintenance and enhancement of the raised mire as a typical habitat.

Site Description

Bankhead Moss is a small remnant of a raised bog. Its vegetation consists of dry bog and acid heath with ling heather, hare's tail cotton grass, purple moor grass and cross-leaved heath as the dominant species. There is a small marginal lagg fen to the north and a marshy area to the west which has high water levels for much of the year and supports interesting sedge communities, such as, *Carex flacca, C. panicea, C. echinata, C. brachyrhyncha* and *C. viridula*. Rough pasture and mixed woodland, to the south of the Moss, complement the range of habitats found in the reserve.

The bog has been affected by peripheral drainage and domestic peat extraction. Lint holes (Figure 6.54), which were dug for the flax industry, were abandoned during the mid nineteenth century (Figure 6.55). During the First World War, *Sphagnum* from the site was collected by the Red Cross for wound dressings.

Background to the Featured Technique

Examination of archive and recent aerial photographs (*see* 4.6.4) clearly shows the encroachment of peripheral birch woodland onto

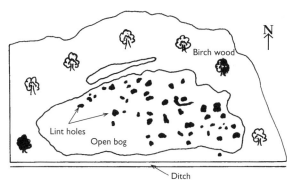

Figure 6.54 A sketch map showing the distribution of lint holes at Bankhead Moss. (Scale 1:3000)

Figure 6.55 A recently excavated lint hole which would have been used for *retting* lint and possibly for collecting *Sphagnum* for use as wound dressings, Bankhead Moss. (Emma Wilson)

the mire surface during the last forty years (Figure 6.56). It is not certain whether disruption of mire hydrology has been followed by birch colonisation, or if colonisation has caused the drying of the site (*see* 1.9, A3.3.2, A3.2.2). By 1983 the problem had become so serious that the voluntary management committee began a scrub-control programme.

Approach

Ditches adjacent to and leading from the site were blocked in an attempt to deal with the root cause of the problem (that is, site hydrology).

Initially, scrub control focused on hand-pulling of saplings (*see* 5.3.2.1) and felling of parent birch and pine trees (*see* 5.3.2.2). The management committee found it increasingly difficult to keep abreast of the problem, and in 1987 they undertook some experimentation with herbicides (*see* 5.3.4) in order to compare the various methods of application for different herbicides and their efficacy.

- In late May/early June – weedwiping with Roundup (glyphosate);
- In early June – painting of cut stumps using a herbicide glove with Roundup (glyphosate) and Amcide (ammonium sulphamate); and
- During September – spraying via a knapsack sprayer using Roundup and 3% Krenite.

The Management Committee then produced a report (Robinson, 1991) suggesting that weedwiping with glyphosate gave good results

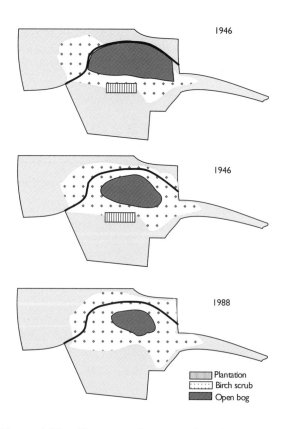

Figure 6.56 The rate and pattern of scrub encroachment at Bankhead Moss. (Not to scale)

6.25

as it was less damaging to surrounding vegetation and less time-consuming than other methods. For this reason 3% Krenite was considered too destructive. Using an individual weedwiper with a soft wick was found to give best coverage and results. Food dyes should be used to ensure treatment of all cut stumps. It was recommended that all dead saplings should be removed to facilitate further applications. Painting with Glyphosate is still necessary for larger trees which have to be felled.

Herbicide suitable for painting cut stumps costs around £15 per bottle and requires approximately five person-days per year. The use of a weedwiper costs £35 per bottle and requires around four person-days per year.

Monitoring Management Success

Monitoring of the effectiveness of the herbicide techniques in use was considered a priority (*see* 4.6.4). Regular hydrological monitoring is carried out, taking just over one day per month to read three WaLRaGs (*see* 4.3.3.3), a dipwell transect (*see* 4.3.3.2) and, piezometer nest (*see* 4.3.4.3).

Appraisal

Weedwiping is not suited to very small plants (hand-pulling will continue), and larger bushes may require subsequent applications (recommended three times annually).

The present Moss occupies less than 50% of its former area, and, if scrub control were to cease, a birch woodland would probably begin to take its place within a decade. Initial attempts at control were too sporadic to make a serious impression on the problem. Scrub control has been carried out each year between 1988 and 1994 and, despite intensive effort, Bankhead Moss remains extremely vulnerable to birch encroachment (Elliott, 1995). The site may require several uninterrupted cycles of cutting and poisoning. Monitoring of the techniques in use has been very good and will provide excellent lessons for future projects. This case shows that careful attention needs to be paid to planning, timing and execution of herbicide programmes to ensure maximum effect.

6.26 GARDRUM MOSS

Featured technique	Transplanting whole plants; spreading propagules
Cross-references	5.2.3
Location	South of Falkirk, Scotland, UK
GB Grid Reference	NS 882754
Contact address	Dr C. Turner William Sinclair Horticulture Firth Road Lincoln LN6 7AH
Telephone	01522 537561
Area	Managed area 2ha
Classification	Raised/blanket bog
Date of featured works	1991 (began)
Management objectives	The rehabilitation of a section of the mire by conversion of bare peat into a valuable wetland habitat.

Site Description

The Slamannan plateau is an area of higher ground in the heart of central Scotland. It is characterised by east–west-oriented drumlins which are farmed as pasture. In between the drumlins are numerous wetland areas comprising open water, fen and mainly bog. The bogs have a topography and vegetation similar to classic raised bogs and are usually classified thus. However, their topography is usually controlled by sub-surface topography, and the existence of shallow peats shows that blanket bog may form in certain areas of the plateau. The National Peatlands Resource Inventory neatly solves the confusion by calling these sites intermediate bogs. The plateau has tremendous ornithological significance as it is the roost and feeding grounds for one of only two of Britain's wintering bean geese flocks. Gardrum Moss is the commercially-worked part of a bog complex which once included Darnrigg Moss SSSI. Like many mosses on the plateau, it has been exploited for peat extraction.

Some 95% of Gardrum Moss consists of bare cut-over peat, having been exploited for peat extraction since the early twentieth century. In 1945, the site was the focus of trials of pressure water-extraction. Now extraction by milling occurs over most of the site and only small areas of vegetation remain, providing a poor source for renaturation of the site.

6.26

Background to the Featured Technique

William Sinclair Horticulture (the site owner) are considering what is to be done with their peat bog sites in twenty to sixty years' time when peat extraction ceases. The most common land use to follow extraction was forestry or poor pasture. Today, the priorities have shifted towards renaturation to a wetland habitat – preferably bog. Sinclair Horticulture are, thus, using part of the site for experimenting with the possibility of recreating wetland and providing the conditions necessary for *Sphagnum* growth. A team of environmental consultants was employed to carry out initial detailed studies and make recommendations.

Approach

Following a detailed ecological and hydrological study, a working method was based on the concept that the degree of waterlogging, nutrient status and microtopography were the most influential ecological constraints on the development of the mire system. The rehabilitation programme would therefore proceed in the following way:

1. Recontouring was carried out using the company's own machinery to create the necessary microtopography.
2. The site has been given the ability to retain water to achieve rewetting by creating six lagoons (Figure 6.57). Embankments were bulldozed into place and plastic tubing was used for overflow pipes. The lagoons filled with water over winter and now hold plenty of water.
3. Vegetation was put in the lagoons in the following year (the milling process meant that very few propagules would exist in the peat itself). Lagoons were inoculated with Sphagna whilst heather and cotton grass were transplanted to the surrounding areas using vegetation from existing parts of Gardrum Moss (which would otherwise be lost). One lagoon was left untreated to act as a control.
4. Emphasis was also placed on the need for monitoring water levels and botanical development.

Monitoring of Management Success

Water levels are measured in the lagoons and vegetation is monitored via regular site observation and photographic record.

Figure 6.57   The constructed lagoons at Gardrum Moss, Scotland. (C. Turner)

Appraisal

Initially, the water-table fluctuated by only 8 cm and some *Sphagnum* growth was evident in 1993/94. However, the dry summer of 1994 caused water levels to drop by about 25 cm. By July 1994, 80% of new *Sphagnum* growth had died. Although much of this growth had been replenished by the spring of 1995, the exceptionally dry summer of 1995 killed off virtually all remaining vegetation. A reinoculation programme was, thus, conducted in Spring 1996. Clearly, a weakness of the scheme is the inability to control water levels during dry weather. The company is considering the possibility of converting two of the six lagoons into reservoirs to supply ombrotrophic water for pumping into other lagoons (a similar method is currently employed at Thorne Moors by English Nature). Three to four years of such experimentation have brought a small improvement to Gardrum Moss, but considerable amount of knowledge and experience has be gained which will be of use in future years when larger areas of cut-over bog begin to be rehabilitated.

6.27 NEUSTÄDTER MOOR

Featured technique	Burning and grazing
Cross-references	5.5, 5.4
Location	Part of the Diepholzer Moor Lowland, Lower Saxony, Germany

Contact address	Dr Reinhard Löhmer Institut für Zoologie Tierärztliche Hochschule Hannover Bünteweg 17 D-30559 Hannover Germany	Friedhelm Niemayer BUND Project Leader Langer Berg 15 D-49419 Wagenfeld-Ströhen Germany
Area	1,600ha	
Classification	Raised bog	
Management objectives	Management of the site is undertaken primarily for the benefit of wild birds, aiming to create a mosaic of open habitat and sheltered habitat whilst preventing the site from scrubbing over.	

Site Description

The majority of Neustädter Moor (Figure 6.58) has been cut-over for commercial peat extraction since 1965. A small area of intact mire remains at the centre and now lies above the water-table.

6.27

Figure 6.58   View of Neustädter Moor showing rewetted peat cuttings. (Stuart Brooks)

Attempts have been made to rehabilitate the site by bulldozing flat the old cutting fields and installing peat dams to raise the water table. *Bunkerde* has been used at this site. When the surface vegetation is removed prior to milling, it is kept aside to be used later in rehabilitation. It is thought that this material will provide a seed source and enhance water retention. Wheeler and Shaw (1995) compared *Bunkerde* fields with those left bare and concluded that *Bunkerde* encourages a more desirable succession to a bog flora which is less dominated by purple moor grass. However, this method does not appear to enhance *Sphagnum* recolonisation in any way.

Background to the Featured Technique

Over the decades, intensive agricultural practices, including drainage and clearance of lagg fen areas, and later peat extraction have led to a decline in bird populations on the bog. As rehabilitation measures appear to have had little success, the bird decline has continued (for example, in 1980 there were twenty pairs of golden plover; this fell to two pairs in 1992). BUND (*Bund für Umwelt und Naturschutz Deutschland*), in close cooperation with the administrative authorities, aim to restore some of the traditional marginal feeding grounds around the site to encourage birds back to breed. They are raising funds in order to acquire peripheral farmland for more environmentally sensitive management. On a site with over 1,000 proprietors, this is no easy task.

Approach

Fire is a traditional tool used by former shepherds to improve grazing conditions and is now used to create the mosaic of open habitat and suitable cover required by the birds.

The mire is grazed by sheep at a stocking density of 0.94 sheep per ha. These are a traditional North German breed (Figure 6.59) specially adapted to grazing mires (Moorschnucke). They are particularly hardy, with splayed toes which, unlike other sheep, are not prone to footrot in wet conditions.

The operation is managed as a project which, although it has to be subsidised by the German government, earns some of its own money. The project uses adjoining areas for hay – sold as a cash crop or used as winter feed for the sheep. Manure from the sheds is spread over the fields. Fleece from the Moorschnucke is not of sufficient quality to be used in the textile trade, but some is currently being sold as loft insulation.

The farm has an annual budget of DM450,000 and must sell the equivalent of 400 sheep a year if it is to make a profit. It therefore markets its produce as organically-produced meat, which is very popular in the Hannover region.

Grazing is a suitable mire management tool as sheep feed selectively; from February to March on the young shoots of hare's tail cotton grass and later on young purple moor grass shoots. In May, the sheep begin to feed on the new growth of birch. The sheep are kept away from the central *Sphagnum*-dominated areas to contain poaching pressure. Careful shepherding is a hallmark of the grazing management of Neustädter Moor. The sheep are kept off the bog at night. Winter grazing is largely peripheral.

Figure 6.59 Moorschnuke sheep whose managed grazing is used to create open habitat suitable for nesting birds, Neustädter Moor. (Lucy Parkyn)

6.27

Monitoring of Management Success

The effects of the management regime are difficult to assess and the effects of burning are not monitored. Small 5 × 5m plots have been established for monitoring grazing effects, but no data is available as yet.

Appraisal

Comparing the various areas of Neustädter Moor indicates that grazing has played a significant part in manipulating the development of secondary vegetation over rewetted fields. Birch and purple moor grass in particular have been kept in check. The effects of trampling, selective grazing and enrichment are difficult to gauge. The severity of impact is reliant upon the skill of the shepherd in controlling the movement of the flock. Data from exclosure experiments may shed some light on this.

6.28   RED MOSS OF BALERNO

Featured technique	Boardwalk and information panels
Cross-reference	5.6.2
Location	Near Balerno, Edinburgh, Scotland, UK
GB Grid reference	NT 163638
Contact address	Reserve Manager Scottish Wildlife Trust Cramond House Kirk Cramond Edinburgh EH4 6NS
Telephone	0131 312 7765
Area	23ha
Classification	Raised bog
Designations	Scottish Wildlife Trust Reserve, SSSI
Date of featured works	1993
Management objectives	To encourage visitor access to the reserve with the provision of suitable interpretation without compromising its nature conservation interest.

Site Description

Most of Balerno Common was enclosed in 1768, although a part of Red Moss remained as a common (used by local villagers). The enclosed bog was cut away and now forms pastoral land, but the common land was only lightly used for grazing, shooting and peat-winning. Over time, though, these activities have cumulatively had a large effect on the site. It is now badly damaged, partly by a defunct aqueduct used to carry water from the Pentlands into an expanding Edinburgh, which crosses the south of the site. Lint holes are also present at the site, showing that the site was used for flax-retting.

Background to Featured Technique

The Moss has a good history of academic and public interest, probably due to its proximity to Edinburgh. Edinburgh University is reported to have used Red Moss as a teaching site for 300 years (although no details are available). Throughout its recent history as a reserve, the Moss has also attracted much interest, particularly following its incorporation into the Regional Park. To encourage public understanding of bogs and their conservation, SWT has recently (1993–5) constructed a boardwalk and four information panels.

Approach

The boardwalk idea offered the opportunity to link access to interpretation in a single project.

The aqueduct is used as the main access point, limiting costs and damage by utilising an existing structure. It is also located away from the more sensitive areas of the bog. An interpretation board at the start of the route (Figure 6.60) deals with peatlands in general, Red Moss in particular and SWT's role in its management. A second board is located on the aqueduct where emphasis is on the industrial archaeology of peatlands and the human threats that they face. When visitors have reached the pond to the west, they have also passed birch woodland and open bog: a good place to emphasise hydroseral succession and how bogs record their own history. A fourth board is placed at a lint hole, where the ecology, fragility and management of the bog system are highlighted. The cost of the four boards was about £4,500.

The 1.2m-wide (this allows wheelchair access) elmwood boardwalk was constructed to

6.28

Figure 6.60 An information panel at Red Moss of Balerno. (Emma Wilson)

Countryside Commission standards using voluntary labour; materials cost £2,500.

Monitoring Management Success

There is little monitoring directly related to the boardwalk, although it is thought that the boardwalk is currently (1995) underused as there were no signs to show that it was there. This has been rectified!

Appraisal

As part of the Regional Park, the Moss can attract many people at weekends and holidays and it provides a good opportunity to promote peatlands.

6.29 GUALIN (STRATH DIONNARD)

Featured technique	Permanent tracks
Cross-reference	5.6.7
Location	Sutherland, Scotland, UK
Contact address	Area Officer Scottish Natural Heritage Knockan Cottage Elphin Lairg IV27 4HH
Telephone	01854 666234
Area	1,540ha
Classification	Blanket bog
Designations	NNR
Date of featured works	1989
Management objectives	The track was constructed to protect the peatland from further damage by ATVs (all-terrain vehicles) and allow the recovery of damaged and eroded areas.

Site Description

The majority of the area is contained within Strath Dionnard. Lewisian gneiss outcrops through a variable thickness of blanket bog. Large pool complexes are common within the thicker, flat areas of peat which occupy the lower slopes of the valley. The vegetation throughout the valley is dominated by deer grass and hare's tail cotton grass with variable amounts of ling heather, cross-leaved heath, *Sphagnum* spp. and *Racomitrium lanuginosum*. The area is noted for its populations of breeding waders, particularly greenshank (*Tringa nebularia*).

Background to the Featured Technique:

In the past, an ATV was used to transport anglers from the A838 road to various drop-off points along the river and up to Loch Dionnard at the head of the valley. From 1962 to the late 1970s, three major routes had been established. As erosion problems increased, lighter and more manoeuvrable ATVs were introduced (1981). These vehicles could travel over wetter areas and increased the area and rate of damage. At least three ATVs were used daily between June and October, transporting five or six anglers on each occasion. This caused considerable damage to surface vegetation as well as sheet erosion, gullying, drainage of pool systems and

6.29

Figure 6.61   ATV's prior to construction of the track caused considerable damage to the surface. In some areas erosion has exposed ancient pine stumps within the peat, Gualin, Scotland. (Rob Stoneman)

downwashing of peat into the river (Figure 6.61). It is estimated that up to 20% of the peatland surface was damaged within a 200m zone of the river. To minimise further damage to the surface and maintain fishing access to the river, it was agreed between the Nature Conservancy Council (NCC), the site owners and the local planning authority that a permanent track should be built. The site owners agreed to finance and instigate the project under guidance from the NCC.

Approach

During August to December 1989, a 3m-wide track was constructed, linking the main A838 road to Loch Dionnard (Figure 6.62). Where possible, the designated route followed existing ATV tracks. However, badly-damaged areas were avoided as they were considered too unstable to carry the weight of the track. Geotextile netting (2.5 cm^2 mesh size) was laid directly onto the remaining surface vegetation. Over bare peat, it was thought necessary to lay Terram matting over the geotextile to prevent the track from sinking under the weight of passing vehicles.

Ditches were cut into the upslope side of the track to prevent flooding and wash-out of the road. Flexible plastic pipes were installed at key water-collection points to carry away excess water beneath the track. Ditches or channels were not constructed on the downslope (river) side of the track. As the track progressed, the excavators used it as a building platform. Deep borrow pits were made immediately adjacent to the track where gravel was excavated for the top dressing. The gravel was laid down and compacted to a depth of at least 20–25 cm (Figure 6.63).

Monitoring and Appraisal

Much of the interest in the site is related to the breeding population of greenshank. From 1964–

6.29

Figure 6.62   The finished track running though Gualin. (Stuart Brooks)

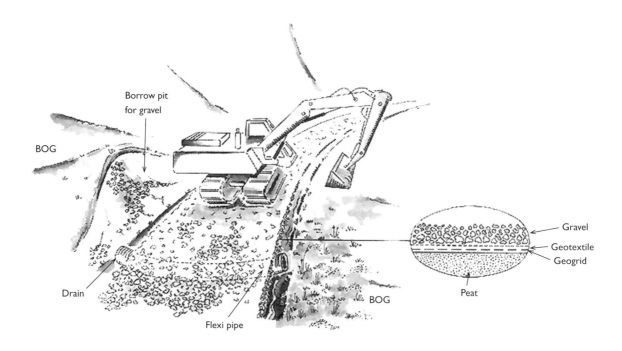

Figure 6.63   Sketch showing the construction principles of the Gualin track.

1990, a detailed investigation into the changing habitat and population dynamics of birds was undertaken by D. Nethersole-Thompson and family.

- Occupation of 'territories', numbers of males and females, timing of breeding, hatching success and subsequent brood movements were recorded.
- Meteorological information was recorded, including ground and air temperatures at 1.0m.
- Habitat changes were assessed through analysis of aerial photographs (1946, 1977 and 1988).
- In 1990, vegetation cover (percentage cover estimates) was measured in 0.3m² quadrats.
- Pitfall traps were sunk along nine transects in June 1990 for one week.

Between 1964 and 1990, the greenshank population varied threefold in number but declined in the 1980s (Thompson and Thompson, 1991). The increase in the numbers during the mid-1970s coincided with a long run of favourable summer weather. The decline in population is thought to be due to large-scale habitat loss from the afforestation of the Flow Country and more directly from the impacts of the all-terrain vehicles. There is a marked decline in activity within damaged areas, and, due to a loss of microtopographical variation, chicks are more likely to fall victim to predation. Detailed information on the rates and extent of habitat recovery are at present unavailable. However, there is evidence to show that revegetation within the lesser damaged areas has started. The main colonists of these areas are common cotton grass and to a lesser extent cross-leaved heath and bog asphodel. The severely-damaged areas are at present showing no signs of recovery, remaining as bare peat surfaces.

The construction of the track has succeeded in its primary objective of preventing further damage to the peat surface from the movement of the ATVs within the valley. This has also allowed some recolonisation of previously damaged areas. The effect of the track on the peatland system is less certain.

6.29

APPENDICES

Appendix 1

Glossary

Acidophilous	Acid-loving.
Acrotelm	The upper semi-aerated layer of a peat bog.
Anaerobic	Airless.
Anion	The positively-charged part of a molecule.
Apices	The top of the *Sphagnum* capitula.
Baulks	Upstanding blocks of peat between peat-cutting fields.
Black peat	Well humified peat.
Blanket bog	A layer of peat, usually 1–8m deep, literally blanketing upland and highly oceanic areas.
Bog	Mires which are fed by rainwater alone (i.e. ombrotrophic).
Bog mats	Wooden boards used to support excavators on peat.
Brown earth	A soil-type commonly found under deciduous forest.
Bulk density	Mass of material per unit volume.
Bund	An embankment (often made of clay or peat) used to hold water – effectively a long dam.
Bunkerde	A German term for the stockpiled remains of surface peat and vegetation – used for rehabilitation purposes.
Caledonian pine forest	The natural forest-type of northern Scotland – dominated by Scots pine.
Capitula	The growing top of *Sphagnum*.
Catchment	The area of land which feeds water into a particular river or stream.
Cation	The negatively-charged part of a molecule.
Catotelm	The lower, permanently saturated layer of a peat bog.
Colloid	A thick suspension of substance in water.
Confined mires	Mires which cannot develop beyond a certain boundary (often a river, lagg stream or hillside).
Countryside Council for Wales	Statutory nature conservation agency in Wales.
Cupola	The peat dome.
Dipwell	A hollow perforated tube, inserted into the bog, used to measure the water level beneath the surface.
Drumlin	A small ice-moulded hill of glacial till.
Dubh lochans	Small dark, coloured lakes found on blanket bog.
Duckboard	Small sections of boardwalk used to stop localised trampling.
Eccentric bogs	Asymmetric peat domes where the highest point is not at the centre; often develop on shallow slopes.
Ecohydrology	The combined study of ecology and hydrology. The term is often used when studying mires because of the close interplay between the ecology and hydrology of mires.
English Nature	Statutory nature conservation agency in England.
Environmentally Sensitive Area	A British designation given to land which can qualify for higher agri-environmental grants because of their special nature.
Ericoids	Plants belonging to the Heath family (Ericaceae).
Eutrophic	Nutrient-rich.
Evapotranspiration	Water lost by evaporation and transpiration.
Fen	A general term for mires which receive water from groundwater and rainwater.
Flow Country, the	A large area of blanket bog covering much of Caithness and some of Sutherland in northern Scotland.

A1

Geographical Information System	Computer software which allows mapped data to be analysed.
Glyphosate	A biodegradable herbicide (sold under the trade-name of Roundup).
Gravimetric samples	Samples on which analyses are related to the weight of the sample.
Groundwater Mound Theory, the	Soil physics: where water adopts a mound in semi-permeable substrates.
Highlands, the	Uplands or north-western unenclosed land in Scotland.
Hochmoor	German word for raised bog.
Holocene	The present interglacial period. It began about 12,000 years ago after the last ice-age.
Humification	The degree of decomposition.
Hyaline cells	Large, water-filled cells in Sphagnum leaves.
Hydraulic conductivity	The rate at which water moves through a material.
Hydromorphology	The study of the interactions between the contours of a landform and its hydrology.
Hydrophilous	Water-loving.
Intermediate bog (1)	Bogs which have characteristics of both blanket and raised bogs (NPRI).
Intermediate bog (2)	Mires which are transitional between fen and bog.
Lagg	The marshland which would naturally surround a raised bog.
Levelling (1)	Measuring surface topography by surveying.
Lint holes	Small hand-cut depressions in the bog surface used to 'rett' (partially rot) hemp fibres.
Loch Lomond Glaciation, the	The last gasp of the last ice-age – a cold period at the beginning of the Holocene.
Lysimeter	A device to indirectly measure evapotranspiration.
Macrofossils	Semi-decomposed remains left in the peat which can be identified under a hand-lens, for example, stems, leaves, seeds and wood.
Macrotope	A series of coalesced mesotopes.
Mesotope	A body of peat which forms a single hydrological unit.
Meteoric water	Water derived from the atmosphere: rain, fog and snow.
Microbore dipwells	Very thin (about 8mm) dipwells.
Microform	A single hummock or hollow.
Microfossils	Semi-decomposed remains left in the peat which can only be identified by using a high-powered microscope, for example, pollen and testate amoeba.
Microtope	A group of hummocks and hollows forming a surface pattern.
Mires	A generic term to cover all wetlands which are normally peat-forming.
Mooratmung	Literally 'bog-breathing' – it relates to the up-and-down movement of the bog surface observed between wet and drought periods.
Morphology	The study of the shape and contours of landforms.
Munsell colour chart	A chart of hundreds of differing colours all named and coded. Commonly used for describing soil and soil-extract colours.
National Vegetation Classification (NVC)	A relatively new (1980s) classification system for British vegetation designed by Rodwell and co-workers at the University of Lancaster. The scheme is now widely used although it should be remembered that the NVC was devised by analysing vegetation data alone. For bogs, hydromorphological classification schemes can be more useful.
Oligotrophic	Nutrient-poor.
Ombrotrophic	Literally rain (ombro) –fed (trophic).
Ordnance Datum (OD)	The mean sea-level at Newlyn, Cornwall, UK – used as 0m above sea-level on British (Ordnance Survey) maps.
Palaeoecology	Literally fossil ecology – the study of organisms and their environment in the past.
Paludification	The development of peat directly onto mineral ground.
Patterning	Most bogs exhibit an undulating topography of hummocks/ridges and pools. These often form distinct patterns.

AI

Peat anchor	Usually a rod pushed through the peat and sunk into the underlying mineral sediments. Peat anchors keep their absolute position regardless of how much the bog surface moves (see *Mooratmung*).
pH	A measure of acidity or alkalinity.
Physiognomy	The characteristic appearance of a plant community.
Phytosociology	The study of relationships between plants.
Piezometers	Equipment used to measure the rate and direction of lateral seepage. They are sometimes arranged in groups known as 'nests'.
Pitfall traps	A device to catch invertebrates.
Podzol	A soil-type found in wet regions. The upper horizons are leached of iron and aluminium in particular. These are deposited lower down in the soil profile often as an impermeable iron-pan.
R-16s	Continuous water level monitoring devices.
Raised bog	Rain-fed domes of peat sitting above (often by 10m) the landscape. These bogs have often developed over former lakes.
Rand	The edge of the peat dome.
Recharge	Water supply.
Red Data Book species	Species which have been identified as particularly rare or threatened.
Renaturation	The colinisation of appropriate vegetation.
Rheotrophic	Fed by groundwater.
Ridge-raised mire	Apparently domed deposits of peat mantling flattened summits and ridges. The dome often reflects underlying topography.
Royal Society for the Protection of Birds	Non-governmental nature conservation organisation based in the UK.
Schwingmoor	A floating raft of peat.
Scottish Natural Heritage	Statutory nature conservation agency in Scotland.
Scottish Wildlife Trust	Non-governmental nature conservation organisation allied to the Wildlife Trusts.
Seepage	Water movement though a material.
Soak system	Where water collects and flows either at the edge or on the surface of the bog.
Stereo-photograph	A set of two photographs showing nearly the same view but taken from different positions. By viewing through a stereo-viewer (or stereoscope), the overlap between the two pictures can be seen in 3-D.
Stob	A wooden support or anchoring post.
Storage capacity	The total amount of water that can be held in a given volume of soil.
Stratigraphy	The peat column representing a neatly-stacked historical and environmental archive.
Tanalised timber	Timber products that have been vacuum-pressure-treated with a *Tanalith*-based preservative.
Terram	A geotextile material used for footpath construction. This is a trade-name of ICI but is commonly used.
Till	Sediment deposited from glaciers. Much of northern Europe was covered in ice during the last ice-age. This has left a mantle of often impermeable till across northern Europe.
Topography	A description of surface relief.
Transpiration	Water lost by the plants. Water is drawn up through the plant roots and evaporated through pores in plants' leaves.
Volumetric samples	Samples on which analyses are related to the volume of the sample.
WaLRaGs	Water-level range gauges – a device used to measure maximum and minimum water levels.
White peat	Poorly-humified peat.

A1

APPENDIX 2
LATIN AND ENGLISH PLANT NAMES

Latin	English
Andromeda polifolia	Bog rosemary
Arctostaphylos uva ursi	Bearberry
Betula nana	Dwarf birch
Betula pubescens	Downy birch
Calluna vulgaris	Ling heather
Carex echinata	Star sedge
Carex panicea	Carnation grass
Carex rostrata	Beaked (bottle) sedge
Chamerion angustifolium	Rosebay willowherb
Cladonia spp.	Reindeer moss
Deschampsia flexuosa	Wavy-hair grass
Drosera anglica	Long-leaved sundew
Drosera rotundifolia	Round-leaved sundew
Empetrum nigrum	Crowberry
Erica tetralix	Cross-leaved heath
Eriophorum angustifolium	Common cotton grass
Eriophorum vaginatum	Hare's tail cotton grass
Juncus effusus	Soft rush
Juncus squarrosus	Heath rush
Ledum groenlandicum	Labrador tea
Menyanthes trifoliata	Bog bean
Molinia caerulea	Purple moor grass
Myrica gale	Bog myrtle
Nardus stricta	Mat grass
Narthecium ossifragum	Bog asphodel
Picea abies	Norway spruce
Picea sitchensis	Sitka spruce
Pinus contorta var. latifolia	Lodgepole pine
Pinus mugo	Mountain pine
Pinus sylvestris	Scots pine
Racomitrium langinosum	Woolly fringe moss
Rhododendron ponticum	Rhododendron
Rhyncosphora alba	White-beaked sedge
Rubus chaemorrus	Cloudberry
Saracenia purpurea	Pitcher plant
Schoenus nigricans	Black bog rush
Scirpus caespitosus	Deer grass
Sphagnum	Bog moss
Ulex europaeus	Gorse (whin or furze)
Vaccinium myrtillus	Bilberry
Vaccinium oxycoccus	Cranberry
Vaccinium uligonosum	Northern bilberry
Vaccinium vitas-idea	Cowberry

Latin	English
Carex rostrata	Beaked (bottle) sedge
Arctostaphylos uva ursi	Bearberry
Vaccinium myrtillus	Bilberry
Schoenus nigricans	Black bog rush
Narthecium ossifragum	Bog asphodel
Menyanthes trifoliata	Bog bean
Sphagnum	Bog moss
Myrica gale	Bog myrtle
Andromeda polifolia	Bog rosemary
Carex panicea	Carnation grass
Rubus chaemorrus	Cloudberry
Eriophorum angustifolium	Common cotton grass
Vaccinium vitas-idea	Cowberry
Vaccinium oxycoccus	Cranberry
Erica tetralix	Cross-leaved heath
Empetrum nigrum	Crowberry
Scirpus caespitosus	Deer grass
Betula pubescens	Downy birch
Betula nana	Dwarf birch
Ulex europaeus	Gorse (whin or furze)
Eriophorum vaginatum	Hare's tail cotton grass
Juncus squarrosus	Heath rush
Ledum groenlandicum	Labrador tea
Calluna vulgaris	Ling heather
Pinus contorta var. latifolia	Lodgepole pine
Drosera anglica	Long-leaved sundew
Nardus stricta	Mat grass
Pinus mugo	Mountain pine
Vaccinium uliginosum	Northern bilberry
Picea abies	Norway spruce
Saracenia purpurea	Pitcher plant
Molinia caerulea	Purple moor grass
Cladonia spp.	Reindeer moss
Rhododendron ponticum	Rhododendron
Chamerion angustifolium	Rosebay willowherb
Drosera rotundifolia	Round-leaved sundew
Pinus sylvestris	Scots pine
Picea sitchensis	Sitka spruce
Juncus effusus	Soft rush
Carex echinata	Star sedge
Deschampsia flexuosa	Wavy-hair grass
Rhyncosphora alba	White-beaked sedge
Racomitrium langinosum	Woolly fringe moss

A2

Appendix 3
Site Assessment of Bogs from the Damage Sustained

Site Assessment of Bogs from the Damage Sustained

A3.1 Introduction

Before the agricultural revolution in the eighteenth century, bogs were held in high regard according to many writers of the time (Smout, 1996). They were valued mainly as a source of fuel but also as providers of winter hay and as ground to provide sheep and cattle with an early 'bite' in spring. Attitudes changed in the nineteenth century as agricultural improvers saw the land as capable of betterment. From this time, until very recently (in the last ten or twenty years), peatlands were primarily considered as unproductive land. This resulted in dramatic changes in landuse on peatlands throughout Europe. Such changes have resulted in widespread damage to peatland ecosystems. This appendix (summarised in sections 1.8–1.14) describes the types of uses to which bogs have been subjected and the resulting damage that they are likely to have sustained. It then goes on to describe the ecological effects and how they can be recognised. This section can thus be used to assess the characteristics of a site in terms of the damage sustained. This helps to construct a useful site description (*see* Part 3) and also sets the basis for setting realistic management objectives and prescriptions for achieving those objectives.

A3.2 Peat Extraction

A3.2.1 Introduction

Peatlands have long been used as a mineral resource. Peat is high in organic matter (nearly 100%), light, has excellent water-retention properties and is easy to cut. Peat has probably been used as fuel for many thousands of years, and many peat bogs show signs of a long history of domestic peat-cutting. More recently, the properties of peat have been exploited by the horticultural industry. For the bog conservation manager, the effects of peat extraction (whether recent or ancient) are often one of the main causes of bog degradation. In this section, the types of peat-cutting and their effects are considered.

Over the years, peat production/extraction techniques have developed and adapted to accommodate changes in the market. Peat extraction via hand-cut domestic peat banks has been superseded by large commercially-run operations which mill peat into piles across a bare surface. Central Ireland provides a spectacular example of this change where the Great Bog of Allen has been turned into a seemingly black and featureless desert (*see* Figure 1.12).

Peat use is dictated by the properties of the peat itself which vary according to site characteristics and bog-type. Fuel peat is derived from both blanket (mainly) and raised bogs whilst peat for the horticultural industry tends to emanate mainly from raised bogs. Whatever type of bog is used, or techniques employed, there are several common features: drainage, provision of access routes, removal of surface vegetation and drying of cut peat on the surface (Wheeler and Shaw, 1995).

Hand-cutting of peat for domestic fuel has been a traditional and widespread method of extraction resulting in extensive areas of cut-over blanket and raised bog. This traditional activity has declined as communications have improved and other fuel-types have become more widely available. However, active domestic peat-cuts are still a feature of many parts of rural Scotland and Ireland. In some areas, traditional hand-cutting has been replaced by modern techniques such as sausage extraction. Small-scale cooperative ventures by people owning adjacent peat banks have accelerated this process, and in some cases a cottage industry of semi-commercial, small-scale ventures has been established.

A3.1

Other uses for peat include animal bedding (moss litter), whisky production, fuel for power stations and production of charcoal briquettes for barbecues. More recently, peat extracted from raised bogs has been used as a growing medium and soil conditioner for the horticultural and amateur gardening industries. Varying uses require different extraction techniques to result in differing degrees of damage. The extraction technique then influences the types of after-use an exploited area can be used for, and its potential for rehabilitation towards a bog habitat.

A3.2.2 General Effects of Extraction

Many of the effects of peat-cutting are common to different extraction techniques. This is partly the result of similar methods required to prepare a site for extraction, for example, drainage and vegetation removal. Common features are detailed below.

Drainage (*see* A3.3.2) results in drying, compaction, oxidation, wastage and a changed water-table response pattern to rain events. In effect, an uncharacteristically highly fluctuating water-level pattern is produced which is unsuitable for many bog plants such as *Sphagnum* spp.

Enrichment can be caused by three interrelated effects of peat-cutting:

- Peat-cutting may expose underlying rich fen peat (more likely on former raised bogs), the mineral substrate or groundwater leaving the resulting surface relatively richer in nutrients (*see* Figure 5.50).
- Extensive removal of peat may change the local hydrology of an area considerably. For example, a formerly water-shedding dome may be converted into a water-collecting basin following extensive removal of peat. Water from surrounding land is likely to be of a higher nutrient status than ombrotrophic bog water.
- Drainage and exposure of bare peat surfaces may mobilise nutrients sufficiently to affect the vegetation. The exact nature of this release and utilisation needs further investigation (Wheeler and Shaw, 1995).

Loss of stratigraphic record either entirely or at least in part.

The following effects are common to only some of the extraction techniques.

Steep hydrological gradients: Block (sod) and domestic peat-cutting often give rise to unnaturally steep hydrological gradients at an unnaturally abrupt edge to the peat body. On raised bogs, this changes the 'ground-water mound' (*see* 2.5) of the whole peat body, though the main effects are confined to the edge of the bog where lowered water levels should be apparent. Peat-cutting within the peat body may also result in an uneven land surface. Raised blocks act in a similar way to an individual 'raised bog'. Within each block of peat, water levels fall to an equilibrium based upon the block's ground-water mound. As a result, the surface of the bog becomes drier. Resultant atypical vegetation establishment may then exacerbate the drying effect (Wheeler and Shaw, 1995).

Extensive bare peat surfaces: Exposed dark peat surfaces absorb more heat than a vegetated surface, causing increased water loss and higher levels of microbial activity. Bare peat areas are also susceptible to wind and water erosion. Blanket peats forming in cool and wet climates, often on sloping ground, are particularly vulnerable.

Additionally, high temperature and water-level fluctuations coupled to a generally smooth surface topography of bare peat surfaces makes plant colonisation difficult. Commercial extraction operations often camber the peat fields for enhanced drainage. As a result, water-collection areas are rare, hindering recolonisation by bog vegetation.

A3.2.3 Domestic Extraction

Peat-cutting for use as a domestic fuel (Figure 1.9) is a traditional rural activity which is still carried out in many parts of Europe. Even though peat-cutting by hand methods can be labour intensive and hard work, it is still pursued in many localities where there is a strong cultural connection to the use of peat. This is despite the advent of mechanical methods for peat extraction such as the DIFCO cutter which can be operated using a farm tractor.

The techniques employed require the use of special peat spades which are characteristically flat rather than curved (*see* Figure 5.13). The surface vegetation is removed and laid to one side.

Peat below this layer is then cut out in blocks and laid on the vegetated surface to dry. On raised bogs, peat-cutters may discard the upper, less humified ('white') peats and dig deep faces to extract the darker, more humified 'black' peat which is more suitable for burning. Gradually, the peat face moves forward and vegetation is relaid on the bare peat surface exposed behind the bank. Extraction is fairly slow, allowing recolonisation to keep up with the forward extraction of the bank. On blanket bogs, worked faces are generally orientated down the slope to facilitate drainage so that little or no artificial drainage is required.

The effect of peripheral peat-cutting on raised peatland has probably been seriously underestimated in the past. The position of the water-table in raised peatland is governed in part by the shape and depth of the peat deposit and in part by the hydraulic properties of the peat. The height of the groundwater mound is poised in equilibrium. This idea, proposed first by Ingram (1982), suggests that changes to the shape of a deposit, for example by a reduction in the basal area by domestic peat-cutting, influences the equilibrium height of the groundwater mound. The expected trend based on model predictions is for the water-table to fall below the original equilibrium height until a new equilibrium establishes. The rate at which the groundwater mound readjusts to the new height is unknown. It is suggested that oxidation of peat limits readjustment to a few centimetres per year. Compression of peat, collapse and subsidence could assist the process further, though in many cases this may be insufficient to prevent changes in the typical flora from occurring (for example, from bog to heath). Some of the drying effects may be moderated in areas of higher rainfall.

For example, domestic cutting around Raheenmore (Ireland) seems to have caused a progressive loss of pool communities within the last thirty years.

Cut-over areas may support a variety of vegetation types depending on the severity of the cutting. An often uneven surface is characteristic, supporting a variety of 'acid' vegetation communities ranging from heath, in drier areas, through to bog pools. If extraction has been sufficient to reach underlying fen peats, mineral deposits or groundwater, then a fen community is likely to develop.

The ecohydrological effects of domestic peat cutting on blanket bog may be less severe. Blanket bogs (more accurately blanket mire – see 2.3.2) are more diverse than raised bogs composed of a variety of differing vegetation assemblages. The practice of relaying vegetated turfs on bare peat behind the peat bank facilitates rapid recolonisation. However, eventually an unnaturally uneven surface results, leading to a mosaic of wetter (cut-away areas) and drier (remaining uncut baulks) areas.

Where cutting has ceased, recognition depends on the following factors:

- *Time since abandonment*. Very old peat faces may be masked by recolonised vegetation. Shrinkage, cracking and wastage of peat allied to slumping gradually reduces the height of the peat bank.
- *Type of vegetation established after cutting*. Certain vegetation assemblages such as fen, fen carr and trees (both self-sown and planted) may mask cutting activities.
- *Extent of cutting*. Extensively cut areas may be difficult to recognise if a wide area has been cut away to leave flat surfaces. Careful examination, however, usually reveals the remains of peat-cuts or baulks. A useful tool to identify such cut-over sites is stereo air photography which often reveals straight or slightly curved lines of old peat-cutting banks. A 3-D stereo image will also reveal hitherto hidden small height differences, often arranged in a regular pattern, across the surface of the peat bog.

A3.2.4 Peat Extraction by Extrusion – Sausage Cutting

A3.2

Traditional hand-cutting of peat is now being gradually replaced by sausage extraction (*see* Figure 1.14). This extraction technique uses a machine to drive over a peat bog to cut a series of angled slits at a depth of about 1m. Peat is then extruded, from the base of the slit to the surface, as a long 'sausage' which is divided into lengths of 20–30 cm and left on the surface to dry. Dried peat 'sausages' are typically used for domestic fuel and also in the whisky industry.

In the past, it was common to dry 'sausages' on vegetated surfaces. However, problems relating to the peat 'sausage' becoming entangled with vegetation during mechanical removal has meant that commercial operators now strip surface vegetation away. Where peat is dried on a vegetated surface, the combined actions of driving machinery across the bog surface and the physical presence of drying peat alters vegetation communities and may lead to extensive areas of bare peat. Significant damage to surface vegetation has been recorded after only one harvest; further changes result from continued cutting (Meharg et al., 1992).

Before extraction, peripheral and/or widely-spaced drains are cut in order to drain the bog sufficiently to allow the passage of heavy machinery. Drainage is assisted by sub-surface slits which act as 'mole' drains. Note that the slits usually seal at the surface but may well be open below ground. Commercial extractors also camber extraction fields to improve surface water run-off, although this is difficult to discern in the field.

Drainage, vegetation removal, repeated travel across the bog surface by machinery, large amounts of peat lying on the bog surface and sub-surface drainage channels all serve to badly damage the bog. The peat archive is disturbed and gradually destroyed, whilst intense physical disruption of the peat structure may even result in peat liquefaction preventing further cutting and hindering vegetation colonisation.

Active sausage-cut sites are easy to discern by the presence of peat sausages (thin cylinders 20–30 cm long by approximately 10 cm in diameter) left on the surface to dry. Extrusion slits are less obvious where they have sealed at the surface, given that they are usually cut at an angle. Slits become more obvious in dry weather as the surface cracks along slit lines. After abandonment, vegetation recolonisation of bare peat surfaces is slow. Initially, a species-poor vegetation assemblage of sedges and the mat-forming mosses form. Hare's tail cotton grass is particularly common. Soft rush colonisation indicates extensive removal of peat and an increasing influence of groundwater.

A3.2.5 Baulk and Hollow/Block (Sod) Cutting

A major historical use of peat was as moss litter for livestock bedding. Moss litter was usually extracted from bogs with poorly-humified peat (raised bogs, in the main). Originally, peat was cut by hand – a highly labour-intensive industry. After sufficient drying, peat was milled or shredded to produce a bulky, highly absorbent and odourless material for animal bedding.

As the litter industry declined, block cutting of peat was used to supply a burgeoning horticultural demand. From the 1960s, block cutting by hand was replaced by mechanical cutters, although the same pattern of baulks and hollows (see Figure 1.15) was still produced.

Before the late 1960s, most operations were carried out by hand. Bogs were cut in a regular pattern of baulks (low ridges) and cut-out hollows or peat fields. Sites were drained by a regular network of drains. More recently, commercial operations have switched away from block cutting to milling.

The resulting block-cut pattern leaves a very unnatural surface. Cutting fields or hollows may stay reasonably wet depending upon drainage characteristics. Upstanding baulks do, however, dry considerably as a result of steep hydrological gradients between baulks and hollows. Baulks are usually too dry for *Sphagnum* recolonisation. Repeated passage of machinery across cutting fields compacts peat, further altering its hydrological properties. Once extraction activities cease, drier areas such as the baulks are prone to colonisation by scrub, notably birch, or dry heath vegetation. Hollows tend to be wetter and may even flood as drains infill.

The extraction system results in a distinctive pattern of baulks (raised ridges) and hollows (areas from which peat has been removed). The resultant pattern consists of a series of parallel and rectangular channels, of similar length and width (length is variable, but width is generally 2–3m) cut to a depth of 1–2m. Each cutting field is drained by ditches placed at the end of each field. There may also be additional mole or slit drains which are less obvious. Hollows/trenches are separated by ridges/baulks of similar length and width. Additional raised baulks usually exist which were used for access and storage of cut peat.

Hollows are often revegetated by hare's tail cotton grass and common cotton grass whilst drier baulks are usually characterised by ling heather, wavy-hair grass and birch. If drains

A3.2

become blocked, cutting fields may flood, allowing Sphagna to colonise – *Sphagnum recurvum* is particularly common, reflecting enhanced nutrient levels probably relating to peat mineralisation. If the drainage system remains effective, both the baulks and the cutting fields dry out to become dominated by heath vegetation. Many block-cut sites are, thus, dominated by leggy heather across the entire site. Species not normally associated with bogs may also colonise these dry peat surfaces such as dock and bracken.

A3.2.6 Milling

Milling was originally pioneered in Scotland in the 1930s. It has subsequently become the most important commercial peat-extraction technique and is widely practised in central and eastern Europe, Scandinavia, Germany and Ireland. Peat is milled to produce horticultural products and fuel for peat-fired power stations. Milling is devastating and turns open natural bog into highly-drained, bare landscapes (*see* Figure 1.16). Peat is removed layer by layer, gradually stripping away the stratigraphical archive. Additionally, any archaeological finds, which may have been unearthed by extraction, are destroyed by the milling machinery.

The first phase of a milling operation involves drainage of the site to allow machinery to pass across the surface. A series of regularly-spaced parallel drains (usually 1m wide and 1.5m deep) are dug every 15–20m. These drains are fed into larger collector drains. Sites are often left for five to ten years prior to further activities. Once the upper peat has dried sufficiently, surface vegetation is removed leaving a bare peat surface. The resulting peat surface is then gently cambered between drains to stop any water from collecting on the cutting fields.

The top 10–50mm of peat is then rotavated (milled) and left to dry for twenty-four hours; under dry conditions, moisture content drops to 70%. Further drying is promoted by turning the milled peat several times before bulldozing it into long ridges. Peat is then removed from the site. The length and efficiency of the process is weather-dependent. In Britain, eight to twelve harvests are possible within an extraction season

(Wheeler and Shaw, 1995). In eastern European countries, a more continental climate allows for twenty to twenty-five peat extraction cycles (Peat Producers Association, 1992).

Many operations transport milled peat to central processing and packing plants, or direct to power stations, using a network of railway tracks across the bog surface.

Milling has severe ecohydrological effects and drastically alters the functioning of a bog. Removal of successive layers of peat gradually lowers the perched water mound whilst intensive drainage of upper peats dries the top surface. However, drainage systems are only designed to dry upper layers and are deepened annually. Following cessation of milling, a layer of wet peat may be left whose hydrophysical properties have altered due to changes in water-storage capacities and permeability. One important effect of peat extraction is the exposure of underlying darker, more strongly-humified peat. These 'black' peats suffer greater falls in water levels than upper, lighter 'white' peats for the same amount of evapotranspiration (Schouwenaars and Vink, 1990).

The depth of peat remaining after milling also has an influence. If the bog is underlain by permeable sediments, the site loses water through vertical seepage. Whilst initial depths have not been established, Blankenberg and Kuntze (1987) suggest that at least 50 cm of high humification (>H7) peat is required to keep downward seepage losses to an acceptable rate for rehabilitation purposes. The depth of ombrotrophic peat is also important in preventing enrichment from underlying base-rich substrate. Again, critical depths have not been established, though Eggelsman (1980) again suggests 50 cm. However, by taking into account sub-surface topography and the final topography required for rehabilitation, several metres of peat may be required, and then of the appropriate quality.

A3.3 AGRICULTURE

A3.3.1 Introduction

Peatland areas have long been regarded as wastelands. The wettest areas viewed as hazardous to both man and beast. This has

A3.3

resulted in a desire to reduce the wetness of the areas and if possible to convert them to something regarded as useful and of economic value. As a result, many areas have been drained and/or burnt in an effort to dry the ground and *improve* the vegetation.

Some activities such as reseeding and/or fertiliser application (particularly after peat-cutting) can result in the complete loss of the peatland. Other activities, such as drainage or grazing, may cause only a gradual and (possibly) reversible change in vegetation assemblages.

A3.3.2 Drainage

Before drainage, fire and grazing were possibly the principal tools for manipulating the vegetation of bogs. With drainage, however, additional advantages have been perceived. Foremost is the effect on the local water-table. Although the drawdown is small, over long time periods drainage can improve ground conditions to support stock and improve moderately the quality of herbage. Drainage always demands a sustained effort. Drains can quickly infill either through collapse of the peat or through revegetation. Often the gradients on bogs are so slight that unless sophisticated systems of arterial drains are established, there is a strong likelihood of failure. In Britain, agricultural subsidies encouraged the expansion of peatland drainage onto hill peat-lands, though the agricultural benefits from this practice have been negligible or slight.

The initial effects of drainage of virgin bog are probably slow to express themselves, but if sustained the following effects can be expected.

Ecohydrological effects of agricultural drainage

Process	Response
Direct drainage	• Alters flow patterns.
	• Dewaters peat body.
	• Increases amplitude of water-table fluctuations.
	• Lowers average water table.
	• Increases microbiological activity and hence oxidation of peat.
	• Induces mineralisation of peat and releases nutrients.
	• Changes physical properties of peat, for example, increase in bulk density, compression and subsidence.
	• May induce slumping, irreversible drying and cracking.
	• Encourages a narrower range of bog species (heathers, cotton grasses).
	• Restricts the full range of typical bog mosses, resulting in extinctions and replacement by others less typical of open bog.
	• Encourages colonisation by alien species.
Peripheral drainage	• Lowers perched water-table of bog as a whole.
	• Alters functional role of lagg fen.

Air photos (*see* 4.6.4) are a very useful tool to identify and locate drains, as they show up as distinctive dark, straight lines across the peat. Even when the drains are blocked by vegetation, aerial photographs may still indicate the position of drains, as they can remain visible for hundreds of years (Goodwillie, 1980) (Figure A.1).

Where drains have become filled in by vegetation, they are less obvious but can usually be picked out by different vegetation associated with the drain line. Distinct lines of bright green aquatic Sphagna or scrub and trees indicate drain-lines. The presence of trees or scrub usually indicates some degree of drying-out of the surface (in the oceanic conditions of the Atlantic region). Spoil resulting from drain construction can often be identified as a distinct ridge running along one side of the drain. With the passage of time, the ridge oxidises and diminishes. The physical wastage (oxidation) of the peat resulting from drainage is apparent as slumping or sloping of the ground down into the drain. This physical change occurs alongside all drains but is often not noticeable.

The ecohydrological effects described above can also be destructive to archaeological artefacts as well as altering the palaeoecological record contained within the peat (*see* 1.6).

A3.3.3 Grazing, Poaching and Enrichment

Introduction

Ombrogenous peat is, by definition, poor in nutrients and thus supports vegetation of low nutritive value to grazing animals. Despite this,

Figure A.1   Re-vegetated drain which, although infilled, still acts as an effective drain, Tailend Moss, Scotland. (Stuart Brooks)

most bogs are grazed by various animals including sheep (in particular), cattle, deer, rabbits, hares, goats and birds. Some upland farms, in Britain, consist almost entirely of poor-quality grazing land, much of which may consist of blanket bog.

The impacts of grazing vary considerably, especially given its interaction with other forms of land management, notably burning (Rawes, 1983) and drainage. The historical management of blanket bog for the benefit of domestic grazing animals has resulted in a change in species composition and structure. This is exacerbated by increasing grazing pressure from wild herbivores, which, in Scotland, has come largely from the rising populations of red deer (Staines et al., 1995).

General ecohydrological effects relate to grazing (herbage removal), poaching (trampling) and enrichment. They are summarised below:

Process	Response
Herbage removal	• Selective removal of more palatable species at specific times of year (for example, cotton grass, or tips of purple moor grass). • Encourages growth forms to protect growing tips from grazing. • Encourages species tolerant of grazing pressure.

Trampling	• Damage to microtopography. • Damage to sensitive pool systems. • Exposes bare peat (prevents revegetation). • Creates new niches for alien species. • Increases risk of small-scale erosion.
Enrichment	• Local enrichment from congregating animals, feeding areas, deaths and so on • Widespread enrichment at high stocking levels.

Grazing

Plant species are selectively grazed by herbivores due, in part, to their variable palatability, resulting in uneven structure and composition of communities (Rowell, 1988; Grant et al., 1976; Grant et al., 1987). Additional variables include grazing species (sheep, cattle and so on), stocking density, composition of habitat, timing and other management practices (such as drainage and burning).

Animals browse in various ways, and this has differing effects upon the structure and composition of species. Sheep tend to produce an even, short sward as they move back and forwards across a site. In comparison, cattle tend to produce a more uneven vegetation structure, due mainly to their browsing methods (Table A.1).

The dietary requirements of cattle and sheep vary throughout the year though several communities are commonly selected (Grant et al., 1987). Cattle diets contain a greater proportion of cotton grass than sheep although, in spring, sheep selectively browse immature flowers of hare's tail cotton grass. Red deer can exert considerable grazing pressure on upland bog communities. The hinds prefer a similar habitat to those of sheep, providing competition for desirable species and

A3.3

Table A.1:   Functional grazing attributes of animals.

Species	Biting method	Selective ability	Grazing height
Sheep	Biting/shearing	High	Short
Red deer	Biting/shearing	High	Short
Cattle	Wrap tongues around vegetation and pull	Low	Longer
Goats	Biting/shearing	Highly selective	Short
Rabbits	Biting/shearing	Very high	Very short

exacerbating damaging impacts of domestic animal grazing. Seasonal variation in species selection is characteristic for all browsing herbivores and is shown in Table A.2. Preference for certain plant communities or species also relates to digestibility at particular times of the year.

Table A.2: Selection of peatland species by hill sheep (MAFF, 1983).

Species selected	Parts eaten	Season
Ling heather	Tips	Late summer and late winter
Bilberry	Leaves/green stems	Spring to late summer and late winter
Purple moor grass	Green	Early summer
Heath rush	Green	Winter
Mat grass	Green	Late winter and spring
Hare's tail cotton grass	Young heads	Late winter and early spring
	Leaf butt	Spring
	Green-leaf	Spring
Crowberry	Green	Autumn and early winter
Deer grass	Green	Spring

Other observed preferences, not related to digestibility, are also evident and are summarised in Table A.3.

The preferential selection by herbivores of desired species imposes uncharacteristic species assemblages and structures. The control of these impacts is largely down to stocking densities, timing of grazing and interaction with other management practices.

A3.3

Table A.3: Observed grazing preferences not related to digestibility (after Armstrong and Milne, 1995).

Species	Preferences
Sheep	Avoid mat grass generally but graze small plants as part of a short sword. Avoid rushes.
Red deer	Graze heather more than sheep.
Cattle	Eat more mat grass than sheep or deer.
Goats	Eat rushes in spring; will eat mat grass.
Rabbits	Avoid aromatic or prickly species.

Poaching

Poaching is the term given to damage caused from trampling by animals. Relative levels of poaching are determined by the following:

- Animal size – the worst poachers are cattle.
- Pressure points – poaching is evident along fence lines, in areas of desirable vegetation, at and around gates and around supplementary feeding stations (Figure A.2).
- Ground conditions – wetter areas are more susceptible.
- Vegetation type – *Sphagnum* is particularly susceptible to trampling.

Another consequence of poaching is the disruption of the physical structure of the surface, encouraging areas of bare peat around tussocks.

Enrichment

Enrichment through grazing may be localised or diffuse. Most enrichment results from animal faeces. Usually the addition of faecal matter to an area merely represents a recycling or loss of nutrients rather than any net gain to the system. However, supplementary feeding is often necessary especially during the winter. This can lead to a transfer of nutrients from extra feed onto the bog. Supplementary feeding directly on the bog, in the form of hay bales and so on, concentrates enrichment effects (and trampling) around feeding stations. Additionally, animals may be taken in overnight and fed off site. Faeces, deposited on the bog, emanating from overnight feeding also causes a net nutrient gain. Even if grazing is restricted to peatland only, the

Figure A.2 Poaching damage caused by grazing cattle. (Jonnee Hughes)

deposition of nutrients in the form of dung and urine is locally (Rowell, 1988) variable, leading to changes in community composition. Nutrient-level increases cause a shift from ombrotrophic to mesotrophic communities (for example, rushes, *Sphagnum recurvum* or bog asphodel-dominated stands) (Figure A.3).

Another form of enrichment results from decomposition of animal carcasses.

Note that the principal threat to the survival of the archaeological resource lies in possible changes in vegetation allowing the development of deep-rooted species or erosion. Enrichment may stimulate microbial activity, which may jeopardise the survival of fragile organic deposits.

A3.3.4 Direct Improvement – Agricultural 'Reclamation'

To 'improve' bogs for agriculture, fertilisers are often applied in combination with drainage to boost the nutrient supply available to vegetation. Prior to any fertiliser application, natural vegetation may be flailed to reduce its cover and vigour. Enhanced nutrient status changes vegetation communities and also enables a site to be reseeded to support an entirely different type

Figure A.3 Localised enrichment causes a shift from ombrotrophic to mesotrophic vegetation communities. Isolated stands of bog asphodel are often a good indicator of point source enrichment in the UK. (Richard Lindsay)

of vegetation (pasture or arable crops). Despite fertiliser application, pasture on peat is usually poor and continued fertiliser applications are necessary to avoid a reversion to poor acidic pasture characterised by abundant rush growth.

Conversion to agricultural land has had a major impact on lowland raised bogs where the peat has been cutaway. Deep peat areas are more difficult to 'reclaim'. Where agricultural conversion has been attempted, the land tends to revert to poor acid grassland, often with abundant growth of soft rush, eventually reverting to bog.

Reseeded or heavily-fertilised bog stands out as bright green, often fenced areas, generally with a short grassy sward. Extensive areas of soft rush are also indicative of past fertiliser input, particularly where there is a grassy sward between rush tussocks. Depending on the time elapsed since fertiliser applications ceased, there may be elements of heath or bog vegetation re-emerging in the vegetation.

A3.3.5 Burning

Introduction

Fire is used as a management tool to control or manipulate the vegetation of bog peatland in a number of ways. Perceived benefits of burning bogs include:

- Improving the grazing value of herbage for domestic livestock through the provision of spring bite, removal of coarse grasses, preventing the build-up of litter (for example, purple moor grass) and the renewal of heather.
- Sustaining habitat for red grouse through the provision of a multi-structured and multi-aged heather-rich habitat.

In effect, these two objectives are frequently combined in Britain.

Fire is also sometimes employed even when the agricultural use has ceased because it is considered 'traditional' to do so. Drain-clearance and reduction of fire risk to adjacent cash crops are also reported. Malicious fires are a common feature, as are accidental ones. The cumulative effects of repeated and regular burning tend to promote a succession which favours heath and grass vegetation communities and suppresses the abundance and diversity of bog mosses.

A3.3

Even without the deliberate use of fire, wildfires or natural fires have occurred at intervals throughout the history of bog development. Such fires have to some degree influenced the development of the vegetation of the British uplands (Stevenson and Thompson, 1993). The magnitude and significance of the effects of fire as an ecological factor remain unquantified, although natural fire frequency is low in comparison to deliberate burning frequency. A long cultural use of peatlands in historic and prehistoric times makes it difficult to separate the effects of natural from deliberate burning. Evidence of fire can be found throughout the profiles of all lowland raised bogs (for example, Barber et al., 1994) and blanket bog (for example, Charman, 1992).

Most controlled burning of upland peatland occurs between February and March and is linked to management of heather moorland to improve grazing for sheep and habitat for red grouse. Controlled burning, if conducted in accordance with the Muirburn Code (SNH, 1994), should result in small-scale, low-intensity fires. However, uncontrolled burning can be highly damaging to the ecology and economy of peatland areas.

The deliberate and continued use of fire in the management of bog vegetation has distinctive ecological effects. These are described below:

Process	Response
Combustion of vegetation and moss mats and hummocks	• Results in complete or partial removal of above ground vegetation. • Promotes a flush of nutrients which may encourage species such as purple moor grass, hare's tail cotton-grass and deer grass. • Damages bog moss species which form high hummocks, such as the rare *Sphagnum imbricatum*.
Litter and peat combustion	*Frequent fires* • expose bare peat, creating new niches for species such as S. tenellum; and • increase firmness of the peat which reduces water holding capacity; *Intense fires* • remove bog moss mulching layer, altering capacity to modulate precipitation;

• expose peat and increase risk of erosion;
• consume shallow seed bank; and
• form tarry surfaces on peat which reduce water-holding capacity.

Vegetation succession	*Frequent fires encourage* • shrubs such as heather, crowberry and bilberry; • tussock-forming species such as purple moor grass and hare's tail cotton grass; • hypnaceous mosses (*Pleurozium schreberi* and *Hypnum cupressiforme*); and • tight cushions of S. compactum, and S. capillifolium, and woolly-hair moss. *Intense fires encourage* • bottle-brush mosses (*Polytrichum, Camplyopus* and so on), algal mats and crustose lichens; and • unstable and eroding surfaces.

There are several variables which influence the ecological and hydrological responses outlined above. Foremost are the intensity of an individual fire and the frequency of burning. Other variables include the time of year, the amount of combustible material, and the pattern and speed of fire spread.

Intensity

The intensity of a fire is controlled largely by the amount of combustible material, though environmental conditions such as moisture content, the position of the water-table and wind speeds are also involved. On ground that is often burnt, the amount of combustible material relates to the time since the last fire.

Typical signs of fire include partial or complete scorching and bleaching of bog mosses, charred heather stems and charcoal. Particular bog mosses are considered very susceptible to fire. *Sphagnum imbricatum* and *S. fuscum* are considered to be the least-tolerant, possibly because they grow in high hummocks. The decline of *S. imbricatum* on Cors Fochno in Wales is attributed largely to fire (Slater, 1976).

More intense fires may be shown up by partially-consumed bog-moss hummocks and charring of fence posts and trees, if these occur. Particularly intense fires often lead to the

A3.3

formation of a skin of tarry bitumen formed by chemical reactions following ignition of peat waxes (Mallick et al., 1984). Crustose lichens such as *Lecidea granulosa* and *Lecidea uliginosa* and several species of algae may form over unconsolidated peat, significantly reducing germination rates of seeds (Legg et al., 1992). However, algae growths and crusts may serve to prevent excessive erosion across bare peat surfaces.

Frequency

Regular burning has quite distinctive effects and, in most cases, rather long-lasting impacts on vegetation even if the intensity of fires is low. Regular burning prevents the build-up of combustible material in litter and keeps dwarf shrubs in check. Frequent fires also produce flushes of plant nutrients which encourage sedges and grasses. Such flushes are thought to be lost if burning takes place in late autumn or early winter, though the cotton grasses can grow at low temperatures. Plants such as purple moor grass and hare's tail cotton grass tolerate low- and medium-intensity fires since their growing bud is usually below ground or well protected in the heart of a tussock. A short fire rotation is considered to favour cotton grasses above heather. Where purple moor grass is present, there may be a build-up of litter. Fire is often then used to control this build up. Paradoxically, fire favours purple moor grass, which can then overwhelm most other species.

Less frequent fires at low intensity have more subtle effects. A light, controlled winter burn, for example, removes most above-ground plant woody material, although basal stems of the heather plants remain largely intact, protected by a layer of dead plant material and a wet, or frozen, bryophyte layer. After a fire, heather quickly regrows from both basal stems and seed – the desired objective of moorland management. Effects on other plants are varied. Some species such as purple moor grass, deer grass and hare's tail cotton grass are largely unaffected and if anything are encouraged or favoured by burning regimes given their growth form.

A single fire can provide the conditions for the invasion of scrub and trees, while rotational burning destroys seedlings and saplings (Hester and Miller, 1995).

Time of Year

Time of year affects the temperature of a burn, primarily through the moisture content of combustible material and waterlogging of peat. Autumn fires are thought to encourage heather and may discourage cotton grasses and deer grass. Conversely, later winter fires may stimulate the latter. Summer fires on the other hand are likely to burn hot, risk burning peat and inflict longer-lasting damage, for example, through erosion.

Other Factors

Interactions with other factors such as grazing, hydrology, erosion and climate are also important. The interaction effects of burning and grazing may reinforce the effects of each. Even limited grazing after fire may retard the regeneration of heather. Species which are normally tolerant of fire, such as cloudberry, are likely to be absent given grazing.

Severe burning reduces water storage capacity (Robinson, 1985). This affects the regeneration of many bog species as well as altering the general hydrological behaviour of bog (less water is stored in the upper horizons, and discharge following rainfall events may be greater). Erosion may have a drying effect also. Past erosion and drying may explain the severity of fire in a number of documented cases (for example, Legg et al., 1992). Climate, particularly the length of the growing season and exposure, may be an important variable in the regeneration of bog after fire.

Recolonisation after Fire

The recolonisation of *Sphagnum* species onto bare peat surfaces is dependent upon:

- proximity of available seed (spore) source to bare/burnt area;
- hydrological and physiochemical conditions – water-table, pH and nutrient status of the bare surface;
- ability of different species to colonise from spores; and
- ability of different *Sphagnum* species to compete with other colonising species.

A3.3

Very little information exists on the ability of *Sphagnum* species to colonise bare areas, although anecdotal evidence suggests that *Sphagnum* species are poor colonisers. Vegetative regeneration, notably of the aquatic species *Sphagnum cuspidatum*, provides the quickest method of recolonisation of bare and waterlogged surfaces. Evidence from one study (Lindsay and Ross, 1994) suggests that *Sphagnum tenellum* is a good coloniser of bare, burnt areas, though this is dependent both on the hydrological conditions of the surface being suitable (that is, wet) and on a reasonable community of the species existing in the locality. It is unclear from the study whether colonisation is vegetative or from spores.

A3.3.6 Lint Holes

The cloth-production industry has left a legacy on some lowland raised bogs in the form of *lint holes* (*see* Figure 6.55). These were dug to soak or 'rett' flax to remove tough outer layers of the plant and soften the fibres beneath. The acid water of bogs enhanced the procedure, with an added bonus that the process, which was considered smelly and polluting, was carried out away from habitation and also from drinking water supplies. With the decline of the industry, lint holes were abandoned.

Lint holes are small (not more than 2–3m across), straight-sided and regular-shaped. Since the abandonment of the flax industry, at the beginning of the twentieth century, most lint holes have filled with vegetation although they often still support a more hydrophilous vegetation than the surrounding peat surface. Aquatic *Sphagnum* hollows, often associated with lush growths of common cotton grass, are characteristic. Often, the surface is unconsolidated and is unable to bear the weight of a person.

These features are small, and their impact on a site as a whole is limited. They probably have an effect on water levels immediately around them, enhancing shrub growth due to reduced water levels. The effect also relates to their size and distribution – some relatively small sites may have large numbers of lint holes, causing a more pronounced effect (*see* 6.25).

A3.4 COMMERCIAL AFFORESTATION

Trees can be a natural component of bog flora. In continental climates of hot and dry summers and cold winters, water levels fall sufficiently to allow trees to become established, although those that do are often rather stunted and often form only sparse cover. In more maritime climates such as those found in Britain, trees are rarely (if at all) a natural component of bog vegetation, although palaeoecological evidence shows that, in the past, conditions on bog surfaces were dry enough to allow tree growth.

However, the introduction of the Cuthbertson plough, in the 1950s, allowed deep peats to be drained sufficiently to allow tree-planting (*see* Figure 1.19). Within the UK, large estates in northern England and Scotland were purchased for forestry, leading to substantial areas of upland blanket bog being afforested, such as, Kielder Forest, Northumberland (England) and the Galloway Forest (Scotland). New tax concessions, set up in 1980 to encourage forestry, were used by private individuals and companies to offset tax losses by investing in forestry. This had the undesired effect of afforesting parts of the Flow Country (this tax concession was removed in 1988). Raised bogs have been afforested in a more piecemeal way. Large raised bogs in Scotland – such as, Racks Moss, Lochar Mosses and West Flanders Moss – were afforested in the 1960s and 1970s. Threats from new forestry to British raised bogs have largely ceased.

Commercial planting of trees on deep peat has been largely restricted to conifers. The main species used – lodgepole pine and sitka spruce – can tolerate a high degree of wetness, although some artificial drainage is still required. The simplest form of drainage may be provided by deep ploughing. The young trees are planted on the plough mounds. As trees mature to form a closed canopy, up to 30% of rainfall is intercepted on leaf surfaces (Gash et al., 1980), significantly drying the peat body. Better initial growth is obtained by utilising systematic drainage systems (*see* Figure 1.19) where a number of deep drains run into an arterial system (sometimes natural stream courses).

The direct ecohydrological impacts of forestry planting are summarised below.

A3.4

Process	Response
Ploughing	• Destroys the acrotelm. • Creates a drier mound inhospitable to bog vegetation. • Encourages non-bog species such as wavy-hair grass or tussock-forming species such as purple moor grass. • Exposes bare furrows acting as drains.
Drainage	• Dries mound further and increases water-table drawdown and water-table fluctuations. • Increases moisture deficits and lowers summer water-table. • Increases mineralisation of peat. • May induce slumping of material into drains, scouring, and sedimentation downstream.
Canopy closure	• Increases interception and evaporation. • Increases transpiration. • Induces cracking. • Root development and cracking create new pathways for water-flow. • Needle fall and canopy shades out most vegetation, except in rides. • Peat compaction.
Fertiliser application	• Favours competitive species. • Increases microbial activity, mineralisation, and plant nutrient run-off of plant.

Forestry on peatland is not always successful. Foremost is the breakdown of the drainage system. Should this occur prior to canopy closure, tree growth can be set back. If drains infill and become revegetated with bog species, trees may die and the plantation fail. While outright failures are localised, stressed plantations are much more common.

Unplanted areas which are surrounded either completely or partially by forestry may also be affected. Smith and Charman (1988) showed that the vegetation of ombrotrophic mire sites in the Kielder Forest – the Border Mires – changed considerably after the forest was planted. In general, moorland species appear to be outcompeting ombrotrophic bog species. Significant increases of wavy hair grass, *Pleurozium schreberi* and *Polytrichum commune* have been matched by decreases in *Sphagnum magellanicum*, *S. papillosum*, *S. cuspidatum*, round-leaved sundew, bog asphodel, common cotton grass, bog rosemary and cross-leaved heath. This could be due to cessation of grazing and burning following afforestation or due to effects of adjacent afforestation on remaining open areas. Long-term grazing exclosures have been set up to test this. Initial data analyses suggest that cessation of grazing may have a more important role (Charman and Smith, 1992).

Run-off from afforested peatlands also affects associated freshwater systems. Palmer (1988) lists a series of effects on watercourses resulting from afforestation on blanket bog:

- *Run-off*: Run-off rates from afforested peat differs from unplanted areas and changes during different stages of afforestation. After initial drainage, run-off is typically 'flashy' – quickly peaking and reducing after a rain event (Robinson, 1980). As trees reach closed canopy, run-off decreases due to increased interception and higher transpiration rates by trees. This may result in lowered water levels in associated streams and rivers, causing downstream effects on the fauna and flora.
- *Sedimentation*: Sediment released into watercourses increases as a result of increased erosion rates in drained peatlands (Robinson and Blyth, 1982). Enhanced turbidity and silt deposition in streams and rivers also affect plant and animal life.
- *Fertiliser application*: Afforestation also elevates nutrient levels through mineralisation of peat (due to ploughing and drainage) and the addition of fertilisers to encourage tree growth.

Afforestation, commercial or semi-natural, is detrimental to archaeology and the palaeoenvironmental record. Both can be degraded or destroyed due to physical and chemical changes resulting from afforestation. Tree roots can cause physical damage to organic materials and cause microbiological change within the rhizosphere.

A3.5 **DEVELOPMENT**

A3.5.1 **Introduction**

In many cases, the pressure of direct development leads to outright destruction of bogs. However, other types of development may only cause transient changes or only affect part of a peat area.

A3.5

A3.5.2 Roads and Railways

Peatlands have long formed a barrier against travel. The oldest trackways, uncovered within the peat, are prehistoric. The Sweet Track, found in the Somerset Levels, for example, is dated to 3806 BC (Coles, 1995) (*see* Figure 6.7). More recently, peatlands have also proved difficult for road and rail construction. Routes are sometimes 'floated' across bogs using wool bales or birch platforms, although in modern times the preference is to remove peat before construction.

Given the extent of blanket bog areas, it is inevitable that roads and railways are routed through peatlands. These routes may have a long history. In the Pennines, pack-horse trails, sometimes existing as flagstone-paved pathways, have been excavated and restored for use as bridleways.

Process	Response to floating roads
Pressure	• Route sinks. • Subsidence/slumping. • Local flooding. • Compaction. • Imposition of new slope on groundwater mound.
Drainage	• Drainage and drying of intact peat. • Drying beneath road – cracking (needing frequent repair).
Enrichment	• Local or widespread eutrophication.

Process	Response to roads cutting through to mineral
Cutting of peat to mineral base	• Creates unstable peat face liable to erosion and bog burst. • Dissection or severance of groundwater mound. • New groundwater mound establishes with risk of whole site drying.
Effluent and nutrient run-off	• Local or widespread eutrophication.
Revegetation of damaged surfaces	• Mixing of peat with mineral soil. • Establishment of rushes.

A3.5.3 Housing

Housing has had a limited impact on peatlands given that peat is a very unstable substrate for house construction. However, encroachment by housing or industrial estates is encountered. In these cases, peat is stripped away before construction. Clearly, such actions have a dramatic impact on the ecohydrology of the sites in question. The likely effects of house construction are:

- *Hydrological*: Even where peat is stripped away, a site is still likely to be subject to waterlogging and possibly flooding. Housing developments have to incorporate intensive and effective drainage systems, disrupting the hydrological regime of the remaining bog. An additional problem is that where peat has been removed from a raised bog, the original shape and size of the peat dome is altered, causing further hydrological change (*see* 2.5.3).
- *Chemical*: Housing adjacent to peatlands may also cause nutrient enrichment either directly as water floods onto peatlands as a result of altered hydrology or indirectly via dust from construction.

A3.5.4 Mining

In Britain, there are many peatland areas which overlie economic mineral deposits; open-cast coal mining has had a particular impact in central Scotland, for example.

Underground or deep mining creates a network of underground galleries often extending many miles beneath the surface. Once mining has ceased, and mines are no longer maintained, galleries close up and may collapse to result in surface subsidence. One effect of subsidence is the creation of pools as water collects in subsidence depressions. Another effect is the creation of numerous deep and circular depressions (shakeholes) often vegetated by a mixture of grass and dwarf shrub, found, for example, on Conistone and Grassington Moors (Yorkshire, England).

Open-cast mining is necessarily much more devastating, usually resulting in total destruction of a peatland site. As underlying minerals are usually of greater economic value than peat, the latter is usually removed as quickly as possible. Even where small volumes of peat are removed, they cannot be replaced, as the structure and properties are irrevocably modified. Clearly, the archive within removed peat is virtually destroyed, as is the context for any archaeological

A3.5

remains which may be found. Rehabilitation work to recreate bog, after mining has ceased, has been tried with little success, although other wetland areas may be created.

Ecohydrological effects of mining are:

Process	Response
Pumping galleries	• Lowers water-table in permeable substrates.
	• Causes drying of bog surface.
Pumping onto bog surface	• Local nutrient enrichment.
Collapse of galleries	• Causes subsidence and creates surface depressions.
	• Depressions may fill with water.
	• Alters topography of peat surface increasing locally drying effects.
Dumping or removal of spoil	• Eutrophication from dust during working.
	• Compression of peat, local flooding.

In most cases, the effects of mining are extremely obvious. However, where underground mining has ceased, surface features and historic records should be checked. The presence of numerous large surface depressions, some of which may be water-filled, are indicative of deep mining activity. Shake-holes should not be confused with 'swallow' or 'sink holes' which are associated with naturally-occurring sub-surface channels on blanket bogs.

A3.5.5 Waste (Rubbish) Disposal

Peat bogs, having little economic value, have been used as areas for waste disposal. Fly tipping is a frequent problem on bogs. Further problems are found where agricultural waste has been dumped on bogs. Some raised bogs have been used for tipping local authority waste. Bolton Metropolitan Borough Council, for example, was attempting to use Red Moss SSSI in this way.

A3.5.6 Development and Archaeology

All of the activities described in section A3.5 inevitably result in damage to or destruction of the archaeological resource within peatlands. Outright or partial destruction, hydrological or chemical change, as described above, all impact upon archaeological remains including the palaeoenvironmental record.

A3.6 OTHER FORMS OF DAMAGING ACTIVITIES

A3.6.1 Introduction

Some activities, if carried out sympathetically, can have a positive effect on a habitat for example, grouse-moor management maintains moorland whilst additional habitats can be created such as open water areas for duck decoys. Others, however, can be extremely detrimental to this delicate habitat if not properly controlled. For instance, trampling by walkers has led to severe erosion problems along popular long-distance walks which cross blanket peat, for example, the Pennine Way (northern England).

A3.6.2 Grouse Management

Large areas of upland blanket bog in Britain are managed for grouse shooting, particularly in northern England and southern and eastern Scotland. Grouse feed mainly on young shoots of ling heather or crowberry. Sporting interests have created heather moorland areas through limited drainage, burning and grazing to increase grouse numbers. This habitat is far from 'natural'. Peat macrofossil diagrams demonstrate that moorlands were originally dominated by *Sphagnum* mosses and sedges with occasional heathers.

However, heather moorland is recognised as a valuable wildlife habitat in its own right, and agricultural incentive schemes exist in Britain to encourage its maintenance (such as, the Heather Moorland Scheme). Setting conservation objectives for heather moorland is difficult. For example, *British Wildlife* reported that *Sphagnum* growth, which was threatening to overwhelm heather on Dartmoor, could be curtailed by second burning. If the conservation objectives are to work towards more 'natural' systems, the manager would want to encourage *Sphagnum* growth. However, in this case, the objectives are to manage the peatland as heather moorland rather than as active blanket bog. Priorities may change in blanket bog areas which have been declared as possible Special Areas of Conservation under the EC *Habitats Directive*. Conservation objectives are clearly defined to conserve active blanket bog.

A3.6

A3.6.3 Shooting and Clay Pigeon Shooting

Clay pigeon shooting is not a huge problem but is included here as it has been found on some bogs. Main effects relate to trampling and pollution from shattered clays. On Ballynahone Bog (Northern Ireland), for example, shattered clays appear to have altered the chemistry of one part of the site. Poor *Sphagnum* growth may be due to lead pollution from shot.

A3.6.4 Duck Decoys

Many duck decoys are quite old, although there are also examples of recent attempts to create open water areas for shooting purposes. Duck decoy pools may not have always been deliberately cut; some have been created by mining subsidence and peat-cutting.

A3.6.5 Trampling by People

The physical effect of trampling may be to change the surface microtopography. Hummocks may be destroyed, ridges flattened and depressed to create artificial areas of open water. A good example of the effect of trampling is found near permanent quadrat monitoring stations (*see* 4.6.3) where peat compression and trampling serves to alter the vegetation being monitored.

Repeated trampling, as may occur along footpaths, can cause the total loss of vegetation. In the wet upland areas dominated by blanket peat, the exposed bare peat is particularly susceptible to erosion. This can result in extensive areas of erosion, further exacerbated by people seeking drier routes around the bare, unconsolidated peat, and extending the damaged area (Figure 5.79).

A3.6.6 Vehicle Damage

In the past, access onto peatland areas would have been primarily by foot although some journeys, particularly to peat banks, would have been made by horse and cart. Damage would, therefore, have been limited to distinct trackways to peat banks.

More recently, access onto peatlands may be by tractor or by all-terrain vehicles (ATVs). ATVs come in various sizes and designs: some with caterpillar tracks and others with low-ground-pressure tyres (*see* 5.6.9).

Vehicle traffic on peatlands is associated with both commercial afforestation and some forms of peat-cutting such as milling or 'sausage' extraction. In these situations, drainage usually precedes other activities to allow heavy machinery to pass safely across the bog surface. However, heavy machinery has been known to sink into peat despite drainage. This often relates to disruption of the peat/water matrix which causes liquefaction of peat to form a highly unstable surface. Increasingly, ATVs are also used to transport people to hunting and fishing sites. This often involves repeatedly using the same tracks (*see* 6.29).

The main forms of damage resulting from vehicle pressure are physical damage to the plants and disruption of the peat surface. Studies on the effect of off-road vehicles on tundra in North America by Richard and Brown (1974) have shown that a number of factors are important in determining the degree of damage caused to plants and the peat structure:

- Operational and vehicle perameters such as speed, acceleration, wheel-track pressure and so on
- Surface topography characteristics – uneven surfaces can become accentuated due to the action of vehicles across an area. On level terrain, compaction or the formation of ruts are common results of repetitive vehicle passes.
- Degree of slope – sloping terrain is more susceptible to erosion than level ground and, once initiated, the action of water on bare peat can result in extensive gully formation.
- Time of year – damage may be expected to be more severe when the ground is wetter.
- Type of vegetation – wet marshy areas experience greater disturbance than well-drained areas.
- Level of microbial activity – compaction of peat results in increased transfer of heat into, and out of, the underlying soil which may alter the rate of microbial activity.

A3.6.7 Moss-gathering

Sphagnum moss absorbs water extremely well. As a result, *Sphagnum* has been put to a variety of differing uses. In the past it has been used as a sterile dressing, filling for babies' nappies and to clean up oil spills and other contamination. More recently, large quantities of *Sphagnum* moss have

A3.6

been used in the horticultural industry. Wet *Sphagnum* is often used as a packaging around plants during transportation. In a dry state, it is used to line hanging baskets, as, once wetted, it releases water to growing plants at a slow and steady rate. *Sphagnum* also prevents the growing medium, contained within the hanging basket, from drying out too quickly.

Sphagnum moss is an important component of a functioning acrotelm (surface layer). Its removal, therefore, can have a considerable damaging impact. Terrestrial *Sphagnum* removal exposes bare peat, causing drying (through higher evaporation rates) and erosion. Removal of aquatic species from pools has less effect, although if aquatic species are removed from revegetating drains, the drain is likely to become more efficient.

A3.7 INDIRECT FORMS OF DAMAGE

A3.7.1 Pollution

Bogs are rain-fed, and thus nutrient-poor, making them particularly vulnerable to the effects of chemical pollution. Pollutants may enter the system in a variety of ways:

- via the atmosphere: fertiliser drift from agriculture and forestry or acid deposition from industrial activities and vehicle emissions.
- via drains or surface run-off: agricultural effluent, sewage, industrial waste and so on.
- via direct application: fertiliser for agricultural improvement, liming, manure and so on.
- via faecal enrichment: from bird roosts, grazing animals and so on.

Atmospheric Pollution

The addition of nutrients and pollutants from the atmosphere may have an effect on both the development of peat and the vegetation of a mire. There are three main sources of atmospheric nutrient enrichment: the surrounding land, industry and the sea.

Glaser and Janssens (1986), for example, consider the surprisingly *Sphagnum*-rich bogs of mid-continental Canada to be the result of dust from the North American prairies fertilising the bogs to favour the growth of *Sphagnum* over lichens. Further, Van Geel and Middeldorp (1988),

attempting to explain the local extinction of *Sphagnum imbricatum* from Carbury Bog, Eire, around AD 1400, note that this may be related to the intensification of agriculture, reflected in the pollen diagram, increasing dust and charcoal aerosols. Rudolf and Voigt (1986) have shown that for several *Sphagnum* species a nitrate concentration of 100µM is favourable but that *Sphagnum magellanicum* can tolerate up to 322µM. This may explain the increase and dominance of *Sphagnum magellanicum* in recent peat layers at Carbury Bog and also at many other sites in the UK. Stoneman et al. (1993) and Stoneman (1993) also found evidence to suggest that agriculturally-derived atmospheric nitrogen deposition may have caused the decline of *Sphagnum imbricatum* across the British bogs.

In the southern Pennines, Moss (1913) listed eighteen *Sphagnum* species of which only two were rare. By 1964, Tallis recorded only five *Sphagnum* species of which only *Sphagnum recurvum* was common. Industrial pollution may have had a significant effect on the ecology of the southern Pennine blanket peatlands. Conway (1948) found that at Ringinglow Moss, Derbyshire, *Sphagnum* disappeared when industrially-derived soot spheres became prevalent.

The sensitivity of Sphagna to industrially-derived sulphur pollution is well documented (Ferguson et al., 1978; Ferguson and Lee, 1979 Ferguson et al., 1984; Press et al., 1986). Twenhoven (1992) looked at the effect of nitrate and ammonium addition on *Sphagnum magellanicum* and *Sphagnum fallax* (*Sphagnum fallax* is known as *Sphagnum recurvum* in Britain) on a mire in Germany. Where pollution is low, the two species occupy a similar niche and are often found growing together. The addition of nitrogen, however, caused *Sphagnum fallax* to out-compete *Sphagnum magellanicum* in hollows and on lawns. On hummocks, the better water-holding capacity of *Sphagnum magellanicum* allowed the moss to out-compete *Sphagnum fallax* during drier periods. Increased atmospheric nitrogen deposition may therefore explain the recent success of *Sphagnum fallax* across central and north-eastern Europe. It is worth noting that the only *Sphagnum* species found on much of the southern Pennines is *Sphagnum recurvum* (Ferguson et al., 1978).

A3.7

Deposition of minerals can affect bog ecology. In the southern Pennines, there seems to be a fairly clear connection between *Sphagnum* decline and industrial and agricultural pollution. Elsewhere in the UK, the decline of *Sphagnum imbricatum* with a concurrent increase of *Sphagnum magellanicum* and *Sphagnum papillosum* may also be due to pollution (Stoneman, 1993).

Eutrophication

Elevated nutrient levels (eutrophication) result in increased plant growth rates and species change which in turn have significant effects on numbers and types of micro-organisms present (Maltby, 1992). This can lead to changes in decomposition rates, possibly preventing peat formation. Enrichment may come from a variety of sources: farm waste, domestic refuse, sewage, road surface water drainage and bird roosts.

A3.7.2 Cumulative Impacts

Theoretically, both raised and blanket bogs are stable climax systems (Godwin, 1975; Moore, 1987). Occasionally, natural perturbations occur (fire and bog bursts, and so on) which temporarily disrupt the equilibrium; although, with time, a stable state re-establishes. Bog sites in their natural and undamaged state, therefore, do not require active management to sustain a natural vegetation cover.

However, sites are often encountered where the vegetation cover is distinctly unnatural yet there are no obvious forms of damage. On these sites, it is highly likely that there has been damage although it was so long ago that the direct evidence is difficult to discern. Drains, for example, may be well vegetated but still function well. Past fertiliser application and past repetitive burning are also often difficult to identify yet may still be affecting the site's ecology. Atmospheric pollution and changes in surrounding water levels are particularly difficult to isolate as causal agents for ecological change, although they may have profound effects.

In Britain at least, every raised bog in the country and most areas of blanket bog have been damaged in some way. Areas of seemingly 'near-natural' vegetation are nearly always surrounded by more damaged areas. As different parts of the same bog are intimately connected through the same hydrological systems, damage in one area of a site is likely to affect another (*see* 2.5). Consequently, many sites are probably continuing to degrade due to forms of damage that may have occurred many years ago.

A3.7

APPENDIX 4
HEALTH AND SAFETY

Health and Safety

A4.1   Introduction

Peat bogs are a potentially hazardous environment for both site workers and recreational users. The habitat is characterised by open water and saturated soils, creating hazards for even basic management operations.

Health and safety must be a primary consideration in the management planning process and also in on-site training programmes. Hazards, and their associated risks, should be identified and appropriate precautions and procedures established. To avoid or minimise the risk of hazards usually requires nothing more than an awareness of the situation and common sense.

This section identifies some of the common hazards that are associated with bogs, but it should not be used as an exhaustive list. For general information, contact your local office of the Health and Safety Executive (listed in the phone book) or, for specific information and publications ,contact:

HSE Information Centre
Broad Lane
Sheffield
S3 7HQ.
Telephone: 01742 892345
Free Leaflet Line: 01742 892346

A4.2   The Bog Environment

There are a number of features that could be a potential hazard when walking or working on a bog.

Pools, either natural or man-made, can represent a significant drowning hazard. Their depth can be deceptive as wind-blown detritus builds up on the bottom. What appears, at first glance, to be a shallow pool may, in fact, turn out to be four or five times deeper. Many pools are also steep-sided, so once you are in, it may be difficult to get out.

Precautions:
• Make site visitors aware of pool locations and potential hazards.
• Provide a lifeline and danger signs where heavy public use is encouraged.

Ditches are a common feature on many bogs. Small ditches are often concealed by overhanging vegetation and it is very easy to end up with either a wet foot or, more seriously, a twisted ankle. These are especially important to look out for when carrying materials and tools over the site. Larger ditches, especially those which have been blocked, represent a drowning hazard similar to pools.

Precautions:
• Avoid carrying bladed tools or heavy materials over areas with concealed drainage.
• Make everyone aware of the hazard, and where necessary provide marked pathways.

Subsidence often occurs on drained or cut-over bogs. This can result in uneven or cracked ground which is often concealed by leggy heather.

Bare peat surfaces can be deceptively hazardous. Without a binding mat of vegetation, they are often incapable of supporting the weight of a person. People can quickly get 'stuck' as suction holds and pulls them in further. Bare peat which is saturated with water is particularly hazardous.

Precautions:
• Test any bare peat with one foot before walking across it.
• Be particularly cautious when alone.
• Where site workers or the public have to cross bare peat, provide temporary or permanent access facilities.

Tree stumps can quickly become covered by growing vegetation. They can become a hazard

A4.1

to walkers and especially site workers carrying tools or materials.

Adders, although uncommon, still present a potential threat on some bogs. Site visitors should be made aware of this and of the appropriate procedures in case of emergency.

Precautions:
- Never attempt to pick up an adder.
- If bitten, try to stay calm. Running will only speed up the movement of the venom around the body.
- Try to keep the bitten area below the level of the heart.
- Seek immediate medical assistance.
- If there is a realistic threat of coming into contact with adders, make sure that everyone is aware of the correct emergency procedures and establish the location of the nearest medical facility capable of dealing with snake-bites.

Navigation over unfamiliar bogs can sometimes be difficult and can be a particular hazard to people working alone. Bogs have very few reference features and it is easy to get disoriented or lost, especially on large areas of blanket bog or sites completely surrounded by uniform conifer plantations.

Precautions:
- Always carry a map and compass.
- Avoid working alone.
- Carry a mobile phone or other means of communication.
- Carry a whistle to attract attention if you become injured.
- Always tell someone where you are going and when you should get back.
- Always carry a rudimentary first aid kit.

A4.3 WORKING ON BOGS.

A number of the techniques mentioned within this handbook could represent a threat to the health and safety of the workforce.

Blocking large ditches by hand can sometimes be awkward. Instead of over-reaching and risking overbalancing and falling in, construct a suitable platform to work from.

Impounding large volumes of water behind dams or bunds creates a potentially significant safety hazard. In the UK, impoundment of large volumes of water (>25,000m^3 above the natural level of adjoining land) is regulated under the 1975 Reservoirs Act and must be implemented under the guidance and supervision of a qualified civil engineer. It is recommended that advice should also be sought for much smaller operations, particularly where there is a potential threat to the general public or neighbouring landowners.

Excavators are often used to construct dams, bunds and embankments. When rewetting a site it is important to identify the correct construction sequence. As areas can rapidly rewet, the driver should be made aware of the correct and safest route off the site.

Hazardous substances such as herbicides are recommended for the control of invasive species. Their use in the UK is controlled under COSHH (Control of Substances Hazardous to Health – Regulations, 1988). Complying with these regulations involves:

- Assessing the risks.
- Defining precautions.
- Preventing and controlling the risks.
- Health surveillance.
- Informing, instructing and training.

Full details of COSHH regulations can be obtained from the HSE Information Centre or by consulting HMSO (1993), *Approved Codes of Practice: Control of Substances Hazardous to Health and Control of Carcinogenic Substances.*

Power and bladed tools are often required to clear scrub from bogs. Unstable ground, open water and concealed ditches and stumps can increase the risks involved in using these tools.

APPENDIX 5
ABBREVIATIONS USED IN THE TEXT

Abbreviations Used in the Text

API	Aerial photograph interpretation
ATV	All terrain vehicle
BBS	British Bird Survey
BTO	British Trust for Ornithology
CBC	Common Bird Census
CCW	Countryside Council for Wales
CMS	Countryside Management System
DG	Dutch Guilder
DoE	Department of the Environment
DWT	Depth to water-table
EDM	Electronic Distance Measurer
EEC	The European Economic Community
EN	English Nature
EU	European Union
FA	Forest Authority
FC	Forestry Commission
FE	Forest Enterprise
FoE	Friends of the Earth
GCR	Geological Conservation Review Site
GPS	Global Positioning System
GRC	Glass-reinforced concrete
HMSO	Her Majesty's Stationery Office
H-value	Humification value
IPCC	Irish Peatland Conservation Council
LNR	Local Nature Reserves
MAFF	Ministry of Agriculture, Fisheries and Food
MLURI	Macauley Land Use Research Institute
NCC	Nature Conservancy Council
NCR	Nature Conservation Review Site
NGOs	Non-governmental organisations
NPRI	National Peatland Resource Inventory
NVC	National Vegetation Classification (UK)
PPA	Peat Producers Association
pSAC	Possible Special Protection Area
pSPA	Proposed Special Protection Area
RSPB	The Royal Society for the Protection of Birds
SLR	Single-lens reflex camera

SNH	Scottish Natural Heritage
SOAFT	Scottish Office, Agricultural and Fisheries Department
SPA	Special Protection Area
SSSI	Site of Special Scientific Interest
SWT	Scottish Wildlife Trust
UK	The United Kingdom of Great Britain and Northern Ireland
WaLRaG	Water-level range gauge
WOAD	Welsh Office, Agriculture Department
WWF	The World Wide Fund for Nature

A5

APPENDIX 6
COMMON METHODS

COMMON METHODS

A6.1 INTRODUCTION

This section describes in more detail a number of methods and techniques set out briefly in Part 4. Where methods and techniques are common to many habitats, for the sake of clarity, they have been summarised in the main body of the text. However, more detailed descriptions are included here.

The following methods are included in this appendix:

A6.2 Topography
A6.3 Hydrological Methods
A6.4 Vegetation

A6.2 TOPOGRAPHY

A6.2.1 Introduction

This section presents methods for investigating a wide range of topographic features. Topographic survey is particularly used for baseline survey, although a number of the techniques can also be used for repeated monitoring. It is often time-consuming, and thought should be given before embarking on any survey. However, many characteristics of bog ecosystems (hydrology, vegetation and so on) are dependent upon the morphology of a bog.

A6.2.2 Ground Survey

A6.2.2.1 General Applications

Ground survey techniques are used to investigate topographic features and their distribution. The size, distance and type of feature influences the choice of technique or instrument. Full information about using the more specialised survey instruments is not given. Reference should be made to specialist texts and the instruments

demonstrated by someone familiar with their use. There is a large range of ground survey equipment available. The instruments most frequently used are described below.

A6.2.2.2 Levelling Frame

Levelling frames are suitable for surveying small features up to 1m across such as a *Sphagnum* hummock; with care, they can be used across distances of two to three times the length of the frame. They are easy and quick to use, can be used by one person and are capable of fine vertical and horizontal resolution.

The frame (Figure A.4) consists of a horizontal bar supported by a fixed or adjustable leg at either end. A spirit level is either secured to the bar or placed on it when necessary. A rule or self-adhesive scale should be secured to the bar or a distance scale inscribed. Vertical holes to take needles can also be drilled at intervals as and if required. Dimensions vary but a horizontal length of 1.0 to 1.5m is the most practical size. Wood and aluminium are suitable materials for the horizontal bar, although 4.25 cm diameter plastic pipe (fall-pipe) is also suitable. Fall-pipe is light and does not warp. Legs can be made of any suitable rod-shaped material such as, wood dowel or aluminium rod.

A levelling frame is used in the following way:

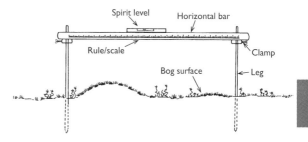

Figure A.4 A levelling frame.

A6.1

247

- Place the frame over the feature to be surveyed and push legs into the peat until they are secure.
- Ensure that the horizontal bar is level and the legs are vertical.
- Insert needles through holes in the bar at measured intervals until the tip is in contact with the bog surface and measure the length of needle protruding below or above the bar.
- or: use a weighted (plumb) line to obtain a true vertical and measure distance from the bar, or a line inscribed along its side, to the bog surface.

> **Repeated measurements should be from fixed points which can be relocated.**

A6.2.2.3 Hand Levels (Abney Level and Stadia)

Hand levels are pocket-sized easy-to-use instruments. They can be used to measure both slope (Abney) and height (Abney and Stadia) changes and are suitable for investigating topographic detail over short distances of a few metres or for carrying out less detailed rapid surveys over greater distances. Over short distances, they can provide surprisingly accurate results if they are used with care and their limitations recognised.

An Abney level comprises a short viewing scope to which a 180° scale is attached. The scale incorporates a movable indicator to which a spirit-level is attached. A windowed mirror in the scope enables the spirit level to be viewed alongside the target. A stadia level comprises a scope and a fixed spirit-level only.

These levels are used in the following way:
Setting zero: For those with access to the seashore or a large lake, zero on an Abney Level can be checked by setting the angle scale to zero and sighting the level on the horizon of the sea or lake with the horizontal wire in the scope lying along the horizon. The spirit-level bubble should then appear to bisect the wire. Adjust the bubble, if necessary, using the adjustment screws situated on the spirit-level.

Method 1 (for short to long distance using an Abney Level)

- Set the angle scale to zero.
- Hold the level firmly against a pole or on a support of known height.

- Sight on to a surveying staff with the spirit-level bubble bisected by the wire.
- Read height on surveying staff.
- Subtract height of level from height reading on staff to give height difference of bog surface between level and staff position (Figure A.5).
- The level can be sighted onto a staff or pole of the same height as the one on which the level is held. The angle at which the bubble is bisected by the wire is recorded. The surface height difference is calculated trigonometrically (Figure A.6).

Method 2 (rapid survey method for short to long distances using an Abney Level)

- While standing on a level surface, look through the scope holding it horizontally and note exactly where the cross-wire lies on the assistant. Assistant walks out a measured distance and the operator sights on to the same position on the assistant, bisects bubble with the wire and records the angle of slope.
- Using the measured distance and angle of slope, the height difference is calculated trigonometrically.

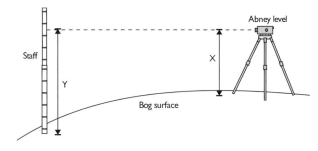

Figure A.5   Using an Abney level (method 1). The change in surface height between the level and the staff = y - x.

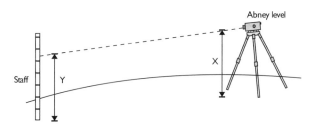

Figure A.6   Using an Abney level to calculate height trigonometrically. In this case, x = y.

A6.2

248

Method 3 (for measuring slopes over short distances using an Abney Level)

- An Abney level can be used with a slope pentameter to measure angles of slope. The slope pentameter was developed for use on moderate to steep and intricate slopes. It is particularly suitable for measuring both transverse and longitudinal angles of erosion gullies.

A slope pantometer can be made from well-seasoned wood or lightweight alloy and consists of a pivoting frame in the form of a parallelogram. The frame enables standard units of slope to be measured. Slope angles are recorded via a protractor scale (Figure A.7).

A6.2.2.4 Dumpy, Quick-set and Similar Levels

Over long distances, these levels are time-consuming to use, but a closing error of just a few centimetres is achievable over a levelling circuit of one or two kilometres. They are suitable for surveying a wide range of features including microtopography, erosion gullies, surface shrinkage alongside drainage ditches and the overall macrotopography and morphology of bogs. In addition, some levels can be used to map the position and extent of features using tachometric techniques. This type of level is expensive but can usually be borrowed from educational and research institutions (or hired).

Dumpy and similar levels require mounting on a tripod (Figure A.8). They have a larger and better-quality scope than Abney levels but similarly rely on a built-in spirit-level to ensure that the scope is horizontal. A circular spirit-level on the base of the instrument ensures that it is horizontal in all directions. Some instruments have a 360° scale within which the instrument can be rotated which can be used to fix the direction of a transect or a survey point. The scope contains a graticule with three horizontal lines. The centre line is the equivalent of the cross-wire in an Abney level. Readings for the upper and lower lines are used to calculate the distance from the instrument to the staff. Using tacheometry and the 360° horizontal scale, the spatial distribution of features can be mapped.

Figure A.8 An optical level being used to assess the gradient of a ditch prior to dam construction. (Stuart Brooks)

A6.2

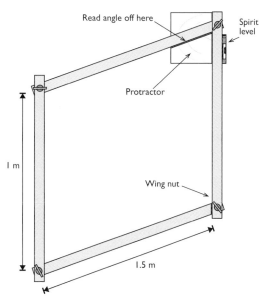

Read angle off here
Spirit level
Protractor
1 m
Wing nut
1.5 m

Figure A.7 A simple slope pantometer can be constructed from wood or alloy.

These levels are used in the following way:

Setting up the Tripod and Instrument

- Place tripod on as firm a stand as possible.
- When all readings are to be made from one or a few locations, a platform can be constructed for the tripod using three planks and a few wooden pegs.
- When the instrument is located on one of the points of a survey grid or line, use a plumb-line or built-in sight to centre the tripod over the marker, and measure the instrument's height above the bog surface.
- The instrument's height must be measured accurately, as it links the foresight and backsight.
- The level has to be levelled by using the footscrews to bring the bubble into the middle before taking the reading.
- Make sure you have focused the graticule by focusing it on infinity.
- Write readings down on standard booking forms (refer to surveying texts or instrument instruction manual).

Setting out a line or grid

- Survey lines – mark at measured intervals using garden canes or similar.
- Survey grid – measure and mark out a baseline at one side or across the site. Set out grid lines at right angles, to the baseline. To obtain a right angle, use the 3, 4, 5 triangle system (Figure A.9) or a right-angle sight (Figure A. 10).
- The baseline should be permanently marked (*see* 4.1.3.2)

Levelling a Line or Grid

- Set up the tripod and instrument as described.
- Place the staff on the survey points. Attach plastic, metal or wooden disks to the base of the tripod to help prevent it from sinking.

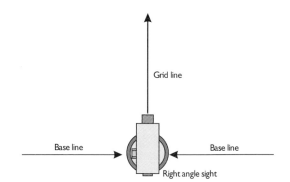

Figure A.10   Use a right angle sight to position a grid line at a right-angle to the baseline.

- Sight the instrument onto the staff, focus and adjust the spirit-level (if the instrument is not self-levelling) and read the staff height scale (make sure the bubble is still centred – if it drifts, read as it crosses the centre and take an average of a few readings).
- Over distances greater than 30m, it is advisable to move the instrument, 'leap-frogging' with the staff person, foresighting and backsighting onto the staff without moving the staff position before and after moving the level (Figure A.11).
- Surveys that require repositioning of the instrument must be 'closed'. The first and last staff positions of the survey or section of the survey coincide. This acts as a check on the accuracy of the survey.
- The difference between the start and end heights for each closed survey or survey section is known as the closing error. This error is apportioned equally between all survey points except the start point.

Tacheometric Surveying

Tacheometric surveying techniques can be employed when time is short and the precision of a measured grid is not required. The stadia wires within the telescope are manufactured so that they represent a fixed angle. If the telescope is level, then the distance between them, as measured on the staff, can be directly converted to determine the distance that the staff is from the instrument. With most instruments, the ground distance is calculated by multiplying the interstadial distance by 100.

Feature Mapping

- Instruments with a 360° horizontal scale can be used to provide a location map of features such as pools, ditches, monitoring sites and so on

A6.2

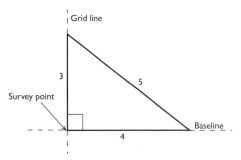

Figure A.9   Align a grid-line at right angles to the baseline by using the 3-4-5 triangle method.

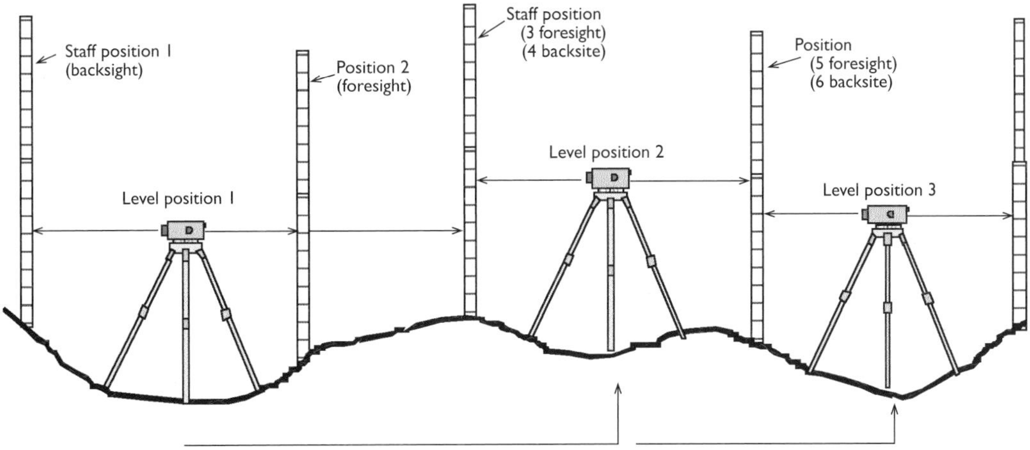

Figure A.11   A 'leap frog' survey used for surveying long distances requires foresighting and backsighting when the level is moved.

- Hold the staff alongside a feature and point the scope at the staff. Read the angle of orientation on the horizontal scale and measure the distance between the instrument and staff tacheometrically.
- Repeat at a number of points along or around a feature to determine the extent of the feature.

A6.2.2.5 Theodolites

The advantages of using theodolites are that they are accurate and versatile, measurements can be made over long distances and surveys require, therefore, fewer instrument stations. Disadvantages are their size, weight and cost and that the operator needs adequate training in their use. If a survey using a theodolite is required, it may be appropriate to bring in a skilled volunteer or contracted specialist. Theodolites have the same uses described for simpler instruments but come into their own when used for large or whole-site surveys.

There are two principal types of theodolite: those that are purely optical and those that incorporate an electronic measuring system. Refer to specialist texts for details on how to operate theodolites.

A6.2.2.6 Plane Table

This is a simple and relatively inexpensive form of survey which uses visual and graphic techniques for one person to produce a map in the field. It is most appropriate for mapping topographic detail in small areas. Over larger areas, the errors are too great. The equipment is simple: tripod and flat wooden board covered by drawing surface (paper or similar). The board is held on the tripod by screws which allow it to be rotated and clamped. The sighting ruler (alidade) allows rays (lines) to be drawn from the known point (where the plane table is situated) to unknown ones.

There are several methods for using a plane table. The simplest is to set down a number of known points on the paper as a control framework. These are plotted accurately at the scale of the desired end map (for example, 1:500/ 1:1,000) and also marked in the field (for example, using ranging poles). The plane table is then set up over one of these control points and orientated by sighting to another, checked with a third. Once correctly orientated, the alidade is used to sight onto unknown points and draw rays on the map. By transferring the plane table to another control point, reorientating it, then sighting onto all the unknown points again, a set of intersecting rays are produced (that is, points are located by triangulation). These procedures can be repeated from a third point to produce 'triangles of error' on the unknown point locations.

Plane tabling can be enhanced to include height information using an *Indian Clinometer*. However,

A6.2

more commonly a *microptic alidade* is used. This uses the stadia principle and this needs a staff. So the basic simplicity of the method is lost!

A6.2.2.7 Storage, Analysis and Display of Ground Survey Data

Topographic survey data can be stored on paper or electronically. For most purposes, the results can be plotted by hand using graph paper.

Repeated measurements along transects associated with, for example, erosion gullies, drainage ditches and *Sphagnum* hummocks, can be stored on computer spreadsheets. The data can then be processed and plotted using the spreadsheet to show change and entered into statistical packages if required. The results of detailed grid, whole-site/study-area surveys can be plotted manually or entered into specialist computer packages to give surface and basal contour maps. An example is shown in Figure A.12 which displays the topography and water levels (*see* 4.3.3) of an area of blanket bog at Shielton (*see* 6.8).

A6.2.2.8 Equipment Costs

Costs in 1996 are approximately:

Stadia	from £25
Abney Level	from £40
Dumpy type levels	from £600
Theodolites	£1,600–£10,000
Plane tables	£170
Metal detectors	from £200

A6.2.2.9 Electronic Equipment

Note that many of the surveying techniques described above have now been superseded by newer electronic equipment. Of these, the most useful are Electronic Distance Measurers (EDMs) and Geographic Positioning Systems (GPS). EDMs use reflective plates which reflect light back at the instrument to record exact distances. Measurements can be downloaded directly into computer software allowing much quicker survey. GPS relies on satellites. Instruments search and fix on a series of satellites orbiting above. GPS is becoming more and more accurate, with positions now being fixed to within a few metres – usually good enough for the survey requirements of conservation management.

A6.2.2.10 Aerial Photogrammetric Survey

The other method of obtaining detailed contour maps is to use aerial photogrammetric survey.

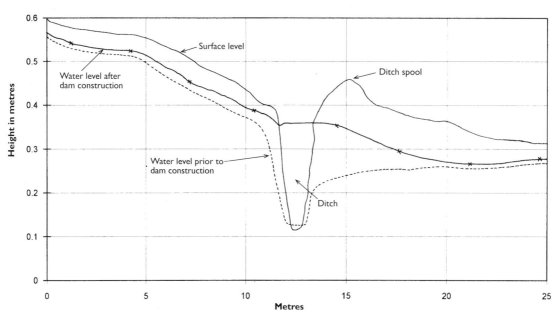

A6.2

Figure A.12   The topography and water-levels of an area of blanket bog at Shielton (see 6.8). The surface levels were measured using a dumpy level and the water-table measured using microbore dipwells (see 4.3.3.2).

These surveys use stereo-images to construct topographical maps. This is specialist work and should be contracted out. The costs are around £5,000 per site. Bear in mind that the method maps the top of the vegetation, not necessarily the ground surface. This is fine for *Sphagnum*- or heath-dominated bogs but is very inaccurate for woodland.

A6.3 HYDROLOGICAL METHODS

A6.3.1 V-notch weir

A6.3.1.1 Purpose

A V-notch weir is an instrument for measuring the amount of water flowing along a ditch or down a stream. In terms of the water balance of an area of bog, this represents the lateral seepage component, since water moving sideways through a bog usually moves near the surface and is intercepted by a ditch. The rate of flow, known as the discharge, is measured indirectly using a V-notch weir and a water-level recorder.

A6.3.1.2 Description and Appraisal

V-notch weirs are widely used in the water industry and in hydrological research. They are specialist hydrological instruments and their use can involve considerable financial outlay and commitment of staff time.

The weir forms a dam in the stream or ditch, and the V-shaped notch in its top edge acts as a spillway. The discharge of the ditch can be calculated from a standard formula and is related to the stage or head of water above the base of the notch. A water-level recorder is used to monitor the stage (*see* Appendix 7 for costs and suppliers).

The method of recording the water level determines the cost. Home-made clockwork chart recorders have been used, but these need a lot of maintenance to work reliably. Many different types of water-level recorder are available commercially. Chart recorders (*see* 4.3.3.4, Appendix 7) do not require mains or battery power and are reliable, although extra work is involved in reading off the levels and times from the chart. A more advanced type uses a float, counterweight and pulley arrangement similar to that of a chart recorder but converts the rotation of the pulley to a varying electrical signal using a multi-turn potentiometer and records it on a data logger. Water-level recorders based on pressure sensors are available commercially. These monitor the pressure difference between an underwater sensor and the atmosphere to convert it to a water level, usually relative to the sensor position. Other types of water-level recorder based on capacitance sensors are also available.

Expect to get some unreliable records during cold weather. Ice can form in the weir pool, and, although water usually continues to flow over the notch, the relationship between discharge and stage changes as ice impedes the notch. The water-level recorder may also record incorrectly during freezing conditions. If it has a float, this may become frozen into the ice and will not float properly until it thaws.

A6.3.1.3 Method

Some aspects of the design and calibration of V-notch weirs are very complicated. More information about design, calibration, hook gauge design and so on, can be found in British Standard 3680.

A weir suitable for ditches and small streams on bogs can be made from any sheet material that can withstand constantly wet conditions and is resistant to corrosion by acid bog water. Marine plywood, plastic, aluminium or stainless steel are all appropriate. It should be strong enough to resist bending (thin sheets can be strengthened by fixing horizontal stiffening bars) and big enough to cut into the undisturbed sides and base of a stream or ditch by about 50 cm. The notch may be cut out of the top edge of the weir plate, or alternatively a separate notch plate can be bolted over a cut-out in the weir plate and the gap sealed with silicone sealant. The latter arrangement allows the use of a relatively cheap material, such as plywood, for the weir plate with a more robust and expensive, stainless steel notch plate.

The plate is inserted into a groove cut through the vegetation at both sides with a spade and is pushed or hammered down so that the notch base is 15 cm or so above the stream or ditch base. This

A6.3

may be easier if the leading edge is bevelled. Use a wooden or metal strip to protect the top edge of the sheet if you have to hammer it in.

A small stilling pool is needed to slow down the flow of water immediately upstream of the weir so that the relationship between stage and discharge is not affected by changing flow paths in the ditch or stream. The pool should be at least two notch-lengths deep (that is, two notch-lengths below the level of the notch base) by four notch-lengths wide by six notch-lengths long, and it must be prevented from filling up with sediment, either by using a sediment trap or by emptying it out when it gets half-full. If necessary, line the bed of the stream or ditch with a board angled away from the weir plate to prevent undercutting of the weir on the downstream side.

The shape of the notch determines how accurately small discharges can be measured; the commonly-used 90° notch does not allow accurate measurement of low flows, although a much narrower 20° notch has to be much deeper to cover the likely range of discharge. Discharge is low most of the time, although short, sharp flood peaks occur when it is raining. Low flows need to be recorded accurately whilst not missing any of the peaks. A notch with a narrow angle at its base and a wider angle further up fulfils both requirements but makes it difficult to obtain a calibration equation from a limited number of stage and discharge measurements. The steeper the gradient of the ditch or stream, the easier it will be to use a straight-sided narrow V-notch because a deeper notch can be used.

Calibrate the weir by measuring both the stage and the volume of water collected in a pail in a known time period during a range of different flow conditions. This presents certain difficulties. First, a hook gauge is required to measure the water level relative to the notch base. Second, there must be enough room, below the notch base on the downstream side, to get a bucket or basin in to catch the water. Third, a channel needs to be fixed onto the downstream side of the plate, below the notch, to allow low flows to be caught which would otherwise trickle down the weir plate. This channel may interfere with the higher flows. Fourth, it is difficult to be on site at the right time to catch any of the short flood peaks.

During low flows, the notch tends to get blocked by debris, such as dead vegetation or insects. This leads to false readings, so it must be avoided. A screen made from a suitable mesh material (for example, expanded aluminium stitched onto a fencing wire frame) should be used to minimise blockages. It needs to prevent airborne and submerged debris as well as floating material from blocking the notch. Floating and submerged debris has an uncanny ability to find its way to the notch by passing through the narrow gap between the screen and the weir plate, so fit the screen carefully to make this gap as small as possible.

A6.3.1.4 Data Analysis, Display and Interpretation

Chart recorder charts hold a continuous record of water level, although the data will at some stage have to be digitised (that is, discrete readings taken from the chart and stored as numbers on paper or computer). This can be time-consuming, more so when done manually than when using a computer-linked digitiser. The time taken depends on the digitising frequency (the number of readings taken per day or per week). As a rough guide, digitising a one-week chart takes about five minutes and a one-month chart takes twenty minutes using a computer-linked digitiser.

When digitising charts, the interval between readings can be varied. During dry periods, when the trace has no discharge peaks, daily readings should suffice; more frequent readings are needed where rain has produced peaks in the trace. As a bare minimum, the lowest and highest points of a water-level rise need to be read, followed by several points during the subsequent fall.

Convert water-level measurements to discharge using the calibration line on a graph of discharge against water level. The line can be obtained mathematically by a regression of the logarithm of discharge on the logarithm of stage (Figure A.13), or drawn less accurately by eye. The equation of the calibration line can be used to perform the conversion in a computer spreadsheet.

To get the volume of water flowing over the weir in a given period, multiply the mean discharge between each pair of readings by the

A6.3

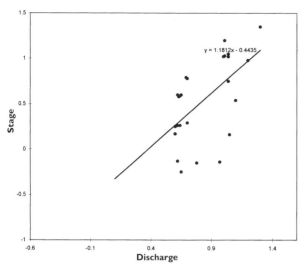

Figure A.13 The relationship between the measured water-level (x) and the discharge (y) can be obtained using a calibration line.

time interval between them and then calculate the sum of these products for the period. This can be done in a spreadsheet. Finally, divide the volume by the catchment area above the weir to get a figure that can be compared directly with rainfall.

A6.3.2 Tipping Bucket Flow Gauge

A6.3.2.1 Purpose

Water usually runs off undrained bogs in small natural streams, above ground as overland flow in very wet weather and mostly below ground as lateral seepage (*see* 2.5.2). On drained bogs, ditches intercept overland flow and lateral seepage so that ditchflow partly replaces these components of the water balance. If you know the catchment area of a stream or a ditch, you can use the measurements of discharge to calculate what proportion of the rainfall is leaving the bog by this route. A tipping bucket flow gauge measures discharge and can also be used to monitor drainage from a natural lysimeter.

A6.3.2.2 Description and Appraisal

A bucket with an internal partition pivots on an axis running through its base. A pipe leads water from a dam and pours it from a point directly

above the pivot into one half of the bucket (Figure A.14). When it is nearly full, its weight causes the bucket to tip, emptying the one half and bringing the other to the filling position below the pipe. Each time the bucket tips, a magnet on one end swings past a reed switch causing it to close momentarily so that an electrical current flows for an instant. This is detected by a counter, which stores the number of tips, or by a data logger which records the time of each tip.

Tipping buckets work well and are reliable provided they are well designed, carefully built and properly maintained. The pivot, in particular, must be designed not to corrode in the harsh environment of a bog ditch. Stainless steel is more resistant to corrosion then galvanised metal in these conditions. The bucket can become choked with ice in freezing weather, and this causes it to tip more often than it should or to freeze up and not tip at all. Tipping buckets suitable for ditches need to hold 2–5 litres in each half and they have to be strongly built to withstand the force of the bucket crashing down with each tip.

A tipping bucket designed for monitoring ditchflow costs between £800 and £1,100 or can be hired for around £300 per year. A tip-counter costs around £180 and is easy to use. Alternatively, record the time of each tip on a data logger (*see* 4.3.3.4).

Figure A.14 A tipping bucket flow gauge.

A6.3

A6.3.2.3 Method

- Measure the height of the central partition above the ground when it is at the half-way position (that is, directly above the pivot).
- Also measure the height of the lowest point of the emptied bucket above ground.
- When damming the ditch, use the first measurement to indicate how much clearance is needed between the outlet pipe and the ditch base on the downstream side. You can dig out the base slightly; the second measurement tells you how high the water level can be above the base before preventing the bucket from emptying.
- Arrange the outlet pipe of the dam at the lowest level that allows the tipping bucket to work properly. This minimises the extent of ponding of water above the dam, thus minimising evaporation from the ditch.
- Install the tipping bucket with its pivot directly below the end of the outlet pipe and level it so that both halves of the bucket fill to the same level. Make sure that the water from the pipe only enters the half of the bucket in the filling position and that the bucket partition does not touch the pipe when it tips.

Two types of calibration can be used: static and dynamic. Static calibration involves temporarily blocking the outlet pipe from the dam or extending it to take the water down past the tipping bucket. Each bucket is filled slowly using a one litre measuring cylinder, and the volume needed to make it tip is recorded. The mean of the two sides can be used later to convert the number of tips to a water volume. Repeat this calibration at regular intervals.

During floods, water may be gushing out of the pipe so fast that a substantial volume goes into the bucket between the time it starts to tip and the time it reaches the half-way position. In these conditions, the buckets hold more water than the amount measured, thus underestimating the discharge when using the static calibration. This underestimation is small enough to be unimportant for most purposes, although when monitoring discharges very accurately it is advisable to use a dynamic calibration.

A6.3.2.4 Data Analysis, Display and Interpretation

Use the calibration to convert the number of tips in a period to a water volume. Given an estimate of catchment area of the ditch or stream, divide the total volume in litres by the catchment area in square metres to give the run-off in millimetres. Display the period discharge measurements using a bar chart. Use unshaded bars to display a series of weekly, fortnightly or monthly rainfall and shade the lower part of the bar representing discharge.

A6.3.3 Lysimeters

A6.3.3.1 Purpose

Evapotranspiration rates are markedly different on undisturbed and disturbed bogs. More natural bogs, dominated by *Sphagnum* mosses, exhibit low evapotranspiration rates, as *Sphagnum* lawn and hummocks have tightly-packed capitula at the surface. Under dry conditions, *Sphagnum* wilt to a white colour reflecting heat. Vascular plants, which characterise more disturbed bogs, have higher transpiration rates and can dry a bog further. Monitoring evapotranspiration rates requires the use of a lysimeter.

A6.3.3.2 Description and Appraisal

A lysimeter consists of an area of representative vegetation and underlying peat which is isolated from its surroundings by a waterproof barrier which prevents lateral seepage (*see* 2.5.2) into and out of the area. Small lysimeters are sometimes constructed by cutting out a block of peat with the surface vegetation and fitting it tightly into a container such as an oil drum or plastic tank with an outlet pipe and some means of monitoring the discharge from it. It is normally used in conjunction with a rain-gauge and a few dipwells so that evapotranspiration can be estimated by subtracting the total seepage, as indicated by the outlet discharge, from the rainfall and a correction can be made for any change in the amount of water stored in the peat as indicated by a change in the dipwell water level. One type, known as a weighing lysimeter, has a built-in weighing device, so that the amount of water in and on the soil and vegetation can be monitored accurately. A natural lysimeter has no artificial lining below but uses an impermeable peat or clay layer to minimise vertical seepage.

A6.3

A tipping bucket (*see* A6.3.2) or a pipeflow gauge based on a V-notch weir built into a weir box (*see* A6.3.1) are alternatives for measuring the discharge from the outlet pipe.

Lysimeters are difficult to construct. A successful lysimeter must measure total seepage without affecting evapotranspiration. Except in very small lysimeters, it is usually not possible to seal off the underside although, where the waterproof barrier around its edge reaches down to an impermeable layer, this is adequate. Avoid disturbing the vegetation and make sure that the lysimeter does not lower the water-table below its previous level, otherwise the measurements are atypical and worthless.

A6.3.3.3 Method

- Decide on the size of lysimeter you need. Ones less than 1 m² in area have been used in uniform vegetation while others of 5 ha have been used in mature conifer plantations. The scale of variation of most bog vegetation dictates a size in the range 10 to 20 m² although it may have to be larger (up to 100 m²) if there are trees or tall shrubs because the scale of variation of these types of vegetation is larger.
- Choose a fairly flat area with vegetation typical of the surrounding bog. It helps if there is a slope leading to lower ground nearby so that the outlet pipe can lead water to a place where there is at least a 40 cm fall – the minimum necessary to install a suitable discharge measuring device.
- Mark out the lysimeter area; it can be circular, oval, square, rectangular or any regular shape.
- If the peat beneath the fibrous surface layer is pseudofibrous or amorphous or shallow and overlies heavy clay, dig a ditch right round your lysimeter area which is deep enough to reach this layer.
- Use a blunt-edged board to push a waterproof barrier, such as a doubled-over sheet of thick polythene, into the centre of the ditch base. In the clay layer (or well-humified lower peat), dig a narrow trench, insert the barrier and backfill with clay, stamping it well down to form a seal.
- Carefully seal the ends together where they meet, using a water-resistant sealant, and strengthen this joint. Fill in the ditch evenly on both sides of the barrier, stamping the peat down to fill up any air spaces.
- If the peat is relatively undecomposed and therefore fairly permeable, dig out blocks of peat complete with vegetation from the lysimeter area and replace them after lining the hole with a waterproof barrier such as a sheet of thick polythene.
- Make good the surface afterwards and, if the vegetation shows any signs of suffering from the disturbance, allow a period of a few weeks for it to recover before starting monitoring.
- From knowledge of the site or from previous dipwell readings, estimate how far below the surface the water-table lies during the winter. Make a hole in the barrier at this depth and seal a pipe onto it to lead water away to the discharge measuring device.
- Install four or five short dipwells, within the lysimeter, taking care not to puncture the barrier if you have laid one as a base.

A more detailed description of the design and use of a lysimeter is given by Calder (1976).

A6.3.3.4 Data Analysis, Display and Interpretation

Calculate weekly or daily evapotranspiration by subtracting the outlet discharge plus the increase in the peat water store from precipitation. An example is shown below for a lysimeter covering 16m² over one day.

Step 1: Convert outflow (U) (measured in a tipping bucket gauge) to millimetres depth.
Average tip of 0.261 litres
Number of tips in a day = 174
Volume = 174 x 0.261 = 45.4l
Outflow = 45.4l divided by 16m² = 2.84mm

Step 2: Calculating change in water store (ΔW).
Four dipwells – average rise of 3.25 cm.
Use a conversion factor (below) to calculate change in peat water store.

Peat type	Factor	% pore space
Undecomposed, surface	0.3	33
Fibrous	2.0	5
Well humified	5.0	2

Factor of 2.0 used: 3.25 divided by 2.0
Change in peat water store = 1.625mm

Step 3: Calculate daily rainfall (P)
Rain-gauge showed 5.5mm of rainfall

Step 4: Calculate evapotranspiration (E)
Note: vertical seepage (G) = 0
Use the water balance equation (*see* 2.5.2)

$$E = P - U - G - \Delta W$$
$$1.035 = 5.5 - 2.84 - 0 - 1.625$$

Evapotranspiration = 1.035mm

A6.3

For a pipeflow gauge, use its weir calibration equation to convert the series of stage readings to discharge rates. For each period, multiply the mean discharge by the time interval and sum the volumes in litres before finally dividing by the lysimeter area.

A6.4   VEGETATION

A6.4.1   Introduction

Diverse methods and scales are used in vegetation monitoring. As in other aspects of monitoring, techniques should be matched to the scale and type of analysis. For instance, loss of bog to agriculture and forestry can be monitored, both retrospectively and in the future, using satellite imagery or high-level aerial photography; the encroachment of birch scrub or bracken can be followed using aerial photography or floristic quadrats; and cover changes of plants such as *Sphagnum* and heather are best monitored using floristic quadrats.

In the following account, ground-monitoring techniques are presented first and are followed by remote techniques, namely photography and other imagery. To set up and run a vegetation ground-monitoring programme, choices concerning plot or study area, quadrat type, data collection and processing need to be made. These aspects of a monitoring programme are presented under separate subsections.

Quadrat monitoring frequency is also an important consideration. Vegetation responds relatively slowly to environmental changes. Monitoring vegetation once a year or even once every two years may be sufficient in most situations. To ensure comparable results from year to year, record at the same time each year or when the vegetation reaches a specified growth stage, for example, a set week in the summer or when heather starts to flower.

A6.4.2   Study Area and Plots

Selecting study areas and plots is necessary for a number of monitoring activities. It is included here, as vegetation monitoring is often the principal monitoring activity of site managers and also because other monitored data, such as, chemical and hydrological data, may be interpreted in terms of floristic effect.

A study area is simply an area in which monitoring is carried out. It may be self-defining, for example, the boundaries of a bog. Within large bog expanses, it can be impracticable or even unnecessary to spread monitoring throughout the bog. In these cases, natural features such as streams, watersheds or slopes can be used to define a study area or, if monitoring is related to particular features, such as erosion channels or drainage ditches, the area defined by the feature may also define the study area. In many cases, it is necessary or possible to monitor only small, selected study areas or plots within a much larger bog.

Plots are either of regular shape (for example, square, rectangular) or their shape is determined by surface features. They range in size from a few square metres to many thousands of square metres. Study areas can also be linear, that is, they may comprise transects (for example, centre to edge) across a bog. Transects of dipwells and vegetation quadrats are examples. Whatever its size or shape, a study area must adequately represent the bog or part of the bog requiring monitoring. Adequate representation may be obtained by setting out a number of plots or transects on a site.

Plots can be either fenced or unfenced. For general monitoring and in most situations, fencing is not necessary. However, it is advisable to fence in certain situations and to meet certain criteria:

- To exclude domestic or wild large herbivores when they may interfere with monitoring devices;
- To monitor grazing or trampling effects of large herbivores. If grazing is reduced to lessen damage or increased to prevent excessive litter accumulation, for example, then set up a monitored comparison between grazed plots and ungrazed (and fenced) plots.

Within large bog areas, refinding unfenced study areas and plots is made easier by noting their position in relation to obvious physical features or marking their position with permanent reference markers (*see* 4.1.3.2).

One important consideration is the effect of monitoring on those plots. Permanent quadrats on Glasson Moss revealed an unusual pattern of lush cotton grass growth at the four corners of the quadrat. These related to the posts which marked the plots, which were used by birds. Droppings had eutrophied the bog, causing lush cotton-grass growth. Monitoring had, in effect, monitored the effect of monitoring! Further, trampling around the plot obviously damages delicate vegetation anyway (*see* A3.6.5) and can also affect vegetation within the quadrat. As a rule, always use some form of protection such as duckboarding or sections of aluminium ladder (*see* 5.6.6).

A6.4.3 Quadrats

A6.4.3.1 Introduction

Vegetation quadrats are areas or space in which attributes of plants are recorded. Consideration must be given to the location or positioning of quadrats and to the type of quadrat and recording scale to be used.

A6.4.3.2 Location/Positioning

At the outset, the method for locating quadrats needs to be determined. Common positioning strategies are: random, stratified random, along a transect or on a grid. Whether to resurvey in the same or different locations must also be determined. These decisions relate primarily to the objectives of the monitoring programme (*see* 3.4.3.2) but also to the size and complexity of the study area and the time and personnel available.

Random Quadrats

A random quadrat pattern is not affected by other features and is, theoretically, the most objective way to locate vegetation quadrats. However, quadrat site location can involve much trampling, and relatively large numbers of quadrats may be required to adequately characterise a study area. It is recommended that random numbers be used to locate quadrat positions. Random number tables are found at the back of some statistics books or they can be generated by personal computers. Except when 'needs must' it is not recommended that the 'throw over the shoulder'

approach is used. This can introduce a degree of selectivity as the practitioner has to decide where to stand before throwing.

For speed and ease, or if only one person is available, distances can be paced. A long measuring tape can be used if two people are available and if greater precision is required. Procedure:

- Pace or measure the length and width of the study area.
- Select random numbers.
- Mark out a baseline along one side of a study area.
- Pace or measure along the baseline and place garden canes at positions identified using the random numbers.
- If transects of quadrats are being located, use these baseline positions as the start of the transects and pace or measure along the transects marking quadrat positions using random numbers.
- If a totally random scatter is being located, pace or measure a random distance at right angles to each of the baseline markers to locate one quadrat. Repeat until the required number of quadrats has been located. In this case, random numbers should be paired, one number along the baseline and one offset from the baseline.
- Alternatively, a random 'zig-zag' can be walked across the study area and at intervals canes left to identify quadrat positions.

Stratified Random Quadrats

Stratification implies some degree of preselection based on existing knowledge of a study area, for example, knowledge of vegetation types, surface features, drainage pattern, and so on.

If, for example, it is decided to monitor the vegetation of hummocks and wet hollows or of intact and damaged areas, a stratified random approach may be suitable. Although slightly less objective than a totally random approach, it does allow a degree of targeting of effort. Again, much trampling can result from this method. It permits easier comparison of different features, as equal numbers of quadrats are located in each 'stratified' feature. Procedure:

- Position a baseline along one side of the study area or along each of the stratified features as appropriate.
- Pace or measure the study area or features, select random numbers and randomly mark the baseline as described above.

A6.4

- Using random numbers, pace or measure out from the baseline positions until the required and equal numbers of quadrats have been located in each stratified feature or area.
- Or, if the size and distribution of the stratified features allow, quadrats can be located by the random 'zig-zag' method described above.
- Or, if features are small or scattered, it may be appropriate to throw a cane to randomly select quadrat sites.

Grids and Transects

A grid pattern is suitable for monitoring whole site changes or for relatively uniform study areas. The grid intersects determine quadrat locations. A grid is sometimes considered to give a better representation of vegetation than a totally random approach (Greig-Smith, 1952). Because quadrats are at regular intervals, grids may not be suitable for use where the study area has a regular or repeated pattern of surface features. Procedure:

- Install reference markers at the ends of grid lines.
- Hold a measuring tape between two reference markers and temporarily mark quadrat positions, at regular intervals along the tape, with canes.

A grid is in effect a series of parallel transects; therefore, the same approach can be used to locate transect quadrats. Quadrats can be located along the transects at regular intervals or randomly.

Targeted Quadrats

At times it may be necessary to target quadrat locations. For example, there may be too few examples of a particular feature for random selection to be carried out.

Relocating Permanent Quadrats

The relocation of quadrats is an important consideration. In a random or stratified random design, a completely new set of quadrats could be located for each recording period. However, detected change may just reflect the differences between quadrat positions each time the quadrats are monitored. Usually quadrats are marked in some way to facilitate their relocation (*see* 4.1.3.2). Siting canes or posts a fixed distance away from the quadrat minimises the risk of eutrophication from perching birds.

Visible markers may not be necessary for grid- or transect-based quadrats. Place visible markers at either end of grid lines or transects so that, when recording quadrats, a tape can be laid out between the end markers and a cane placed at the quadrat position. Precise relocation can then be achieved with metal rods or even wooden pegs or canes raised only slightly above the ground surface over which the corners of a quadrat frame or against which the legs of a point quadrat frame are placed.

A6.4.3.3 *Quadrat Types*

There are three main types of quadrat: area, point and line. All are useful for monitoring purposes, but area and point quadrats are the most widely used. The type of quadrat and its size and shape may depend on characteristics of the bog and on the objectives of the monitoring programme. Factors or questions to be considered are:

- Vegetation community mosaic – is there one, and what size are the component vegetation types?
- Should the mosaic be monitored as an entity or as a number of associated vegetation types?
- Which data are most appropriate – percentage, cover-scale or other?
- How much time is available for recording the vegetation?
- Are intersite comparisons to be made, and, if so, will the techniques or datasets be comparable?
- How much detail is required?

Area Quadrats

Area quadrats can vary in size and shape. They are mostly within the range of 10×10 cm to 10×10m. The commonest size is 1×1m, but this is often considered too large for bog monitoring as recording would result in trampling damage along at least two sides of the quadrat. A small square or rectangular quadrat frame (Figure A.15) used singly or in pairs is recommended.

Quadrat frames can be constructed from 2 cm plastic tubing joined by elbow connectors or from lengths of angle iron held together by wing-nuts. Whatever the chosen material, 3 or 4mm holes should be drilled along each side at 5 or 10 cm intervals. Elasticated thread can be secured through the holes to subdivide the frame. Subdivisions of 10×10 cm are generally suitable.

A6.4

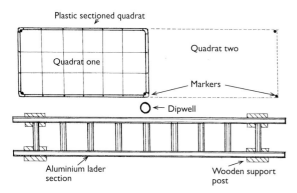

Plastic sectioned quadrat

Quadrat two

Quadrat one

Markers

Dipwell

Aluminium lader section

Wooden support post

Figure A.15 An area quadrat suitable for monitoring bog vegetation. The quadrat is only 45cm wide so that the whole quadrat can be examined without trampling the vegetation. The aluminium ladder further minimises trampling.

Table A.4: Domin values and their equivalent cover percentage ranges.

Domin value	Cover (%)
1	<1
2	1 – 2
3	2 – 3
4	3 – 10
5	10 – 20
6	20 – 33
7	33 – 55
8	55 – 75
9	75 – 95
10	95 – 100

The abundance of each species or of selected key species is estimated visually. This can be done for the quadrat areas as a whole or for each individual subdivision separately. Estimations based on subdivisions are more accurate, and mean and variance values can be computed.

Species abundance (not to be confused with relative frequency) can be estimated as a cover percentage, a cover value or a frequency value. There are a number of cover abundance value scales. The ten-point Domin scale (Table A.4) is the most widely used. Other scales based on four or five points are used, but they may be too coarse to detect all but major vegetation changes; although some workers find the narrow middle bands of the Domin scale difficult to apply. It may be just as useful to opt for gross changes as recorded by a five-point scale, for example. It should be noted that the National Vegetation Classification (Rodwell, 1991–6) uses the Domin scale.

Species frequency can be calculated by recording the presence or absence of each species in each subdivision of a quadrat. This is not recommended, as the cover or quantity of a species can change substantially without the frequency value changing, particularly if plants of a species are scattered rather than clumped. Also, species with the same frequency values may have hugely different percentage covers. Species with frequency values of 50, for example, may have cover values ranging from just a few per cent to nearly 50 per cent.

Mapping

An advantage of establishing permanent area quadrats is that the distribution and cover of plant species can be mapped sequentially with time. Sequential mapping gives a strong visual impression of vegetation change (for example, Lindsay and Ross, 1994).

Point Quadrats

When visual estimates of percentage cover and cover abundance values are not detailed enough, it may be necessary to monitor using point quadrats. Point quadrat work can, however, be very intensive and time-consuming. This method is considered to be the most objective and quantitative means of estimating species composition and change, and it is particularly useful for monitoring vegetation changes associated with management changes (Grant, 1993).

Point quadrats (Figure A.16) are recorded using a frame which supports one or a row of regularly-spaced, sharpened needles. The frame may incorporate a height scale. The needles are slowly pushed through the vegetation, one at a time, towards the ground and all contacts with the tip of the needle are recorded. To avoid errors, use very sharp needles, only record contacts with the

A6.4

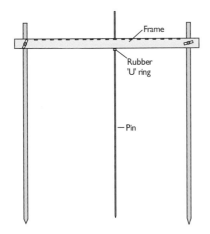

Figure A.16   A point quadrat frame constructed from plastic pipe with one pin in position. The ends of the frame are solid plastic and the legs are held with wing nuts. The pin is held by a rubber ring to prevent it from slipping.

tip, and incline needles at 32.5° to the horizontal (Warren Wilson, 1959).

As well as recording species, plant structures such as flowers, leaves and woody stems can be noted. Cover percentage and relative frequency calculations are generally based on a minimum contact number of 500. In peatlands, this will require between 100 and 200 needles. Either each cover figure should be based on a set number of needles or recording should continue until a specified number of contacts is achieved.

Percentage cover is based on the number of needles that contact a species, and cover abundance is based on the total number of contacts made by a species.

$$\text{Percentage cover} = \frac{\text{No. of needles contacted}}{\text{Total no. of needles}} \times 100$$

$$\text{Relative frequency} = \frac{\text{No. of contacts}}{\text{No. of needles}} \times 100$$

For example, if 200 needles are used and of these 100 needles make 300 contacts with species A, then percentage cover is 50% and relative frequency is 150%.

Point quadrat frames with height scales cost about £800 and £2,000 for single-pin and multi-pin frames respectively (*see* Appendix 7).

Line Quadrats

Line quadrats are particularly suitable for monitoring mosaics or for monitoring vegetation transects across bogs. A measuring tape is a convenient line quadrat marker. Within vegetation mosaics the line quadrat should be long enough to include the principal features of the mosaic.

Line quadrats along a transect of a bog can be contiguous or at regular or random intervals. A line quadrat can be of any reasonable length, although lengths of 5 or 10 m should be useful. There are two main ways of recording plants along a line quadrat:

- at regular (for example, 10 cm) or random points along the tape, record the species in contact with one edge of the tape; or
- measure the distance along the tape of each species contact.

Line and point quadrats can be combined. Hulme (1986) recorded quadrats using a 10m line with frames of pins (for example, 10 pins × 10 frames) randomly or regularly placed along the line. As well as recording the overall species composition, he was able to measure the proportion of the vegetation mosaic occupied by particular vegetation types and physical features (such as, wet hollows and pools).

A6.4.4   Data Storage and Processing

Vegetation data can be stored on paper or on a computer spreadsheet. Either medium can be used to process the data to express cover as percentage or relative frequency values. When cover values have been calculated for a number of quadrats or plots and for a number of years, they can be analysed or processed further. Two main approaches can be employed, namely simple graphing of results and numerical computer analysis of results.

A6.4.4.1   Graphic Representation

The response of vegetation to management, land-use pressure, site reinstatement, and so on, can be determined by graphing the cover of the principal or more significant species. This is illustrated in Figure A.17, which shows the

A6.4

response of *Calluna* and *Molinia* in a heavily-grazed wet heath/blanket bog to a 60% stock reduction and to no grazing. Such graphs must be derived from adequate-sized datasets. Each point on the Figure A.17 graphs represents a cover value for twenty quadrat frames with five needles each and a average of at least five contacts per needle, that is, for at least 500 contacts.

A6.4.4.2 Numerical Analysis

Numerical analysis is carried out using computers. Computer packages such as Minitab, Genstat, VESPAN (University of Lancaster) and MVSP (Kovach Computing) contain a range of statistical and ordination routines suitable for analysing and representing vegetation changes. Correlation, regression and variance analyses, and so on can, be useful interpretative tools, as can ordination techniques such as principal component, principal coordinate and correspondence analyses, Decorana and Canoco and so on (for example, Ludwig and Reynolds,

1988; Parker, 1991; Bailey, 1992; Kent and Coker, 1992).

A6.4.5 Remote Sensing

A6.4.5.1 Introduction

The science of environmental remote sensing covers all means of detection and measurement from a distance (including camera and film). There are an increasing number of instruments that operate over both visible and non-visible wavelengths. Although the use of many of these instruments is highly specialised, it is important that the land manager be aware of their existence and their potential applications to mapping and monitoring problems.

This section deals with general principles, common satellite remote sensing systems, video cameras, and some more specialised instruments, including thermal imagers.

A6.4.5.2 General Principles

Most remote sensing instruments utilise electrical sensors to detect variations in light

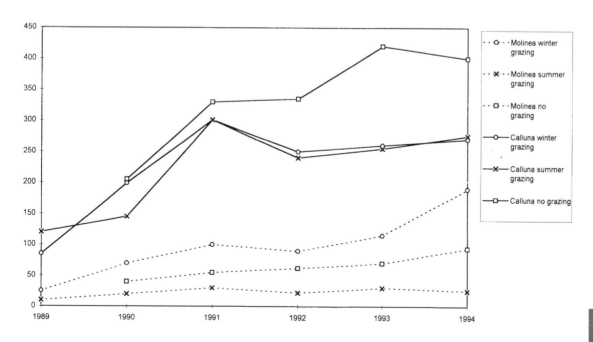

Figure A.17   A graphical representation of plant species cover changes relating to a reduction in grazing level by 60%. The graphs show the effect on heather and purple moor grass in summer (x) and winter (0) as well as a complete cessation of grazing (♠).

A6.4

(electromagnetic radiation). These variations are recorded as an electrical signal which is subsequently converted to a digital reading. (It helps to think of these instruments as being similar to a camera light meter). As the instrument scans or moves over the ground, the readings vary according to the amount of light being reflected back from the ground. Through geometrically controlled readings, the instrumentation can be used to build up an image of light variation over a geometric grid. Each grid cell, called a picture element or pixel, has a single digital number. These digital numbers can be displayed either using a computer or through specialised film-writing equipment to produce an image of the ground, which is like a photograph.

Remotely-sensed images can be used to map vegetation. The basic idea is that each vegetation type has a unique signature in relation to how it reflects radiation at different wavelengths – its spectral signature. So if you identify a known vegetation type on the digital imagery and determine its reflecting properties, it is then possible to identify all the other areas of the image with the same properties. This process is called image classification.

The very simple system described above provides a basic insight into digital spectral imaging systems. In reality they tend to be more complex! Most vegetation features are green – so at visible wavelengths they are quite hard to tell apart. Most imaging systems, therefore, do not simply produce one digital number per pixel. Instead, they record reflected radiation over a range of discrete wavebands – for example, visible blue, green, red and invisible infra-red. It is the response of the vegetation across the range of wavebands that really enables discrimination between different vegetation types.

Remotely-sensed imagery comes in two forms: as raw digital data on a computer disk or tape, or as photo images produced by film-writing equipment. The digital data is more useful if you have access to appropriate computing hardware and image-processing software. However, scaled photo products can be useful as the basis for field mapping over large areas.

Imaging systems are governed by the same laws of physics as photographic ones. In essence, the size of an object on the ground, that can be detected or measured, is dependent upon the height of the instrument above the ground. The resolution of most scanning systems is described in terms of pixel size. Airborne scanners can provide resolutions of the order of 1m (dependent on flying height). Satellite-borne scanners provide resolutions in the range 10m to 4 km.

A6.4.5.3 Satellite Imagery

One very important advantage of satellite-borne sensing systems over airborne ones is that they provide the opportunity for regular coverage of an area at relatively low cost. They are, therefore, potentially useful for monitoring purposes.

The resolution and frequency of coverage is set by the satellite orbit. Polar orbiting satellites operate nearer to the earth, typically around 900 km, to provide higher-resolution imagery. Geostationary satellites are positioned over the equator at altitudes of around 36,000 km, so as to progress at the same speed as the earth rotates – hence geostationary! The trade-off between these two orbital configurations is the frequency of imaging. Geostationary satellites can provide imagery on an hourly basis over very large areas of the earth. Polar orbiting satellites can cover the whole earth in twelve hours although only by using wide-angled viewing and thus trading off resolution for frequency of coverage. By increasing the resolution, using longer-focal length lenses, polar orbiting systems can provide resolutions of 10m, but the time between overpasses is increased to 16–18 days.

Most weather satellites are either geostationary or polar-orbiting with wide-angled imaging systems (these produce the sorts of images that you *see* on television weather bulletins). The typical pixel sizes are 4 km for the geostationary images (for example, Meteosat) and around 1 km for the polar orbiting images (for example, Tiros – N).

Although weather satellites provide daily image cover, the ground resolution of this imagery is so poor that it is unlikely to be of any practical value to the management of small areas of bog. There is some limited use to be made of this sort of imagery, for example, looking at time-series of vegetation development, over very extensive bog

A6.4

areas (such as, northern Canada) but probably not in western Europe.

It is the families of earth-observing satellites which are likely to be of more interest to the bog manager. The principal ones are the US LANDSAT series and the French SPOT series. These are described below.

The first LANDSAT was launched in 1972. Since then, there has been regular imagery available for most of the earth, except high latitudes. All the satellites have multi-spectral scanning instruments. The existing instrumentation, the Thematic Mapper, gives image cover every sixteen days with a pixel size of 30m – or just about one-quarter of the size of a football pitch! It also records in seven spectral bands, across the visible, near-middle and into the thermal infra-red. However, because the thermal band has a poorer ground resolution (c. 100m) and the imagery is taken in mid-morning (c. 09:30 local time), the quality of the thermal data is much poorer.

To make it easy to get LANDSAT data, there is a standard Worldwide Reference System. In this, the orbit is called a path and the image is centred on a row. Each image covers an area 180 km x 180 km. So if you wanted imagery of north-east Scotland you would order Path 205, Row 20. All UK images are obtainable through the National Remote Sensing Centre. They can be purchased on computer media or as film products (prints, negatives and so on).

The French SPOT satellites were first launched in 1986. They carry a similar multi-spectral scanning system to LANDSAT, although there are important differences. First, the SPOT instruments operate in two modes: a black-and-white (pan-chromatic) mode which gives images with a pixel size of 10m, and a multi-spectral mode giving a pixel size of 20m. The scanner is also 'steerable'. These means that it is possible to get, by request, more frequent coverage. (This costs a lot!) It also allows the acquisition of overlapping imagery. So some SPOT imagery can be viewed in stereo. The coverage of a standard SPOT scene, however, is only 60km x 60km or less than one quarter of the LANDSAT equivalent.

Satellite imagery can be expensive. Typical LANDSAT TM scenes cost £3,000 (1996 prices).

Typical SPOT coverage of the same area cost £12,000 (1996 prices). It is worth contacting your local university Geography Department before using such imagery. Some existing images may be available at lower cost.

There are several uses for satellite imagery:

As a base map: A great advantage of satellite images is that, unlike aerial photographs, they are relatively free of distortions and do not have to be merged together to provide coverage of larger areas. It is possible to produce a properly scaled, true-colour photo-product, which can be used as a base map in the field. Bearing in mind the size of the pixels, the most appropriate scale for enlargement is 1:50,000, although 1:25,000 is possible but usually highly 'pixelated', that is, you can *see* the pixels.

For vegetation mapping: Satellite images have been and are routinely used for mapping vegetation. In general, their use in mapping involves the use of a computer and image-processing software.

Scaled photo-products can be used to map vegetation communities. This can be done on colour imagery (true or false-colour, which is similar to infra-red aerial photography in that green vegetation appears red). Alternatively, it can be done on an image for each individual band. The best way to do this is using a gridded overlay and ticking each cell as to whether it is in the vegetation class or not. An interesting and useful output from this approach is that vegetation gradients are realistically represented on the final grid map.

Monitoring vegetation state: Healthy green vegetation absorbs strongly at red wavelengths and reflects strongly at infra-red wavelengths. As vegetation grows and dies there are related changes in the way in which it reflects light. These changes can be exploited as a means of remotely measuring vegetation state (development stage, stress and so on). The most simple vegetation measure is to take a ratio of the infra-red to red reflectance. A high value represents a healthy green cover, a low value represents dead or senescent vegetation. Ideally, for this information to be of most use it should cover a whole growing season and preferably several seasons so that general trends can be established.

A6.4

Monitoring vegetation state using high-resolution satellite imagery is difficult due to the cost of the multiple images and the unreliability of coverage due to cloud cover. A simpler, more controllable alternative is to use ground-based radiometers which simply record light reflectance at red and infra-red wavelengths. These instruments can be incorporated into a routine monitoring programmes and cost around £500–£600. There are well-developed relationships between vegetation index and percentage ground cover; slightly poorer relationships with leaf area index and net primary productivity. There have been very few studies that have used radiometers for monitoring semi-natural vegetation, and they would still have to be considered as 'experimental'.

A6.4.5.4 Video and Thermal Imaging

There are other types of non-photographic imaging systems. These include video and thermal imaging systems.

Video: Video systems operate at visible wavelengths, produce good colour imagery and are generally available in a domestic guise, so their use in monitoring should be considered. Although their image quality is limited by the number of scan lines, this is compensated for by the low cost of video storage. The quality of video cameras has improved greatly in recent years, and some of the limitations of early tube technology have been overcome (for example, early video cameras did not take kindly to being operated vertically!).

To make the most use of video cameras as monitoring instruments, all the same conditions as photography apply (*see* 4.1.3), particularly in relation to viewing geometry and light conditions.

However, because video is essentially recorded onto magnetic tape and played back through a domestic video player, there is a difficulty in making use of the imagery for quantitative assessment.

It is now possible to convert video images to digital images using appropriate 'frame-grabbing' technology. This is becoming increasingly available with microcomputing systems, although be aware of the resolution and quality that this provides. The frame-freeze facilities on most domestic video players are not, however, an alternative. Technical advice can be obtained from your local university or research institute, and it is worthwhile experimenting with the complete cycle of intended use from video capture, through frame-grabbing, to image analysis before embarking on a system of monitoring based on video cameras.

Thermal imaging: Thermal imaging is a very specialised technology. It depends upon new sensors which can measure subtle changes in the radiant temperature of objects. Thermal cameras have been developed by the military and are generally used by emergency services for search-and-rescue purposes. They have had very limited applications in environmental monitoring; these have mostly been to do with heat-loss surveys of buildings. However, they are very sensitive to variations in radiant temperature-detecting to 0.2°C. In Canada, they have been used to detect upwelling groundwater, which has a different thermal regime to surface water. It is conceivable that there are some very specialised applications of this technology to monitoring bogs. The costs of these systems, in the order of £10,000–£20,000, would indicate that they are likely to be used for experimental rather than operational purposes.

A6.4

APPENDIX 7

SUPPLIERS

PART 4: MONITORING AND SITE ASSESSMENT

Hydrology

WaLRaGs:

Barry Imerson
The Old Dairy
Highgreen
Tarset
Bellingham
Northumberland
NE48 1RP
Tel.: 01434 240405

Weirs, Chart Recorders and Data Loggers:

ADAS Land Research Centre
Anstey Hall
Maris Lane
Trumpington
Cambridge
CB2 2LF
Tel.: 01223 840011

R16 Water-level Recorder:

Smail Engineers (Glasgow) Ltd
30 Napier Road
Hillington Industrial Estate
Glasgow
G52 4DR
Tel.: 0141-882 4882

Water Table Logger (and software):

Chambers Electronics
Kaluna House
Nairnside
Inverness
IV1 2BU
Tel.: 01463 790400

Tipping Bucket Gauge:

ADAS Land Research Centre
Anstey Hall
Maris Lane
Trumpington
Cambridge
CB2 2LF
Tel.: 01223 840011

Vegetation

Vegetation Recording Frames:

Scottish Agricultural College
Bush Site
Roslin
Midlothian
EH25 9SY
Tel.: 0131-667 1041

Invertebrates

Malaise Traps:

Watkins and Doncaster
PO Box 5
Cranbrook
Kent
TN18 5EZ
Tel.: 01580 753133

Moth traps:

Watkins and Doncaster
PO Box 5
Cranbrook
Kent
TN18 5EZ
Tel.: 01580 753133

A7

Suction trap:

Burkard Manufacturing Company
Rickmansworth
Hertfordshire
England
Tel.: 01923 773134

PART 5: METHODS AND TECHNIQUES FOR MANAGEMENT

Dams:

Plastic Piling:

Plastic Piling Ltd
Cottars Hall
Nethergate Street
Hopton
Near Diss
IP22 2QZ
Tel.: 01953 688369

Bankmaster Systems
Unit 130
Clydesdale Place
Moss Side Industrial Estate
Leyland
Lancashire
PR5 3QS
Tel.: 01772 456482

Glass Reinforced Concrete sluices:

BCM Contracts Ltd
Unit 22
Civic Industrial
Whitchurch
Shropshire
Tel.: 01948 665321/5322

Scrub Control:

Forest Safety Leaflets for Chainsaws:

The Secretary
Forestry Safety Council
Forestry Commission
231 Corstorphine Road
Edinburgh
EH12 7AT
Tel.: 0131-334 0303

Chippers:

Bandit Chippers
DanEquip
Manor Farm Business Centre
The Street
Tongham
Farnham
Surrey
GU10 1DG
Tel.: 01252 782487

Chipmaster
GreenMech Ltd
The Mill Industrial Park
Kings Coughton
Alcester
Warwickshire
B49 5QG
Tel.: 01789 400167

Dosko
DanEquip
Manor Farm Business Centre
The Street
Tongham
Farnham
Surrey
GU10 1DG
Tel.: 01252 782487

Gandini
Meccanica Chippers International Limited
Little Acres Farm
Kings Lane
Snitterfield
Warwickshire
CV37 0QZ
Tel. 01789 41487

Vehicles:

Vimek Minimaster 101
Forest Machinery Sales
92 Whitelaw Drive
Bathgate
EH48 1RJ
Tel.: 01506 656478

Access:

Recycled Plastic Sections:

Dumfries Plastics Recycling Ltd
College Road
Dumfries
DG2 0BU
Tel.: 01387 247110

Inflatable Path:

AMS Systems Engineering
Unit 3
Bentley Industrial Centre
Farnham
Surrey
GU10 5NJ
Tel.: 01420 23777

Flexible Boards:

Sommerfield Flexboard Ltd
Doseley Industrial Estate
Frame Lane
Doseley
Telford
Shropshire
TF4 3BY
Tel.: 01952 503737

Vehicles:

Vimek Minimaster 101
Forest Machinery Sales
92 Whitelaw Drive
Bathgate
EH48 1RJ
Tel.: 01506 656478

Glencoe ATV
ACV Engineering
Unit 13b
Queensway
Stem Lane Industrial Estate
New Milton
Hampshire
BH25 5NN
Tel.: 01425 629200

Argocat
For local supplier, contact:
Ontario Drive and Gear Limited
P.O. Box 280
220 Bleams Road
New Hamburg
ON Canada
N0B 2G0
Tel.: +(519) 662 2840

A7

REFERENCES

REFERENCES

Aaby, B. and Tauber, H. (1974) Rates of peat formation in relation to degree of humification and local environment as shown by studies of a raised bog in Denmark. *Boreas*, **4**, 1–17.

Agate, E. (1983) *Footpaths. A Practical Conservation Handbook.* British Trust for Conservation Volunteers, Wallingford.

Armstrong, H. M. (1993) The MLURI hill grazing model: using a computer to help set stocking rates. *ENACT – Managing Land for Wildlife*, **1**(4), 7–9.

Armstrong, H. M. and Milne, J. A. (1995) The effects of grazing on vegetation species composition. In: Thompson, D. B. A., Hester, A. J. and Usher, M. B. (eds) *Heaths and Moorlands – Cultural Landscapes*. HMSO, Edinburgh, pp. 162–173.

Atkinson, M. D. (1992) *Betula pendula* Roth (*B. verrucosa Ehrh*) and *B. pubescens Ehrh*. Biological flora of the British Isles. *Journal of Ecology*, **80**, 837–870.

Bacon, J. and Lord, B. (1996) Troublesome trees – taking trees off bogs. *ENACT – Managing Land for Wildlife*. **4** (3), 12–16.

Bailey, N. T. J. (1992) *Statistical Methods in Biology*. 2nd ed. Cambridge University Press, Cambridge.

Bannister, P. (1978) *Birch Survey – Flanders Moss SSSI*. Unpublished report, Nature Conservancy Council, Edinburgh.

Barber, K. E. (1981) *Peat Stratigraphy and Climatic Change: A Palaeoecological Test of the Theory of Cyclic Peat Bog Regeneration*. Balkema, Rotterdam.

Barber, K. E. (1984) A large capacity Russian-pattern sediment sampler. *Quaternary Newsletter*, **44**, 28–31.

Barber, K. E., Chambers, F. M., Maddy, D., Stoneman, R. E. and Brew, J. S. (1994) A sensitive high-resolution record of late Holocene climate change from a raised bog in northern England. *The Holocene*, **4**, 198–205.

Barber, K. E., Dumayne, L. and Stoneman, R. E. (1993) Climate change and human impact during the late Holocene in northern Britain. In: Chambers, F. M. (ed.) *Climate Change and Human Impact on the Landscape*. Chapman and Hall, London, pp. 235–6.

Bibby, C. J., Burgess, N. D. and Hill, D. A. (1992) *Bird Census Techniques*. Academic Press, London.

Birnie, R. V. (1993) Erosion rates on bare peat surfaces in Shetland. *Scottish Geographical Magazine*, **109**, 12–17.

Birnie, R. V. and Hulme, P. D. (1990) Overgrazing of peatland vegetation in Shetland. *Scottish Geographical Magazine*, **106**, 28–36.

Blackford, J. J. (1993) Peat bogs as sources of proxy climate data: past approaches and future research. In: Chambers, F. M. (ed.) *Climate Change and Human Impact on the Landscape*. Chapman and Hall, London, pp. 47–56.

Blankenberg, J. and Kuntze, H. (1987) Moorkundlich-Hydrologische Voraussetzungen der Wiedervernassung von Hochmooren. *Telma*, **17**, 51–58.

Bragg, O. M. and Brown, J. M. B. (in preparation) *A Handbook of Ground Water Mound Theory*. Scottish Natural Heritage, Edinburgh.

Bragg, O. M., Hulme, P. D., Ingram, H. A. P., Johnston, J. P. and Wilson, A. A. (1994) A maximum–minimum recorder for shallow water tables, developed for ecohydrological studies on mires. *Journal of Applied Ecology*, **31**, 581–592.

Brooks, A. (1980) *Woodlands – A Practical Handbook*. British Trust for Conservation Volunteers, Wallingford.

Brooks, S. J. and Stoneman, R. E. (1996) Tree removal at Langlands Moss. In: Parkyn, L., Stoneman, R. E. and Ingram, H. A. P. (eds) *Conserving Peatlands*. CAB International, Wallingford, pp. 315–323.

Cadell, H. M. (1913) *The Story of the Forth*. Maclehose, Glasgow.

Calder, I. R. (1976) The measurement of water losses from a forested area using a 'natural' lysimeter. *Journal of Hydrology*, **30**, 311–25.

Chambers, F. M. (1996) Bogs as treeless wastes: the myth and the implications for conservation. In: Parkyn, L., Stoneman, R. E. and Ingram, H. A. P. (eds) *Conserving Peatlands*. CAB International, Wallingford, pp. 168–176.

Chapman, S. B. and Rose, R. J. (1991) Changes in the vegetation of Coom Rigg Moss National Nature Reserve within the period 1958–86. *Journal of Applied Ecology*, **28**, 140–53.

Charman, D. J. (1992) Blanket mire formation at the Cross Lochs, Sutherland, northern Scotland. *Boreas*, **21**, 53–72.

Charman, D. J. (1993) Patterned fens in Scotland: evidence from vegetation and water chemistry. *Journal of Vegetation Science*, **4**(4), 543–52.

Charman, D. J. (1994) Late Glacial and Holocene vegetation history of the Flow Country, northern Scotland. *New Phytologist*, **127**(1), 155–8.

Charman, D. J. and Smith, R. S. (1992) Forestry and blanket mires of Kielder Forest, northern England: long-term effects on vegetation. In: Bragg, O. M., Hulme, P. D., Ingram, N. A. P. and Robertson, R. A. (eds) *Peatland*

Ecosystems and Man: An Impact Assessment. University of Dundee, Dundee, pp. 226–30.

Clarke, J. L., Welch, D. and Gordon, I. J. (1995) The influence of vegetation pattern on the grazing of heather moorland by red deer and sheep. 1. The location of animals on grass/heather mosaics. *Journal of Applied Ecology*, **32**, 166–76.

Clymo, R. S. (1963) Ion exchange in *Sphagnum* and its relation to bog ecology. *Annals of Botany, London*, **27**, 309–24.

Clymo, R. S. (1992) Productivity and decomposition of peatland ecosystems. In: Bragg, O. M., Hulme, P. D., Ingram, H. A. P. and Robertson, R. A. (eds) *Peatland Ecosystems and Man: An Impact Assessment.* University of Dundee, Dundee, pp. 3–16.

Coles, B. (1995) *Wetland Management. A Survey for English Heritage.* Wetland Archaeology Research Project, Occasional Paper 9. University of Exeter, Exeter.

Coles, B. and Coles, J. (1986) *Sweet Track to Glastonbury: The Prehistory of the Somerset Levels.* Thames and Hudson, London.

Conway, V. M. (1948) Ringinglow Bog, near Sheffield. *Journal of Ecology*, **34**, 131–49.

Cooke, A. S. (1986) *The Use of Herbicides on Nature Reserves.* Focus on Nature Conservation, 14. Nature Conservancy Council. Peterborough.

Countryside Commission for Scotland (1983) *The Treatment of Exterior Timber Against Decay, Information Sheet 13. 1.* Countryside Commission for Scotland, Battleby.

Countryside Commission for Scotland (1989) *Boardwalks, Information Sheet 6. 9.* Countryside Commission for Scotland, Battleby.

Cox, M. J., Jones, B. and Hogan, D. V. (1996) Wet site curation in the Somerset Levels and Moors. In: Beavis, J. and Barker, K. (eds) *Science and Site: Evaluation and Conservation.* Bournemouth University, Bournmouth, pp. 78–92.

Daniels, R. E. and Eddy, A. (1990) *A Handbook of European Sphagna.* Natural Environment Research Council, HMSO, London.

Eggelsman, R. (1980) Ökohydrologische Aspekte zur Erhaltung von Moorgewässern. *Telma*, **10**, 173–96.

Elliott, D. (1995) *Bankhead Moss Management Plan. April 1995–March 2000.* Unpublished report, Scottish Wildlife Trust, Edinburgh.

Emanuelsson, U. (1985) Recreation impact on mountainous areas in northern Sweden. In: Bayfield, N. G. and Barrow, O. C. (eds) *The Ecological Impacts of Outdoor Recreation on Mountain Areas in Europe and North America.* Recreation Ecology Research Group, Wye, pp. 63–73.

Ferguson, P. and Lee, J. A. (1979) The effects of bisulphite and sulphate upon photosynthesis in *Sphagnum. New Phytologist*, **82**, 703–12.

Ferguson, P., Lee, J. A. and Bell, J. N. B. (1978) Effects of sulphur pollutants on the growth of *Sphagnum* species. *Environmental Pollution*, **16**, 151–62.

Ferguson, P., Robinson, R. N., Press, M. C., and Lee, J. A. (1984) Element concentrations in five *Sphagnum* species in relation to atmospheric pollution. *Journal of Bryology*, **15**, 107–14.

Forestry Safety Council (1988) *Clearing Saw – Forestry Safety Guide (FSC 1).* Forestry Commission, Edinburgh.

Forestry Safety Council (1990a) *Chain Saw Snedding – Forestry Safety Guide (FSC 12).* Forestry Commission, Edinburgh.

Forestry Safety Council (1990b) *Felling By Chain Saw – Forestry Safety Guide (FSC 11).* Forestry Commission, Edinburgh.

Forestry Safety Council (1990c) *The Chain Saw – Forestry Safety Guide (FSC 10).* Forestry Commission, Edinburgh.

Fry, R. and Lonsdale, D. (1991) Habitat conservation for invertebrates – a neglected green issue. *Amateur Entomologist*, **21**. The Amateur Entomologists' Society, London.

Gash, J. H. C., Wright, I. R., and Lloyd, C. R. (1980) Comparative estimates of interception loss from three coniferous forests in Great Britain. *Journal of Hydrology*, **48**, 89–105.

Gimmingham, C. H. (1992) *The Lowland Heathland Management Handbook.* English Nature Science Series, no. 8. English Nature, Peterborough.

Glaser, P. H. and Janssens, J. J. (1986) Raised bogs in eastern north America: transitions in landforms and gross stratigraphy. *Canadian Journal of Botany*, **64**, 395–415.

Glaser, P. H., Wheeler, G. A., Gorham, E. and Wright, H. E. (1981) The patterned mires of the Red Lake Peatland, northern Minnesota: vegetation, water chemistry and landforms. *Journal of Ecology*, **69**, 575–99.

Godwin, H. (1975) *The History of the British Flora*, 2nd edn. Cambridge University Press, Cambridge.

Godwin, H. (1981) *The Archives of the Peat Bogs.* Cambridge University Press, Cambridge.

Goodall, D. W. (1963) The continuum and individualistic association. *Vegetatio*, **11**, 297–316.

Goodwillie, R. (1980) *European Peatlands.* Nature and Environment Series, no. 19. Council of Europe, Strasbourg.

Gore, A. J. P. (1983) Introduction. In: Gore, A. J. P. (ed.) *Ecosystems of the World 4A. Mires: Swamp, Bog: Fen and Moor, General Studies.* Elsevier Scientific, Amsterdam, pp. 1–13.

Granlund, E. (1932) De svenska högmossarnas geologi. *Svensk. Geol. Unders. Ser. C*, **373**, 193.

Grant, S. A. (1993) Resource description: vegetation and sward components. In: Davies, A., Baker, R. D., Grant, S. A. and Laidlaw, A. S. (eds) *Sward Management Handbook*, 2nd edn. British Grassland Society, Reading, pp. 69–97.

Grant, S. A, Lamb, I. C, Kerr, C. D. and Bolton, G. R. (1976) The utilisation of blanket bog vegetation by grazing sheep. *Journal of Applied Ecology*, **13**, 857–69.

Grant, S. A., Torvell, L., Smith, H. K., Suckling, D. E., Forbes, T. D. A. and Hodgson, J. (1987) Comparative studies of diet selection by sheep and cattle: blanket bog and heather moor. *Journal of Ecology*, **75**, 947–60.

Greenslade, P. J. M. (1964) Pitfall trapping as a method for studying populations of Carabidae. *Journal of Animal Ecology*, **33**, 301–10.

Greig-Smith, P. (1952) The use of random and contiguous quadrats in the study of the structure of plant communities. *Annals of Botany*, **16**, 293–306.

Habron, D. (1994) *The Effects of Human Trampling on Raised Mire Vegetation Communities at East Flanders Moss*. Unpublished M.Sc. dissertation, Department of Environmental Science, University of Stirling, Stirling.

Hall, D. and Coles, J. (1994) *Fenland Survey: an Essay in Landscape and Persistence*. English Heritage, London.

Harvey, S. (1993) *An Investigation into the Effectiveness of Dams Placed in Drainage Channels in Order to Raise the Water Table on Three Mires Situated in Kielder Forest*. Unpublished B.Sc. dissertation, University of Newcastle upon Tyne, Newcastle upon Tyne.

Heathwaite, A. L. and Göttlich, K. (1993) *Mires, Process, Exploitation and Conservation*. John Wiley and Sons, Chichester.

Hester, A. J. and Miller, G. R. (1995) Scrub and woodland regeneration: prospects for the future. In: Thompson, D. B. A., Hester, A. J. and Usher, M. B. (eds) *Heaths and Moorland : Cultural Landscapes*. HMSO, Edinburgh, pp. 140–53.

Hill, M. O. (1992) *Sphagnum: A Field Guide*. Joint Nature Conservation Committee, Peterborough.

Hillam, J., Groves, C. M., Brown, D. M., Baille, M. G. L., Coles, J. M. and Coles, B. J. (1990) Dendrochronology of the English Neolithic. *Antiquity*, **64**, 210–20.

Holmes, P. R., Boyce, D. C. and Reed, D. K. (1993) The ground beetle (Coleoptera; Carabidae) fauna of Welsh peatland biotopes: factors influencing the distribution of ground beetles and conservation implications. *Biological Conservation*, **63**, 153–61.

Holopainen, J. K. (1990) Influence of ethylene glycol on the numbers of carabids and other soil arthropods caught in pitfall traps. In: Stork, N. (ed.) *The Role of Ground Beetles in Ecological and Environmental Studies*. Intercept, Andover, pp. 339–41.

Hudson, P. J. and Newborn, D. (1995) *A Manual of Red Grouse and Moorland Management*. Game Conservancy Ltd, Fordingbridge.

Hulme, P. D. (1980) The classification of Scottish peatlands. *Scottish Geographical Magazine*, **96**, 46–50.

Hulme, P. D. (1986) The origin and development of wet hollows and pools in Craigeazle Mire, south-west Scotland. *International Peat Journal*, **1**, 15–28.

Immirzi, C. P. and Maltby, E. (1992) *The Global Status of Peatlands and their Role in Carbon Cycling*. A report for Friends of the Earth by the Wetlands Ecosystems Research Group, Department of Geography, University of Exeter. Friends of the Earth, London.

Ingram, H. A. P. (1982) Size and shape in raised mire ecosystems: a geophysical model. *Nature*, **297**, 300–2.

Ingram, H. A. P. (1992) Introduction to the ecohydrology of mires in the context of cultural perturbation. In: Bragg, O. M., Hulme, P. D., Ingram, H. A. P. and Robertson, R. A. (eds) *Peatland Ecosystems and Man: An Impact Assessment*. University of Dundee, Dundee, pp. 67–93.

Ingram, H. A. P. (1995) Conserving the cultural landscape? *Mires Research Group Newsletter*, **1**, 2.

Irish Peatland Conservation Council (1992) *Peatland Education Pack*. IPCC, Dublin.

Ivanov, K. E. (1981) *Water Movement in Mirelands* (*Vodoobmen v bolotnykh landshaftakh*). Academic Press, London.

Joosten, J. H. J. (1995) Time to regenerate: long-term perspectives of raised bog regeneration with special emphasis on palaeoecological studies. In: Wheeler, B. D., Shaw, S. C., Fojt, W. J. and Robertson, R. A. (eds) *Restoration of Temperate Wetlands*. John Wiley and Sons, Chichester.

Jowsey, P. C. (1966) An improved peat sampler. *New Phytologist*, **65**, 245–48.

Juniper, T. (1994) Comment: conservation on the global stage. The Habitats Directive, the Biodiversity Convention and the UK. *British Wildlife*, **6(2)**, 99–105.

Kent, M. and Coker, P. (1992) *Vegetation Description and Analysis – A Practical Approach*. CRC Press, Ann Arbor, Michigan.

Kirby, P. (1992) *Habitat Management for Invertebrates: A Practical Handbook*. RSPB, Sandy.

Ledger, D. C., Lovell, J. P. B. and McDonald, A. T. (1974) Sediment yield studies in upland catchment areas in south-east Scotland. *Journal of Applied Ecology*, **11**, 201–06.

Leech, R., Bell, M. and Evans, J. (1983). The sectioning of a Romano-British saltmaking mound at East Huntspill. *Somerset Levels Papers*, **9**, 74–9.

Legg, C. J., Maltby, E. and Proctor, M. C. F. (1992) The ecology of severe moorland fire on the North York Moors: seed distribution and seedling establishment of *Calluna vulgaris*. *Journal of Ecology*, **80**, 737–52.

Lindsay, R. A. (1977) *Glasson Moss National Nature Reserve and the 1976 Fire*. Unpublished report, Nature Conservancy Council, Peterborough.

Lindsay, R. A. (1993) Peatland conservation – from cinders to Cinderella. *Biodiversity and Conservation*, **2**, 528–40.

Lindsay, R. A. (1995) *Bogs: The Ecology, Classification and Conservation of Ombrotrophic Mires*. Scottish Natural Heritage, Battleby.

Lindsay, R. A., Charman, D. J, Everingham, F., O'Reilly, R. M., Palmer, M. A., Rowell, T. A. and Stroud, D. A. (1988) *The Flow Country. The Peatlands of Caithness and Sutherland*. Nature Conservancy Council, Peterborough.

Lindsay, R. A., Riggal, J. and Burd, F. (1985) The use of small-scale surface patterns in the classification of British peatlands. *Aquilo, Seria Botanica*, **21**, 69–79.

Lindsay, R. A. and Ross, S. (1994) Monitoring of peat bog systems. *Strapfia*, **32**, 73–92.

Lowe, S. (1993) *Border Mires Redefinition of Hydrological Boundaries.* Unpublished report, English Nature, Newcastle upon Tyne.

Ludwig, J. A. and Reynolds, J. F. (1988) *Statistical Ecology: A Primer on Methods and Computing.* John Wiley and Sons, New York.

Lynn, W. C., McKenzie, W. E. and Grossman, R. B. (1974) Field laboratory tests for characterisation of histosols. In: Aandahl, A. R., Buol, S. W., Hill, D. E. and Bailey, H. H. (eds) *Histosols, their Characterisation, Classification and Use.* SSSA Special Publication Series, no. 6, pp. 11–20.

Maas, D. and Poschold, P. (1991) Restoration of exploited peat areas in raised bogs – Technical management and vegetation development. In: Ravera, O. (ed.) *Terrestrial and Aquatic Ecosystems: Perturbation and Recovery.* Ellis Horwood, Chichester, pp. 379–86.

Mallick, A. U., Gimmingham, C. H., and Rahman, A. A. (1984) Ecological effects of heather burning. 1. Water infiltration, moisture retention and porosity of surface soil. *Journal of Ecology*, **72**, 767–76.

Maltby, E. (1992) Microbiological changes resulting from human impacts on peat and organic soil horizons. In: Bragg, O. M., Hulme, P. D., Ingram, H. A. P. and Robertson, R. A. (eds) *Peatland Ecosystems and Man: An Impact Assessment.* University of Dundee, Dundee, pp. 45–58.

Marrs, R. H. (1985) The use of Krenite to control birch on lowland heaths. *Biological Conservation*, **32**, 149–64.

Marrs, R. H. and Welch, D. (1991) *Moorland Wilderness: the Potential Effects of Removing Domestic Livestock, Particularly Sheep.* Department of the Environment, London.

McVean, D. N. and Ratcliffe D. A. (1962) *Plant Communities in the Scottish Highlands.* HMSO, London.

Meade, R. (1992) Some early changes following the rewetting of a vegetated cut-over peatland surface at Danes Moss, Cheshire, UK, and their relevance to conservation management. *Biological Conservation*, **61**, 31–40.

Meharg, M. J., Montgomery, W. I. and McFerran, D. (1992) Potential damage to peatland ecosystems by mechanised peat extraction. In: Bragg, O. M., Hulme, P. D., Ingram, H. A. P. and Robertson, R. A. (eds) *Peatland Ecosystems and Man: An Impact Assessment.* University of Dundee, Dundee, pp. 23–30.

Ministry of Agriculture, Fisheries and Food. (1983) *A System for Hill Sheep in the North of England.* Booklet 2031, MAFF, Alnwick.

Money, R. P. (1994) *Restoration of Lowland Raised Bogs Damaged by Peat Extraction – with Particular Emphasis on* Sphagnum *Regeneration.* Ph.D. thesis, University of Sheffield, Sheffield.

Moore, P. D. (1973) The influence of prehistoric cultures on the initiation and spread of blanket bog in upland Wales. *Nature*, **241**, 350–53.

Moore, P. D. (1979) Next in succession. *Nature*, **282**, 361–62.

Moore, P. D. (1984) *European Mires.* Academic Press, London.

Moore, P. D. (1987) A thousand years of death. *New Scientist*, **1,542** (8 January), 46–8.

Moore, P. D. and Bellamy, D. J. (1974) *Peatlands.* Paul Elek, London.

Morris, J. M. (1990) *Earth Roads: A Practical Manual for the Provision of Access for Agricultural and Forestry Projects in Developing Countries.* Cranfield Press, Cranfield.

Moss, C. E. (1913) *Vegetation of the Peak District.* The University Press, Cambridge.

Nature Conservancy Council (1988). *Site Management Plans for Nature Conservation – A Working Guide.* Nature Conservancy Council, Peterborough.

Ninnes, R., and Keay, D. (1994) *Hydrological Monitoring on Balloch Moss. Report of Methods.* Unpublished report, Scottish Natural Heritage, Angus.

Osvald, H. (1925) Die Hochmoortypen Europas. *Veröff. Geobot. Inst. Eidg. Tech. Hochsch. Stift. Rübel*, Zürich, **3**, 707–23.

Palmer, M. A. (1988) The impacts of afforestation on freshwater habitats. In: Lindsay, R. A., Charman, D. J., Everingham, F., O'Reilly, R. M., Palmer, M. A., Rowell, T. A. and Stroud, D. A. (eds) *The Flow Country. The Peatlands of Caithness and Sutherland.* Nature Conservancy Council, Peterborough, pp. 127–130.

Parker, R. E. (1991) *Introductory Statistics for Biology*, 2nd ed. Institute of Biology Studies in Biology no. 43, Cambridge University Press, Cambridge.

Parkyn, L. and Stoneman, R. E. (1996) The Scottish Raised Bog Land Cover Survey. In: Parkyn, L., Stoneman, R. E., and Ingram, H. A. P. (eds) *Conserving Peatlands.* CAB International, Wallingford, pp. 192–203.

Pearce, F. (1994) Ice Ages: the peat bog connection. *New Scientist*, **1,954**, (3rd December), 18.

Peat Producers Association (1992) *The Peat Industry in the UK. Areas, Production, Imports, Harvesting, Alternatives and Restoration.* Peat Producers Association, Lincoln.

Phillips, J., Yalden, D. and Tallis, J. H. (1981) *Peak District Moorland Erosion Study, Phase 1 Report.* Peak Park Joint Planning Board, Bakewell.

Poschold, P. (1992) Development of vegetation in peat-mined areas in some bogs in the foothills of the Alps. In: Bragg, O. M., Hulme, P. D., Ingram, H. A. P. and Robertson, R. A. (eds) *Peatland Ecosystems and Man: An Impact Assessment.* University of Dundee, Dundee, pp. 287–90.

Press, M. C., Woodin, S. J., and Lee, J. A. (1986) The potential importance of increased atmospheric nitrogen supply to the growth of ombrotrophic *Sphagnum* species. *New Phytologist*, **103**, 45–55.

Pryor, F. (1991) *Flag Fen Prehistoric Fenland Centre*. Batsford and English Heritage, Peterborough.

Ratcliffe, D. A. (1977) *A Nature Conservation Review*. Cambridge University Press, Cambridge.

Ratcliffe, D. A. and Oswald, P. O. (eds) (1987) *Birds, Bogs and Forestry. The Peatlands of Caithness and Sutherland*. Nature conservancy Council, Peterborough.

Rawes. M. (1983) Changes in two high altitude blanket bogs after cessation of sheep grazing. *Journal of Ecology*, **71**, 219–35.

Reid, E., Ross, S. Y., Thompson, D. B. A. and Lindsay, R. A. (1996) From *Sphagnum* to satellite: towards a comprehensive inventory of the blanket mires of Scotland. In: Parkyn, L., Stoneman, R. E. and Ingram, H. A. P. (eds) *Conserving Peatlands*. CAB International, Wallingford, pp. 217–28.

Richard, W. E. Jr and Brown, J. (1974) Effects of vehicles on arctic tundra. *Environmental Conservation*, **1**, 55–62.

Robinson, M. (1980) *The Effect of Pre-afforestation Drainage on the Streamflow and Water Quality of a Small Upland Catchment*. Report 73, Unpublished report, Institute of Hydrology, Wallingford.

Robinson, M. (1985) The hydrological effects of moor-gripping; a re-appraisal of the Moor House research. *Journal of Environmental Management*, **21**, 205–11.

Robinson, M. and Blyth, K. (1982) The effect of forestry drainage operations on upland sediment yields: a case study. *Earth Surface Processes and Landforms*, **7**, 85–90.

Robinson, P. (1991) *Herbicide Experiments on Bankhead Moss*. Unpublished report, Scottish Wildlife Trust, Edinburgh.

Rodwell, J. S. (ed.) (1991–6) *British Plant Communities*, vols 1–5. Cambridge University Press, Cambridge.

Rowell, T. A. (1988) *The Peatland Management Handbook*. Nature Conservancy Council, Peterborough.

Rudolf, H. and Voigt, J. U. (1986) Effects of NH_4^+–N and NH_3^+–N on the growth and metabolism of *Sphagnum magellanicum*. *Physiologia Plantarum*, **66**, 339–43.

Rybnicek, K. (1984) The vegetation and development of Central European mires. In: Moore, P. D. (ed.) *European Mires*. Academic Press, London.

Schouwenaars, J. M. and Vink, J. P. M. (1990) Hydrophysical properties of peat relics in a former peat bog and perspectives for *Sphagnum* growth. *International Peat Journal*, **4**, 65–76.

Scottish Natural Heritage (1994) *A Muirburn Code*. Scottish Natural Heritage, Battleby.

Scottish Natural Heritage (1995) *Boglands. Scotland's Living Landscape*. Scottish Natural Heritage, Battleby.

Scottish Wildlife Trust (1994) *SWT Reserve Management Programme*. Unpublished report. Scottish Wildlife Trust, Edinburgh.

Shaw, S. C. and Wheeler, B. D. (1995) *Monitoring Rehabilitation Work on Lowland Peatlands*. Unpublished report to English Nature, Somerset.

Slater, F. M. (1976) Contribution to the ecology of Borth Bog, Wales. 2. Human influence. *Proceedings of the 5th International Peat Congress*, **1**, 176–81.

Slater, F. M. and Agnew, A. D. Q. (1977) Observation of a peat bog's ability to withstand increasing public pressure. *Biological Conservation*, **11**, 21–4.

Sliva, J., Maas, D., and Pfadenhauer, J. (1996) Rehabilitation of milled fields. In: Parkyn, L., Stoneman, R. E. and Ingram, H. A. P. (eds) *Conserving Peatlands*. CAB International, Wallingford, pp. 295–314.

Smith, R. S. and Charman, D. J. (1988) The vegetation of upland mires within conifer plantations in Northumberland, northern England. *Journal of Applied Ecology*, **25**, 579–94.

Smout, T. C. (1996) Bogs and people since 1600. In: Parkyn, L., Stoneman, R. E. and Ingram, H. A. P. (eds) *Conserving Peatlands*. CAB International, Wallingford, pp. 162–67.

Staines. B. W., Balharry. R. and Welch. D. (1995) The impact of red deer and their management on the natural heritage in the uplands. In: Thompson, D. B. A., Hester, A. J. and Usher, M. B. (eds) *Heaths and Moorlands – Cultural Landscapes*. HMSO, Edinburgh, pp. 294–308.

Stead, I. M., Bourke, J. B. and Brothwell, D. (1986) *Lindow Man, The Body in the Bog*. British Museum, London.

Stevenson, A. C., Jones, V. J., and Battarbee, R. W. (1990) The cause of peat erosion: a palaeolimnological approach. *New Phytologist*, **114**, 727–35.

Stevenson, A. C. and Thompson, D. B. A. (1993) Long term changes in the extent of heather moorland in upland Britain and Ireland: palaeoecological evidence of the importance of grazing. *The Holocene*, **3**, 70–6.

Stoneman, R. E. (1993). *Holocene Palaeoclimates from Peat Stratigraphy: Extending and Refining the Model*. Ph.D. thesis, University of Southampton, Southampton.

Stoneman, R. E., Barber, K. E. and Maddy, D. (1993) Present and past ecology of *Sphagnum imbricatum* and its significance for raised peat-climate modelling. *Quaternary Newsletter*, **70**, 14–22.

Streefkerk, J. G. and Zandstra, R. J. (1994) *Experimental Management Measures in the South-East Corner of the Raheenmore Raised Bog Reserve*. Unpublished report from the Dutch – Irish raised bog study, Office of Public Works, Dublin.

Stroud, D. A., Reed, T. M., Pienkowski, M. W. and Lindsay, R. A. (1987) *Birds, Bogs and Forestry. The Peatlands of Caithness and Sutherland*. Nature Conservancy Council, Peterborough.

Tallis, J. H. (1964) Studies on southern Pennine peats III. The behaviour of *Sphagnum*. *Journal of Ecology*, **52**, 345–53.

Tallis, J. H. (1973) Studies on southern Pennine peats V. Direct observations on peat erosion and peat hydrology at Featherbed Moss, Derbyshire. *Journal of Ecology*, **61**, 1–22.

Tallis, J. H. (1981) Rates of erosion. In: Phillips, J., Yalden, D. and Tallis, J. (eds). *Peak District Moorland Erosion Study,*

Phase 1 Report. Peak Park Joint Planning Board, Bakewell, pp. 74–85.

Tallis, J. H. (1985) Erosion of blanket peat in the southern Pennines: new light on an old problem. In: Johnson, R. H. (ed.) *The Geomorphology of North-west England*. Manchester University Press, Manchester, pp. 313–16.

Tansley, A. G. (1939) *The British Islands and their Vegetation*. Cambridge University Press, Cambridge.

Taylor, J. A. (1983) The peatlands of Great Britain and Ireland. In: Gore, A. J. P. (ed.) *Ecosystems of the World 4B. Mires: Swamp, Bog, Fen and Moor: Regional Studies*. Elsevier Scientific, Amsterdam, pp. 1–46.

Thompson, D. B. A., MacDonald, A. J., Marsden, J. H. and Galbraith, C. A. (1995) Upland heather moorland in Great Britain: a review of international importance, vegetation change and some objectives for nature conservation. *Biological Conservation*, **71**, 163–78.

Thompson, P. S. and Thompson, D. B. A. (1991) Greenshanks *Tringa nebularia* and long-term studies of breeding waders. *Ibis*, **133**, suppl. 1: 99–112.

Trubridge, M. (1994) *Ornithological Surveys of Selected Lowland Raised Mires in East Kilbride, Hamilton, Monklands and Stirling Districts 1994*. Unpublished report. RSPB, Glasgow.

Twenhöven, F. L. (1992) Competition between two *Sphagnum* species under different deposition levels. *Journal of Bryology*, **17**, 71–80.

Van Geel, B. and Middeldorp, A. A. (1988) Vegetational history of Carberry Bog (Co. Kildare, Ireland) during the last 850 years and a test of the temperature indicator value of ^{2}H/^{1}H measurements of peat samples in relation to historical sources and meteorological data. *New Phytologist*, **109**, 377–92.

Walker, D. (1970) Direction and rate in some British post-glacial hydroseres. In: Walker, D. and West, R. G. (eds) *Studies in the Vegetation History of the British Isles*. Cambridge University Press, Cambridge, pp. 117–39.

Warren-Wilson, J. (1959) Analysis of the distribution of foliage area in grassland. In: Ivins. J. D. (ed.) *Proceedings of the Sixth Easter School of Agricultural Science*, University of Nottingham, 1958. Butterworths, London, pp. 51–61.

Welch, D. (1984) Studies in the grazing of heather moorland in north-east Scotland. II. Response of heather. *Journal of Applied Ecology*, **21**, 197–207.

Welch, D. (1996) The impact of large herbivores on north British peatlands. In: Parkyn, L., Stoneman, R. E., and Ingram, H. A. P. (eds) *Conserving Peatlands*. CAB International, Wallingford, pp. 176–83.

Welch, D. and Rawes, M. (1996) The intensity of sheep grazing on high-level blanket bog in upper Teasdale. *Irish Journal of Agricultural Research*, **5**, 185–96.

Werritty, A. and Ingram, H. A. P. (1985) Blanket mire erosion in the Scottish Borders in July 1993. *Bulletin of the British Ecological Society*, **16**, 202–3.

Wheeler, B. D. and Shaw S. C. (1995) *Restoration of Damaged Peatlands – With Particular Reference to Lowland Raised Bogs Affected by Peat Extraction*. HMSO, London.

Yalden, D. (1981) Sheep and moorland vegetation – a literature review. In: Phillips, J., Yalden, D. and Tallis, J. (eds) *Peak District Moorland Erosion Study, Phase 1 Report*. Peak Park Joint Planning Board, Bakewell, pp. 132–41.

INDEX

INDEX

Published by The Stationery Office and available from:

The Stationery Office Bookshops
71 Lothian Road, Edinburgh EH3 9AZ
(counter service only)
0131-479 3141 Fax 0131-479 3142
49 High Holborn, London WC1V 6HB
(counter service and fax orders only)
Fax 0171-831 1326
68-69 Bull Street, Birmingham B4 6AD
0121-236 9696 Fax 0121-236 9699
33 Wine Street, Bristol BS1 2BQ
0117-926 4306 Fax 0117-929 4515
9-21 Princess Street, Manchester M60 8AS
0161-834 7201 Fax 0161-833 0634
16 Arthur Street, Belfast BT1 4GD
01232 238451 Fax 01232 235401
The Stationery Office Oriel Bookshop
The Friary, Cardiff CF1 4AA
01222 395548 Fax 01222 384347

The Stationery Office publications are also available from:
The Publications Centre
(mail, telephone and fax orders only)
PO Box 276, London SW8 5DT
General enquiries 0171-873 0011
Telephone orders 0171-873 9090
Fax orders 0171-873 8200

Accredited Agents
(see Yellow Pages)
and through good booksellers

Typeset by IMH (Cartrif), eh209dx, Scotland
Printed for The Stationery Office Limited by CC 68942